COMPLETE GLOSSARY

TO THE

Poetry and Prose of Robert Burns.

COMPLETE GLOSSARY

TO THE

POETRY AND PROSE

OF

ROBERT BURNS.

WITH UPWARDS OF

THREE THOUSAND ILLUSTRATIONS FROM
ENGLISH AUTHORS.

BY

JOHN CUTHBERTSON.

ALEXANDER GARDNER,
PAISLEY; AND 12 PATERNOSTER ROW, LONDON.
1886.

JOHNSON REPRINT CORPORATION
111 Fifth Avenue, New York, N.Y. 10003

JOHNSON REPRINT COMPANY LTD.
Berkeley Square House, London, W. 1

First reprinting, **1967,** Johnson Reprint Corporation

Printed in the United States of America

PREFACE.

WHILE my aim, in the following pages, has been a little more ambitious than the compilation of a mere Glossary to the Writings of Burns, it is still a humble one.

My endeavour has been to show to English readers that by far the greater number of the Poet's words for which a glossary is generally consulted are to be found in their own authors. For this purpose, I have quoted upwards of three thousand passages from English authors, besides words from old dictionaries and provincial glossaries.

With the exception of a very few words from provincial authors, real or pretended, I have taken no illustrations from works published since Burns's time.

I have not hesitated, when occasion offered, to insert anything which seemed likely to illustrate, in however small a degree, any word or passage, even at the risk of being accused of going beyond the province of the glossarist.

I have not, however, neglected what is the primary purpose of a glossary; and I believe this, which I now offer to the public, will be found to contain a number of words not to be found in any other. Of course, Burns's own glossary has been incorporated.

I do not know whether or not this volume has any philological value, but surely it cannot be altogether uninstructive to see so many words, most of them dead or dying, which have had new life breathed into them by the genius of Robert Burns. To have these words shown, as it were, in their shrouds, and then to behold them "instinct with life" in the pages of the modern Poet, cannot fail to be interesting to many.

If I be successful in removing a single stumbling-block from the path of the readers of the Ayrshire Bard, it will be an ample reward.

J. C.

Umberley, Troon,
June, 1886.

GLOSSARY.

A.

A'. All.

> Listeneth now to Merlin's saw,
> And I will tell to *aw*
> What he wrat for men to come.—*Merlin's Prophecies.*
>
> Somewhere I have had a hugeous faw,
> I'm sure o' that, and, master, that's neet *aw.*—*Cotton.*

Marry, Muff *a'* your counts, and there be no more life in them.—*Dekker.*

Here beginnyth a short tretice to make a tre bere *a* maner frute.—*English MS. quoted by Sir F. Madden.*

Dr. Jamieson says, "*L* after broad *a*, as occurring in English words, is changed (by Scotch writers) into silent *u* or *w*, as malt, *maut*; salt, *saut*, etc."

This is true, but it is equally true of old English authors, e.g.,

> And after hem came a great company of *heraudes.*—*Chaucer.*
>
> And roll with rest in Runes of Ribaudry (ribaldry).—*Spenser.*

And words like *auter, assaute, emeraud,* for altar, assault, and emerald are common down to a comparatively recent time. In Shakspeare's day, the proper name Walter was pronounced Water, as may be seen in "The

Second Part of King Henry VI.; and Dr. Wolcot rhymes *Ralph* with *laugh*.

L is also, sometimes in English and frequently in Scotch, changed into *w* in words ending in *oll*, *l*, or *le*, as *scrow* for scroll, *pow* for poll, *stowe* for stole, and sometimes when followed by other letters, especially *d* and *t*, as *gowd* for gold, *cowt* for colt, &c.

It is also occasionally omitted after *u*, as in *pu* for pull; never after *e* or *oo* in Scotch, wool excepted, and that it is really not an exception, see under *woo*, and after *i* only in the verb *will*, which Shakspeare and other writers change into *woo'*, e.g.,

> *Woo't* thou fight well?—*Antony and Cleopatra*.

Aback. Away, aloof.

> But when they came where thou thy skill didst show,
> They drew *abacke*.—*Spenser*.
>
> Stand *abacke*, stand *abacke*, sayd Robin,
>   Why draw ye me so near.—*Robin Hood: Ritson*.
>
> For drede archeres *abak* they sterte.—*Kyng Alisaunder*.

Abeigh. At a shy distance.

Though I do not intend to make this an etymological glossary, yet as *abeigh* has not hitherto been satisfactorily accounted for, I venture to suggest a not unlikely origin for it in Anglo-Saxon *beág*, or *beáh*, gave way, from *bugan*, *beógan*, or *bigan*, to bow, bend, stoop, to *give way*, to recede, avoid, flee.

Aboon, and *'boon*. Above, up.

> The toke on on ethar hand
>   Be the lyght of the mone;
> Many had no strengt for to stande
>   In Chyveat the hyllys *abone*.
>   *Ancient Ballads of Chevy Chase*.

> Then he put on the old man's shoes,
> Were patch'd both beneath and *aboon*.
> *Robin Hood: Ritson.*

> The rof *abone* unlek
> As hyt wolde asounder.—*Lybeaus Disconus.*

About. Alternately.

> Of lusty women in the route
> A fresh caroll hath song *aboute*.—*Gower*.
> Let every felowe telle his tale *aboute*.—*Chaucer*.

Abread. Abroad, in sight.

> Thine armes shall thou sprede *abrede*,
> As man in warre were forwerede.—*Romaunt of the Rose.*

Abreed. In breadth.

Brede. Breadth.—*Bailey's Dictionary*.

> The streets paved both in length and *brede*.—*Lydgate.*

> Hang me up on your main-mast tree,
> If I miss my mark one shilling *breed*.—*Sir Andrew Barton.*

> He shulde have be larde of that lande a lengthe and *abrede*.—
> *Piers Plowman.*

Ace. The one of cards. In E. literature ace signifies something very small, as, "I will not bate an *ace*." The figure is taken from dice, but Burns uses the word to denote the one of cards. I do not know if he played at cards, but he seems to have been fond of the figure, for he uses it at least three times. In one place he says—

> My heart-warm love to guid auld Glen,
> The *ace* and wale of honest men.

And in another—

> But tent me, Davie, *ace* o' hearts.

It is often asked what was the use of specifying *hearts*, since in all the games likely to be known to the poet or his correspondents the ace, whether of hearts or others, had always the same power, and, when it was a trump, could take any card. The explanation is that in the game called "Twenty-five," once popular in country districts, *hearts are always trumps;* therefore, to call a man the ace of hearts was to pay him the highest compliment that could be drawn from " The devil's pictured beuks," unless " King o' hearts," as he calls Lapraik, surpass it.

A-coming. The prefix does not alter the meaning.

> I was told the queen was *a-coming.*—*Pepys.*

Acquent. Acquaint for acquainted. *E* is often used for *a,* as in

> Whan that ye come *agen* (again) from Canterbury.—*Chaucer.*
> Have thei no *gernere* (garner) to go to.—*Piers Plowman.*
> Ase man that is *queinté* (quaint).—*The Seven Sages.*
> Alle this loude it *smerteth* (smarteth).—*Occleve.*
> Thou also most entirely art *acquaint* with all my ways.—
> *Psalm* cxxxix. *Rous's Version.*
> But I must bannysshe him
> As he that *aquentyth* hym with ydilnes.—*Skelton.*

Advisement. Counsel.

> Ye that I say gyve good *advysement.*—*Skelton.*
> Perhaps my succour, or *advisement* meet,
> Mote stead you much.—*Spenser.*

Addle, adle, or *aidle.* Addle, putrid water, liquid oozing from a dunghill.

Ae. One.

> *Ae.* One; one of several; each.—*Halliwell's Archaic Dictionary.*
> And not to fasten *a* (one) fryday in fyve score winter.
> *P. Plowman.*

> For the world and worldlis life to-gider
> Chaunges & turnes oft hider & thider,
> And in *a* (one) state duelles ful short while,
> Unnethes the space of a myle.—*Pricke of Conscienee.*

> Wele he saw that by na gyn Allane to hir mycht he noght win.
> Thar was bot *a* (one) dur and *a* (one) way, And tharof bare the erl the Kay.—*The Seven Sages.*

Aff. Off. *A* is often used for *o*, as in

> The pope was *nat* profytable for them.—*Froissart.*

> The beggar moht *na* better do,
> But *sald* this corn igain him to.—*E. Metrical Homilies, Small.*

Aff-loof. Off-hand, without premeditation. *Aff* and *loof.*

A-fiel. In the field. *D* is often omitted, as in

> It is a dry *scall* (scald).—*Lev.* xiii. 30.

> A baggepipe wel coude he blowe and *soune.*—*Chaucer.*

> Their heds are hid with *skalls* (scalds).—*Sylvester.*

> For ydell *hyne* (hind) for to fede,
> Thereto hadde we lytyll nede.—*Octovian Imperator.*

A-field, which is literally *on the field*, is used by English writers to signify to the field; thus, "We drove *afield*."—*Milton.* "*A-field* I went."—*Gay;* but it is also found in Burns's sense:—

> Ant hou he sloh *afelde*
> Him that is fader aquelde.—*King Horn.*

> How now, prince Troilus? wherefore not *a-field*?
> Because not there.—*Shak.*

> Rises, full-orb'd, the silver harvest-moon,
> To light th' unwearied farmer, late *afield*
> His scatter'd sheaves collecting.—*Dyer.*

Afore. Before.

> Hang
> Your shield *afore* your heart.—*The Two Noble Kinsmen.*

Let them be as the grass upon the house-tops, that withereth *afore* it groweth up.—*Psalm* cxxix.

And with a crosse *afor* the Kynge comsed thus to techen.
Piers Plowman.

Aft. Oft. This word is often spelled *eft*, which comes near to *aft*.

Eft looking back would faine have runne away.—*Spenser.*

Aften. Often. *A* for *o*; see under *aff*.

Against. Before, by the time.

Against he reached the middle of the arch.—*Burns to Grose.*
Some say that ever '*gainst* that season comes
Wherein our Saviour's birth is celebrated,
The bird of dawning singeth all night long.—*Shak.*

Agee, ajee. On one side. I have not found this word in any E. author, except it may be in a passage in the romance of Richard Cœur de Lion:—

Agee, awry, obliquely, askew. *Ajee*, awry, uneven.—*Halliwell.*

The Sarezynes thoo turnyet *ayee*,
To that other syde off the town,
And cryede, trewes! with gret soun,
To the false Kyng of Fraunse.

It must be remembered that *y* is often used for *g*; thus in the romance quoted we read—

And for joye off this dede,
The cuppes fast abouten *yede*.

Occleve has

Tyme and tyme he *yave* them with his hondes
Of his goode passyngly.

The word will thus not appear to be forced if we spell it *agee*; and the circumstances in which it is used seem to require a word of similar meaning. Let us see what the circumstances were:—Richard of England and Philip of France besieged Babylon, the former on one side of the city, the latter on the other. The inhabitants desired to make a truce with Richard, which he refused, and then they "turnyd *ayee*"—applied to Philip on the other side. I think this is really the so-called S. word *agee*, and not *again* as Weber explains it.

Agley. Off the right line, wrong, wide of the aim.
> To *glie*, to look awry or sideways, to squint.—*Bailey.*
> I garde her gaspe, I garde her *gle*.—*Skelton.*

Ahin. Behind. For elision of *d* see under *a-fiel.* *A* is often used for *be*, as in
> The maister his tale he gan *agin* (begin).—*The Seven Sages.*
> But with outrageous strokes did him restrain,
> And with his body barr'd the way *atwixt* them twain.—*Spenser.*

Aiblins. Perhaps.
> *Aiblins*, perhaps, possibly.—*Halliwell.*

Aik. An oak; *aiken*, oaken.
> *Akehorns*, acorns.—*Tyrwhitt.*
> *Aec*, an oak; *Aecen*, oaken.—*Bosworth.*
> Oundes synkyng oundes uppon the hard *ake* rise.—*Chatterton.*

Ain. Own.
> But some than sat right sad
> That nothynge had
> There of theyr *awn*.—*Skelton.*

He was now come in hys *awne* proper person.—*Hall's Chron. of England.*

Air. Early.
> I griev'd you never in all my life,
> Neither by late or *air*.—*R. Hood.*

Airl-penny, **airles.** Earnest-money.

GLOSSARY.

Arles-Penny, earnest-money given to servants when they are first hired.—*Bailey*.

Arls, or *earles*, earnest.—*Thoresby, Ray Correspondence*.

Arles, or *earles*, money paid to bind a bargain.—*Grose*.

So recently as 23rd May, 1883, at the Petty Sessions Houghton-le-Spring, a servant was accused of having "sent back his *erls* because he had heard the situation was not a good one."

Airn. Iron, a tool of iron. *Plough-irons*, the coulter and share.

> And when they han hir lust gotten
> The hote *ernes* they all foryetten.—*Chaucer*.
> He was armed wele
> Bot with *yrne* and with stele.—*Davie's Venus*.
> For steel, ne *yrne*, in her swerd,
> Ne mighth hem percen, hy weren so hard.—
>
> *Kyng Alisaunder*.

I quote these lines because the seeming peculiarity of the S. word lies not in the change of the vowel sound, but in the loss of a syllable. *Airn* is found in the glossary of the "Voiage and Travaile of Sir John Maundevile," but it does not occur in the text of at least one edition.

Airt. Quarter of the heavens; to direct.

Airt, point of the compass.—*Halliwell*.

> And over all this, full mokell more he thought
> What for to speake, and what to holden inne,
> And what to *arten*, er to love he sought.—*Chaucer*.

Tyrwhitt understands *arten* to mean *constrain*—as Troilus is thinking of his own action restrain would be a better word—but that seems to be expressed by "holden inne." *Arten* appears to refer to the schemes he would devise, the methods he would take to gain the love of Cressid. *Art* occurs again in Chaucer, in the "Court of Love," where it may mean constrain, but may also signify conduct or guide:—

> When I was young,—
> Love *arted* me to do my observance
> To his estate.

Aith. An oath.

> Pride, wrath, and glotonie,
> *Aithe*, sleuthe, and lecherie.—*Arthour and Merlin.*
> Depely has he sworn hys *ath*.—*Ywain and Gawain.*
> But should he evrie *ath* lese kirtel or kote,
> He sholde stande stark naked twyse a day or ene.—
> *The Simonie.*
> The mason sware grete *athes* him to.—*The Seven Sages.*

Aits. Oats. *A* is frequently used for *o* by E. authors. See under *aith.*

> And *hat* (hot) is al Alisaundres blod.—*Kyng Alisaunder.*
> I durst no more say thereto,
> For pure feare, but *stale* (stole) away.—*Chaucer.*

Aiver. An old horse.

Aver, a labouring beast.—*Bailey.*
A work-horse.—*Halliwell.*

Average formerly meant work done for the lord (of the manor) by the *avers*, or draught-cattle of the tenants.—*Wedgewood.*

Aizle. A hot cinder, a red ember.

Ysela, Ysla, a fire spark, spark, ember, hot ashes.—*Bosworth.*

When spelled *eizel*, as it sometimes is, it comes nearer the *Anglo-Sax.*

Ajee. See *agee.*

A'kind. Every kind.

> There's *alkyn* welth ay to weld.—*Pricke of Conscience.*
> And *alkyn* crafty men that konne lyven in treuthe.—
> **P. Plowman.**

Ye sold think over *alkyn* thing.—*Ywain and Gawain*.

Akwart. Awkward.
> *Akwart.*—*Thoresby.* *Aukert.*—*Halliwell.* *Awkert.*—*Barnford.*
>> They make interpretacyon
>> Of an *aquarde* facyon.—*Skelton*.
>> They cut like *marmalet.*—*Fletcher*.

The perpetual change of *T* into *D*, and *vice versa*, is very familiar to all who have ever paid the smallest attention to language. *Horne Tooke.* Crook-backt.— *Lev.* xxi. 20.

> Now poor men to the justices with capons make their *errants*.—
>> *George Wither*.

Alake. Alas, alack. That the change of *ack* into *ake* is not unsanctioned by E. poets, is shown by—
> Sorrow I am ; in endless torments pained
> Among the Furies in the infernal lake
> Where Pluto, God of Hell, so grisly *blake* (black)
> Doth hold his throne.—*The Mirrour for Magistrates*.
> Hire browe broune, hire eghe *blake.*—
>> *Wright's Specimens of Lyric Poetry*.

Alane. Alone.
>> I said what dose you here *allane*.—*Ywain and Gawain.*
>> The knight *allane* went him to play.—*The Seven Sages.*
>> And band her hym *alane*.—*The Felon Sewe of Rokeby*.

Alang. Along. See *lang.*
> Ten myle they yeode *alang.*—*Kyng Alisaunder.*
> He set mirkenes his lurking *lang.*—*Metrical E. Psalter*.

Allegretto forte. Gay, merry, quick, and loud.

Amaist. Almost. See *maist.*
>> Now God, that es of mightes *maste,*
>> Grante him grace of the Haly Gaste.—*Minot.*

Amang. Among.

> At the last thai ordeined twelve
> The thoghtfulest *amang* themselve.—*Cursor Mundi.*
>
> Ane banneist lord wes thame *amang.*—
> *Ane Exclamation maid in England.*

An'. And.

> Pledoures shuld peynen hem to plede for such, *an'* helpe.
> *P. Plowman.*
>
> Betwix the lift *an* the erthe it glade.—*Cursor Mundi.*

D is frequently omitted in E. poetry, even when the rhyme does not require its omission, *e.g.* :—

> 'Tis strange, yet true, her glove, ring, scarfe, and Fan,
> Make him (*unhansome*) a well-favoured man.—
> *House of Correction,* 1629.

Sir Isaac Newton, I think, always wrote *hansome,* and the *d* is still omitted in the pronunciation.

In the house there were many *hansome* ladyes.—*Lord William Russell,* 1654.

An. If.

> This day at least is friendship's—on the morrow
> Let strife come *an* she will.—*Otway.*
>
> Nay, *an* you will not.—*Shak.*
>
> And myght kisse the kyng for cosyn *an* she wolde.—
> *P. Plowman.*

Anana. The pine-apple.

> Where rich *ananas* blow.—*The Farewell.*
>
> Witness thou best *anana,* thou the pride
> Of vegetable life.—*Thomson.*

Anathem. A curse.

> Round your bold master flock, ye mitred hive,
> With *anathems* on Whigs his soul revive.—*The Rolliad.*

Ance. Once.

> Step on thy feet; come of, man, al at *anes.*—*Chaucer.*

>   He said, "Of thir es none so balde,
>   Nowther by day ne by night
>   *Anes* to pas out of mi sight."—*Ywain and Gawain.*
>
>   To Christ *ance* be turning, not use him in jest.—
>   *Black letter Ballads and Broadsides.*

Ane, One.

>   And other trees there was mané *ane.*—*The Squyr of Lowe Degre.*
>   If *ane* were doughty and single man.—*Robert of Brunne.*
>   When every *yean* had taen their place.—*Ritson.*
>   Byhind leved thar noght *ane.*— *Ywain and Gawin.*
>   His harp he hid in *ane* holme tre.—*Orfeo and Herondes.*

Anent. Over against, concerning, about.

>   *Anent*, over against.—*Bailey.*
>   And many a sink poured out her rage *anenst* them.—*Ben Jonson.*
>   For every word schal not be impossible *anentis* God.—*Wyclif.*
>
>   >   Of that down-cast we may bi chaunce
>   >   *Anent* this world get coveraunce.—*Cursor Mundi.*

Aneuch. Enough. See *eneugh.*

Anither. Another. *I* is often used for *o* or the *ŭ* sound, as in—

>   John *Gilden*-moth (Golden-mouth) says.—*Cursor Mundi.*
>   Lordings, quod he, in *chirche* whan I preche.—*Chaucer.*
>   The faurtend day, at a schift
>   Sal bathe *brin* (burn) bathe erthe and lift.—*E. Metrical Homilies.*

Antigua. Rum.

Antithesize. To employ antithesis. This is not stranger than Sterne's *epistolize.*

Aqua fontis. Spring-water. I should not have inserted this had I not found that some country people thought *aqua fontis* and *sal marinum* to be genuine drugs, and even in the "farina of beans and pease" did not recognise an old friend—pease-meal.

Aquavitae. Properly brandy, but applied to whisky.

> The first of them, in many a taverne tide,
> At last subdued by *Aquavitæ* died.—*Rowlands. Warton.*
>
> I will trust an Irishman with my *aqua vitae* bottle.
> *Shakespeare.*

Aqueesh. Betwixt or between. This seems, at first sight, a most licentious spelling of betwixt, but when we remember the various ways in which old English authors wrote the word, it will be found not very far from their pronunciation at least. Take a few examples:—

> Thou schalt part *betwys* hus two
> Of all thyng that thou spede.—*Sir Amadas.*
>
> For all the gold *atwixen* sunne and see.—*Chaucer.*
>
> An the fiend had been a truss of hay
> She wad a swallowed him and mickle mare,
> *Bequeen* the night and the day.—*Ritson.*

X, it must also be remembered, was often used for *sh*, and *vice versâ*.

> No *Lushburghes* (Luxemburghs) payen ye.—*Chaucer.*

The author of "Piers Plowman" has the same spelling, and as late as Henry the Eighth's time we find Skelton writing—

> *Xall* (shall) kyt both wight and grene.
> Thou *xuldst* have been shrynyd.

If *x* in *atwix* be sounded *sh* it is not far from *aqueesh*, to build nothing on the *q* in *bequeen*.

Arioso. A musical term.

> *Arioso*, the movement or tune of a common air.—*Bailey.*

Ase. Ashes. I believe that this word, in Ayrshire at least, is always pronounced *awz.*

Ask, ash, as, do all come from the Saxon *aesc,* an ash-tree.—
Camden.

Ess-hole, or *ass*-hole, the hole under the fire which holds ashes.—
Bamford.

As, or *asse,* ashes.—*Var, dial. Thoresby.*

Esse, ashes.—*Bailey. Ahse, asce,* ashes.—*Bosworth.*

Asklent. Asquint, aslant. Except in the change of *e* for *a,* for which see under *beld,* this word differs from aslant only by the insertion of *k,* which is often in old E. authors placed between *s* and *l,* as in—

Her name men *Sclaunder* call.—*Spenser.*

Her armes long and *sclendre.*—*Chaucer.*

Chichevace is my name,
Hungry, meagre, *sklendre,* and lene.—*Lydgate.*

He schal hym *scle* (slay) with dethes dent.

Octovian Imperator.

He fond a knyght whar he lay
Isclayne (slain) and made full tame.—*Lybæaus Disconnus.*

What we now call *slate* was formerly *sclat.*—*Horne Tooke.*

Many man is *sclepyr* (slippery) of tonge.

Ancient Mysteries. Hone.

Assoilyed. Absolved.

They sende aftur the pope Symonde,
And he schrofe hym and hoselde on that grounde,
And *assoyled* hym, wele y wate.—*Le Bone Florence of Rome.*

Assoyle me yf thou wylte.—*The Erle of Tolous.*

Thilke horrible sinfull dede
Assoiled was.—*Gower.*

Asteer. Abroad, stirring, astir. See *steer.*

Athort. Athwart, abroad, through.

Athurt, athwart, across.—*Halliwell.*

Attour. Besides, over.

Attour, towards.—*Bailey.*

Ded buth my prynces be *atour.*—*Kyng Alisaunder.*

Atween. Between.

Worship not Jove with curious fancies vain,
Nor him despise, hold right *atween* these twain.—*Grimoald.*
Feyr thei partud them *atwen.*—*The Hunttyng of the Hare.*
Pieres for pure tene pulled it *atweyne.*—*P. Plowman.*
Twene hope and drede my life I lede.—*Skelton.*
And seem'st to laugh *atween* thy twinkling light.—*Spenser.*

Aught. Eight. Supposing both words to have the guttural sound *aught* and *achtande*, which means eight, and not eighteen, as a young reader might suppose, come very near each other:—

And al the erthe, the *achtande* day,
Sal stir, and quac and al folc flay.
English Metrical Homilies.

The King was thare with his Knyghtes
Aght dayes and *aght* nyghtes.—*Ywain and Gawain.*
He regnede *ahte* and twente yer.—*Chronicle of England.*

Aught. Possession, as "in a' my *aught*," in all my possession.

An erl wond in that castele
That *aght* the lordship ilkadele.—*The Seven Sages.*
He hyhth hem *aughte* and gret nobleys.—*Kyng Alisaunder.*
This werldes welth, *auht*, and catel.
E. Metrical Homilies. Small.
This stede *aught* Sir Campanus.—*Ipomydon.*

Auld. Old.

Take then thine *auld* cloak about thee.—*Shakespeare.*
He makes both young and *alde*
Bow untill his hand.—*Sir Penny.*

> This dome
> He fand in an *ald* bok.—*Cursor Mundi.*

Auld-farran, or *farrant*. Sagacious, prudent, cunning.

Aud-farrand.—*Grose.*

Aud-farand. Children are said to be so, when grave and witty beyond what is usual in such as are of that age.—*Bailey.*

> She knew non such in hyr londe,
> So goodly a man and wele *farande*.—*Ipomydon.*

Auld lang-syne. Olden time. See *auld*, *lang*, and *syne*.

Auld light. The doctrine of the Church of Scotland and other Presbyterian Churches in Scotland.

Fuller has a sermon on "The Feare of losing the Old Light."

Aumos. Alms, gift to a beggar. For change of *al* into *au* see under *A'*.

Almous, alms; *aumrie*, the place where alms are given.—*Bailey.* *Awmoss.*—*Thoresby.*

Seynt Ione, the *aumenere.*—*Robert of Brunne.*

Aumos dish. A dish for the reception of alms.

Auntie. Aunt. The diminutive in *ie* is rare in English. Spenser has it in the "Shepherd's Calendar."

> Forthy, my *kiddie*, be ruled by me.
> Well heard *kiddie* all this sore constraint.

Ava. At all. Corruption of *of all*.—*Jamieson.*

Awa'. Away. Poets have often omitted *y* and more important letters.

Awa' sometimes means about, as in *here awa'*.
> A royal ghaist that had been cased
> A prisoner eighteen years *awa'*.—*Amang the Trees.*

Our old limes (limbs) now wel ben *unwelde* (unwieldy).—*Chaucer.*

Awauken. To waken. *Au* for *ā* is frequent in old E.

> I am a good *Aungel.*—*Coventry Mysteries.* Hone.
>
> These poetes of *auncyente*,
> They ar to diffuse for me.—*Skelton.*
>
> They to hym came, withouten eny *daungere.*—*Occleve.* Skeat.
>
> His *fraught* (freight) we soon shall know.—*Milton.*

Awe. To owe.

> For faith ye *aw* unto the Kyng,
> Cumandes him his tale to tell.—*Ywain and Gawain.*

Awfu'. Awful.

Awkart. Awkward. For change of *d* to *t* see under *Akwart*.

Awkert.—*Halliwell.*

What silly discourse we had as to love matters, he being the most *awkerd* man ever I met with in my life as to that business!—*Pepys.*

Awn. The beard of barley, oats, etc.

The beard growing out of corn or grass.—*Johnson and Bailey.*

Awns.—*Grose.*

Awnie. Bearded, having awns.

Ayont. Beyond. *B* for *be*, see *ahin*.

> They're going to seek their fortunes *ayont* the salt sea.
> *Jack and Tom Bell.*

B.

Ba'. A ball. See under *a'*.

> At Scales, great Tom Barwise got the *ba'* in his hand,
> And t' wives aw ran out, and shouted, and banned.
> *Hutchison's Hist. of Cumberland.*

The best at thieve craft and the *ba'*.
> *The Fray of Hantwessell.*

Bawer, a maker of balls. *Staffordsh.—Halliwell.*

Bab at the Bowster. Bob at the bolster. A kind of dance in which partners are selected by placing a bolster, or some more handy thing, say a handkerchief, before them, and sealing the engagement by kneeling on it and kissing. Fifty years ago no rustic ball ended without "Bab at the Bowster." A similar dance called the "cushion dance" was known in England.

> Sukey that danced with the cushion,
> An hour from the room had been gone.
> *The Winchester Wedding.*

In King Charles's time, there has been nothing but trenchmore and the *cushion-dance*, omnium gatherum, tolly polly, hoite come toite.—*Selden's Table Talk.*

Backet. A wooden trough for carrying coals, etc.; another form of bucket. *A* for *u*, as in—

But right anon a thousand peple in *thrast* (thrust).—*Chaucer.*

Backlins. Backward; *backlins-comin*, coming back, returning.

Bæcling, backwards; *linga*, adv. termination.—*Bosworth.*

A good deal has been said about the termination *ling*, but as it occurs in a few English words it does not concern us here. What is supposed to be a Scottish peculiarity is the omission of *g*. This letter is by English writers often omitted for the sake of the rhyme, and still more frequently unsounded even when written.

> A ductile *codlin's* skin.—*Herrick.*

> I'll have no dumps, nor *dumplins.*—*Fletcher.*

After this proud foe *subduing*
   When your patriot friends you see,
Think on vengeance for my ruin.—*Glover*.

Some for abolishing black *pudding*
And eating nothing with the blood in.—*Butler*, who also has *pudden*.

Beware of Latin authors all,
   Nor think your verses *sterling*;
Though with a golden pen you scrawl,
   And scribble in a *berlin.*—*Pope*.

Bade. Desired, or asked; past tense of *bid*, to pray.

As meche lande of the Kyng sche *bade*,
As with a bole hyde men mygth sprede.—*Robert of Brunne*.

He *bad* of heom all that he wolde,
Stedis, armes, seolver, and golde.—*Kyng Alisaunder*.

He fel on knees and *bad* a boon.—*R. C. de Leon*.

Baggie. Dim. of bag, the stomach.

Hoo'll no com ogen till *baggin-time* (lunch-time).—*Bamford*.

Baide, or *bade.* Endured, did stay.

Bád, p. of *bidan*, to bide, abide, etc.—*Bosworth*.

This jolly prentys with his mayster *bood*,
Til he was oute neygh of his prentyshood.—*Wright's Chaucer*.

Nan man *bude* be northan him.—*Life of Alfred*.

He *abood* the lyon fers and wood.—*R. C. de Lion*.

Bailie. Magistrate; corresponds to alderman.

Knight, squire, or *bailie.*—*Chaucer*.

As our Saviour sayd by the wicked *baily*, which though he played the false shrewe for his master provided yet wilily somewhat for himselfe.—*Sir T. More*.

He had of bestes the *bailie.*—*Gower*.

Bailie in these passages is not the Scotch magistrate, but the word is the same.

Bailiery. The extent of a bailie's jurisdiction; sometimes the extent of the jurisdiction of a sheriff.—*Jamieson.* In England it is called a *bailiwick* (which sometimes means a county, and sometimes a barony). We still have *baron bailies.*

Bairn. A child.

> Mercy on's! a *barne:* a very pretty *barne!*—*Shakespeare.*
> And every *bairn.*—*Ben Jonson.*
> Has he not well provided for the *bairn?*—*Fletcher.*

Bairn-time. A family of children; a brood.

> Wit-in (within) the toon of Bethleem,
> And utewit (outwith) mani *barntem*
> Did he sacclesli o lyf (life),
> Ful waful made he mani wyf (wife).—*Cursor Mundi.*

> Antenoure was of that *barne-teme.*—*La Bone Florence of Rome.*

Baith. Both.

> I wold hold it for no scathe
> Though thou hadst bow and arrows *baith.*
> *Hartshorne's An. Met. Tales.*

> For the mercy of God is swa mykel here,
> And reches over all *bathe* far and nere.—*Hampole.*

> But I will make a recompence
> Is better for you *baith.*—*R. Hood.*

Bake. A particular kind of biscuit; once the only kind to be found in bakers' shops, and long the principal article for which there was any demand, and hence its name of *bake* as the only thing that came from the bakers. The Scotch people were long before they gave up baking their own bread,—even yet the practice is not altogether abandoned,—and only purchased what they called *tea-bread* for an occasional party, and *bakes*, which were the only kind of baby's food then known.

This explains why, in "The Holy Fair," Burns represents those assembled in the tavern as "crying out for *bakes* and yill," for, unless it might be a few oat-cakes, there was no other bread in the house.

Ballets, ballants. Ballads.

Ballant, a ballad.—*Halliwell.*

This day the House of Peers have committed to preson ye man that printed the scandalous *ballet* concerning the Queen.—*Sir Ed. Nicholas to Ch. I.*

> I make but repetition
> Of what is ordinary, and Ryalto talk,
> And *ballated*, and would be plaid o' th' stage.—*Webster.*
>
> That can sing *ballet* tunes.—*Burton.*

Bamboozle. To impose upon; to deceive; to confound.
—*Johnson.*

You are so *bamboozled* with what you hear, you forget to scold me.—*Smollett.*

Ban. To swear, curse.

> And beggars they *ban*.—*Skelton.*
>
> You bade me *ban*.—*Shakespeare.*
>
> And now they *ban* that they were born.—*The Lover at Liberty.*

Ban', Band. A neckcloth of a particular form worn by clergymen; *Johnson.* A survival of the collar worn in the sixteenth century; at one time part of every gentleman's dress.

> His cloaths rich, and *band* sit neat.—*Ben Johnson.*
>
> A Chrysostom to smoothe thy *band* in.—*Pope.*

Band. A bond.

> Hast thou, according to thy oath and *band*,
> Brought hither Henry Hereford thy bold son?—*Shakespeare.*
>
> Was he arrested on a *band*?—*Ib.*

Chains and *bands* she meant to make them prove.—*Fairfax.*

He sent to her his basenet as a faithfull *band.*—*Spenser.*

Bane. A bone; a small toothed comb.

> Hit had sticked the Yerl of Douglas
> In at the brest *bane.*—*Ancient Ballad of Cheny Chase.*

> The bischop went in-to that toun,
> And come into his knihtes wanes,
> And soht ful gern his hali *banes.*
> *E. Metrical Homilies. Small.*

These demy divines, and friscaioly yonkerkyns, moche better *bayned* than brayned.—*Skelton.*

Banie, or *bainie.* Having large bones, strong.

Bang. An effort, to beat, to strive, to excel.

Bang, to beat, also to excel; "that *bangs* a'."—*Bamford.*

> You will bear me a *bang* for that.—*Shakespeare.*

> My master comes like any Turk,
> And *bangs* me most severely.—*Henry Carey.*

The young uns roaid for th' Ribband, me cusen *banged* awth lads and gat it for sure.—*Westmoreland Dialect.*

She *bang'd* him, she *bang'd* him, for spending a penny when he stood in need.—*Speech at riding the stang in Yorkshire. Ellis.*

Bannock. Flat, round, soft cake. As Jamieson has pointed out, a bannock differs from a cake principally in not being toasted before the fire as well as on it. A *bannock* is also much thicker than a cake or scone.

Bannock, an oat-cake tempered in water and baked under the embers.—*Bailey, Ray, and Grose.*

These definitions, Scotch and English, speak only of bannocks made of oatmeal, whereas, in Scotland at least, they were often made of cheaper material, as witness the song,

> Bannocks o' bear meal,
> Bannocks o' barley!

Indeed, when bannocks were in common use, oat-meal was considered too valuable to form more than a small part—parritch always excepted—of the food of a cottar's or even of a farmer's house. This is well brought out in an incident in the life of Burns's mother, related by Chambers. When a child, " Agnes Brown was sent to live with her mother's mother. When this old person was more than ordinarily pleased with her granddaughter's doings at her wheel, she gave her, as her *ten-hours*, or lunch, a piece of brown bread, with a piece of white as *kitchen* to it, both being only varieties of oat-meal cake."

Now, I believe the brown bread was *mashlum*, a cheaper kind of bread, oat-meal being always, till recently, called *white* meal, and long after Agnes Brown's useful days it was customary to reward deserving youngsters with a piece of oat-cake along with the *mashlum scone*, not as kitchen, but as a *bonne bouche*.

In Ireland they (fairies) frequently lay *bannocks* in the way of travellers.—*Grose.*

The butter, the cheese, and the *bannocks*,
Dissolved like snaw in a fresh.—*The Northumberland Garland, Ritson.*

Bardie. Dim. of bard.

Barefit. Barefooted. See *fit.*

Barkit. Barked. For change of *d* into *t* see under *akwart.*

And shot they with the round, the square, or *forket* pile.—*Polyolbion.*

They withstoden and wel *defendit.*—*Kyng Alesaunder.*

The dame perceiv'd that Tancred breath'd and *sight* (sighed).—
Fairfax.

Barley bree. Barley juice, malt liquor. See *bree.*

Barmie. Of, or like barm, yeasty.

> And their cold stomachs with crown'd goblets cheer
> Of windy cider, and of *barmy* beer.—*Dryden.*
>
> I think my brains will work without *barm.*—*Fletcher.*

Base. Bass.

> Next pans and kettles of all keys,
> From trebles down to double *base.*—*Hudibras.*
>
> *Hor.* Madam, 'tis now in tune.
> *Luc.* All but the *base.*
> *Hor.* The *base* is right.—*Shakespeare.*
>
> The mean (tenor) is drown'd with your unruly *base.*—*Id.*
> The *base* murmurs of the water's fall.—*Spenser.*

Bash. To be ashamed.

> His countenance was bold, and *bashed* not
> For Guion's looks, but scornful eye-glance at him shot.—*Spenser.*

Bashfu'. Bashful.

Batch. The quantity of bread baked at a time; a crew, a gang.

> I ne'er hurt their churnings,
> Their brew-locks, nor their *batches.*—*Thomas Middleton.*
>
> Except he were of the same meal and *batch.*—*Ben Jonson.*
>
> I am a pupil of the same academy. We'll have a noble *batch.*
> —*Garrick.*

Batts. Botts. *A* for *o.* See under *aff.*

Bauckie-bird. A bat.

> The royalle egle with his fetherys dunne,
> Of nature so hihe takith his flyght,
> No *bakke* of kynde may looke ageyn the sunne,
> Of frowardnesse yit wyl he fleen be nyght.—*Lydgate.*

Baudrons. A cat.

"Bawd is a common name for a hare in Aberdeenshire," says Dr. Jamieson, and he asks, "Can Badrans have any affinity?" It seems also to have been applied to a hare in England, if, as has been supposed, *bawd* is so used in the second act of "Romeo and Juliet." If so, then as *cat* or *puss* was often applied to the hare, one of the numerous names of that animal may, with a slight change, have been given to the cat.

Bauk. A cross-beam; a *bauk en'*, the end of a beam.

This is Burns's definition, but I believe a *bauk* is a spar above, and parallel to, a joist.

For change of *l* into *au*, see *a'*.   Balks.—*Johnson.*

Bawks, timbers, beams.—*Bamford.*

Bawks, the large timber beams that support the roof.—*Thoresby.*

The sewe was in the kilne-hoile doone,
And they were on the *bawke* aboone.—*The Felon Sewe of Rokeby.*

Two yards a plaister tumald off at *bawk* onta me head.—*Tom Treddlehoyle.*

Bauld. Bald. See *aff*.

He makes meke that ar was fell,
And waik that *bald* has been.—*Sir Penny.   Warton.*

Show yoursell
To all the shepherds *bauldly.*—*Ben Jonson.*

A prophet of Estrinland,
Heght Balaam, crafti and *bald.*—*Cursor Mundi.*

Bawmy. Balmy. See under *a'*.

The *bawmy* liquor is so commendable.—*Lydgate.*

Bawk. A balk.

A strip of land, of indeterminate breadth, left unploughed.—
Jamieson.

Nor that they set debate between their lords
By earing up the *balks* that part their bounds.—*George Gascoigne.*

Dikeres and delveres digged up the *balkes.*—*P. Plowman.*

Baws'nt. Having a white stripe down the face like a bawson or badger.

His mittens were of *bawson's* skin.—*Drayton.*

> I am a lord of other gear ! this fine
> Smooth *bawson's* cub.—*Ben Jonson.*

Bawtie. Dog, or name of dog.

Be. To *let be*, to give over, to cease.

> Let be that Lady debonaire.—*Spenser.*
>
> Neverthelese he *let be*
> And loked on the chylde so fre.—*Emare.*

Let be, said Amys of the Mountayne.—*Sir Guy. Warton.*

Bear. Barley.

The farmers will not take it from them for their *bere*.—*Swift.*

Orge Paumé, *Beere*-barlie ; big barlie ; barlie with the square ear. —*Cotgrave.*

Beas'. Beasts, specially applied to cattle, but in the "Address of Beelzebub"—lice. Burns applies it to a sheep and a horse.

Beasts, and sheep, and horses.—*Revelation*, xviii. 13.

Meh measter seet store on hur becose o' fotchin the *byess* an sheep.
—*Tim Bobbin.*

> Thoo when scome (I came) home esbote (I bought) some *beass.*
> —*Wright's Political Songs.*

Beastie. Dim. of beast.

Ther wer many *bestys* felle in that forest.—*Octovian Imperator.*

Lene me
An hundred frankes for a weke or tweye,
For certain *bestes* that I must beye.—*Chaucer.*

Kepe the corne fro the *bestes.*—*P. Plowman.*

The words *bestys* and *bestes* are not diminutives, but their use as plurals may have led to the form *beastie*, and probably all our diminutives in *ie* had a similar origin.

Beck. A curtsy.

A *beck* was a *bend of the knee*, as well as a nod of the head.—*Halliwell.*

> My bony on gave me a *bek.*—*Old Song, Ritson.*
>
> Then peine I me to stretchen forthe my necke,
> And est and west upon the peple I *becke.*—*Chaucer.*

Bedevil. To afflict.

> Recruited once more, I forgot all my pain,
> And was jilted, and burnt, and *bedevil'd* again.
> —*Edward Moore.*

Lucretia is so fashion'd and *bedevil'd* that nothing can save her.—*Garrick.*

Beef. Body.

> Chastise that brawny *beef* of thine!—*Shelton's Don Quixote.*

Beek. To bask.

> He had more mystyr of a gode fyre
> To *beyke* hys boones by.—*Le Bone, Florence of Rome.*
>
> That knyght es nothing to set by
> That leves al his chevalry,
> And ligges *bekeand* in his bed,
> When he haves a lady wed.—*Ywain and Gawain.*
>
> And eke agaynst the sonne
> *Bekyth* hym poor Diogenes in his tonne.—*Sir T. More.*
>
> As Abraham was in the playn
> Of Mamre where he dwelt,
> And *beakt* himselfe agaynst the sunne,
> Whose parching heat he felt.—*W. Hunnis.*

Beet. To add fuel to fire, to mend, to become better.

> I will don sacrifice, and fires *bete.*—*Chaucer.*
>
> Anoon a fyer ther was *y-beet.*—*Octovian Imperator.*
>
> Jhesue crist our balys *bete*, and to the blys us brynge!
> —*Chevy Chase.*

Behadden. Beholden. See under *a'* and *haud.*

Behint or *behin*. Behind. See *akwart*.

Beld. Bald. *E* for *a*, as in

> A lion almost *sterved* is not by upland herdsmen driven.
> —*Chapman.*

> Sone after she gan *herk*
> Cokkes crowe and houndes *berk*.—*Lay Le Fraine.*

> And his queene attone
> Was Lady Flora, on whom did attend
> A fayre flocke of faeries, and a fresh *bend* [band]
> Of lovely nymphes.—*Spenser.*

> Duke Gedeon whan it was *derke*
> Ordeineth him unto his *werke*.—*Gower.*

Bellum. Force, impetus.—*Jamieson.* "To ward their bellum" seems to mean "to defend from their assaults."

Belyve. By and by, presently, quickly, immediately, at once.

> *Belive*, anon, by and by, or towards night.—*Bailey.*
> To London the knyghts went *belyve*.—*Rich. C. de Lion.*
> By the same way the direful dames do drive
> Their mournful charet, fild with rusty blood,
> And down to Plutoes house are come *bilive*.—*Spenser.*

Ben. In, into. Into the *spence* or parlour; into any place in which the speaker is; *but and ben*, the country kitchen and parlour. See *but and ben*.

Ben, into.—*Halliwell.*

> & teyy (they) comen eft till Gerrsalem,
> To seken himm thaer *binnin* (within).—*The Ormulum.*

> The King Arthur es redy dight
> To be her *byn* this fowretenyght.—*Ywain and Gawain.*

Benison. A benediction.

Benizon, a blessing.—*Bailey.*

> For which his fadres *benison* he wan.—*Chaucer.*
>
>> Be gone
>> Without our grace, our love, our *benison.*—*Shaks.*
>
> Fadyr, thy *benesoun* with good entent !
> —*Octavian Imperator.*

Benmost. Inmost. See *ben.*

Benorth. To the northward of.

> So that folc *binorthe* durste nour at-route.—*Rob. of Gloucester.*
>
> The army landed two myles *bewest* the town of Lethe.
> *The Late Expedition in Scotland, Lond., 1554.*
>
>> For Horn
>> That woneth her *by-weste.*—*The Geste of Kyng Horn.*

Bent. A kind of coarse grass; the ground on which bent grows.

> Whiles round about thy greedy eye doth look,
> Observing wonders in some flower by,
> This *bent*, that leaf, that butterfly.—*Henry Peacham.*
>
> Her cassock was of scarlet red ;
> Long and large, as straight as *bent.*—*Robert Green.*
>
> Like as the bird, that having close imbarr'd
>   Her tender young ones in the springing *bent*,
> Cries and complains most where she needeth least.—*Fairfax.*

Bent. Stretched, braced, in

>> Till a' their weel-swall'd kytes belyve
>>   Are *bent* like drums.—*To a Haggis.*
>
>> I'll give thanks
>> When my belly's *braced* up like a drum.—*Massinger.*

Besouth. To the southward of.

>> An harpour sange a gest be mouth
>> Of a knyght there *be-south.*—*Sir Cleges.*

Bethankit. Grace after meat. Past tense in *t* instead of *d*, as in—

And soo *invadet* Scotland.—I *commandet* dewe watche to be kepte.—*Earl of Northumberland to Henry VIII.*

Bethankit is similar to Shakespeare's *we-thank-you*—

> Like a cipher,
> Yet standing in rich place, I multiply,
> With one *we-thank-you*, many thousands more
> That go before it.—*Winter's Tale.*

Beuk. A book. Change of *oo* to *u*.

In the line from Gavin Douglas, which Burns has prefixed to "Tam o' Shanter," this word is spelled *buke*. It is more common for both English and Scotch authors to change *oo* to *u* or *ui* than to *eu*.

> Arthur the Kyng of Yngland
> That wan al Wales with his hand,
> And al Scotland, als sayes the *buke*,
> And mani mo, if men will *luke.—Ywain and Gawain.*
>
> Every man his leve *tuke.—Ipomydon.*

His daughter bears away the bell from all the *buke*-sellers wives in London.—*Life and Errors of John Dunton. Lond., 1705.*

I hold hym never no good archer
That *shuteth* at buttes so wyde.—*Adam Bell, Clym of the Clough.*

Bicker. A drinking-cup made of staves and hoops like a tub.

Byker, a beaker cup.—*Haliiwell.*

Jamieson, I believe correctly, says there is no connection between *beaker* and *bicker*. He seems to suggest *beech*, the wood of which it was made, as the origin of *bicker*, and this seems probable when we remember the tendency to change *ch* into *k*, as *bitch* into *bick*, *pitch* into *pick*, *beseech* into *beseke*, etc.

Bicker. A short, rapid race; a strife of any kind; a skirmish rather than a battle.

> Unnumber'd streamlets *bicker'd* through the sunny shade.
> *Thomson.*

Byker, a fray or scuffle. *Bickering*, a tilting or skirmishing dispute, wrangling.—*Bailey.*

> Bomen *bickarte* uppon the bent.

Percy says *bickarte* here means skirmished, but it must mean *ran*, for the Scots had not yet come up, and the *bomen* were running after and shooting the deer.

> As fast as the heels on't could *bicker*,
> It scamper'd on northward away.
> *The Northumb. Garland. Ritson.*

> Thou art to old at (to) *bykyr* and fyght.—*R. C. de Lion.*

> Heore thonkyng they nowe be sikir,
> Y schal heom yelde wel this *bykir.*—*Kyng Alisaunder.*

> We shall begin our ancient *bickerings.*—*Shakespeare.*

Bid. To ask. See *bode.*

> I will *bid* the duke to the nuptial.—*Shakespeare.*

Biel, bield. A shelter.

> *Beeld*, a sheltered place.—*Bailey.*

> This our *bield*, the blustering winds to shun.—*Fairfax.*

> Alweldand God, of mightes maste,
> He be his *beld*, for he mai best.—*L. Minot.*

> None es so wight wapins to welde,
> Ne that so boldly mai us *belde.*—*Ywain and Gawain.*

Bien. Wealthy, plentiful.

> This is *bien* bouse, this is *bien* bouse.—*Broome's Jovial Crew.*

Latham says, "The thieves of London are conservators of Anglo-Saxonisms," and we may assume that Broome would make his *Jovial Crew* speak the language most likely to be understood by a London audience; if so, *bien* may be a good old English word.

Big. To build.

Bigge, to build up.—*Bailey*.

That day is good a myll to *bygge*.—*De Curzione Lunaes*.

On a buke the erl swar
For to restor bath les and mar,
And *big* again both tour and toun.—*Ywain and Gawain*.

Big the a hows, at thi liking.—*The Two Dreams*.

Biggin. Building, a house, from *big*. For omission of *g* see *backlins*.

When he come to his *byggynge*,
He welcomed fayr that lady yyng.—*Emare*.

Vuche burde with her barne the *byggynge* they levez.
Dr. Morris's *Early English Alliterative Poems*.

Biggit. Built. *It* for *ed*, as in—

Thou never *ploughit* the ocean's foam,
To seek and bring rough pepper home.—*Herbert*.

She bringeth me forthe the great *clobbet* staves.—*Chaucer*.

So fell aslepe, *slepet* there all nyght.—*Froissart*.

She *smirkit* and she smyld.—*Heywood*.

Ther was mony a sarsyn, and long-*berdet*. Barbaryn.
Kyng Alisaunder.

Bill. A bull. *I* for *u* sounding as in *bull*, is rare in E. It is, however, to be found, as in—

And with that worde, he for a *quishen* (cushion) ran.—*Chaucer*.

Billie. A brother, a young fellow, a companion, a man.

Billy, a brother, a young fellow, a term of endearment.—
Halliwell.

Billy. Familiar for William. See under *Commutation*.

Had I a great princess been born,
My *Billy* had dear been to me.—*Fielding*.

Bing. A heap of grain, potatoes, etc. Unless a word in Marlow's "Jew of Malta," which is suspected to be a misprint, be relied on, I do not know that *bing* occurs in any English author.

> Here have I purst their paltry silver *bings*.
> Fie, what trouble 'tis to count their trash !
> Well fare the Arabians, who so richly pay
> The things they traffic for with wedge of gold.

Birdie. Dim. of bird ; a young woman.

Holy hath *byrdys*, a ful fayre flok.—*Christmas Carol. Brand*.
That fest lasted fourten night
Of barouns and of *birddes* (ladies) bright.—*Amis and Amiloun*.
    The Justices somme
Busked him to the boure there the *birde* dwelled.—*P. Plowman*.

Birk. Birch. *K* for *ch*, as in—

I'll *pick* (pitch) you o'er the pales.—*Shakespeare*.
Stain or *brack* (breach) on her sweet reputation.—*Fletcher*.
We *beseke* (beseech) you of mercie and socour.—*Chaucer*.
Birk, a kind of birch tree.—*Grose. Bailey*.
He bete her wyth a yerd of *bvrke*.—*Le Bone Florence of Rome*.

Birken. Consisting of birches.

> Still, 'tis said, the fairy people meet
> Beneath each *birken* shade on mead or hill.—*Collins*.

Birkie. A clever fellow. This is Burns's explanation of the word, but it does not agree with his use of it :—

> You see yon *birkie* ca'd a lord,—
> He's but a *coof* for a' that.

And a *coof*, he tells us, is "a blockhead, a ninny." Now a person cannot well be a clever fellow and a blockhead. Cunningham says it means "a clever, a forward conceited fellow," yet Burns says of himself—

> There was a *birkie* born in Kyle,

and of Creech—

> We've lost a *birkie* weel worth gowd.

The truth seems to be that *birkie* simply means fellow, and, like fellow, depends for its signification on the adjective joined with it. Had birch or *birk* ever been used as an instrument of punishment in Scotland we might have supposed a *birkie* to be a person possessing some good qualities, but likely to be benefited by an occasional use of the birch.

Birl. To club money for the purpose of procuring drink; to pour out.—*Jamieson.*

> Some dame Elynour entrete
> To *byrle* them of the best.—*Skelton.*

> The olde God of wyne called Baccus *birlyng* the wyne.
> *Hall's Chron.*

In these extracts *byrl* or *birl*, though the same word as the S. *birl*, has not exactly the same meaning. The one signifies to draw liquor, the other to provide for its being drawn.

Birnie. Ground covered with the scorched stems of heath.—*Jamieson.*

Birnie. Burns uses this word, which Chambers translates *lively*, in a jocular letter to Nicol. I have not met the word elsewhere, but from the context and the fact that *birn* is a form of burn, lively or spirited seems the meaning.

Birring. The noise of partridges when they rise.

Beere and *birre*, force or might, as *with all my beere*, i.e., with all my might.—*Bailey.*

> To him he stirt, with *birful* grim.—*Ywain and Gawain.*

> With the mouth he made a *bere*
> That al the halle was afered.—*Kyng Alisaunder.*

> Good wife, let be all this *beare,*
> That thou makest in this place here.—*Chester Mysteries.*

And the unclene spiritis entridden into the hoggis, and with greet *bire,* or haste, the floc was cast down in-to the sea.—*Wyclif.*
Morris and Skeat.

> Richard gaff
> To labourers, and to trumpours,
> Hors and robes to *ber* (sound) her los.
>
> *R. C. de Lion.*

> Bi that time was the barn for *bere* of that hounde
> Draw him in to his den.—*R. of Gloucester.*

Birse. A bristle.

Byrst, a bristle.—*Bosworth.* Burst.—*Thorpe.*

Bit. Crisis, nick of time.

Bizz. To buzz, a bustle. *I* for *u*, as in—

> That we be not exyled
> To the *dyne* (dun) dale
> Of boteless bale.—*Skelton.*

Of him ye might be *trist* (trust) enough.—*Ywain and Gawain.*
The tayl they *kyt* (cut) of hundredis fyve.—*Kyng Alisaunder.*
And was war
Of the fir in the *chirche-haw* (church-yard).—*The Seven Sages.*
Biez, to buzz.—*Halliwell.*

Bizzard. A buzzard.

Bizzie. Busy. Differs only in spelling. In some districts of England *z* is often used for *s*. Thus in "Tummas and Meary," by John Collier, we find *yezzier* for easier, *uz* for us, etc.; but this is not quite analogous, for *busy* and *bizzie* have the same pronunciation. There are also some very old writings in which the flat is used in the spelling instead of the sharp *s* in the plural of nouns, thus—

> Bukkez, bausenez, and bulez, to the bonkkez hyghed.
> *Dr. Morris's Early English Alliterative Poems.*

Black. Disastrous, evil, in "Black be your fa!" i.e., "May your lot be unfortunate."

> I will to France, hoping the consequence
> Will prove as bitter, *black*, and tragical.—*Shakespeare.*

Black-art. Mysterious rite; conjuration; union with evil spirits.

Black-art, necromancy.—*Halliwell.*

The *black art* of dark antiquity.—*James Heath.*

> Let's also flee the furious-curious spell
> Of those *black-artists* that consult with hell.—*Sylvester.*
>
> He (Chillingworth) was called the King's *Black-art man.*
> *Life of T. Fuller.*

Black bonnet. A name given by Burns to the elder who stands at the plate for receiving the offerings of those entering the church. I believe it was the poet's own invention, for the oldest people I have met never knew the term till they saw it in "The Holy Fair." From that poem it is plain who is meant, but it is not so easy to find out why he is called Black Bonnet, for I do not suppose that an elder had any distinctive dress. It is not quite certain that Burns did not mean a clergyman as well as an elder by the term. In his Epistle to Mr. M'Math he says,

> My music, tired wi' mony a sonnet
> On gown, and ban', and douse *black bonnet.*

Gown and *ban'* mean minister, and I rather think so does *black bonnet.*

Black-lippit. Black-lipped, bitter tongued, foul-mouthed.
He's noble. He had a *black mouth* that said other of him.
Shakespeare.

Blade. A reckless fellow. This is one of those words that depend for their meaning on the adjective with which they are joined.

Despatch me, I pri'thee this *troublesome blade.*—*Prior.*
He is a *bonny blade,* and master of his trade—*R. Hood.*
If all the gods should now a fancy take
Some one of us a raw young *blade* to make.
Duke of Buckingham.

Blae. Livid; the colour of the skin after a blow with the fist or a blunt instrument. In old E. this word is spelled *blo.*

O pereles Prynce, payned to the deth,
Rufully rent, thy body wan and *blo.*—*Skelton.*
That fyre shall falle, and brenne al to *blo* askes
The houses and the homes.—*P. Plowman.*
And bett hym tille his rybbis braste,
And made his flesche fulle *blaa.*—*Sir Isumbras.*

Blastie. A shrivelled dwarf; a term of contempt. *Blast* is a minced oath, and so blastie, in American phrase, is a *little cuss.*

Quick, d—mme, take away your nasty sheep.
. . . . . , . .
You *blast* (i.e., d—n, as above) the sheep, good Master Skinner!
. . . .
Have I brow-beaten each thief and strumpet,
And *blasted* on them?—*Dr. Wolcot.*

Blastit. Blasted.

Blate. Bashful, sheepish.
Blait or *blate,* bashful.—*Grose.*

> If they have supt e'er I come in,
> I will look wondrous *blate.—R. Hood.*

The old E. form seems to have been *blade :—*

> And they meet in her mirth whan mynstrals ben styl
> Whan telleth they of the trinitie a tale or twaine
> And bringeth forth a *blade* reason and take Bernard to witness.
> *P. Plowman. Warton.*

Blather. The bladder.

> There's nothing gained by being witty : fame
> Gathers but wind to *blather* up a name.
> *Powell to the Memory of Master Fletcher.*

The use of *th* for *d* is not a Scottish peculiarity. In a letter to Parliament Cromwell speaks of the Earl of *Lautherdale* (Lauderdale).

> Well *couth* (could) he tune his pipe.—*Spenser.*
> The dore was all of *athamant* (adamant) eterne.—*Chaucer.*
> Him was lever have . .
> Twenty books . .
> Then robus riche, or *fithul* (fiddle).—*Wright's Chaucer.*
> At Oxforth (Oxford).—*Skelton.*

Murther for murder is still used.

> Though he wer *thoghtyer* (doughtier) gome
> Than Launcelot du Lake.—*Lybeaus Disconnus.*

Blaud. A flat piece of any thing, to slap, to dash ; a slap or blow.

Blaw. To blow, to boast, to flatter.

> The princes that war rich on raw,
> Gert nakers strike, and trumpets *blaw.—Minot.*
> In shynyng of the sonne whan March *blaweth*,
> The aitches upward them thraweth.—*Kyng Alisaunder.*
> Gret bost he gan to *blawe.—Amis and Amiloun.*

I do not know that *blow*—as *blaw* does—means to flatter, but that seems to be the sense in—

> Whyle I was ryche inow at home
> Grete bost then wolde they *blowe*.
> And now they renne awaye fro me.—*R. Hood*.

To blaw south. When sentence of banishment was passed on a Scotsman, unless he had considerable means, he could go nowhere but to England, that is, south; so, to *blaw south* means *to banish*.

Blearie and *blear ee.* Wet eye. See *ee*.

A *bleery-eed* fowler trust not though he wepe.—*Lydgate*.

Bleer. To bedim, to deceive.

> You your forces bend
> To *bleer* men's eyes
> With fopperies
> Which fools embrace and wiser men despise.
> *Thomas Ellwood*.

Gold's radiant lustre never *blears* his eye.—*Sylvester*.

Ambition *blearde* myne eyes, I could not see.
The Flower of Fame.

Bleerit. Bleered; *bleerit een*, eyes hurt with weeping. *It* for *ed.* See *Biggit*.

Bleeze. Blaze, flame. *E* for *a*, as in—

> He held virginitee
> More parfit than wedding in *freeltee* (frailty).—*Chaucer*.

Their tresour and their *meles* (males)
He toke to his own deles.—*R. C. de Lion*.

I wud the deil had had their craigs,
And a' things in a *bleeze* o' fire.—*The Fray of Hantiwissell*.

Blellum. An idle talking fellow. Of this word, which Burns uses twice, nobody seems to know anything, and I suspect it must be placed in the same category as Butler's *slubberdegullion*, Chaucer's *viretote*, his own *ramfeezled*, and similar words which are perhaps none the less effective that they cannot be exactly defined.

Blether. To talk idly. See *blather.*

Blether, to make a great noise.—*Halliwell.*

I blunder, I bluster, I blowe, and I *blother*.—*Skelton.*

Blin. Blind. *D* is often omitted after *n* by E. authors.

Through the worlde went the *soun* (sound).—*Chaucer.*

And she shalt out, thus said heere and *houn* (hound).—*Ib.*

An *almon* (almond) now for Parrot.—*Skelton.*

His bestes hym folowed by the *sowne*.—*The Frere and the Boye. Ritson.*

Blink. A little while, a smiling look ; to look kindly; to shine by fits.

Pers of hys slepe gan *blynke*.—*Robert of Brunne.*

The dame who thought that one *blink* of her eye
Could make the stoutest heart feel love's sweet pain.—*Fairfax.*

Though she bee a vixen, she will *blenke* blithly on you for my cause.—*Two Lancashire Lovers.*

Blinker. A term of contempt; a young woman. Jamieson says "a lively engaging girl."

A blinkard, *blinker, strabo. Blinker, straba.* She that is squint-eyed, or has a cast in her eye. *Si qua straba est, Veneri similis.*—*Ovid. Ainsworth.*

Is it possible that Burns, on one of those occasions when he turned to his "Latin again," found this passage ?

Blinkin. Smiling, shining.

Blirt. Out-burst of grief.

Blirt, to cry.—*Grose.*

Blue-gown. One of those beggars who get (now got) annually on the King's birth-day a blue cloke or gown, with a badge. (No new member has been added since 1833).

> A *blue coat* with a badge does better with you.
> *Green's Tu Quoque.*

Bluid. Blood. *U* for *oo*. See under *beuk.*

Blid, blood. *Bamford*. This is the Ayrshire pronunciation.

Yt was marvele ande the redde *blude* renne not.—*Chevy Chase.*

The red *blude* gan out glyde.—*Sir Guy.*

They are less *bluddy* than ever they were.—*De Mornay.*

> In his right hand a naked sword he had,
> That to the hiltes was al with *blud* embrewed.
> *The Mirrour for Magistrates.*

Bluntie. A sniveller; a stupid fellow. *Bluntie* seems to be a noun formed from the adj. *blunt* by the addition of *ie*,—a rare form of derivation, so rare that I recollect only two other instances: *brownie* (the spirit) and *crummy*, and both of these may be disputed, for it is not universally conceded that brownie comes from *brown*, the colour; and *crumb*, though an adj. in Anglo-Saxon, was not used as such in English; *crummy* is still not a noun but an adjective, with the subaddition *cow* or *staff.*

Blunt, ignorant, or uncivilized.—*Todd. Blunt*, clownish.— *Bailey.*

As base or *blunt*, unmeet for melodie.—*Spenser.*

Blutter. The heather-bleater, or blutter; the mire-snipe.

Blype. A shred, a large piece; anything peeled off.

Board. A plank on which a corpse is stretched.— *Jamieson.* This is his definition of *board trees*, which he says is a Northern term. In the South it is called a *straughtin-board*.

> The Laird o' the Ford will *straught on a board* (will die)
> If he canna get her.—*The Tarbolton Lasses*.

Bob. The obeisance made by a lady, a curtsey; to move up and down.

> When she drinks, against her lips I *bob*.—*Shakespeare*.

Bock. To vomit, to gush intermittently.

> They looked him all round about,
> But wound on him saw nane,
> Yet at his mouth came *bocking* out
> The blood of a good vein.—*R. Hood*.

Agrunting and drinking, *reboking* up again.—*Barclay*.

His stomak stuffed ofte tymes dyde *reboke*.—*Skelton*.

To *boken*, to nauseate, ready to vomit.—*Thoresby*.

Bode. An offer made for anything on sale. The old past tense of bid.

> Another come and *bode* more.—*Rob. of Gloucester*.
>
> Hour King *boden* him gold and fe,
> With (if) that he wil with him be.
> *Horn Childe and Maiden Rimnild.*
>
> And we pray
> That ye wolden take our *bode*.—*Rich. C. de Lion*.

Bodle. A copper coin of the value of two pennies Scots, or the third part of an English halfpenny.—*Jamieson*.

Boadle, an old English word for half a farthing, is still in use in Lancashire.—*Sir John Sinclair, 1782*.

Bodle.—*Halliwell, Bamford, and Grose*.

Bogie. Dim. of *bog*.

Bogle. A spirit, an apparition.

Boggart, a spirit, an apparition.—*Bamford*.

Potato-*bogle*, a scarecrow.—*Halliwell.*

Bogle-boe, which seems, at least in sound, to bear some affinity to *Hobgoblin*, is said to be derived from the Welsh *Biogwyl*, to terrify.—*Ellis.*

Boggle. To start, to fly back; to fear to come forward.—*Johnson.*

Theer wur a *boggle* in it, I often 'eered 'm mysen.—*Tennyson.*

Bole. An aperture in a wall for holding small articles in frequent use.

Bole-holes. The openings in a barn for light and air.—*Halliwell.*

Bolus. A form of medicine.—*Johnson.*

Take one of these *boluses* every six hours, washing it down with six spoonfuls of the best Holland's Geneva.—*Fielding.*

Bonnie, bonny. Handsome, beautiful. Burns seems to have generally written *bonie.*

And be ye blithe and *bonny.*—*Shak.*
And he wolde, after fyght,
Bonie landis to hem dyght.—*Kyng Alisaunder.*

Bonnet. This word needs no explanation, but one passage in which it occurs may deserve a line. In "The Cottar's Saturday Night" it is said—

The cheerfu' supper done, wi' serious face,
The *bonnet* reverently is laid aside.

Does the poet mean us to understand that, in Scotland in his day, men remained covered at meat? This was once the custom in England, and I suppose in Scotland, but except for this passage I should not have thought it had continued till so recent a period. Pepys, under date 1664, says—" Home to bed; having got a strange cold in my head, by *flinging off my hat at dinner.*" And his editor remarks, in a note on this passage—" In Lord

Clarendon's Essay on the Decay of Respect paid to Age- he says that in his younger days he never kept his hat on before those older than himself except at dinner." And Bishop Hall mentions among the degradations to which a chaplain in a great man's house must submit, he has " to sit bare at meals."

Hee dyd come in to diner, and dyd *put on hys cappe.—Merie Tales of Skelton.*

Now *hats fly off* (after dinner), and youths carouse.
Sir John Suckling.

Bonnock. See *bannock.*

Since *Bannock* was in type, the following paragraph appeared in the newspapers:—

At an election meeting in Wiltshire, a labourer said, "Wasn't it six shillings a week and *barley bannocks* when the corn were taxed?"

This shows that *bannock* is an E. word, and that it was not always made of oatmeal.

Boord. A board. The digraph *oo* in *boord, broose,* etc., sounds like *u* in Fr. *fut, début.*

Aïs, a planke or *boord.—Cotgrave.* Board, see *boord.—Sherwood.*

We ben entred into schippes *boord.—Wright's Chaucer.*

An house of timber and *boord* being there erected.—*Stows.*

Now have at all that lyeth upon the *burde.—Skelton.*

The King and myself of all the Councell *Boord* were, etc.—*Sir E. Nicholas.*

Boord-en, Board-end. The head of the table. For omission of *d,* see under *blin.*

With Marchauns to beon were hend
Ne weore accountis at the *bordis eynde.—Kyng Alisaunder.*

Item, it is thought good that no plovers be bought at no season but only in Christmas and principal feasts, and my lord to be served therewith, and his *board end*, and none other.—*Household Book of the Earl of Northumberland quoted by Hume, Hist. of E.*

> Take here the golde in a bagg,
> I schall hyt hyng on a knagg,
> At the schypp *borde ende.*—*Le Bone F. of Rome.*

Boortree. The shrub elder, planted much of old in hedges of barn-yards, etc.; literally a bowertree.

Boor, the parlour, bed-chamber, or inner room.—*Grose.*

A *bur-tree*, an elder, or dog-tree.—*Thoresby.*

> Ful many a maide bright in *bour*
> They mourned for him *par amour.*—*Chaucer.*

And the boys were armed in general with *bore-tree* or elder pop-guns.—*Hutchison's Hist. of Cumberland.*

Boost. Behoved, must needs.

Buse, behoves.—*Sir F. Madden.*

> And sen ye wil that it be thus,
> At yowre likynge habide me *bus.*—*The Seven Sages.*

Nedes *bus* you have sum nobil knyght
That will and may defend your right.—*Ywain and Gawain.*

Another form of *boost* is *bud*:—

Fer might thai noght fle, but thaire *bud* tham bide.—*L. Minot.*

This explains

Ne *bode* I never thence go.—*Chaucer. Romaunt of the Rose.*

Boot. The balance of value in barter.—*Scott.*

Boot-hose. Stockings to serve for boots; spatterdashes.—*Johnson.*

His lacquey with a linen stock on one leg, and a *boot-hose* on the other, gartered with a red and blue list.—*Shak.*

Bore. A hole in a wall, a cranny.

> A sonne bem ful bryht
> Schon opon the Quene
> At a *bore.*—*Sir Tristrem.*

> Lo, he saide, water hi can stop,
> That hit ne mai nowt bi *bores* drop.—*The Seven Sages.*
>
> Your franchise, wherever you stood, confin'd
> Into an augre's *bore.*—*Shakespeare.*

Bother. To tease, to trouble.

> *Bother*, to tease, confuse, perplex.—*Dr. Hooper.*
>
> Round the yard, a thousand ways,
> Beasts in expectation gaze,
> Catching at the loads of hay
> Passing fodd'rers lug away.
> Hogs with grumbling deafening noise
> *Bother* round the server boys.—*Clare.*

Bouse. To drink. *Bowze*, a convivial meeting, a heavy drinking.

> *Bouse*, to drink lavishly; to tope.—*Johnson.*
>
> Then seke another house
> And there wyll byb and *bouse.*—*Skelton.*
>
> Drynke to hym deirly of fol god *bous.*
> *A Song on the Man in the Moon.*
>
> Come, prythee let's shog off,
> And *bowze* an hour or two: there's ale will make
> A cat speak at the Harrow.—*Beaumont and Fletcher.*
>
> Up rose the *bousy* sire.—*The Dunciad.*

Bow-hought. Bow-legged.

Bowk. The body.

> *Bowke*, the body.—*Bailey.*
>
> The clotered blood, for any leche-craft,
> Corrumpeth, and is in his *bouke* ylaft.—*Chaucer.*
>
> Philotas mette Laban the duyk,
> And bathed his spere in his *bouk.*—*Kyng Alisaunder.*
>
> Smothered it within my panting *bulk.*—*Shak.*

Bow-kail. Cabbage. See *Kail.*

Bow-Kail, cabbage, so called from the circular (?globular) form of the plant.—*Jamieson*.

Bow in *bow-kail* is not the same word as *bow* in *bow-hought*, and is indeed in no way allied to it. The only modern E. word which retains something of its appearance, and is from the same root, is *bowl*, a round drinking cup, and a ball for rolling on the ground. It is from *boll* (A.-S. *bolla*), by the change of *ll* into *w*, as are many words, e.g., roll into *row*, poll into *pow*, knoll into *knowe*, etc., both in S. and E. One example may suffice here.

Or use any charmes in gadering of herbes, or hanginge of *scrowes* (scrolls) about man or woman for any sicknesses.—*Dialogue of Dives and Pauper*.

In Exodus ix. it is said "The flax was *bolled*," that is, *bowed*. Johnson says *boll* is "to rise into a stalk," whereas it means to form into a pod or *bowl*.

Whose feet were *bowlne*
With the streight cordes wherewith they haled him.
Surrey.

New ale will their bellies *bowne* (swell).—*Watkin's Ale*.

It may be mentioned that *bow* in *bow-kail* rhymes to *now*, and *bow*, to bend, to *too*, the difference of pronunciation indicating a difference of origin.

Bowster. A bolster.

Bowster, a bolster, a pillow.—*Bamford*.

Taken by Collard MacCulloch , . a feder *bouster*.—*Deposition of a Manxman, quoted by Sir W. Scott*.

To Judith White, a feather bedd and *bowlster*.—*Will of Bish. Davenant, 1637*.

Bow't. Bowed, bended, crooked. *T* for *d*, as in *biggit*.

A threepence *bow'd* would hire me.—*Shakespeare*.

Then taking fourth a *bowed* Groat, and an old Pennie *bowed*, he gave it her.—*The Third Part of Couny-Catching*.

Brackens. Fern.

Bracken, female fern.—*Bailey*. *Brakons*, fern, brakes.—*Thoresby*. *Breckins*.—*Grose*.

> The hartt was in a *bracken* ferne,
> And hard the houndes and stode full derne.—*Sir Gawaine*.

Brae. A declivity, a precipice, the slope of a hill.
> Up that steep *bray*, Lord Guelpho would not then
> Hazard his folk.—*Fairfax*.

An old traveller and poet translates

> Ipse inter ripas demisso flumine Nilus
> Curretiners,

Slow Nile with low sunk streams shall keep his *braies*.—*Sandys*.

Sandys uses *brae*, as Allan Ramsay sometimes does, for the bank of a river.

> Making down the *brae* he was killed by a random shot.
> *Memoirs of Cap. J. Creichton. Swift.*

Braid. Broad.
> His face was full *brade* and flat.—*Ywain and Gawain*.
>
> His horns been as *brade* as rainbow bent.—*Spenser*.
>
> Without the diche were listes made,
> With wall battailed large and *brade*.—*Chaucer*.
>
> With eghen that war ful bright and clere,
> And *brade*, ilkone, als a sawsére.—*Maister Gemes*.

Braik. A kind of harrow (a heavy one). A different spelling of *brake*.

Brake, a harrow.—*Halliwell*.

Braik. An instrument for rough-dressing flax. From *break*.

Brake, an instrument with teeth, used in dressing flax or hemp.—*Bailey*.

Brainge, or *braindge*. To run rashly forward, to draw unsteadily.

Brak. To break, made insolvent.
> By helping of a friend *brak* his prisoun.—*Chaucer*.
> The chancellor the wex *to-brak*.—*R. C. de Lion*.
> The horse of his company *brak* lowse.—*Surrey to Henry VIII*.
> He blesside and *brak* and gaf looues to disciplis.—*Wyclif*.
> Brake was formerly written *Brak*.—*H. Tooke*.

Brankie. Gaudy; pranked up. —*Jamieson*. Allan Ramsay has "*Brankand*, prancing." Perhaps it means, spirited, forward, needing to be restrained by the *branks* or bridle; or can it be the same as *prankie* in—

> So, that is somewhat like, but *prankie* cote, nay whan?
> *Ralf Roister Doister*.

Branks. A kind of wooden curb for horses. *Cheeks o' branks*, the wooden or side part of branks.

As this kind of halter,—for bridle it could not be called,—has been long disused, it may be worth describing, especially as Jamieson's account of it is not quite accurate. The head-stall was of rope, and the nose-band consisted of two pieces of wood about a foot in length and about four inches thick, fastened in front with a strong cord or other ligature. To one of these sticks a rope was fastened and passed through a hole in the other. When this rope was pulled the nose-band pressed the nostrils more or less tightly according to the force employed. It needed no bit, indeed could admit of none. Animals could be readily enough stopped by it, but could not be guided so steadily by it as by a bit, and hence the force of Burns's line, in which he speaks of himself as "Gaavin, as if led wi' branks," that is, with head now up, now down, and moving from side to side, like an animal under imperfect control.

Branks, a kind of halter or bridle, used by country people on the borders.—*Halliwell*.

Brash. A sudden and short illness.

Brash, a fit, or tumbling one about.—*Grose*.

Brat. A worn shred of cloth; *brats*, coarse clothes, or simply clothes.

Brat, a rag..—*Bailey*. *Brat*, a coarse apron, a rag.—*Grose*.

For ne had they but a shete
Which that they might wrappen hem in a-night
And a *bratt* to walken in by day-light.—*Chaucer*.

Brattle. A short race, hurry, fury.

Braw. Fine, handsome. This is the *brave* or *braue* of old E. writers.

Right over stood in snow-white armour *braue*
The Memphite Zorous, a cunning clark.—*Grimoald*.

There is a great concourse of *braw* lads and lasses.
Bishop of Ossory to Earl of Northumb.

Not many people need to be told that in old writings *u* stands for both *u* and *v*. I suspect that in modern E. many words which formerly had the *u* sound are spelled with a *v*.

Brawlie, or *brawly*. Very well, finely, heartily.

Braxie. A morkin sheep, etc.

This explanation, whatever may have been the case when Burns wrote, is now as obscure as the word it was designed to interpret. "Morkin, a wild beast that has died by sickness or mischance," was taken from Bailey by Johnson, who would not have been indebted to him if he had found the word anywhere else; and more recent Dictionaries, if they have the word, mostly use Bailey's definition.

Braxie is a sheep that has died of splenic fever.

Query—Had Burns a Dictionary when his first volume was published? If not, where could he have got such words as *morkin*, *tenebrific*, and *melancholious*?

Thenne *mourkne* (rot) in the mudde.—*Early E. Alliterative Poems.*

Breast. To spring up or forward, to oppose. E.

The hardy Swiss
Breasts the keen air, and carols as he goes.—*Goldsmith.*

Breastie. Dim. of breast.

Brechame, or *brechan*. A horse-collar. *Brechan* is altogether unknown in Ayrshire.

Bregham, a horse-collar.—*Bailey.*

Brauchin, a collar for a horse, made of old stockings stuffed with straw.—*Grose.*

In "Willie Chalmers," "a braw new *brechan*," as part of the equipment of a saddle-horse, if it means a horse-collar,—and if it does not mean that, I know not what it means,—seems to be a burlesque.

Breckan. Fern. See *brackens.*

Bree. Juice, liquid; *barley bree*, malt liquor.

Bree, the liquor of a stew.—*Bamford.*

Brewis the *bree* of swine's meat.—*Ib.*

A Cambridge lass, Venus-like, born of the froth
Of an old half fill'd jug of *Barley-Broth.*—*Cleaveland.*

Breef. An invulnerable or irresistible spell or charm, a short writing.

This is a *brief* how many sports are rife (giving a paper).—*Shak.*

With his *carecte* would him *enchaunt.*—*Gower.*

Characts seem to have been charms in the form of Inscriptions (i.e., short writings, *breafs*).—*Brand.*

By *carectes* . . .
Whiche constrayned hym forcibly
To love a certayn body.—*Skelton.*

I think you have charms.—*Shakespeare.*

The Divels or wicked spirits delight in furnishing folke with *love charms.*—*De Mornay.*

I do not know that the word *breef* occurs in English as Burns uses it, but the *thing* is described in Sir Bevis of Hampton:—

> I shall go make me a *writ*,
> Thorough a clerk wise of wit,
> That there shall be no man have grace,
> While that letter is in place,
> Against my will to lie me by,
> Nor do me shame nor villany.

This is the *warlock breef* of Burns, though used to repel instead of to attract.

Breeks. Breeches.

> I have linen *breeks* on.
> False gelden, gang thy gait,
> And du thy turns betimes; or I'se gar take
> Thy new *breikes* fra thee.—*Ben Jonson.*

Hastily that maiden meke
Took hose, and shose, and serk, and *breke.*—*Ywain and Gawain.*

It cometh out on smale Trees, that ben non hyere than a Mannes *breek-Girdill.*—*Sir John Maundeville.*

Breere. Briar. When Burns wrote "The rose upon the *brier* by the water running clear," he plainly intended that brier should be pronounced *breere*, as it is written by many E. authors.

Hard by his side grew a bragging *Brere.*—*Spenser.*

Now in the crop, and now doun in the *breres.*—*Chaucer.*

An other shape apperes
Of Greedy Care, stil brushing up the *breres.*—*Lord Buckhurst.*

Brent. Smooth, not wrinkled.

Some etymologists think this is a corruption of *bent*. Both forms are found in English authors.

With browes *brent.—The Squyr of Lowe Degree.*

Thou hast the right arched *bent* of the brow.—*Shakespeare.*

So spak the Knight, the geaunt sed,
Lead forth with the the sely maid,
   And mak me quit of the and she ;
For glaunsing ee, or brow so *brent*,
   Me lists not fight witb thee.—*Romance of the Falcon.*

Dr. Mackay says, "*Brant, brent*, steep, high, precipitous. In the song of 'John Anderson my Jo,' the goodwife says to her husband—

> When we were first acquent,
> Your locks were like the raven,
> Your bonnie brow was *brent*,

a high compliment both to his personal graces and his intellect." But she speaks as if his brow were no longer *brent*, because he has become *bald*, which could not diminish the height of his brow, but rather appear to add to it. *Brent*, however, does mean high, as in—

> Bowed (went) to the hygh bonk there *brentest* hit were.
>   *Early E. Alliterative Poems. Morris.*

Brent-new. Quite new, brand new. Shakespeare has *fire*-new ; and *brent* means burned.

Your *fire-new* stamp of honour is scarce current.—*Richard III.*

For with long travel I am *brent* in the sun.——*Spenser.*

Brie. The eye-brow.

Bree, an eye-brow.—*Halliwell. Breg*, a brow—*Bosworth.*

A great fot was betwix hys *bryn* (old plu. in n).—*Octovian Imperator.*

Shaw's Brow, in Salford, is still (or was lately) called *Shee Brees.*

Brig. A bridge.

Brigbote. A contribution made towards the repairing or rebuilding bridges.—*Bailey.*

And yet the fire consumed the *Brigg.*—*Loves of Hero and Leander.*

> She helped him opon his hors ryg,
> And sone thai come until a *bryg.*—*Ywain and Gawain.*
>
> Franche men put tham to pine
> At Cressy, when thai brak the *brig.*—*L. Minot.*

Bring to. To amend, to cure.

Brither. Brother. *I* for *ŭ* sound. See *bizz,* and *wirk* for work, in—

> Without mesure may non artificere
> In his *wirkyng* parfitely procede.—*Lydgate.*
>
> If any of the *bretherhode* be a-losed, etc.
> —*Chartulary of the Guild of the Holy Trinity.*
>
> Trew luf suld be us bytwene,
> As suld bytwyx *brether* bene.—*Ywain and Gawain.*

Brock. A badger.

> As big as *brocks* or badgers.—*Holland's Trans. of Pliny.*
>
> Marry, hang thee *brock!*—*Shakespeare.*
>
> And go hunte hardiliche to hares and to foxes,
> To bores and to *brockes.*—*P. Plowman.*
>
> It es ful semeli, als me think,
> A *brok* omang men for to stink.—*Ywain and Gawain.*

Brogue. A hum (a cheat), a trick.

I do not think the word is used in this sense in Scotland, but Halliwell gives "*brog,* a trick," as a word found in the east of England. Coleridge uses it in a peculiar way in his "Sonnet on the House that Jack built,"—

> Still on his thighs their wonted *brogues* are worn,
> And through those *brogues,* still tattered and betorn,
> His hindward charms gleam an unearthly white.
> —*Biographia Literaria.*

If we allow Coleridge to make breeches of brogues, which are really coarse shoes, Burns's use of the word may be permitted. It is quite possible that Coleridge had some authority for his substitution of brogues for breeches.

Broo. Broth, liquid, water. See *bree.*

Tak a knyfe, and schere it smal, the rute and alle, and sethe it in water; take the *broo* of that.—*MS. quoted by Halliwell.*

Brode, broth, *brue.*—*Cotgrave.*

Broose. A race at country weddings (to determine) who shall first reach the bridegroom's house on returning from church. *Broose* seems originally to have meant *broth*; thus—

> Wheune he has a good tast,
> And eeten weel a good repast,
> And soupyed off the *brouwys* a sope.—*Rich. C. de Lion.*

And *brewis* is frequently found:—" What an inundation of *brewis* shall I swim in!"—*Fletcher.*

When Burns speaks of the Broose as a race "on returning from church" after the marriage, he must refer to the practice of a time anterior to his own: for though the "Directory for Public Worship" directs that "the minister is publickly to solemnize it (marriage) in the place appointed by authority for publick worship," the ceremony has long been generally, it may almost be said universally, performed in the house of the bride's parents; and it was from this house, and not from the church—which would have been a somewhat unbecoming "starting-post"—that the race began. Marriages in churches are now growing fashionable. Let us hope this arises from an increase of respect for the "Directory for Publick Worship."

In the North of England a similar race *did* start from the church:—

> Four rustic Fellows wait the while
> To kiss the bride at the Church stile :
> Then vigorous mount their felter'd steeds—
> To scourge them going, head and tail—
> To win what country call the *kail*.
> —*The Collier's Wedding. Newcastle.*

"Broose," says Sir Henry Ellis, "has the same meaning as kail."

Brownie. A domestic goblin.—*Sir W. Scott*, according to whom that which differentiates Brownie from other spirits—embodied or disembodied—is his inclination to labour without desire of recompence.

The Cornish to this day invoke the spirit *Browny* when their bees swarm.—*Antiquities of Cornwall.*

Browst. The quantity of malt liquor brewed at one time. *Ew* is often changed into *ow*, examples in this very word being found.

> A sorye beverage ther was *browen* (brewed !)
> Quarelles and arwes thykke *flowen* (flew].—*R. C. de Lion.*
>
> Thou schalt suffre kare and howe,
> And drinke that thou hast *i-browe.*—*The Seven Sages.*

Browster-wives. Ale-house wives ; lit. female brewers, a name originating when every seller of ale was also a maker of it.

Bakerys, *browsterys*, vyntenerys, with fressh liccour.—*Lydgate.*
Bothe Bontyng the *browster* & Sybyly Slynge.—*Coventry Mysteries.*
Ac Beton the *brewestere* bad hym good morwe.—*P. Plowman.*

Brugh. A burgh. This transposition of *r* is quite commen in E. authors, as in *Vanbrugh*, a proper name.

Briddis (birds) of hevene comen and eeten it.—*Wyclif.*
Crull (curled) was his here, and as the gold it shone.—*Chaucer.*

Also Arestens fonde first the usage
Of mylke and *cruddis* (curds) and of honey swote.—*Lydgate*.
Every *brid* (bird) has chose his make.—*Gower*.

Bruilzie or *brulzie*. A broil, a combustion.
> *Brulliment*.—*Halliwell*.
> *Bruzzle*, to make a great ado, or stir.—*Thoresby*.

I do not know that *bruzzle* has any connection with *bruilzie*. It has the same meaning, and they are not unlike in appearance.

Brunstane. Brimstone. *Brunt* and *stane*.
> The blaste of the *brynston* blew away his brayne.—*Skelton*.
> Then the fendes made a fyre an one
> Of blakke pyche and of *brenstone*.—*St. Patrick's Purgatory*.

Brunt. Did burn. See *brugh*.
> The castell of Forde was *brunte*.—*The Battle of Flodden Field*.
> His blistered hands amongst the cinders *brent*.—*Spenser*.
> And of face of him *brent* the fire.—*Metrical English Psalter*.

Brust. To burst. See *brugh*.
> Who into England seld did *brust*,
> But they were *brust* in battle sore.—*Bat. of Flod. Field*.
>
> Eftsoones she grew to great unpatience,
> And into terms of open outrage *brust*.—*Spenser*.
>
> If Renaldo
> Have the sacred love of war so *brust*,
> Take you the charge.—*Fairfax*.

Buchan-bullers. The boiling of the sea among the rocks on the coast of Buchan (in Aberdeenshire).—*Cunningham*. That the flowing of water in a well was sometimes compared to the boiling of a pot, the following couplet will show:—

> Fro silver *wellys that boyle* up with fresshenesse
> Cometh crystal watir renning a gret pas.—*Lydgate*.

Bullyne, to boil.—*Prompt. Parv.*

> And she to *builen* caste ham in,
> And let it *buile.*—*Gower.*

If I had any malice against a walking spirit, instead of **laying** him in the Red Sea, I would condemn him to reside in the *Bullar of Buchan.*—*Johnson's Tour.*

Buckie. A spiral shell; a person, generally with some depreciatory adjective, as *daft buckie, thrawn buckie,* etc.

Buckskin. An inhabitant of Virginia.

You call yourselves *Buckskins*, and you call your neighbour Brother Jonathan.—*Sir Ed. Seaward's Narrative.*

Buckskin Kye. Virginian negro slaves.

Buff. To strike. *Buff our beef*, beat our bodies.

> The giddy ship
> Shoots amain
> Till counter*buff'd* she stops.—*Dryden.*
>
> The Sarazin, sore daunted with the *buffe.*—*Spenser.*
>
> The *buffs* and boxes made the room to ring again.
> *Trans. of Scarron's Comical Romance.*

Buff and blue. The colour of the Whigs in Fox's time.

> Now e'en the reptiles of the *Blue and Buff*,
> In rural leisure, scrawl their factious stuff.—*The Rolliad.*

Bught. A pen, a sheep-fold: lit., something bent or bowed. It is another form of *bight*, as the *Bight* of Benin, of Biafra, etc.

Bucht, a milking or herding place for sheep.—*Halliwell.*

Jartier, the fourth branch of the thigh veine descending unto the *bought* of the hamme.—*Cotgrave.*

And wrapt her scalie *boughts* with fell despight.—*Spenser.*

Bughtin-time. The time of collecting the sheep in the pens to be milked.

Buirdly. Stout-made, broad-built.

Buredely, forcibly, swiftly.—*Halliwell.*

Bum. Bottom.

They (spiders) will often fasten their threads in several places to the things they creep up; the manner is by beating their *bums* or tails against them as they creep up.—*Ray Correspondence.*

All but the wight of *bum* y-galled, he
Abhorreth bench and stool, and fourme, and chair.—*Shenstone.*

A Barbary shape, and a jet with her *bum*, would stir an Anchorite.—*Congreve.*

Bum. A humming noise; the sound emitted by a bee.

Bumbeth, making a humming noise.—*Bailey.*

I *bomme* as a bombyll be doth.—*Palsgrave.*

And I hallus comed to's choorch afoir may Sally was deäd,
And 'eerd un a *hummin* awaäy like buzzard clock ower may yeäd.
Tennyson.

They had assembled themselves to the full number of *bumbees.*
Rabelais. Pantagruel.

From the hedge in drowsy hum,
Heedless buzzing beetles *bum.*—*Clare.*

A *bumble*-bee's soft plush.—*Herrick.*

Bum-clock. A humming beetle that flies in the summer evenings. *Bum* and *clock.*

Bummle. To blunder.

Bummle, to blunder.—*Halliwell.*

Bummler. A blunderer.

Bunker. Any thing used for sitting on, not constructed for that purpose, which may or may not be also used as a chest.

Allan Cunningham, Sir John Sinclair, and other glossarists define a *bunker* to be "a window seat." If they are correct, Burns was guilty of a gross piece of tautology in the line, "A *winnock-bunker* in the east," that is, a *window window-seat* in the east. Chambers again, in relating an anecdote of Burns's friend Robert Ainslie, treats bunker as if it were a chest, and not a seat. "He had already a cellar—certainly, however, not an extensive one, as it consisted simply of the recess under a *bunker seat* in one of the windows of his apartment; an arrangement long ago common in Scotland, but now only seen in old-fashioned houses." Whether a bunker took its name from being promoted to the dignity of a chest, or from serving in the humble capacity of a stool, —chair it could never be—it is not easy, perhaps not possible, to discover. Probably the former, if there be any connection between bunker and the sailor's "Bunk, a bed-place formed of boards."* Like it, it is applied to concealed, or at least not conspicuous places.

In point of fact, however, the *bunker* in which the grim musician sat in "Tam o' Shanter," had nothing to do with a chest, as it is ready to this day to testify, but was simply the *window-sole*, that is, a sill the whole thickness of the wall, a thing which has gone out of fashion in dwelling-houses, but may still be seen in churches and other public buildings.

Scott seems to have considered a bunker an enclosed seat: "They sat cosily niched into what you might call a *bunker*, a little sand-pit surrounded by its banks, and a screen of whins in full bloom."—*Redgauntlet.*

Bunter. A worthless woman.

Bunter, a gatherer of rags in the streets.—*Bailey.*

---

* Bunks are, I believe, also found in lunatic asylums.

Bunter, a cant term for a woman who picks up rags about the streets; and used, by way of contempt, for any low vulgar woman.
Johnson.

Where Fielding met his *bunter* muse. *Horace. Walpole.*

Burdie. Dim. of bird; a woman. *U* for *i*, as in—

> Thus is *thurst* (thirst) of false getting.—*Chaucer.*
>
> *Burde* on of the best;
> This wommon (woman) woneth by west.
> *Wright's Specimens of Lyric Poetry.*
>
> I chot (I know) a *burde* on boure bryght,
> That fully semly is on syht,
> Menskful maiden of myht.—*A Love Song. Ritson.*
>
> Vuche (each) *burde* with her barne, the bygging thay lever.
> *Morris's Early E. Alliterative Poems.*
>
> Than answered that *burd* bright.—*Amis and Amiloun.*

Bure. Did bear.

> His steed was goode
> And *bure* hym ouer that hydious floode.—*Sir Guy.*

Burn. A name given to water used in brewing, and seemingly put by Burns for spirituous liquour in the line—

> An' just a wee drap spiritual *burn* in.

Burn. Water, a rivulet. I think that, except in the case referred to above, *burn* is never applied to other than running water, a stream, that is; a burn is not water, but *a* water.

This word was once common in English poetry as *bourne*, and survives in the names of such streams and places as Ravensbourne, Kelburn, Blackburn, etc.—*Dr. C. Mackay.*

Burne, a brook, a small stream of water.—*Grose.*

> And soone wythynne a lytyll space
> Ranne *bournes* all on blode.—*Le Bone F. of Rome.*
>
> Think of the ring by yonder *burn*,
> Thou gav'st to love and me.—*Dr. Wolcot.*

Burnewin, i.e., *burn the wind.* A blacksmith.

Burnie. Dim. of burn.

Burro. Borough.

Burr-thistle. The spear-thistle.

Bur, a rough head of a plant.—*Johnson.*
Burr, the head of a thistle.—*Bamford.*
Bur-thistle, the spear-thistle.—*Halliwell.*

Boar thistle, a widely-spread popular name for the *carduus lanceolatus*, is a corruption of *Bur Thistle.*—*Palmer.*

Busk. To dress; to make ready.

> The noble Baron whet his courage hot,
> And *busked* him boldly to the dreadful fight.—*Fairfax.*
> *Busk ye*, my merry young men.—*R. Hood.*
> Rise up, Joseph, and *busk* and go.—*Cursor Mundi.*

Buskie. Bushy.

Busk, a bush.—*Bailey.* *Busky*, woody.—*Johnson.*
How bloodily the sun begins to peer
Above yon *busky* hill!—*Shakespeare.*
And every *bosky* bourn from side to side.—*Milton.*
His browes was litel *buskes* (bushes).—*Ywain and Gawain.*

Bussle. A bustle, to bustle. This differs only in spelling, not in sound, from the usual way of writing the word, but instances of omission of *t* in similar words are not uncommon in old E. authors. A curious one occurs in the "Metrical Romance of Richard Coer de Lion":

> And the emperour of evil *trusle* (trust perhaps)
> Carved off his nose by the *grusle* (gristle).

A reformado began to *bussle*, and said he would cut the throats of those round-headed dogs.—*Rushworth.*

Buss. Bush, shelter. *S* for *sh*, as in—

In him ai hope I *salle* (shall).—*Metrical E. Psalter.*

All they ren in a *lees* (one leash), but in divers maners.—*Chaucer*.

The lyon hungered for the nanes,

Ful fast he ete raw *fless* and banes.—*Ywain and Gawain*.

Horn the wyket *puste* (pushed).—*The Geste of Kyng Horn*.

He *frussed* (frushed) alle his sides.—*Horne Child and Maiden Rimnild*.

Confessours approched, . . .
Fressly (freshly) embrodred. *Henry Bradshaw. Warton.*

The riche man *Cherissith* the poore to robbe and reve.—*Lydgate*.

The more *ssame* (shame) be ido.—*R. of Gloucester*.

Ssoldren, shoulders.—*Ib*.

But. Without.

And as blive (quickly) *bout bod* (without delay) he braydes to the quene.—*William of Palerne*.

Bout bod is Blind Harry's *but baid*.

The beggar thought him dead *but* fail.—*R. Hood*.

We dye, lewed and lered, *but* we be stoute.—*Octovian Imperator*.

But is used for than, in—

I asked for no more *but* a soger laddie.—*The Jolly Beggars*.

The same use of it is found in English.

The full moon was no sooner up *but* she opened to me the gate.
Guardian.

But-an-ben. The country kitchen and parlour. Lit., the outer and inner. The name was given when the kitchen, or outer apartment, had to be passed through to reach the parlour. But it came to have a wider signification,—Burns himself being witness,—than to a house, whether in town or country, of two rooms. He says in "The Holy Fair"—

Now *but an' ben* the change-house rings,

meaning that every part of the house was filled. In "The Calf," too, it means the whole house, even the manse: "Your *but an ben* adorns." But-an-ben seems to be used in some parts of England, for Halliwell has it.

Butch. To butcher, to kill.

Butche, to kill.—*Halliwell.*

Er in such words is sometimes omitted by E. writers, as in

> Now may men se mordre and *manslaught*.—*Gower.*
>
> He hadde *prisons* (prisoners) so y fynde,
> Gentil men an hundred thousand.—*Kyng Alisaunder.*
>
> Heo tolde the *slaught* and the brennyng.—*Id.*

Butt. So Burns writes when speaking of the outer apartment by itself, and uses it as if it were a preposition—

> I pray and ponder *butt* the house.
> *Epistle to James Tennant.*

By. Past, as in "May he haud you *by* the covert snare of deceit."

> I did hear
> The galloping of horse. Who was't came *by*?—*Shakespeare.*

I went *by* the field of the slothful, and *by* the vineyard of the man void of understanding.—*Proverbs, xxiv. 31.*

I found it hard to come *by* the lions' mouths.—*Bunyan.*

By himsel. (By himself); lunatic, distracted, beside himself. Under considerable provocation it is said in "The Geste of Kyng Horn"—

> Rimenild hine *bywent.*

These words taken literally are "She went by herself," and she was at the same time distracted, for it is afterwards said,—

> Ther seh he Rymenild sitte,
> Ase (hue) she were out of wytte.
> For he was nouther there ne here
> But clene *out of himself* awey.

By and beside have often the same meaning. *By* the rivers of Babylon.—*Psalm 137, 1.*

If thou be found *by* me thou art but dead. To did *by* thee were but to die in jest.—*Shakespeare.*

Bye attour. Besides, in addition. A distinguished etymologist who, for an Englishman, has a considerable knowledge of Scotch, has lately mistaken *attour* for "*tire*, an old word for a head-dress."

Byke. A wild bee, or wasp nest.
> A *byke* of waspes bredde in his nose,
> And Vaspasian is called by cause of his waspes.
> —*The Siege of Jerusalem.*

Bike, a building, a hive of bees.—*Weber's Note on Beau. and Fletcher.*

Bypast. Past, a term of the Scotch dialect.—*Johnson*, who, however, quotes an example of its use by an English author.

Byre. A cow-stable.
Byre, a cow-house.—*Grose.*

C.

Ca'. To call, to name, to drive. For omission of *ll* see under *a* and—
Sha't (shalt) have thy mortgage.—*Beaumont and Fletcher.*
All this *sha'* not bribe my conscience.—*The Coronation. Shirley.*
Near arcir ver az hie sa geude ;
And piple *kaud* im Robin Heude, *i.e.*,
Ne'er archer were as he so good,
And people called him Robin Hood.—*Robin Hood's Epitaph.*

In came there a tike, they *cau'd* him Grim.
—*The Northumberland Garland. Ritson.*

Ca, to drive; *Caw*, to call; *Caw'd*, called.—*Grose.* To call cattle home, next to bring, whether by calling or otherwise, then to drive, seems to be the process by which call is brought to signify to drive.

Ca'. To calve. See under *ca't.*

Ca' through. To drive on any business with spirit.

Cadger. A carrier. Not, I believe, a common carrier, but one who carries his own goods. If the term survives, it has the same meaning in Scotland as in England.

Cadger. One who brings butter, eggs, and poultry from the country to market.—*Johnson.*

Cadie or *caddie*. A person, a young fellow, a messenger.

Cadet, Cadee.—*Bailey.*

This is the word, but it has not the meaning given above.

Caff. Chaff. For change of *ch* into *k* sound, see under *birk.*

> Me list not of the *caf*, ne of the stre
> Make so long a tale as of the corn.—*Wright's Chaucer.*

Caird. A tinker.

Cairn. A loose heap of stones.

Kairns, rude heaps of stones.—*Halliwell.*

There was (in the grounds of Otterbourne) a large *cairn* of stones, computed to be about 60 ton.—*John Horsley, author of Britannica Romana*, 1729.

Cake. Oatmeal bread baked on a *girdle* and toasted before the fire. Bread not so prepared does not get the name of cake. This so-called Scotch cake must have been well known in England in Shakspeare's time, for one of the watch in " Measure for Measure " is called Hugh *Oatcake*.

I have cruddes and creem, and an haver (oat) *cake.—P. Plowman.*

Calces. Properly lime or chalk.

Calf-ward. A small enclosure for calves.
Ward, a division.—*Johnson.*

Calimanco. A kind of cloth.
Calimanco, a strong woollen stuff.—*Bailey.*

As if it concerned people to know that a man had the honour to be driven into Paris by a postilion in a tawny yellow jerkin turned up with red *calamanco.—Sterne.*

Calker. The hinder part of a horse-shoe sharpened and turned downwards, so as to prevent slipping on ice.— *Jamieson. Dyce* says, " turned up."
Coaken, the sharp point of a horse-shoe.—*Grose.*

On this horse is Arcite
Trotting the stones of Athens, which the *calkins*
Did rather seem to tell than trample.—*The Two Noble Kinsmen.*

Callan and *callant.* A boy.
Callant, a lad, a stripling.—*Halliwell.*

Caller. Fresh, sound.
Caller, fresh, cool; the *caller air*, the fresh air; *caller ripe grosiers*, ripe gooseberries freshly gathered.—*Grose.*

Callet. A loose woman.—*Johnson.*

Gog's head ! and thinks the *callet* thus to keep my neele me fro !
Gammer Gurton's Needle.

Make the shameless *callet* know herself.—*Shak.*

Cam. Did come.

> A prowd potter
> *Cam* dryfyng owyr the ley.—*R. Hood.*
> And thanne *cam* kynd wytte.—*P. Plowman.*
> There was a mayde *cam* out of Kent.—*Ritson's Ancient Songs.*

Cankrie, and *Cankert.* Ill-humoured.

> *Cankart,* ill-tempered, peevish.—*Bamford.*
>> He rages and he raves,
>> And calls them *cankered* knaves.—*Skelton.*
>> The beggar answer'd *cankardly,*
>> I have no money to lend.—*R. Hood.*

Canna. Cannot. *Can* and *na.*

Cannie. Gentle, mild, dexterous.

> *Canny,* nice, neat, housewifely, handsome.—*Grose.*
> O the bonny pit laddie, the *cannie* pit laddie,
>   The bonny pit laddie for me.—*Old P. A. Song. Durham.*

"Owre cannie," meaning *poetically inspired,* is used by Burns in a letter to the author of "Tullochgorum."

Cannilie. Dexterously, gently.

Cant. A merry story. Connected with *canty,* merry.

Cantharidian. Made of cantharides.

Cantie or *canty.* Cheerful, merry.

> *Canty,* cheerful, chatty.—*Bamford.*
> *Cant,* strong, lusty.—*Bailey.*
> The King of Beme was *cant* and kene,
> But there he left both play and pride.—*L. Minot.*
> From the mention of play, *cant* probably means playful, *canty.*
> Lest Peter should grow *canty.*—*Northumberland Garland. Ritson.*

Cantraip, or *Cantrip.* A charm, a spell.

Cape-stone, cope-stone. Key-stone. *Cape* is nearer A.-S. *cæppe* than cope.

Cape, the coping of a wall.—*Grose.*

To *cape* a wall, to crown it.—*Thoresby.*

Caput mortuum. Worthless remains.

He was little better than a *caput mortuum.*—*Garrick.*

Card. A chart.

Sure if my *card* and compasse doe not fail.
We're near the Port.—*Sylvester.*

On life's vast ocean diversely we sail,
Reason the *card*, but passion is the gale.—*Pope.*

Care na by. To be indifferent.

Cark. A load, a burden.—*Jamieson.* Care, anxiety, solicitude, concern, heedfulness.—*Johnson.*

It is not easy to say how *cark* differs from care, yet all writers who have used the word have looked upon it as dissimilar in meaning. Burns has *carking cares.*

Esmay, carke. care, thought, sorrow.—*Cotgrave.*

For hire love y *cark* and care.—*Poem of 13th Century. Ritson.*

Yet to toyle itself in the *cark* and care, etc.—*De Mornay.*

Waile we the wight whose absence is our *carke.*—*Spenser.*

He for us is *carking* and thinking.—*Nahum Tate.*

Carl. An old man.

Carl, a mean, rude, rough, brutal man.—*Johnson.*

The miller was a stout *carle* for the nones.—*Chaucer.*

Obstreperous *carle !*
If thy throat's tempest could o'erturn my house.—*Fletcher.*

A knave and a *carle*, and all of one kynde.—*Skelton.*

Carl-hemp. The male stalk of hemp.

Carle, a kind of hemp.—*Johnson.*

Karle Hemp, the latter green hemp.—*Bailey*.
Carle-hemp, the hemp that bears the seed.—*Grose*.
The female to spin and the *carl* for seed.—*Tusser*.

Carleton.   Charlestown in—

> Down Lowrie's burn he took a turn,
> And *Carleton* did ca', man.—*When Guildford Good*.

Carlin.   A stout old woman.

> Why said'st thou
> It was a boy, and sold'st him then to me
> With such entreaty, for ten shillings, *carlin?*—*Ben Jonson*.

Cartes.   Cards.

> Our ancientest *carte* is for the sin of gluttony.—*Fuller*.

> And forth withall
> As it is written in the *carte*,
> Complexion he taketh of Marte.—*Gower*.

Cartie.   Dim. of cart.

Case.   To confine, as in *case-knife*.

Cast at the Cocks.   To waste, to squander.—*Jamieson*.

Castock.   The stalk of a cabbage.

Castock, the heart of a cabbage.—*Halliwell*.

> Not worth a shyttel cocke,
> Nor worth a sour *calstock*.—*Skelton*.—

Cast out.   To disagree, to quarrel; a quarrel.

Ca't or *ca'd.*   Calved.

There being only three words, *halve*, *salve*, and *valve*, which rhyme to calve, the chance of a variation in the spelling and pronunciation is smaller than in most other words.   But *v* is very often omitted.   Not to speak of *brave* and *salve*, which in Scotch become *braw* and *saw*, or of e'er, ne'er, and o'er, we find in English writers *gie* for give, *ha* or *hae* for have, *lea'e*, for leave, etc.

> And as I prune my feathered youth, so I
> Do *mar'l* (marvel) how I could die.—*Herrick.*
>
> The Naseby *mar'ls* (marvels)
> To see herself now drowned in the Charles.—*Fuller.*

Cattle. Used in reproach of human beings.—*Johnson.*

Boys and women are for the most part *cattle* of this colour.
Shakespeare.

The Dutchess of Portsmouth, Nelly, . . concubines and *cattell* of that sort.—*Evelyn's Diary.*

Caudron. A caldron.

> And there such ghastly noyse of yron chaines
> And brasen *caudrons* thou shalt rumbling heare.—*Spenser.*

I have seen in the infernal partyes a great number of wyd *cauderons* and ketels.—*St. Patrick's Purgatory.*

Cauf. A calf.

Cauk. Chalk.

Cawk stone, a mineral.—*Bailey.*
Cauk, a coarse talky spar. *Cauky, adj.*—*Johnson.*

They hadden walled cité townes,
And *calke* trappen maden ynowe.—*Kyng Alisaunder.*

The word *caulk* is still (1810) used in the north of England for chalk.—*Weber.*

Cauld, cold.

> The storm rase ful sone onane
> With wikked wedders (weathers) kene and *calde.*
> *Ywain and Gawain.*
>
> For now es *cald*, now es hete,
> Now es dry, and now es hete.—*Pricke of Conscience.*

Caup. A wooden drinking vessel (of cooper's work).

Cawpe, a cup.—*Halliwell.*

> And gaf uchone
> *Coupes* of clene gold.—*P. Plowman.*

It seems probable that *cup*, *caup*, or *coupe*, was the name of any drinking vessel, and that the peasantry having only wooden dishes, the term became specific and was applied to these alone.

Cavie. A hen-coop. Perhaps this is a dimin. of *cave*, for Lat. *cavea* is defined "a cage, or coop for birds." —*Ainsworth.*

Caw. To drive, to hammer; *cawd* and *cawt*, driven, as in

> He has cooper'd and *cawt* a wrong pin in't.—*The Kirk's Alarm.*

This is the same word as *ca'* but has generally a different spelling when used as in the line quoted from Burns. To *caw a pin* and *Ca' the yowes to the knowes* do not differ more than *the hammer drives the nail* does from

> A shepherd's boy
> *Driving his sheep* to the fold.

I do not know if *cawthe* in the following verse of an old E. song be the word under consideration. Ritson, who gives it in his "Ancient Songs," did not know what to make of it. It seems to signify *beat*, *strike*, or *thump*, which is not far from hammer or drive. The song describes a convivial meeting of some gossips, one of whom when she comes home is so overcome that

> Sche muste as for anowe go sclepe (sleep).
> Off her slepe when sche dothe wake
> Faste on hey (haste) then gan sche a rake (start up),
> And *cawthe* (? caweth) her servants abowte the bake (back),
> Yff to here they outhe (ought) had sayd.—*Lytyll Thanke.*

Centum per centum. A hundred per cent.; a usurer.

Certes. Certainly.

> And, *certes*, sire, though non auctoritee
> Were in no book.—*Chaucer.*
>
> For *certes*, these are people of the island.—*Shakspeare.*

Chamer or *chaumer*. A chamber. *B* is sometimes omitted.

Ye weren children of God, and *limmes* (limbs) of the regne of God.—*Chaucer.*

Timmer, timber.—*Barnford.*

Dysdayne, I wene, this *comerous* (cumbrous) crabes hyghte.
Skelton.

Change-house. A public-house, but why so called I have never heard, nor can I guess, unless from the change, not always for the better, produced on its frequenters. Probably it is in some remote way connected with small coins, sometimes called *change*. The word occurs in the life of John Metcalf, the blind roadmaker, soldier, card-player, etc.

> The brosteris (brewers) hes na *change* for aill.
> *A Satire. Pub. by Pinkerton.*

Changer-wife. An itinerant female huckster.—*Halliwell.*

Chanter. Part of a bag-pipe.

Chap. A fellow; abbreviation of *chapman*.

Chap, a man.—*Bamford.*

Are we so run out of stock, that there is no one lumber-headed, muddle-headed, mortar-headed, pudding-headed *chap* amongst our doctors?—*Sterne. Let. to Garrick.*

> By gleaning pretty little scraps
> Of Cæsar, Alexander, and such *chaps*.—*Wolcot.*

Chap or *chaup*. A blow, a knock.

Chap, a knock.—*Percy.*

Anon her hedes wer off *chappyd*.—*R. C. de Lion.*

Chapel. A place of worship; in Scotland a chapel was a church built for the accommodation of those who could not get room in the parish church. It was in connection with the Established Church, but had no parish assigned to it. I believe there was only one such church known to Burns, the meeting-house, now the High Church of Kilmarnock. Russell was the pastor in those days, and it was to this chapel Burns refers in "Gie her name up in *the* chapel," alluding to the custom of requesting to be prayed for by name in dangerous illness. The satire is lost when it is translated *let her be prayed for in church.*

Cheep. A chirp; to chirp.

> *Pepier,* to peepe, *cheepe* or pule like a young bird. *Pioler,* to pule, *cheepe,* or chirpe.—*Cotgrave.*

> Notwithstanding *cheeping* of mice.—*Rabelais.*

> And sparrows *chelp* glad tidings from the eaves. Chelp, *cheep.*
> *Clare.*

Cheese and bread. Supposed to be a Scotticism for bread and cheese.

> Here is one dead that will give us *cheese and bread.*—*R. Hood.*

Chiel, chield, or *cheel.* A young fellow. *Odd kind chiel,* strange sort of person. After what Bishop Percy and others have said on this word, it may be assumed that it is another form of *child;* but I am not aware that it has been noticed that child was sometimes spelled *chield.*

> A *chield* to thryve that is unchastisable
> And ever inconstaunte and lightly changeable
> It may well ryme but it accordeth not.
> A *chield* without noryce to be upbrought.—*Lydgate.*

> A wanton *chyld*
> Spake words myld
>   To me alone.—*Ritson's Ancient Songs.*
>
> That oon thefe callyd a knyght,
> He was a feyre *chylde* and a bolde,
> Twenty wyntur he was olde.—*The Erle of Tolous.*

Chimla or *chimlie.* A chimney.

Burns himself says, " a fire grate," and the word must have been used in that sense at one time, otherwise *chimla-lug* could never have existed any more than *chimla-neuk*, *chimla-cheek*, etc., all of which refer to the fire-place, and not to what is now considered the chimney or vent for smoke. This is by Burns and old Scotch people styled the *lum*, and the *chimla* is the fire-place rather than the grate. In England chimney was used for fire-place, *lum*, and that part of the vent which is above the roof. Shakspeare says—

> "Our *chimneys* were blown down,"

i.e, the tops ; and

> " The *chimney* (fire-place)
> Is south the chamber " ;

and his contemporary, Bishop Hall, uses chimney for vent—

> " Look to the towered *chimnies*, which should be
>   The wind-pipes of good hospitalitie."

Chimley, chimney.—*Bamford.*

Chimley, a chimney or fire-place. This form is very common in the provinces.—*Halliwell.*

I knows that ere *chimley* from a hinfant.—*Sweep's evidence in a Police Court in London, 1826. Book of Days.*

Gilbert Burns makes a distinction between a chimney and a fire.

Chimla cheek. A stone pillar at the side of a fire-place. *Cheek* is often used for side.

Yet came my foot never within those door *cheekes.*—*Gammer Gurton's Needle.*

Chimla-lug. The fire-side. See *chimla* and *lug.*

Chitter. To shiver, to tremble; having the same meaning, if it is not the same word, as "*chatter*, to sound as the teeth when one shivers." There is also a word *chitre*, glossed chirp, used by Gower—

> But she with all no word may soune,
> But *chitre* and as a brid (bird) jargoune.
> (She) *chitereth* out in her langage.—*Confessio Aman.*
> I trowe it be a frost for the way is slydder
> So (I avowe), for cold I *chydder.*—*Skelton.*
> Sithen that day I have *chivered* oft.—*Chaucer.*

I have quoted this line from Chaucer, because I believe *chiver* is more common in Ayrshire that *chitter*. Jamieson says—

"Boys are wont to call that bit of bread which they preserve for eating after bathing, a *chittering* piece, or a *chittering dole.*"

I am certain that my contemporaries will bear me out when I state that sixty or seventy years ago—very near to the time when Jamieson published his great work—the *piece* so eaten was always called a *chivering chow;* as for *dole*, it was utterly unknown to the youngsters of Kyle and Cunningham.

Perhaps my remark on *chiver* in connection with *chitter* may seem out of place, but it is a peculiar word, and almost the only one which old writers wrote with *ch* instead of *sh*, and that whether it meant to *shake* or to *shatter*:—

> Thair shaftes *chevered* to thair hand.—*Ywain and Gawaine.*

Divynaciones by *chyterynge* of birdes or fleynge of foules.
Dives and Pauper.

Some useth strange wlaffyng, *chyteryng*, harryng, etc.
John of Trevesa.

Chow. To chew, a quid of tobacco; *cheek for chow*, side by side, close. *Ow* for *ew*, see *browst*.

Chow, to chew. *Var. dial.—Halliwell.*

The trampling steed—
Chawing the foming bit there fiercely stood.—*Earl of Surrey.*

Cheek for chow seems at first sight to mean the same as *cheeke by cheeke* in Spenser, and Shakspeare's *cheek to cheek*. Bailey has "Jig by Jowl, i.e., *cheek by head*, very close together," and Maundeville uses *jowe* for jaw, and an Englishman of his day might have said *cheek for jowe*, which is very near *cheek for chow*. Butler has—

> An by him in another hole
> Afflicted Ralpho, *cheek by jowl.*

All these phrases have been formed, or are supposed to have been formed, on the notion that *jowl* means jaw. Dr. Jamieson, too, whose opinion on such a subject is entitled to great respect, thinks that *chow* as well as *jowl* means jaw; but I rather think it means neck, and *cheek for chow* will mean *cheek on neck*, being in effect head on shoulder—a much more natural and likely attitude to be assumed by "a chuffie vintner," to "a blackguard smuggler" than to put his cheek to his jaw, a thing difficult to do, and which I question if any body ever saw done.

The following passages will, I think, go far to prove that the meaning of *chol* or *chow* is throat. The first gives an account of the dragon encountered by Sir Bevis of Hampton.

> Eighte toskes at 'is mouth stod out
> The leste seventene ench about,

> The her (hair) the *cholle* under the ching (chin):
> He was bothe leith (loathsome) and grim.

Here *cholle*—from Fr. *col*, the neck—being under the chin, it cannot be the jaw, and changed, as it has been shown under *Bow-kail* that words in *ll* often are, it becomes *chow*.

Another passage is from "The Awntyrs of Arthure":

> Who that myghte that hedows see, hendeste in haulle,
> How hir *cholle* chatired, hir chaftes, and hir chyne.

Sir F. Madden says *cholle* here is jowl, jaws, and *chatired* gives countenance, I must acknowledge, to this inter reration. But the philosophers who, we are told on good authority, are of opinion that the "lips are parcel of the mouth," must also hold that the chin is a part of the jaws, and then we have three words, *cholle*, *chaftes*, and *chyne*, for the same thing, or at least for parts of the same thing, a degree of tautology or at best minuteness of detail not easy to parallel in the old Metrical Romances.

Sir Richard Steele, in No. 147 of "The Tatler," says, "I had a bribe sent me of a collar of brawn and a *jole* of salmon."

Jole or *jowl* is generally explained *cheek*, not *jaw*, by the way. Now, what sort of a bribe would the cheek of a salmon be? An epicure might be supposed capable of being corrupted by a cut of the neck or shoulder of an early salmon, but only the most stupid of fishmongers could fancy that a favourable effect could be produced by the present of a fish's cheek.

Christendie. Christendom. *Ie* for *m*, as in—

> This epitaph, which here you see,
> Supplied the *epithalamie.—Herrick.*
>
> So rych a jewell ys ther non
>   In all *crystyante.*
>   *Christentye. King Estmere. Cristente. Launfal.*

Chuck. A hen; a familiar name for a woman.

> Be innocent of the knowledge, dearest *chuck*,
> Till thou applaud the deed.—*Shak.*

Chuck seems to have been applied to men as well as to women. In "The Twelfth Night" Sir Toby Belch says to Malvolio; "How dost thou, *chuck?*" and in "Love's Labour's Lost," Armado, addressing the king and lords, says, "Sweet *chucks*, beat not the bones of the buried."

Chuckie. Dimin. of chuck.

Chuffie. Fat-faced.

Chuffy, clownish, rough, rude.—*Bailey.*

Blunt, surly, fat.—*Johnson.*

Joufflu, chuffie, fat-cheeked, swolne, or puft up in the face.
Cotgrave.

Ye fat *chuffs*, I would your store were here.—*Shakspeare.*

Circumvolute. To circumvolve; to use circumlocution.

Clachan. A small village about a church, a hamlet.

Claise, or *claes.* Clothes. A common pronunciation of clothes by the peasantry throughout England is *close,* which by the change of *o* into *a,* as in *bane,* becomes *claise.*

Clooas, clothes.—*Bamford.*

Pope seems to have pronounced clothes *close :*—

> Poets make characters, as salesmen clothes;
> We take no measure of your fops and beaux.
> *Prologue to " Three Hours after Marriage."*

Claivers, or *clavers.* Idle stories.

Clavers, din, noisy talking.—*Halllwell.*

Claith. Clothing, cloth ; to clothe.

When he unto the chamber yede,
The chamber flore, and als ye bede,
With *klathes* of gold were all ouer sprede.—*Ywain and Gawain.*

And here he comes new *claithed* like a prince
Of swine herds.—*Ben Jonson.*

Whan thai had eten and dronken inoughe,
Thai toke up mete and *clathes* drogh.—*The Seven Sages.*

Clamb. Did climb.

Tho behind gone up lepe,
And *clamben* up on other faste.—*Chaucer. House of Fame.*

The fatal gin thus over*clambe* our walles.—*Earl of Surrey.*

Thence to the circle of the moone she *clambe.*—*Spenser.*

For hit *clam* uche a clyffe cubites fyftene.—*Early E. Alliterative Poems.*

Clankie. Dim. of clank, a severe stroke ; a sharp blow that causes a noise.—*Jamieson.*

Clap. The clapper of a mill. A piece of wood shaking the hopper.—*Johnson.*

> Some be soft and still
> As *clappes* in a mill.—*Image of Ipocrisy.*

Clarkit. Wrote (literally clerked) ; common spelling at one time.

The same was acknowledged by Mr. Taylor and all the *clarks* of that board.—*Sarah, Duchess of Marlborough.*

Some *clarkes* doe doubt in their deviceful art.—*Spenser.*

Is the sonnelyht darke,
Or ignorance a *clarke?*—*Imagery of Ipocrisy.*

Clartie or *clarty.* Dirty, filthy.

Clart, to spread, smear, or daub ; *clarts,* mud ; *clarty,* muddy, sticky.—*Grose.*

Clatty, nasty, dirty, defiled by whatever means.—*Id.*

Clatty, which Mr. Halliwell gives as a Lincolnshire word, and which, Dr. Jamieson says, " seems to be more ancient than *clarty*," is, I believe the only form used in Ayrshire, and suggests a remark on the language of Burns, probably not left for me to make for the first time.

Burns's language is generally that of Ayrshire, with only a few words that are altogether unknown in that county. These words he may have acquired from Ramsay, Ferguson, and others, but some of them he in all probability learned from his father, who, when he left Kincardineshire, was nineteen years old, an age at which, for all the ordinary purposes of life, a man's vocabulary is generally pretty complete, and which hardly any change of circumstances, perhaps not even a change of country, causes him altogether to abandon. We may therefore presume, indeed it was impossible it should be otherwise, that William Burness would occasionally give utterance to a word brought from his native county, and thus his gifted son would catch a note from the east which he mingled with the music of the west, and fitted himself to be the poet, not of the east or the west, but of the whole of Scotland.

Clash.   An idle tale, the story of the day.

About this time some that had run out from the truth and *clashed* against Friends, were reached by the power of the Lord.—*Journal of George Fox*.

Clatter.   To tell idle stories ; an idle story.

Now, siker, I see thou dost but *clatter.*—*Spenser.*

Spite of all your *clatter*,
The tedious chime is still ground, plants, and water.
Mason.

> Tibullus, friend and gentle judge
> Of all that I do *clatter.—Thomas Drant.*

To prevent their noise and *clatter.—The Drunkard's Legacy.*

Much *clatter* was about preparations for the child's cradle, etc.—
Bishop Goodwin.

Claught. Snatched at, seized, clutched.

Claight, snatched.—*Northumb. Halliwell.*

Claut. To clean, to scrape; what is clauted or scraped together, as a *claut o' gear*, property amassed.

Claut, to scratch, to claw.—*Bailey.*

Claver. Clover.

Clafer, clover.—*Bosworth.*

Claver-grass, a kind of three-leaved grass.—*Bailey.*

Clover, more properly *claver.—Johnson.*

> And every one her called-for dances treads
> Along the soft flower of the *claver*-grass.—*Chapman.*

Clavers, claivers. Idle stories.

Clavers, din, noisy talking.—*Halliwell.*

Clavers. John Graham of Claverhouse.

Claw. To scratch.

I do not know why this word should be accounted a Scotch one.

> Bush, why dost thou bear a rose, if none must have it?
> Why thus expose it, yet *claw* those that crave it?—*Bunyan.*
>
> A beggar
> Hath with his pyke-staff *claw'd* my back.—*R. Hood.*

Clean. Entirely, completely. Only in this sense, which, according to Johnson, is obsolete, does Burns's use of *clean* differ from that of E. writers.

Clean, elegant, neat, not encumbered with anything useless or disproportionate.—*Johnson.*

A *clean* instep,
And that I love as life.—By the mass, a neat one.—*Fletcher*.
A *clean* made gentleman.—*Beaumont and Fletcher*.
　　All his lineaments
Strong and clean.—*The Two Noble Kinsmen*.
Thy waist is straight and *clean* as Cupid's shaft.—*Waller*.
To doe a thing *cleane* (entirely) kamme.—*Cotgrave*.

Cleckin. A brood of domestic fowl. Literally what is *clocked* or hatched.

Clocan, to cluck.—*Bosworth*.
Cleckin, a chicken. *Clekyt*, hatched.—*Halliwell*.

Cleed. To clothe. *Th* and *d*, as has already been pointed out, are often interchanged. Compare *klething* with *clodys*, both meaning clothes, in the following passages:—

Vmlapped (enclosed) als *klething* with light.—*Met. E. Psalter*.
The ape thorgh *clodys* and also his schert
　　Brayde (bit) of his pappys.—*Octovian Imperator*.

When we infer, as we are justified in doing, that when we find the past tense of a verb in *a*, as in *clad*, there must once have been also a present tense in *a*, as *clathe* or *clade* (Anglo-Saxon *clath*, cloth, we are, by a parity of reasoning, entitled to conclude, when we find a past tense in *e*, as *cled*, that there must also have been once a present tense with a corresponding vowel, as *bled* suggests *bleed*, and *bred breed*. But *cled* is an English word and so probably is *cleed*.

This Troilus up rose and fast him *cled*.—*Chaucer*.
Ful klenly was he *cled* and dyght.—*The Seven Sages*.
It is not so natural a thing in man to *clad* himself.—*De Mornay*.
Cleeds, clothes.—*Grose*.

Cleek. Hook, catch.

Cleek, to catch at hastily.   *Cleekin*, catching. —*Bamford*.

He smate away al his left cheke,
His sholder als of gan he *kleke*. — *Ywain and Gawain*.

This is the first word that has occurred of " They *reel'd*, they *set*, they *cross'd*, they *cleekit*," a line which to a Scotsman old enough to have taken part in the "fierce vanities" of a *foursome reel*—for I suspect the dancers of the present day are too genteel to give way to the rush and *abandon* of *auld lang syne*—comes with something of the feeling with which the remembrance of a successful charge may inspire an aged soldier, and as an explanation of the terms, reel, cross, set, and cleek, is among the "things unattempted yet in prose or rhyme," this seems a convenient place to endeavour to give it.

The *foursome* reel, to which alone all the terms apply, was danced by two couples, one at each end of the apartment. When they *reeled* they "moved to the music of the Doric reed" from end to end of the apartment, and the gentlemen exchanged places and partners.

They *set*, means that the partners danced in front of each other.

When they *cleeked*, the partners bent their right and left arms alternately, and linking, hooking, or *cleeking* each other, danced in a circle, moving on their own centres. They were not face to face, as in the following description by Sir John Davies, but rather appeared as if chasing each other.

> Yet is there one the most delightfull kind,
>   A loftie jumping, or a leaping round,
> When arme in arme two dancers are entwined,
>   And whirle themselves, with strict embracements bound.
> *Orchestra.*

Crossing, which required two sets of dancers, that is, two couples at each end, was done by each of the dancers at the same end stretching over, taking the hand of the other's partner, and dancing as in cleeking. This crossing is mentioned in the old song, "Arthur O'Bradley's Wedding":

> There was lead up and down, figure in,
> *Four hands across*, then back again.

Clegs. Gad-flies.

Hornets, *clegs*, and *clocks.—Sylvester.*

Clever. Handsome.

Clever, well shaped.—*Batley.*

Clew. Did claw. Old past tense, as,

With teeth he *gnew* (gnawed) the flessch ful harde.
Rich. C. de Lion.

He *clew* the bor (boar) on the rigge.—*The Seven Sages.*

Cling. To shrink, as vessels made with staves do, from heat or drought.—*Jamieson.*

The sunne ariseth, and fallith the dewyng;
The nesche clay hit makith *clyng.—Kyng Alisaunder.*

Upon the next tree shalt thou hang alive
Till famine *cling* thee.—*Shak.*

His fete waxes calde, his bely *clynges.—P. of Conscience.*

Evermore thai grene springeth,
For winter no somer it no *clingeth.—Sir Owain.*

Clink. To jerk, to chink, to rhyme; money.

Clink, to strike so as to make a small sharp noise.—*Johnson.*

In

> O happy is the man
> Whose ain dear lass
> Comes *clinkin* down beside him,

Burns uses the word in the secondary sense, to indicate the action that produces the sound described by Johnson, the nimble motion, for instance, employed in testing a coin by ringing it.

> Five years! a long lease for the *clinking* of pewter.—*Shak.*

> I shal *clinken* you so merry a belle,
> That I shal waken all this compagnie.—*Chaucer.*

They who attempted verse in English down to Chaucer's time made an heavy pudder, and are miserably put to it for a word to *clink*.—*Rymer.*

> Writing what we do not think,
> Merely to make the verse cry *clink*.—*L'Estrange.*

I have not found *clink* for money, but *chink* similarly formed occurs often—

> Those lack'd drink for want of *chink*.—*John and Joan.*

Clinkumbell. He who rings the church bell.

> And as they sat they heard a *belle clinke*,
> Beforn a corps was carried to his grave.—*Chaucer.*

Clips. Shears.

Clips, shears, scissors.—*Northumb. Halliwell.*

Clishmaclaver. Idle conversation. Compound of *clash* and *claver.*

Clock. To hatch.

Clousseuse, a *clocking* henne, or a henne that uses to clocke muche.—*Cotgrave.*

I am aware that *clousseuse* means a *clucking*, not a *brooding* or hatching hen; but the passage shows that the spelling *clock* was known.

> "Nay then," replies the feeble fox,
> "But hark, I hear a hen that *clocks*!
> Go, but be moderate in your food:
> A chicken too might do me good."—*Gay.*

> Our serving-men (like spaniels) range to spring,
> The fowl which he had *cluck'd* (hatched) under his wing.
> —*Cleveland.*

Clock. A beetle.

Clock, a beetle.—*Bailey.* Sort of beetle.—*Johnson.*

Clo:k, a dor. or beetle.—*Grose.*

Hornets, clegs, and *clocks.*—*Sylvester.*

I 'eerd 'um a bummin' away loike a buzzard-*clock* ower my 'eäd.
—*Tennyson.*

Clomb. Did climb. An old past tense of *climb.*

They *clomb* that tedious height.—*Spenser.*

He on his throne was set, to which on hight
 Who *clomb* an hundred ivory stairs first told.—*Fairfax.*

To a huge rock that *clomb* so high in air.—*Gilbert West.*

Cloot. The hoof of a cow, sheep, etc.—*Burns.* The half of a hoof.—*Jamieson.*

Perhaps the word *clowen* in the following passage, rhyming as it does to *drowen* (drew), indicates as clearly as any that has been given how the Anglo-Saxon *cleofa*, that which is cloven, became *cloot*, a cloven hoof.

This Thebes seyghen (saw) how men heom *clowen* (clove):
To heore gates they drowen.—*Kyng Alesaunder.*

Clootie and *Cloots.* Having *cloots*, or cloven hoofs. Old names for the Devil.

I do not know that the English ever had a word expressive of the idea of a hoofed Satan, but the notion was prevalent enough; thus Othello says,—

"I look down towards his feet; but that's a fable;
 If that thou be'st a devil, I cannot kill thee."

The *cloven-footed fiend* is banish'd from us.—*Dryden.*

Tell me who *cleft* the *divels foot.*—*Donne.*

And so late as 1648 a tract was published in London with the title, "The Devil as seen at St. Albans. Being a true relation, how the Devil was seen there, in a Cellar, in the likeness of a Ram," of course with *cloots.*—*Ancient Mysteries Described.*

Have you not *cloven hoofs?* Are ye not devils?—*Massinger.*

Clour. A bump or swelling after a blow.

Clud. A cloud.   *U* for *ou* is quite common in old E. authors.

> I have you *fun* (found) so sone.—*Ywain and Gawain.*
> Bot wend haf *funden* (found) that thai socht.—*Cursor Mundi.*
> The abbesse lete clepe a prest anon,
> And lete it cristin in *funston* (a stone fount).—*Lay Le Freine.*
> To hawke, or els to hunt From the aulter to the *funt.*—*Skelton.*
> Thai said, He sal be *bun* (bound) or slain.—*Launfal.*

Clunk. To emit a hollow and interrupted sound, as that preceding from a nearly empty cask when violently shaken.

The advocates of what has been called the "Bow-wow" theory of the origin of language could not find a better illustration than this word affords, for it does not imitate, but is, the very sound.

Coalition. Union, alliance.

The coalition to which Burns refers in the "Earnest Cry and Prayer" was the union formed by the party of Lord North and that of Mr. Fox. To this alliance he again alludes in "A Fragment":—

> North and Fox united stocks.
> Gay Wilmot joined with thee,
> Shall shew the world that such a thing can be
> As, strange to tell! a virtuous *coalition!*—*The Rolliad.*

Coatie. Dim. of coat.

Coble. A fishing-boat.

> Coggle and *coble*, a small fishing boat.—*Bailey.*

Cock. The mark for which curlers play, now generally called the *tee.*

Cockie. Dim. of cock, a fowl, a familiar, perhaps vulgar name, for an elderly friend.

He has drawn blood of him yet; well done, old *cock.*—*Massinger.*

Cockernony. A lock of hair tied up on a girl's head, a cap.

I do not think this word was in use, at least in Ayrshire, in Burns's day. It is an echo from an older time.

Cod. A pillow.

Cod, a pillow.—*Bailey.* *Cod*, a bag.—*Tyrwhitt.*
Faire *coddis* of silk.—*MS.* quoted by *Halliwell.*
Selling of counterfeit *cods.*—*Fletcher.*

Weber, an editor of an edition of Beaumont and Fletcher, says "cods are pillows."

Co'er. To cover. For omission of *v* see under *ca't.*

> At last, him turning to his charge behight,
> With trembling hand his troubled pulse gan try;
> Where finding life not yet dislodged quight,
> He much rejoyst and *cowred* it tenderly,
> As chicken newly hatcht, from dreaded destiny.—*Spenser.*
>
> Officers full busily them cast
> In the hall bordes for to *cure.*—*Lydgate.*

Coft. Bought.

Cog. A wooden dish of cooper's work, a pail.

This word I take to be the same as *cog*, a small boat, from which we have *cock-boat.* That *cog* should signify both a dish and a *boat*—not to speak of a dish called a *butter-boat*—is not more strange than that *coffin* should mean a box for the dead, part of the foot of a horse, and also a mould of paste for a pie.

> Agaynes hem comen her naveye,
> *Cogges*, and dromoundes, many galeye.—*R. C. de Lion.*

> And for the *cog* was narrow, small, and strait,
> Alone he row'd, and bade his squire there wait.—*Fairfax.*

> Found Jason and Hercules also,
> That in a *cogge* to lond were ygo.—*Chaucer.*

Coggie.   Dim. of Cog.

Coila.   From Kyle, a district in Ayrshire; so called, saith tradition, from Coil, or Coilus, a Pictish monarch.

Sche was Doughtre of Kyng Cool (or *Coyle*), born in Colchester.
—*Maundeville.*

Collie.   A general and sometimes a particular name for country curs; a shepherd's dog.

Collies are not now considered curs, but are fashionable dogs. They probably received their name from being generally black—the colour of Luath in "The Twa Dogs." They seem to have been more so formerly than they are now, being under the law that the longer animals are domesticated the more varied their colours become. This is not Jamieson's opinion; but *colly* in Shakspeare means to blacken, as in *Collied night*, and—

> Passion having my best judgment *collied*,
> Assays to lead the way,

which is something in favour of what, like his, is only a guess.

Colfox, a black fox.—*Bailey.*   Ran *Colle* our dog.—*Chaucer.*

He was colored as the *cole* corbyal untrwe.
—*Early E. Alliterative Poems.*

> He made foule chere,
> And *bicollede* is swere, i.e., blackened his neck.
> —*The Geste of Kyng Horn.*

The newe Testament for them? and then for *cowle* my dog.
—*New Custom.*

Collieshangie. Quarrelling, a tumult, uproar ; such a disturbance as is caused by a dog running through a crowd with a *shangan* (q.v.), tied to his tail.

Shangy, a riot, a row.—*Halliwell.*

Commauṇ. Command. The insertion of *u* between *a* and *n* is common in old E. writers. In a single page before me, I find *daunce, launce, advauntage,* and *demaund.*

As his Grace shall *commaund.*—*The Owlde order of makyng the Kynges* (Henry VIII.) *bedde.*

It is right easy to *commaund.*—*Gower.*

Compleenin'. Complaining.

Where Burns uses it, it may mean *ailing.* *E* for *a*, as in—

> This is all and som, he held virginitee
> More parfit than wedding in *freeltee* (frailty).—*Chaucer.*

Cood. The cud. *Oo* for *u*, as in—

> He *strook* (struck) so hard, the bason broke.
> *The Noble Acts of Arthur and the Knights of the Round Table.*

> Or as a stalon in the fennes,
> Which goth amonges all the *stood* (stud).—*Gower.*

> Swyn, Hares, and othere Bestes, that chewen not here *code.*
> *Maundeville.*

Coof. A blockhead, a ninny.

When the word is spelled *cufe*, as it often is, it is seen to be the same as *chuff* when it has undergone the change of *ch* into *c*, as of *churl* into *carl*, of *chalk* into *calke*, etc. See *cauk.*

> Troth, sister, I heard you were married to a very rich *chuff.*
> *The Honest Whore.*

Cook. To appear and disappear by fits.

Cook seems to be nearly the same as *keek*. To *keek* is to see by fits, and to *cook* to be seen by fits.

Cooser. A stallion.

Coost and *Cuist.* Did cast. The digraph *oo* for *a* does not occur often in English, though it is found in *strook* for *strake,* *schoof* for *shaved,* etc., but it is quite possible that in such words *oo* may represent the long sound of *o*. There are, however, a great variety of spellings of this word.

> And *kest* water opon the stane.—*Ywain and Gawain.*
>
> Ye *kyst* a shepys ie.—*Skelton.*
>
> *Gussen,* cast, dejected.—*Halliwell.*

It requires to be noted that *oo*, in words like *coost, coof,* and *coot*, has an entirely different sound from the same digraph in *boord, foord,* and *hoord*, and is not easy to explain. *Cuist* more nearly represents the pronunciation, and this is not far from Skelton's *kyst* in the line quoted above, and the same word in—

> He *kyst* a down the bores hed.—*Carol for St. Stephen's Day.*

Coot. The ankle.

Cutes, the feet.—*Halliwell.*

Cootie. A wooden kitchen dish or tub; also those fowls whose legs are clad with feathers are said to be *cootie.*

I believe that the word *cootie* always includes the idea of shortness. A *cootie* hen, or domestic fowl, is always short-legged as well as feathered. Is it another form of *cutty?*

Corbie. A species of crow.

Corby, a crow.—*Grose.*

> Slitteth anon
> The belly to the side, from the *corbyn* bone,
> That is corbyn's fee, at the death he will be.
> —*Dame Juliana Berners.*

> He watz (was) colored as the cole *corbyal* un-trewe.
> —*Early E. Alliterative Poems.*

> To her resorted many a beak,
> And birds of sundry sorts of hue;
> Sir Ingram *Corby* he came first there
> With his fair lady clad in black.
> —*The Northumberland Garland. Ritson.*

Core. Corps, a party, a clan; differs only in spelling from corps.

Cork-rumps. Stiffening for dresses; a "dress improver" of the time.

> You have my thanks for the inquiries you have made upon the subject of male *rumps corked.*—*Cowper.*

> Pleased with nature's hips, she scorns *cork rumps.*—*Wolcot.*

Corn. Oats, to feed with oats.

Corn is, or was, the S. name for oats, but although Burns always means oats when he says corn, there is only one passage in his poems which cannot be translated grain, and be quite plain to an Englishman. That passage is—

> When thou was *corn't,*

which, to an ordinary Englishman, and, I suspect, to many a Scotsman, is suggestive of salting rather than feeding. But though Englishmen do not speak of *corning* their horses, they nevertheless feed them with corn:

> A proud Bayard beginneth for to skippe
> Out of the way so pricketh him his *corne.*—*Chaucer.*

> Later age's pride, like *corn-fed* steed,
> Abused her plenty.—*Spenser.*

But after all it appears that corn was used as far south at least as Bedfordshire for a particular kind of grain, probably oats, for John Bunyan says—

He had them into his field, which he had sown with *wheat and corn.--Pilgrim's Progress, Second Part.*

> I've a bag for meal, and a bag for malt,
> And a bag for barley and *corn.—R. Hood.*

Cors, corse, or *corss.* The cross or market-place. For transposition of *r* see *brugh.*

Cottar. The inhabitant of a cot-house, or cottage.

Countra. Country.

This word was spelled by old E. writers, *countrey, countray, countré,* etc.

Country. County.

In his letters Burns often uses country for county, once a common practice, but now disused.

He is a justice of peace in his *country.—Shak.*

Her personal estate alone will buy,
Upon good rates, a thousand pound a year.
Where must that be? Not in our *country.—The Old Couple.*

There was neither tree, nor gate, nor stile, in all that *country*, to which I did not feel a relation.—*Cowper.*

Drayton addresses Warwickshire as "My native *country.*"
Polyolbion.

Court-day. Rent day.

I have at last met with the procedings of the *court-baron.--Specta'or.*

The *court-baron*, though in it the lord of the manor had much greater power than in its successor, was the *court-day's* ancestor.

Couthie. Kind, loving.

Couth, known, or skilful in. *Coutheutlaughe*, one who knowingly, cherishes, entertains, or hides any outlawed person.—*Bailey.*

This uncouth word, *coutheutlaughe*, is just " a person *couthie*, kind, or loving, to an outlaw."

> Loke, boy, be naught betrayed
> Of *kouth* ne strange.—*Octovian Imperator*.
>
> And to the peples eres all and some
> Was *couth* eke.—*Chaucer*.

Here as well as elsewhere *couth* means *known*, which is the fundamental idea of *couthie*, loving, which follows, or ought to follow, knowledge, being only a secondary idea.

Cove. A cavern.

> In this wild, dark, and drearie *cove*,
> Of wife, of children, and of health bereft,
> I hailed thee, friendly spider, who had'st wove
> Thy mazy net on yonder mouldering raft.
> —*To a Spider who inhabited a cell. Anthologia Bor. et Aus.*
>
> In her barm scho (she) ledd hir child,
> Till thai come at a *cove* was depe:
> Thar tham thoght to rest and slepe.—*Cursor Mundi*.

Cowe. To terrify, to keep under; to lop; to fright; a fright, a bunch of furze, broom, etc.

All these meanings, diverse as they may seem, spring from the first, to terrify and keep under. To lop, is to keep under by cutting off the top, and a bunch of furze is here thought of as a means of terrifying, and a most efficient one it has often proved, as most people who have been brought up in the country can testify, many of whom can say with Burns—

> Ae dreary, windy, winter night,
> Wi' you, mysel, I gat a fright,
> Ye like a *rash-bush* stood in sight,

and can tell how relieved they were when the fearful object " squatter'd awa," or its innocence was discovered.

To *cow* one, to put one out of heart, or keep one in awe.—*Bailey*.

It hath *cow'd* my better part of man.—*Shaks*.

For when men by their wives are *cow'd*,
Their horns, of course, are understood.—*Butler*.

Johnson quotes this passage under *cow*, to terrify, but it seems more properly to mean lop, for horns may be cut, but cannot well be frightened.

Colle to me the ryshes grene, *colle* to me.

Ritson in his "Ancient Songs" has one with this burden, and says *colle* means cull. I think it means *cowe* or cut. For change of *ol* into *ow*, see under *a'*. This old E. song will thus appear to be similar to the old S. song, "*Cow* the me the rashes green."

At that I was held a master in, he has *cow'd* me.—*Fletcher*.

The people were annoyed by the pranks of a bogle called the Hedley *kow*.—*Richardson's Table Book*.

Cowp. To barter; to tumble over; a fall; a gang.

Coup, to exchange, or swap.—*Bailey*.

To cope or *coup*, to chop or exchange.—*Grose*.

Coup, to empty or overset.—*Halliwell*.

Flemings began on me for to cry,
"Master, what will you *copen* or buy.—*The London Lickpenny*.

Since in horse *couping* he began,
He had great cause to crack of wealth.—*The Northumb. Garland. Ritson*.

She *cowp'd* him o'er the kale-pot.—*Ib*.

Cowp the cran. To overset. See *cowp* and *cran*.

Cowrin. Cowering.

To *cour*, to squat down, to kneel.—*Bailey*.

As you creep or *cowr*, or lie, or stoop, or go,
So, marking you with care, the apish bird doth do.—*Polyolbion*.

Emere stroke in to that stowre,
And many oon made he for to *cowre*.—*La Bon Florence of Rome*.

Treowe love in heorte durith,
Ac nede coward byhynde *kourith.—Kyng Alisaunder.*

Cowte. A colt. For change of *ol* into *ow*, see under *ci* and *bow-kail.*

Cowt, a colt.—*Bamford.* *Cowt*, a colt.—*Var. dial. Halliwell.*

Cozie. Snug.

Cosey, snug, comfortable.—*Halliwell.*

Crabbit. Crabbed.

Crack. Conversation; to converse; a *crack*, a short time.

> Hereat thy friends will *crack* full crouse.—*R. Hood.*
>
> Here's mother Maudlin come to give you thanks,
> Madam, for some late gift she hath received,
> Which she's not worthy of, she says, but *cracks*
> And wonders of it.—*Ben Jonson.*

Crack, discourse.—*Weber.*

In a crack, immediately.—*Halliwell.*

> I con show thee in a *crack*, sed he.—*John Collier.*

Crack credit. To lose character and confidence in any respect.—*Jamieson.*

Seeing that the intent of all writers of Stories is to be beleeved; what els had this beginning of an History at that point beene, but a *cracking of his credit* at his first entrance in, if the majesty of the author had not served for a warrant.—*The Truenesse of the Christian Religion.*

> How many things there are to be observed
> Which seem but little; yet by one of us
> Neglected, *cracks our credits* utterly.—*Fletcher.*

Shall she be clapt upon his back too, as though one wasn't enough to *crack his credit?*—*Echard.*

Craft or *croft.* A field near a house. *A* for *o*, see under *aff.*

G

Craig, craigie. The neck.

> Thy ewes that woont to have blowen bags,
> Like waileful widowes hangen their *crags.*—*Spenser.*

> I wad the deil had had their *craigs.*—*The Fray of Hantwessell.*

I cannot see so far into a mill-stone as black-hooded and red-*craiged* rabbies.—*Life of Monmouth.*

Craigy. Craggy.

Craig, the top of a rock.—*Bailey.*

Craik. Name of a bird; to whine.

Craik. Creak, a corn creak, a landrail; so called from its creaking note.—*Grose.*

The landrail or corn-*crake* is a bird of passage.—*Markwick.*

The *crakes* sal ly if I may.—*The Seven Sages.*

I cannot *crakell* so in vaine.—*Chaucer.*

Crambo-clink, or *crambo-jingle.* Rhymes, doggrel verses.

Crambo, a play in rhyming in which he that repeats a word that was said before forfeits something.—*Bailey.*

A little superior to them are those who can play at *crambo,* or cap verses.—*Spectator.*

> He pass'd his time
> In virtuoso-ship, and *crambo*-rhyme.—*Walter Harte.*

They were miserably put to it for a word to *clink.*—*Rymer.*

Crampet. An iron with small spikes to keep the foot firm on ice.—*Graeme.*

In Burns's letter to Mr. Cunningham, the definition which Johnson gives of *cramp*—though the above is what in Scotland is understood by a *crampet*—seems to suit his meaning better. The passage in which the word occurs is—" If I choose to bind down with the *crampets* of attention the brazen foundation of integrity, I may rear up the structure of independence." Johnson says—
" *Cramp,* a piece of iron bent at each end, by which two

bodies are held together." Burns's figure implies the holding of the foundation and the building together, and a *crampet* is not used for that purpose.

Cran. An iron instrument, laid across the fire, reaching from the ribs of the grate to the hinder part of it, for the purpose of supporting a pot or kettle. It seems to be denominated from its form, as it bore some resemblance to a crane.—*Jamieson.* In some parts of England a similar instrument is called a *crab.*

"Coup the *cran*," go to wreck like a pot on the fire, when the cran upon which it stood is upset.—*Sir W. Scott.*

Crank. The noise of an ungreased wheel.

Crank, to creak.—*Halliwell.*

Crankous. Fretful, captious.

This is Burns's own definition of a word which, so far as I am aware, is not to be found in any other author. But he uses it, I think, in a stronger sense than his definition implies. The times did not admit of his saying Scotland was in a rebellious, fighting mood, so he said she was "fretful, captious." Examine the passage in which it occurs—

> This while she's been in *crankous* mood,
> Her lost militia *fir'd her bluid.*

What is the state of mind intended to be indicated by "fired her bluid"? He has the same expression in another passage—

> Gie him strong drink until he wink,
> That's sinking in despair;
> And liquor gude to *fire his bluid,*
> That's prest wi' grief an' care.

Surely this prescription was not intended to make the

patient fretful and captious, but bold and sanguine, to make him

> Forget his loves or debts,
> And mind his griefs no more.

Crank, healthy, sprightly; sometimes corrupted into *cranky*.

Johnson.

> Like chanticlere he crowed *cranke*
> And piped full merrilie.—*Dousabelle.*

> As cocke on his dunghill crowing *cranke.*—*Spenser.*

Upton's note on this is, "*Crank* is lusty, courageous."

Cranreuch. The hoar-frost.

Crap. A crop, to crop, the top. *A* for *o*, see under *aff*, and in—

> Be ye nevere the *balder* (bolder) to breke the ten hestes.
>
> *P. Plowman.*

Craps o' heather. Heather-tops.

Crop once meant top.

> Man es a tre
> Of whilk the *crop* es turned donward.
>
> *P. of Conscience.*

Craw. A crow of a cock; a rook.

> With shame and grief adawed
> That of a weed he was over-*crawed.*—*Spenser.*

> He hath queintise white so snawe,
> With foules blac as ani *crawe.*
> With sik werk it is wrought.
>
> *Horn Child and Maiden Rimnild.*

Creel. A basket; *to have one's wits in a creel*, to be crazed, to be fascinated.

To be in a creel, with the same meaning, is more common.

Creel, a wicker basket.—*Halliwell.*

He has made a cleek but and a *creel.*—*Bell's Ancient Poems.*

Creepie chair. The stool of repentance.

Creeper, a small stool.—*Halliwell.*

Creepie, a three-legged stool in North English and Scottish.—*Rev. A. S. Palmer's Folk Etymology.*

Creeshie. Greasy. *C* for *g*, as in "Crussel, a gristle."—*Bailey.* For *sh* instead of *s*, see under *fleesh.*

Creuks. Crooks, a disease in horses. *Eu* for *oo.* See under *beuk.*

Crinkum-crankum. Burns applies this reduplication to "Robin Adair," which he also styles a "cramp, out-of-the-way measure."

Crincum-crancum occurs in the Spectator, No. 623, with a very different meaning.

Here's none of your straight lines here—but all taste—zig-zag—*crinkum-crankum*—in and out.—*Garrick.*

Crocks. Refuse; old sheep.

Croke, refuse, the bad or useless part of anything. *Crock*, an old ewe.—*Halliwell.*

> He sought not the world's *croke,*
> For vaine honour ne for richesse.—*Gower.*

Crood or *croud.* To coo as a dove.

To *croo*, to *crookle*, to make a noise as a dove.—*Bailey.*

Croon. A hollow continued moan, to make a noise like the continued noise of a bull, to hum a tune.

On a time it happened that his bull fell a bellowing, which in the language of the country is called *cruning*, this being the genuine Saxon word to denote that vociferation. Thereupon he said to one of his neighbours, "Hearest thou how loud this bull *crunes?* If these cattle should all *crune* together, might they not be heard from Brough hither?" "Yea." "Well, then," says Brunskill, "I'll make them all *crune* together."—*Nicolson and Burns's History and Antiquities of Cumberland and Westmoreland.*

Cross. Across, over. For *cross* in a dance, see under *cleek*.

Cross, over, from side to side.—*Johnson*.

Enter Parley, running *cross* the stage.—*Farquhar*.

Crouchie. Crook-backed.

Crouch, crooked.—*Bailey*.

> Feol bores, and eke wilde swyn ;
> And *croched* dragons saunfaill.—*Kyng Alisaunder*.
> He is a *crooching* fool.—*Rabelais*.

Crouse. Cheerful, courageous.

Crowse, brisk, lively, jolly.—*Bailey*.

Crowse, as Bailey ; as *crowse* as a new-washen louse.—*Grose*.

How cheer my hearts? Most *crowse*, most crapingly.
Richard Browne.

> And now of late Duke Humphrey's old allies,
> With banished Eleanor's accomplices,
> Attending their revenge, grow wondrous *crouse*,
> And threaten death and vengeance to our house.
> Drayton.

Crousely. Cheerfully, courageously.

Crowdie. Meal and water in a cold state stirred together so as to form a thick gruel.—*Jamieson*.

Sir W. Scott defines crowdie, "Meal and milk mixed in a cold state, a kind of pottage"; but in his "Two Drovers," when describing their food, he says nothing of milk, and there can be no doubt that Jamieson's definition is the correct one. It would be more accurate to say *was*, for the dish is now unknown, and even in Burns's day the word was only employed as a sort of jocular name for "the halesome parritch." Indeed, there is not a particle of evidence to show that it ever was used, except when more carefully prepared food was not attainable, and it would surprise me to find a single Scotsman who believes the following statement :—

Crowdie, a dish very common in Scotland, and accounted a very great luxury by labourers, is a never-failing dinner in Scotland with all ranks of people on Shrove Tuesday, . . . it being considered the most substantial dish in the country.—*State of the Poor, by Sir Frederick M. Morton Eden, Bart.*

Crowdie, oatmeal, scalded with water, and mixed up into a paste.
Grose.

There is not a herd-laddie in Scotland but would say, "That's brose!"

Crowdie-time. Breakfast time.

> But Mars
> In *pudding time* came to his aid.—*Butler.*

Crowlin. Crawling. *Ow* or *ou* sound for *aw* or *au*, as in—

And look that they be nought *rowe* (raw).—*Kyng Alisaunder.*

Chaucer has *doughtren* for daughters, *rought* for raught, Skelton *cought* for caught, and *Powles* continued for a long time to be used for Paul's.

Syr Garcy went *crowlande* for fayne.—*Le Bone Flo. of Rome.*

I do not know that *crowlande* means crawling, though, as Syr Garcy was more than a hundred years old, that word might, in all likelihood, describe his motion.

Crucks. See *creuks.*

Crummie, crummock, crummit. A cow with crooked horns.

Crump, crooked.—*Bailey.*
> This is the cow with the *crumpled* horn.
> *The House that Jack built.*

> Rise up and save cow *Crumbock's* life.
> *Old Song. Percy.*

Crummock. A staff with a crooked head.

Crump. Hard and brittle, spoken of bread (and other easily broken things).

> Toiling in the naked fields,
> Where no bush a shelter yields,
> Needy Labour dithering stands,
> Beats and blows his numbing hands;
> And upon the *crumping* snows
> Stamps in vain to warm his toes.—*Clare.*

She took some little cakes out of her basket which she gave him, and he *crump'd* them between his teeth.—*The Power of Love.*

This is a translation of Longus's *Daphnis and Chloe*, when or by whom made I know not. My copy is dated Dublin, 1763.

Crunt. A blow on the head with a cudgel. This word is common in Ayrshire, though not known in literature till Burns used it.

Cuif. See *coof.*

Cummock. A short staff with a crooked head.

> Your wynde-schakyn shankes, your longe lothy legges,
> Crokyd as a *camoke*, and as a kowe calfles(s).—*Skelton.*
>
> All that he dothe is ryght,
> As right as a *cammoke* croked.—*Ib.*
>
> This is clean *kam* (crooked).—*Shak.*

Curch. A covering for the head. A corruption of *kerchief.*

Curchie. A courtesy, or curtsy, an old-fashioned female reverence.

> Then every man did put his hat off to his lass,
> And every girl did *curchie, curchie, curchie,* on the grass.
>   *Bell's Ancient Poems and Songs of the English Peasantry.*

Curler. A player at the game of curling.

Curling. A well-known game on ice. To those who have not seen it, it may be said that it is something like the game of bowls; but the stones used slide instead of rolling like bowls.

Curlie. Curly: whose hair falls naturally in ringlets.

Curmurrin. Murmuring, slight rumbling noise.—*Burns.* Applied to the motion of the intestines which is produced by slight gripes.—*Jamieson.*

This is another word which cannot, I suspect, be traced farther than the pages of Burns, who would probably have been amused at the learned lexicographer's praiseworthy attempts to find its parentage in *kurrar i magen,* stomachus latrat, etc.

Curpin or *curpon.* The crupper, the buttock or haunch.

Curple. Same as *curpin.*

Cushat. The dove or wood pigeon.—*Burns.* *Cushat* is never applied to any but the wood-pigeon.

Mansart, a culvert, *cooshat,* ring-dove.—*Cotgrave.*

Cushets, wild pigeons.—*Grose.*

Cutty. Short; a spoon, certainly not one broken in the middle, as Allan Cunningham says, or anywhere.

Cutty is applied to various things, a cutty-pipe, a cutty-stool, etc. In English it is *cut,* as cut and long tail.

His wyf walked him with
In a *cutted* cote.—*Peres the Ploughman's Crede. Skeat.*

I set not by the worlde two Douncaster *cuttys* (short-tailed horses).
Skelton.

Cutty-stool. A low stool; stool of penance or repentance.

Cannot sentence
To *stools,* or poundage of repentance.—*Butler.*

D.

Daddie. Father; dim. of dad.

> Formal Patrick is transformed to Paddy,
> And Father by the children christen'd *Daddy*.
> *Dr. Wolcot.*
>
> Dicky your boy, that, with his grumbling voice,
> Was wont to cheer his *dad* in mutinies.—*Shak.*
>
> It says that *daddy* is a false man.—*Farquhar.*

Daffin. Daffing, merriment, foolishness.

> And when this jape is told another day,
> I shall be holden a *daffe* or a cokenay.—*Chaucer.*
>
> Thou dotest, *daffe*, quod she, dull are thy wittes.—*P. Plowman.*
>
> *Daffin*, merriment.—*Northumberland. Halliwell.*

Daft. Merry, giddy, foolish.

> *Daft*, stupid, blockish.—*Bailey. Daft*, foolish.—*Grose.*
> Noo, thou *daft* fule!—*Specimen of Durham Language.*

Dails. Deals. *A* for *e*, as in—

> His bones *crake* (creak),
> Leane as a rake.—*Skelton.*
>
> To make illusion,
> By swiche an *apparance* (appearance) or joglerie
> That she and every wight should wene and say,
> That of Bretagne the rockes were away.—*Chaucer.*
>
> He so longe criede and bade,
> That him com from heven *rade*, i.e. rede, counsel,
> How he scholde heom distroye.—*Kyng Alisaunder.*

Daimen. Rare, now and then; *daimen-icker*, an ear of corn now and then.

This seems to be another word for which Burns alone

is responsible. Jamieson quotes no other authority for it, and says it is perhaps derived from "*diement*, counted, from A.-S. *deman*, to reckon."

Now, granting that *deman* means to reckon, "counted" seems but a poor explanation of *daimen*, which is always used as equivalent to something not worth taking into consideration, and might well be translated a *chance one*.

As Jamieson introduces his derivation with a modest— perhaps, I may, with the same saving adverb, suggest a less recondite origin for the word.

In Burns's time and later the servants on a farm were invariably engaged for the half-year, and the reapers as invariably hired for the harvest, not for a fixed time, but till the crop was secured. A person paid by the day was never seen save in an emergency. Hence to denote a thing of rare occurrence, especially as his visit formed a sort of epoch in the monotonous lives of a farmer's household, a dayman was a convenient and (to them) expressive term. Anything seldom occurring would be said to be like a *dayman*, and in the natural course of language the sign of the simile would be dropped. It may be said that if it were so "daysman" would have been more natural, but the Scottish peasantry knew their Bibles too well not to be aware that daysman had been already appropriated.

Day-man, a labourer hired by the day.—*East. Halliwell.*

Day-woman in "Love's Labour Lost" is generally explained a *dairy-woman*, which is a mere guess. Chaucer has—

<blockquote>She was as it were a maner *dey*.</blockquote>

Tyrwhitt thinks *dey* was originally a day-labourer.

Dainty. Pleasant, good-humoured, agreeable; a delicacy, primarily something for eating better than common food.

His life abhorreth bread, and his soul *dainty* meat.—*Job xxxiii. 20.*

Be not desirous of his *dainties.*—*Proverbs xxiii. 3.*

Dainties, delicacies, niceties, tidbits.—*Bailey.*

This seems to be a good English word, and yet Burns has it in his glossary; it is in Jamieson's Dictionary, and in Halliwell's valuable Archaic Dictionary. What can be wrong with the word?

> And Martilmass Beefe doth bear good tack
> When countrey folke do *dainties* lacke.—*Tusser.*

Among other *dainties*, I saw something like a pheasant.—*Addison.*

Daise or *daez*. To stupify. Does not seem to differ, except in spelling, from E. *daze*.

Dazed, confused, amazed.—*Bamford.*

Dasing after dottrellers like drunkards.—*Skelton.*

For in good faith thy visage is ful pale;
Thine eyen *dasen*, sothly as me thinketh.—*Chaucer.*

Poor humankind, all *daz'd* in open day,
Err after bliss, and blindly miss the way.—*Dryden.*

Dander. To wander.

Dander, to wander about.—*Chesh. Halliwell.*

Dare. To threaten, in "Straight the sky grew black and daring."

Dare, to threaten.—*Somerset. Halliwell.*

What dares not Warwick if false Suffolk *dare* him?—*Shak.*

Darklins. Darkling. The omission of *g* in such words as *backlins* and *darklins* is quite common, and easily explained; not so the addition of *s*, but that is also found.

>   The wakeful bird
>   Sings *darkling*, and, in shadiest covert hid,
>   Tunes her nocturnal note.—*Milton*.
>
>   O, wilt thou *darkling* leave me?—*Shak*.
>
>   He will go *darkling* to his grave.
>   *Ralph Roister Doister*.
>
>   All thair idels, in a stund,
>   *Grovelings* fel unto the grund.—*Cursor Mundi*.
>
>   For the mouth he had grinninge,
>   And the tong out *flatlinge*.—*Arthour and Merlin*.

Dash. To depress.

>   Some stronger power eludes our sickly will;
>   *Dashes* onr rising hope with certain ill.—*Prior*.

A foolish mild man; an honest man, look you and soon *dash'd*.
Shak.

He was quite *dash'd* out of countenance.—*Echard*.

Daud. To thrash, to abuse; to drive forcibly.

Daunton. To tame, to subdue, intimidate.

Beholding him above the common course of other men, *dauntyng* a fierce and cruell beaste.—*Sir Thomas Elyot. Skeat*.

And David shal be diademed, and *daunten* hem alle.—*P. Plowman*.

Daur. To dare.

>   In picturing the parts of beauty daynt,
>   So hard a workmanship adventure *darre*.—*Spenser*.
>
>   As they that *dor* nought schewen his presence.
>   *Wright's Chaucer*.
>
>   This wicked man of warr,
>   So haultis that he *darr*,
>   As he lyste, make and marr.—*Image of Ipocrisy*.
>
>   To hym *dar* no man doo no thyng.—*R. C. de Lion*.

Daurk or *darg*.   A day's labour.   *Han' darg*, work of the hand.

The contributed ploughing days in Northumberland are called "*Bone dargs*."—*Ellis*.

"I'll do my *darg* before I arg" (i.e., argue), is a proverb current in the eastern counties (of England).—*Dr. C. Mackay*.

Daut or *dawt*. To caress or fondle.

Dawted, fondled, caressed.—*Halliwell*.

Davoc. Dim. of Davie.

Daw. To dawn.

>Long or the day began to *dawe*.—*R. C. de Lion*.
>Hit ginneth to *dawe ;* highe the henne.—*The Seven Sages*.
>And on the other side, from whence the morning *daws*.
>*Polyolbion*.

Dawd. A large piece.

Dauds, pieces, fragments.—*Halliwell*.

Dawin. Dawning, dawn. Dunbar has *dawing*. See *daw*.

>And so befell, that in a *dawening*.—*Chaucer*.

Dead. Death.

>Thou shalt die an evil *dede*.—*Guy of Warwick*.
>And by the *ded* that I sall thole.—*Ywain and Gawain*.
>E is the first letter and the hede
>Of the name of Eve that began our *dede*.
>*Pricke of Conscience*.

Dead sweer. Very reluctant. See *sweer*.

Dead, like *clean*, *stark*, etc., is often used as an intensive adverb, as in "You could (like a Suffolke man) answer at the second question *dead* sure."—*A Search for Money*.

>And when he shall but doubt I dare attempt him,
>*Dead* sure he cuts me off.—*Fletcher*.

Dead-lights. Lights seen in places such as churchyards, proceeding from decaying bodies.

Dearie. Dim. of dear.
  Deary, little.—*Bailey*.
       Deores (lovers) with huere derne rounes,
          Domes forte deme.
              Wright's Specimens of Lyric Poetry.

Dearthfu. High-priced. *Dearth* and *fu*.
Dearthful is a regularly formed E. word like healthful, dreadful, etc.

Deave. To deafen. *V* is often used for *f*, as in—
    Their vapour *vaded* (faded).—*Spenser*.
    Unware till that he be *mischeved*.—*Gower*.
    And many of hem became blynde, and many *deve*.
                        Maundeville.

    They ben dombe, and thereto they ben *deve*.—*Chaucer*.

Besides the change of letters, *deave*, by the substitution of a flat for a sharp consonant, has from an adjective become a verb. Verbs are frequently formed from nouns in this way, as grieve from grief, graze from grass, etc., but the formation of verbs from adjectives in this manner is not so common. It is found, however. Thus close, by the change of sharp into flat *s* or *z*, becomes a verb. *Deave* is therefore not un-English. Indeed, many authors have used this very word deaf, without the *en*, which is the characteristic of verbs formed from adjectives.

    When suddenly we heard a dreadful sound
    Which *deaft* the earth.—*Fairfax*.
    A wizard dame, the lover's ancient friend,
    With magic charm has *deaft* thy husband's ear.—*Hammond*.
    And fluttering round his temples *deafs* his ears.—*Dryden*.

I cannot help asking, "would '*deaves* his ears' not sound better?" Shakspeare has also "*deafs* his ears," but the following passage deserves special notice:—

> If sickly ears,
> *Deaf'd* with the clamour of their own dear groans,
> Will hear your idle scorns, continue them.
>
> *Love's Labour Lost.*

The *fd* in *deaf'd* is unpronounceable. One of the letters must be altered. Which? Did Shakspeare say *deaft* or *deaved*?

Deeave, to stun with noice.—*Tim Bobbin.*

Dee. To die.

> And thofe scho *dee* as wyle as hee.—*Octovian Imperator.*

Deil. The devil.

> From fire-drakes and fiends,
> And such as the *deil* sends.—*Fletcher.*
>
> Perhaps he'll sneer or break a jest,
> But *deil* a bit to break your fast.
>
> *Dean Percival on Dean Swift.*

> "Well, I'm at leisure to attend you!"
> "Are you?" (thought I) "the *Deil* befriend you!"
>
> *Cowper.*

Deil-ma-care! No matter! for all that! Sterne's "Le diable l'emporte, said I," is near it.

Deil-sticket. Not one.

Deil tak the hindmost! Each for himself; haste. Great wits jump. Pope has—

> So take the hindmost, Hell!—*The Dunciad.*

Deil's yeld nowte. Sheriff's officers and other executors of the law.—*Gilbert Burns.*

Deleerit. Delirious.

Delirate, to dote; to rave; to talk or act oddly.—*Johnson.*

Den. A hollow, a dingle.

Dene, a small valley.—*Bailey.*

> With flowers fresh their heads bedeckt,
> The Fairies dance in fielde;
> And wanton songes in mossy *dennes*
> The Drids (Dryads) and Satirs yielde.
> *Barnaby Googe.*

> Ther wer slayn, in playn and *den,*
> Two hundryd thousand hethene men.—*R. C. de Lion.*

Dern. To hide, secret.

> Of *derne* love he cowde and of solas.—*Chaucer.*

> I pray thé
> In thy chaumbre thou woldest kepe me *dern.*
> *How a Merchante dyd hys Wyfe Betray. Ritson.*

> He soght and fand a *dern* wicket.—*Ywain and Gawain.*

Descrive. To describe.

> Of me, whose wo ther may no wight *descrive.*—*Chaucer.*

> Oft I wisht some would their woes *discryve.*
> *The Mirrour for Magistrates.*

> How shall frayle pen *descrive* her heavenly face.—*Spenser.*

> And thanne cam coveytise, can I hym nougte *descryve.*
> *P. Plowman.*

Deuks. Ducks. *Eu* is often used by old E. authors for *u*, as in—

Hostage y-take, and *treuth* y-plight.—*Kyng Alisaunder.*

I me repente of my *mysreuled* lyfe.—*Thomas Occleve. Skeat.*

Deuk, to bend down. Bedfordshire.—*Halliwell.*

They conne wel also *duke* (in the water).—*Caxton.*

Dr. Mackay, whose slightest remark on the Scottish language is entitled to respect, says that in the line,

> The deuks dang o'er my daddie,

deuk should be *deuch*, i.e., drink. But I am afraid this cannot be accepted, for the "auld wife," evidently in the humour to say all the ill she can of the "paidlin' body," does not charge him with drunkenness, and the old song from which Burns took the idea says—

> The wife and her cummers sat down to drink
> But *ne'er a drap gae the gudemannie.*

So willingly or otherwise he was sober, and *deuk*, if it was drink, could have found others to "ding o'er."

Devel. A severe or stunning blow.

Devilship. This termination is occasionally used to turn a noun to a species of vocative case.

Does your *rogueship* understand me now?—*The Fair Andrian.*

I'd reward your *bawdship* according to your deserts.—*The Brothers.*

Dictionar. Dictionary.

Diddle. To shake, to jog.—*Jamieson.*

Differ. Difference.

Dight. To wipe, to clean corn from chaff; cleaned from chaff.

Chapman uses *dite* for winnow.—*Iliad V.*

Dight, dressed.—*Johnson.*

Let Piers the Ploughman dwell at home and *dyght* us corn.—*Political squib of the time of Rich. II. Turner's Hist. of England.*

Johnson says:—"The participle passive is *dight*, as *dighted* in *Hudibras* is perhaps improper." He therefore would have sanctioned—

> The cleanest corn that e'er was *dight*
> May hae some pyles o' caff in.

I do not know that it has ever been pointed out that for the figure in these lines Burns was indebted to a poet whom he has praised enough to entitle him to borrow this small matter from him. Allan Ramsay, in his preface to the "Evergreen," says—"The cleanest corn is not without some chaff, no not after often winnowing."

What fouler object in the world than to see a young, fair, handsome beauty unhandsomely *dighted*, and incongruently accoutred.
The Fatal Dowry.

Din. Dun, sallow. *I* for *u*. See under *bizz*.

> O goodly chyld
> Of Mary mylde,
> Then be our shylde!
> That we be not exyled
> To the *dynne* dale
> Of boteles bale.—*Skelton.*

Dine. A dinner, dinner-time.

> They ben so poor, and full of pine,
> They might not ones give me a *dine.*—*Chaucer.*

Ding. To worst, to push.

> From highest Fortunes sudden down they *ding*,
> Who'd or presume a Prince's grace to abuse.—*Sylvester.*

> 'Slight! *ding* it open.—*Ben Jonson.*

> He bad thai sold let for nothing,
> His son with scourges for to *dyng.*—*The Seven Sages.*

> His head he strook, his hands he wrang,
> And each hand on another *dang.*
> *Sir Eger, Sir Grahame, and Sir Gray-Steel.*

> Always *ding, dinging* Dame Grundy into my ears!
> *Speed the Plough.*

Dink. Neat, trim.

Perhaps from *digne*, by the addition of *k*, as *chink* from *cinu* or *chene*.

Dinna. Do not. *Do* and *na*. *Dunno.*—*Bamford.*

Dinsome. Noisy.

Dirl. A slight tremulous stroke or pain.

Th and *d*, as already pointed out, were used indifferently by both S. and E. authors. Burns has—

> Roof and rafters a' did *dirl*,

and also—

> It *thirl'd* the heart-strings.

Burthen and *murther*, though somewhat antiquated, are still occasionally used for burden and murder. John Bunyan writes, "I must say to the puddles in the foot-*pads* (paths), Be dry." Sometimes both spellings are found in the same line—

> I compass the conveyaunce unto the capitall
> Of ower clerke Cleros, *whythyr*, *thydyr*, and why not hethyr?
> *Skelton.*

> With a spere was *thirled* his brest bone.—*Chaucer.*

> So *thirled* with the point of remembrance.—*Id.*

The prayer of hym that loweth hym in his prayer *thyrleth* the clowdes.—*Dives and Pauper.*

Disgeested. Digested. A common spelling.

> Lucilius he coulde not *disgest*.—*An. Ballads and Broadsides.*

Disrespecked. Disrespected.

T is often omitted by careless speakers, and comic writers, after a sharp consonant, e.g.

> T' amend his natural *defects*,
> And perfect his recruiting sex.—*Butler.*

> Who made you so bolde to *interrupe* my tale?—*Skelton.*

Dizzen or *diz'n*. Dozen. *I* for *o*. See *anither*, and—

> (Cerberus) *lilled* (lolled) forth his bloody flaming tongue.
> *Spenser.*

Dizzie. Dizzy, giddy.

If Burns had not put words which differ from the ordinary orthography only in having *ie* instead of *y* in his glossary, *dizzie* would hardly have found a place here.

Dochter.   Daughter.

Douchtrin, daughter.—*Bailey*.   An. Sax., *Dóchter*.

Myne own good *doughter*, I am in good helthe of bodye.—*Sir T. More.*

His *dohter* stode on the city wall.—*Merlin.*

He tok it to his *douhter.*—*Lay le Freine.*

> That riche douke that y of told,
> He had a *douhter*, fair and bold.
> *Amos and Amilon.*

Doited.   Stupified, hebetated (doted).

Where did Burns get "hebetated"? And for whom did he intend it to be an explanation? To the most of his readers hebetated given to explain doited would be like Dugald Dalgetty, after he had desired his Highland guide to go on, saying, "To be more plain, *I prae, sequar.*" Is it likely he had a dictionary from which he could get this and similar "words of learned length, and thundering sound"? So late as 1789 we find him writing to Mr. Hill, "I want an English dictionary."

Doited, superannuated.   *Various dialects.*—*Halliwell.*

Doiting and doyting.   Walking sillily.

Donsie.   Unlucky, dangerous, troublesome.

Doodle and *doudle.*   To dandle.

Doodle-sack, a bagpipe.   Kent.—*Halliwell.*

Dool.   Sorrow; to *sing dool*, to lament, mourn.

Dool, dolour, pain, grief.—*Bailey*.

> On th' other side they see that perilous Poole,
> That called was the Whirlepoole of decay;
> In which full many had with hapless *doole*
> Been sunke of whom no memorie doth stay.—*Spenser.*

> (He) made the most *dool* that man might divise.
> *William of Palerne.*

Doos. Doves. For omission of *v*, see under *ca'*.
>The fauconer then was prest,
>Came runnyng with a *dow.*—*Skelton.*
>
>The giftes called of the Holy Ghost
>Outward figuryd by seven *dowys* white.—*Lydgate.*

On ark on an eventyde drovez the *downe* (old E. plural of dow).
Early E. Alliterative Poems.

Dorty. Saucy, nice.

Douce or *douse.* Sober, wise, prudent.
Doose, thrifty, careful, also cleanly, though coarsely clothed.
Grose.

Douse French of Parryse Parrot can lerne.—*Skelton.*
>*Douse* men chatt and chide it,
>For they may not abide it.—*Image of Ipocrisy.*
>
>Drynke to hym deorly of fol god bous,
>And oure dame *douse* shal sitten hym by.
>*A Song upon the Man in the Moon. Ritson.*

Doucely. Soberly, prudently.

Dought. Was or were able. Preterite of *dow.*
Dohte, done good. *Dohtig,* doughty, valiant.—*Bosworth.*

There has been considerable controversy as to whether the celebrated metrical romance of "Sir Tristrem" is of English or Scottish origin. It is allowed by all that it was once very popular in the south. If so, the language must have been understood, and I shall here give myself the benefit of the doubt and consider it an English production.

>Three yer in care bed lay,
> Tristrem the trew him hight,
>That never he *dought* him day,
> For sorwe he hadde o day.

Jamieson has quoted this passage under *dought,* which he thought was unquestionably a Scotch word, as was

GLOSSARY. 119

natural when he wrote, most people then accepting Sir Walter Scott's theory without hesitation.

The high courage of Douglasse wan that addition of *Doughty* Douglasse.—*Drayton.*

>Sir Amis sent, full hastelye,
>After many a knyght hardy,
> That *dowty* were of dede.—*Amis and Amiloun.*
>
>The Kyngis knyghtis therwhiles *dought,*
>On the lond every day fought.—*Kyng Alisaunder.*

Doup.   The breech ; the extremity, the butt-end.

Whether this word bè E. or S., it must be familiar to thousands of Englishmen from—" Was not Minerva born of the brain, even through the ear of Jove? and Castor and Pollux of the *doupe* of that egg which was laid and hatched by Leda ? "—*Rabelais, Book II.*

Doup-skelper.   One that strikes the breech.

>Like a dub-*skelper* he trotted.— *The Northumb. Garland.*

Doure.   Stout, durable, stubborn, sullen.

>O Alisaundre ! *dure* sire,
>Over alle men y thé desire !—*Kyng Alisaunder.*
>
>Fast he strake them in that stour,
>Might thare none his dintes *dour.*— *Ywain and Gawain.*

I am aware that *dour* here is a verb and not an adjective, but it indicates the origin of the spelling, and perhaps of the adjective.

Dow.   Am, or are able, can.

Ther watz moon forto make when meschef was cnowen
That noght *dowed* but the deth in the depe stremez.
                Early E. Alliterative Poems.   Morris.

Atrophe, one with whom his meat *dowes* not.—*Cotgrave.*

Yiff he have ony thing *dow* ylle,
He schal amend it at thy wylle.—*R. C. de Lion.*

> Yif eny hit wiste heigh or lowe,
> I cholde be brent and done of *dow*.
>> Yif I forsoke my lay.—*The Kyng of Tars and the Soudan of Damas.*

Ritson left *dow* unexplained, but there can be little doubt that it is the verb used as a substantive. As the word is rather a curiosity, and old metrical romances are little read by the present generation, it may be as well to tell the story as far as necessary to elucidate the word.

The Soudan, or Sultan, of Damas, a Mahometan, marries the daughter of the Christian King of Tars. By a very extraordinary miracle, he becomes convinced that he has been holding an erroneous faith, and requests his wife to send for a Christian priest to instruct him in the doctrines of the religion which he is now willing to profess, but charges her to do it secretly, for if his Moslem subjects knew what he was about to do he should be burned and lose his authority or power, i.e., *dow*. The only objection to this explanation is that it seems unnatural to speak of losing his power after saying he should be "brent"; but the old romancers cared little for the ordinary sequence of events, to say nothing of the exigencies of rhyme, when the language was still very imperfect.

Dowff.   Pithless, wanting force.

> To have a galle, and be clepid a *douffe*
> To breke myn hede, and yeve me a houffe,
> It may wele ryme, but it accordeth nought.—*Lydgate.*

Dowie.   Worn with grief or fatigue, crazy, dull.
 Dowly, melancholy, lonely.—*Bailey.*

Downa.   Am or are not able.   See *dow* and *na*.

Downa-do.   Inability.

Down-sittin. Downsitting; a meal.

Thou knowest my *downsitting.—Psalm cxxxix. 2.*

Doylt. Stupified, crazed.

Doyled, spiritless, careworn. Cumb.—*Halliwell.*

I am nere hand *dold*, so long have I nappyd.—*Townley Mysteries. Folk Etymology.*

Dozen. To stupify, to benumb.

Doze, to stupify, to dull.—*Johnson.*

Doze, to make or grow dull, heavy, or sleepy.—*Bailey.*

Dozent. Dozened, p. participle of dozen.

Dozened, spiritless, impotent, withered.—*Halliwell.*

Dozand leuake, an old withered look.—*Grose.*

Draigle. Draggle, differs only in spelling.

Drap. To drop, a drop, a pellet of lead. For change of *o* into *a* see *aft*.

> And neygh to dede we gan *drappe*
> Wythout lesyng.—*Octovian Imperator.*

Draunt or *drant.* To drawl, a drawl.

Drant, draunt, a drawling tone. Suffolk.—*Halliwell.*

Drave. Drove.

Drave. The preterite of drive. Drove is more used.—*Johnson.*

I *drave* my suitor from his mad humour of love.—*Shaks.*

> Who *drave* his oxen yesterday,
> Doth now over the noblest Romans reign.—*Cowley.*

Dree. To suffer, to endure.

To *dree*, to be able to go through till the end of the journey.—*Thoresby.*

Dree, to hold out, to be able to go. *Dree* always signifies long beyond expectation.—*Grose.*

> Of pure sorrow which I *drie*.—*Gower.*

> A true herte will not plie
> For no manace that it may *drie*.—*Chaucer*.
>
> He telde him the sorewe that he *dregh*.
>
> *The Seven Sages.*

Dreep. To ooze, to drop (perhaps rather drip).

> Thou seest the see to over-*dreep* the earth.—*De Mornay*.

Spenser also has over-*dreep*, and he often uses *e* for *i*, as in his "Verse to Lord Hunsdon"—

> Of which apparaunt proofe was to be seene,
> When that tumultuous rage and fearfull *deene* (din)
> Of Northerne rebels ye did pacify.

> We shall be sure to meet there with many *creeples* and beggars.
>
> *Fuller.*

Dreigh. Tedious, long.

> *Dree* (spoken of a way), long, tedious beyond expectation.
>
> *Bailey.*

This and *dree* as given by Grose are just *dreigh* as a modern Englishman would pronounce it.

> In that Cite for sothe as saith us the story,
> Mony gaumes were begonnen, the grete for to solas,
> The draughtes, the dyse, and other *dregh* gaumes.
>
> *Guido de Colonna. Early E. Text Society.*

> The King was locked in a field
> By a river broad and *dreghe*.—*Morte Arthur*.

> Ho wyrles out on the weder on wyngez ful scharpe,
> *Dreghly* alle a long day.—*Early E. Alliterative Poems.*

Dregh. — *Thoresby. Dretche.* — *Gower. Drecche.* — *Chaucer. Dreych.*—*Lib. Dis.*

Dress. To chastise, to punish.

> As for the boyes that frump and scoff,
> And at my holynes doe laugh,
> I mynd to *dresse* them wel enough,
> Yf case I had them here.
>
> *Ancient Ballads and Broadsides.*

> Thider he wendeth with gret pres,
> This stordy citeis for to *dres.—Kyng Alisaunder.*

Dribble. Drizzling, slaver.

This is another word which has no right to a place here, had not Burns inserted it in his glossary.

> The rain
> *Dribbled* on every academic nob.—*Dr. Wolcot.*

Driddle. To move slowly ; to be constantly in action, but making little progress.—*Jamieson.* The motion of one who tries to dance, but moves the middle only.—*Cunningham.* To play.—*Chambers.*

This is a great diversity of definition. The only word calculated to throw any light on this and the somewhat similar vocable *diddle*, is *didder*, which Bailey says means "to shiver or shake with cold." Johnson gives it the same signification, and says it is a provincial word. These three words, *diddle, driddle,* and *didder,* have all the idea of a silly motion in them, and the three authorities, and I do not know of three greater, might each find support in his definition of the word from the other two. We must, therefore, to find what Burns meant by *driddle,* examine his own words.

> A pigmy scraper wi' his fiddle
> Wha used *at* trysts and fairs to *driddle.*

If this is the true reading, then to play or to move slowly would make sense. But if it is, as in some editions we find it—

> Wha used *to* trysts and fairs to *driddle,*

the idea of playing is excluded, and to *driddle* means to go from place to place, to saunter. In the " Epistle to Major Logan " it undoubtedly means to move slowly—

> Until you on a crummock *driddle,*
> A gray-hair'd carl.

Drift. A drove. In the line " Poor hav'rel Will aff the *drift*," it seems to mean company.

Drift, a drove of sheep. Sometimes a flock of birds, etc.
Halliwell.

The Earl of Carlisle prayed the King to grant a moderate toll on cattle coming over the bridge with their great *drifts.*—*Life of T. Fuller.*

Droddum. The breech.

Droddum, the breech.—*Halliwell.*

Droop-rumpl't. That droops at the crupper. See *rumple.*

Drouk. To drench, to soak. *Droukit*, wet.

> *Drowking* lies the meadow-sweet,
> Flopping down beneath one's feet.—*Clare.*

I suspect Clare's word does not mean wet but dry. If so, it is worth putting here for the singularity. *Droukit* is probably a form of *druken*, drunken.

Drouth. Thirst, drought.

> Single none
> Durst ever, who returned, and dropt not here
> His carcass, pined with hunger and with *drouth.*—*Milton.*
>
> Thou life of strife, thou Horse-leach sent from Hell,
> Thou *Drouth*, thou Death, thou Plague of Israel.
> *Sylvester.*

Druken. Drunken.

In Anglo-Saxon *drican* as well as *drincan* signifies to drink, and from the former *drouk* and *druken* may have sprung.

Drucken, tipsy.—*Halliwell.*

N is sometimes omitted before *k*, e.g.—

> With botches and *carbuckyls* (carbuncles) in care I them knyt.
> *Skelton.*

A *druccan* man nivver wants a lantern.—*Yorkshire Proverb.*

Drumlie. Muddy.

Drumly, muddy, or thick water.—*Grose.* *Drumbled*, disturbed, muddy.—*Halliwell.*

Draw me some water out of the spring.
Madam, it is all foul, it is all *drumly*, black, muddy.
French and English Grammar, 1623, quoted by Dr. Mackay in " Lost Beauties of the English Language."

Drummock. Meal and water mixed raw. This is another name for *crowdie*, though they are sometimes spoken of as if they were different.

Drumossie moor. Culloden.

Drunt. Pet, sour humour.

Dub. A small pond.

Dub, a pool of water.—*Bailey. Grose.*

Dub, a puddle, or plash of water.—*Thoresby.*

They stoutly ran with all their might,
Spared neither *dub* nor mire.—*R. Hood.*

Duds. Rags of clothes.

Dudds, rags, also clothes.—*Grose.* *Dud*-man, a scare-crow.—*Bailey.*

In *dud* frese ye were schrynyd,
With better frese lynyd.—*Skelton.*

Crossing the road was a square called the *Duddery*, chiefly taken up with woollen drapers, wholesale tailors, sellers of second-hand clothes, etc.—*History of Stourbridge Fair.*

Harry was country neat as could be,
But his words were rough, and his *auds* were muddy.
Harry's Courtship. Bell.

Tell us
If it be milling a lag of *duds*.—*Fletcher.*

Duddie. Ragged.

Dune. Done. *U* for *o*, see under *huird*.

Dung, dang. Worsted, pushed, driven. Past tense of *ding.*

> I sai yow lely how thai lye
> *Donged* doun all in a daunce.—*Minot.*

> Be not fear'd, our master,
> That we two can be *dung.*—*R. Hood.*

He *dung,* or *dang* it down, threw it down.—*Thoresby.*

> With his tayl the erth he *dang.*—*Ywain and Gawain.*

Dunt. To strike, to beat, a stroke.

> To the Soudan he rode ful riht,
> With a *dunt* of much miht
> Adown he gan him bere.
> *The King of Tars and the Soudan of Damas.*

> The stones (in the ring) beoth of such grace,
> Thet thu ne schalt ın none place
> Of none *duntes* beon of drad
> Ef the loke ther an.—*The Geste of Kyng Horn.*

> Moni was the gode *dunt* that duc William gef a dey.
> *Rob. of Gloucester.*

Durk. A dirk. *U* for *ı.* See under *burdie.*

> The other he held in his sight
> A drawen *durk* to his breast.—*R. Hood.*

Dush. To push as a bull, ram, etc.

> Ryche harburgens all to-rusched,
> And stele helmes all *to-dusched,*
> And bodyes brake out to blede.
> *Le Bone Florence of Rome.*

Dush, to push violently. *Dsos,* to attack with the horns.—
Halliwell.

> That law of yours standes talking of Beasts,
> Of Pastures, of Oxen that *dosse* with their horns, etc.
> *Trewnesse of the Christian Religion.*

Duty. Prayers, in "Min' your *duty* duly, morn an' night."—*Cottar's Saturday Night.*

In all our *duty* we beg the Divine assistance.—*Jeremy Taylor.*

Dwalling. A dwelling, a house. *A* for *e*, as under *dail* and in—

> They conne not stinten, til no thing be *laft* (left).
> *Chaucer.*

> Duke Gedeon *whan* it was derke
> Ordeined him unto his werke.—*Gower.*

Dwalt. Dwelt.
> And us amonge, in payne and famyne
> *Dwalte.*—*Poem attributed to Skelton.*

Dyke. A hedge, a stone wall without mortar, a fence of turf—not a ditch, as is plain from—

> He was a gash an' faithfu' tyke
> As ever lap a sheugh (ditch) or dyke.

Dike, a dry hedge. Cumberland.—*Halliwell.*

Now round his dores
Hang many a badger's snout and foxes tail,
The which had he through many a hedge persewd,
Through marsh, through meer, *dyke*, ditch, and delve and dale.—*Mickle's Sir Martyn.*

Dyke-back. The slight elevation on which a hedge used to be planted, as described in Dodsley's lines; the side opposite to that on which is the open drain or ditch, called in Scotland the *dyke-sheugh.*

> Then low as sinks thy ditch on th' other side
> Let *rise in height the sloping bank;* there plant
> Thy future fence.—*Dodsley's Agriculture.*

Dyvour. A bankrupt.

E.

Eastlin. Eastward. See under *darklins.*

E'e. The eye, to eye, to watch; *een,* the eyes.
> The teres sterte from his *ee.*—*Sir Cauline.*

> Then a noble gunner you must have,
> And he must aim well with his *ee*.
>
> *Sir Andrew Barton.*

> The knight tho up cast his *een*
> And when he saw it was the Queen.—*Chaucer.*
>
> I'll cut my green coat a foot above my knee ;
> And I'll clip my yellow locks an inch below mine *ee*.
> *The Two Noble Kinsmen.*

Ee-bree. Eyebrow. *E'e* and *bree.*

Ee-bree, eyebrow.—*Bamford.*

E'en. Evening. *Night at e'en*, evening, between the cessation of labour in the country and bed-time, sometimes called the *forenight.*

Good *e'en*, neighbours.—*Shak.* Good *e'en*, then.—*Fletcher.*

Ee'nin. Evening.

Mirk i' th' *e'enin*, dark in the evening.—*Thoresby.*

Eerie. Frightened, dreading spirits.

Earh, A.-S. fleeing through fear. *Earh-lice*, fearfully.—*Bosworth.*

Eerie, frightened. *Eery*, unearthly.—*Halliwell.*
> These ben the *eyrishe* beests.—*Chaucer.*

Eyrish, aerial, belonging to the air.—*Tyrwhitt.*

Effectual Calling. One of the questions in the Shorter Catechism, formerly the all but universal, and still to a large extent, the theological text-book of Scotland.

Eild. Old age.

> And from his eyes (not yet made dim with *eild*)
> Sparkled his former worth and vigour brave.—*Fairfax.*

> Now leave we Robin and his men
> Again to play the child,
> And learn himself to stand and gang
> By halds for all his *eild*.—*R. Hood.*

> Who scorns at *eld* peels off his own young hairs.
> *Ben Jonson.*

Elbuck. The elbow.

Elboga, the elbow.—*Bosworth.*
Botones from his *elbouthe* to his hands.—*Warton.*

Elder. See *ruling elder.*

Eldritch. Ghastly, frightful.

> For the *Elridge* knyghte, so mickle of myghte,
>   Will examine you beforne ;
> And never man bare life awaye,
>   But he did him scath and scorn.—*Sir Cauline.*

In some copies of this old romance, *Elridge* is spelled *eldrich.*

Eleckit. Elected.

Elf-candles. Lights carried by elves or fairies.

> Through this house give glimmering light
> By the dead and drowsy fire,
>   Every *elf* and fairy sprite.—*Shak.*

Ell. A Scotch ell is thirty-seven inches.

Eller. An elder. For omission of *d* see under *afiel*, and—

> Judas he Japed with Juwen silver,
> And sithen on an *eller* (elder tree) honged hym after.
> *P. Plowman.*

Elshin. An awl.

Elson, a shoemaker's awl.—*Grose.*
Elsin, a sort of awl.—*Bamford.*

Embryotic. Rudimentary.

This word has not found a place in the dictionaries.

It seems as good as embryonic. So much cannot be said for the next word.

Embryoth. Unformal.

En'. End. For omission of *d*, see under *afiel*, and in—

Rather than thu sholdest faile he wolde *spenne* (spend) of his own goode xx. marcis.—*Royal and Historical Letters.*

For hym I knowe for suffycyent to *expoune* (expound) every diffyculty.—*The Boke of Eneydos.*

Enbrugh and *Embro'.* Edinburgh.

Eneugh or *aneuch.* Enough.

> For he that haveth is god ploh (plough)
> And of worldes wele *ynoh*
> Ne wot he of no sorewe.
>
> *The Proverbs of Hendyng.*

Had he said for nine months, I should think them *enew,*—*John Byrom.*

> There they gave them fighting *eneugh.*
> *The Bishopric Garland. Ritson.*

Enfauld. Infold. See *fauld.*

Engine. Genius.

Very homely poets, such also as made most of their works by translations out of the Latin and French toung, and few or none of their own *engine.*—*Puttenham's Art of English Poetry.*

> Art thou, my son, of such *engin!*—*Gower.*
>
> A tyrant erst but now his fell *engine*
> His graver age did somewhat mitigate.—*Fairfax.*

I ne usurpe not to have founden this werke of my labour nor of myne *engyn.*—*Chaucer.*

> (Virgil) past them all for deep *engyen.*—*Churchyard.*

Enlightened few, the. Freemasons.

Ensuin. Ensuing.

Especial. Especially.

Ether. An adder. For the use of *th* for *d*, see *blather.*

A *nether* or *nedder*, an adder.—*Thoresby.*

Snakes and *nederes* thar he fand.—*English Metrical Homilies.*

It is hardly necessary to say that an adder was once *a nadder.*

> And from Megeras *edders*
> From rufflynge of Philips fethers.—*Skelton.*

The word to which it rhymes shows that *edders* was pronounced *ethers.*

Ether-stane. A stone supposed to be formed by adders; ancient beads. *Ether* and *stane.*

Ettle. To try, to attempt; an endeavour.

Ettle, to intend. *Ettlement*, intention.—*Grose.*

> Themperour entred in a wey evene to *attele*
> To have bruttenet (slain) that bor.
> *William of Palerne. Morris and Skeat.*

> The chorl grocching forth goth with the gode child,
> And evene to themperour thei *ettelden* sone.—*Id.*

> May I traist in thé
> For to tel my prevete
> That I have *aghteld* for to do?—*The Seven Sages.*

Expeckit. Expected.

Extent. Valuation for the purpose of assessment. *Old extent*, old valuation.

> Let my officers
> Make an *extent* upon his house and land.—*Shak.*

Extent is part of a legal phrase from the Sheriff appraising land to its full value.—*Malone.*

Eydent. Diligent.

Sir W. Scott seems to suggest *aye-doin*, always doing, as the origin of this word.

F.

Fa'. Fall, lot ; to fall. For omission of *ll* see under *a'*.

> But somewhere I have had a lungeous *faw.—Cotton.*
> I wot it made him quickly *fa'.—The Fray of Hantwessell.*

I do not remember seeing the noun fall used for *lot*, but the verb is often used to imply it, e.g.

> Nought fully a furlong fro that fayre child,
> Cloughtand kyndely his schon as to here craft *falles* (belongs).
> *William and the Werwolf.*

> Then 'tis most like
> The sovereignty will *fall* upon Macbeth.—*Shak.*

Perhaps fall means lot in—

> I pray, God yeve thé evil *fall!—Octovian Imperator.*

Fa' that. To get that, to have that fall to him, to do.

Thomson, to whom Burns sent his famous "A man's a man for a' that," though in general ready enough to object to any of the poet's expressions which did not please him or the associates to whom he showed the verses, had no fault to find with the line—

> Guid faith he maunna *fa'* that,—

so that we may infer that it was well enough understood at the time. It has been much animadverted upon since those days, and deserves some examination. I hope to prove that it means to *do*, allowing the usual modifications claimed by all poets. First of all, it is to be remembered that fall is a transitive as well as an intransitive verb.

> Each drop she *falls* would prove a crocodile.—*Shak.*
> Fill up that reverend unvanquish'd Bowl,
> Who many a giant in his time has *fallen.—Crowe.*

To *fall* a thing, may then be to produce an effect on it. But I believe the word *fa'*, or its more common form *faw*, was used in English poetry long before Burns's day. According to an old writer, to whom I have already referred, the daughter of the King of Tars had married the Mahometan Soudan of Damas, who, by a miracle, was converted to the faith of his spouse. He had no sooner abjured Islamism than he determined his subjects should do the same.

> And hosé (whoso) wole not crisnet be,
> Sholde be honged on a tre
> Withouten any delay.

Not being certain, however, that they would yield submissively to this summary conversion, or that he could compel them to be thus suddenly "cristened," he requested his father-in-law to come to his help "With al the pouwer that he mouht," and the tale goes on thus—

> A gladór mon mighte not ben (than his father-in-law)
> He clepte his barouns and his qwen,
>   And tolde hem in his sawe,
> The Soudan that was stout and kene
> Cristnet was withouten wene,
>   And leevede (believed) on Cristes lawe,
> And he to me hath isent his soude, i.e., message,
> He wol cristene al his londe,
>   Yif he mihte wel *fawe ;*
> He (who) nil not come to cristenyng,
> Weore he never so heigh lordyng,
>   He scholde be to drawe.

Ritson explains *fawe* fain or glad, as if the King of Tars were speaking of himself, whereas it is plain that he is speaking of the Soudan, and telling his "barouns" that he would "cristene" all his people if he could *fawe*, or do it. This receives corroboration from a passage in another romance. It leads to another story, but to establish the meaning of this important word in the glorious shout of humanity is worth a little detail, and the risk of being tedious.

Launfal, an amiable Knight of the Round Table, upon some dislike to Arthur's queen, leaves the court, and retires to a town at some distance, where, through too great liberality, he gets into debt. Even in those days to be " short of cash " was a decided disadvantage, and Launfal found that poverty is not favourable even to devotion, at least in its social aspect, for on one occasion he says—

> To-day to cherche y wolde have gon,
> But me fawtede hosyn and schon,
>   Clenly brech and scherte.

One day, while in this impoverished condition, he went to the country, and encountered a most beautiful lady, who, with the frankness of her sex in those days, declared her affection for him, and, on his consenting to forsake all women for her, endowed him with unlimited wealth, and gave him gifts such as no mere mortal could bestow. But she added a caution—

> But of othyng, Sir Knyght, i warne the,
> That thou make no bost of me,
>   For no kennes mede ;
> And yf thou doost, y warny the before,
> All my love thou hast forlore.

Some time afterwards, Arthur sends for him to court, and while conversing with Gwennere the Queen, she makes love to him, and provoked by his rejection of her proffer, she taunts him and says, " Thou lovyst no woman, ne no woman the." Irritated by these words, and forgetful of the warning he had received, he said—

> I have loved a fayryr woman,
> Than thou ever leydest thy ney (eye) upon,
>   Thys seven yer and more.

He had no sooner said these words, than what the lady foretold happened—

> He softe (sought) his leef (love) but she was lore,
> As sche hadde warnede hym before,
>   Tho was Launfal *unfawe*.

Now, what is the meaning of *unfawe?* Ritson says *fawe* is fain, but he saw that *unfain* would be a very weak expression for Launfal's state of mind, and he left *unfawe* as one of the words which he confessed he could not interpret. If my conjecture concerning *fawe* is correct, then *unfawe* becomes *undone* or *ruined*, which exactly denotes the knight's condition, for he had lost his beautiful lady, his inexhaustible purse, his invaluable servant, and his matchless war-horse.

> All that he hadde before ywonne,
> It malt as snow agens the sunne;

and he said—

> All my joye I have forlore;

and—

> He bet hys body and hys hedde ek,
> And cursed the mouth that he wyth spek (spoke).

Surely this indicates a man *undone*, rather than *unfain*.

Fac't. Faced.

Factor. A land-steward.

Faddom. To fathom. *D* for *th*, see under *cleed*.
  Fadom, fathom.—*Bailey*.
> Thyrty *fadom* he sanke adowne.—*Sir Guy of Warwick*.
> And twenty *fadome* of bredth.—*Chaucer*.

Fae. A foe.

> Of *fase* may he mak frendes.—*Sir Penny*.
> Mi leser (deliverer) artou, night and dai,
> Fra mi *faes* ben wrathful ai.—*Metrical E. Psalter*.
> Na preson yow sal halde,
> Al if your *fase* be many falde.—*Ywain and Gawain*.
> He ouercome al the erles *fase*.—*The Two Dreams*.

Faem. Foam. *A* for *o*, see under *bane*.

> Foam, *faem*.—*Horne Tooke*.
> Fame, the foam of the sea.—*Grose*.

Faiket. Forgiven, spared, abated.

This word, which Burns has not given in his glossary, has been the occasion of some diversity of opinion as to its meaning. Chambers suggests that the line—

> Sic hauns as you sud ne'er be faiket,

should run—

> Sic hauns as *yours* sud ne'er be faiket;

that is—

> Such hands as yours should never be folded.

One objection to this is, that it is rather too soon to begin "new readings" of Burns. A hundred years hence they will have a better chance of acceptance. A more serious objection is that it is altogether unnecessary, and, to an Ayrshire man, at least, destroys the force of the line.

Jamieson gives the meaning which ninety-nine of every hundred Scotsmen who know Scotch attach to the word, though he does not do it in connection with the line quoted here, but with what he supposed to be a different word. Like Chambers, he says Burns's *faiket* means folded. He seems also to have been puzzled about the derivation, and hence possibly his mistake about the meaning, for though etymology throws much light on the meaning of words, it is occasionally a "light that leads astray." He will not allow that *faik* comes from Fr. *defalquer*, Lat. *defalcare*, and yet he gives this as the derivation of the compound *defaik*, the two differing only in this respect that a person *defaiks* something in or of himself, but *faiks* something in or of another. The examples given by him under the two words (if two they be) illustrate this:—"Will ye no *faik* me?" "He will not *faik* a penny;" "he will not abate a penny of the price," i.e., "the price demanded from some one."

Perhaps Dugald Graham, the "Literary Bellman" of Glasgow, will be accepted as a good authority in a matter of this kind. He makes one of his rough but thoroughly Scottish characters of a remote time say— "If a poor beggar body had a bit wean to chrisen, the deil a doit they *feike* him o't."—*The Coalman's Courtship.*

I think we may conclude that "Sic hauns," etc., means, "From such men as you, we must have what you can accomplish, the full tale of bricks must be exacted, your work shall not be minished."

I have not met with *faik* in an E. author, but Johnson has *defalk*, and quotes as his authority "The Practice of Piety." "What he *defalks* from some insipid sin, is but to make some other more gustful."

In the following extract from a letter of one of Charles II.'s admirals, the word comes very near our *faik*—

"Sir—Please to mynde Mr. Pepys to prepare a bill against the next meeting for two thousand pounds to me out of the fower-penses *defalked* (apparently saved, not spent) for Ministers (chaplains) remaining in his hand, or that shall come to his hand, by reason of the want of ministers in divers of His Majesty's ships. Jo. Lawson."
—*Pepys Correspondence.*

Defalked was sometimes used in Scotland in the same sense as *faiket*. In the " Old Records of the Kilmarnock Bonnet-makers," given in the *Kilmarnock Standard*, Jan. 8, 1881, after " Ane acompt of Money Given to buy a Morcloath," it is stated "there was some reversions of welvat and silk that *defalked* something from the prieses."

Fain. Glad ; merry ; cheerful; fond. It is still retained in Scotland in this sense.—*Johnson.*

> And this faire couple eke to shroud themselves were *fain*.
> *Spenser.*
>
> In all the hous ther n' as so litel a knave, that he n' as ful *fain*,
> For that my lord Dan John was come again.—*Chaucer.*
>
> Yea, man and birds are *fain* of climbing high. —*Shak.*
>
> And when thai wist it was sertayn
> Ayther of other was ful *fayn.*—*The Two Dreams.*

Fainness. Fondness.

Fair fa'. Good luck to you !

> *Fair fo*, fair fall ; good attend you !—*Bamford.*
>
> > Then answeryd the Kyng with crowne,
> > *Fair fall* the for thyn avise !—*The Erle of Tolous.*
> > *Fair fall* the face !—*Shak.*

Fairin. Fairing, a present.

The word no doubt originally meant a present brought from a fair, or more correctly, as Jamieson and Johnson put it, " a present *at* a fair." Indeed, except in very large towns, nothing that could be properly given as a present could be purchased except at fairs. But fairing had lost that sense long before Burns's day. There was no fair at which the fairings spoken of by the Princess in " Love's Labour Lost," could have been bought.

> Sweethearts, we shall be rich ere we depart,
> If *fairings* come thus plentifully in.—*Shak.*
>
> I have gold left to give thee a *fairing* yet.—*Ben Jonson.*

Faith. Oath.

To which Mr. Burns is willing to make *faith.*—*Burns's answer to the petition of T. I.*

Faithfu'. Faithful.

Fallow. Fellow. *A* for *e*, as in—

> Lewdly complainest thou, lasie lad,
> Of winter's *wrack* for making thee sad.—*Spenser.*

Theophrast, the greatest *clark* of all his disciples.—*De Mornay.*

Felawe and *felaw* are often found.

> Welcome, quod he, and every good *felaw.*—*Chaucer.*
> He *halt* (held) no word of covenant.—*Gower.*
> The glorious standard last to heav'n they *sprade* (spread).
> *Fairfax.*

Fand. Did find.

> Searching about, on a rich throne he *fand*
> Armida set.—*Fairfax.*
>
> They shall her tell how they thee *fand*
> Curteous and wise and well doand.—*Chaucer.*
>
> Tha spak na word to na man born,
> Of al the folk tha *fand* byforn.—*Ywain and Gawain.*

Farl. A cake of bread.—*Burns.* Properly, the fourth part of a thin cake, whether of flour or oatmeal (or any other kind of meal); but now a third, according to the different ways in which a cake is divided before it is fired.—*Jamieson.*

Farrel, the fourth part of a circular oat-cake, the division being made by a cross.—*Halliwell.*

A *fardel* of land is the fourth part of a Yard Land.—*Bailey.*

In our ancient law books a *farding-deale* of land means the fourth of an acre.—*Horne Tooke.*

Fash. Trouble, care, to trouble, to care for.

Fash, trouble, etc.—*Halliwell.*

Fash, to trouble or tease ; *donna fash me.—Grose.*

Ne'er fash your head, and *ne'er fash your thumb,* think not of it.

Fasheous.   Troublesome.

Fashious, troublesome.—*Craven. Halliwell.*

Fasten-e'en.   Fastens Even.

Fastens-Een or Even, Shrove Tuesday.—*Bailey.*
Fastne's een, the Tuesday before Ash Wednesday.—*Thoresby.*

Fatterels.   Ribbon ends, etc.

Fatters, tatters.—*Craven. Halliwell.*

Faugh.   Land ploughed and left unsown for the season ; fallow.

This word has, I believe passed out of the farmer's vocabulary, green-cropping having put *faughing* out of fashion.   In some places it means a slight ploughing.

Faugh-ground. Ground which has lain a year or more unplowed.—*Bailey.*

That is one E. dictionary-maker's account of *faugh.* Here is another view of it—

To *faugh,* to plough (the land), and let it be fallow a summer or winter.—*Thoresby.*

Faught.   A fight.

> Up to the ancle they *faught* in here blood.—*Chaucer.*
> Lyke marciall Hector, he *faught* them agayne.—*Skelton.*
> Nygusar *faughte* as he weore wod.—*Kyng Alisaunder.*

Fauld and *fald.*   A fold, to fold.

Fald fee, a composition paid anciently for the privilege of setting up folds for sheep in any field.—*Bailey.*

The right the lord of the manor claimed to fold his tenants' sheep was called *faldage.*

> More curtaysi and mor honour
> Fand he with tham in that tour,
> And mor comforth, by mony *falde*
> Than Colgrevance had him of talde.
> *Ywain and Gawain.*

> Yet be they called
> To the charge of the *fald*,
> Because they be balled
> And be for bishops stalled.—*Image of Ipocrisy.*

Fause. False.

Fause, false, cunning, subtle.—*Bailey. Grose.*

Fa:use, cunning, also false.—*Bamford.*

I had rather be hanged in a withie, or in a cowtaile, than to be a row-footed Scot, for they are ever fare and *fase.*—*Dr. William Bullein's Dialogue both Pleasant and Profitable. Lond., 1564.*

Fause-house. An empty space in a corn-stack.

Burns's note on this word makes any remarks unnecessary, but I place it here to give me an opportunity of quoting a passage which shows that the *fause-house* was not confined to Scotland—

> Thus leaving in the midst (of the stack)
> An *empty space*, the cooling air draws in,
> And from the flame, or from offensive taints
> Pernicious to thy cattle, saves their food.—*Dodsley.*

Faut. Fault, offence.

He could then very well reherse his *fautes* himself.—*Sir T. More.*

> My scole is more solem and somewhat more haute
> Than to be founde in any such *faute.*—*Skelton.*

Faut. Fault, want, lack.

> She swouned for *faute* of blood.—*Chaucer.*
> In us schal be no *fawte.*—*R. C. de Lion.*
> Me *fawtede* hosyn and schon.—*Lannfal.*
> If he dythe for *faute* of flesch
> With a staf y wol the thresche.—*Octovian Imperator.*

Fautor.   A transgressor, one who commits a *faut* or fault.

There is an English word *fautor*, but it means favourers—

> To the general, and the gods and *fautors*,
> The country owes her safety.—*Massinger.*

But *fatour*, *faitour*, or *faytour*, means ill-doers.

> And fostor none *faytoures* ne swiche false freres.
> *Peres the Plowman's Crede.*

> My scoles are not for unthriftes untaught,
> For frantick *faitours* half mad and half straught.—*Skelton.*

> These *fatours* little regarden their charge
> While they letten their sheepe runne at large.—*Spenser.*

Fawsont.   Decent, seemly, orderly; lit. fashioned.

> A corone wern all of the same *fasoun.*—*Warton.*

> Than com ridende Lentilioun,
> A was maister and of fair *fazoun.*—*The Seven Sages.*

> Ther that the mayde set,
> That was fayr of *fasoun.*—*Lybaeus Disconus.*

Feal.   Loyal, stedfast, faithful.

Fealty, loyalty.—*Johnson.*

Tenants by knyghts' service were wont to swear to their lord to be *feal* and leal, i.e., to be faithful and loyal.—*Bailey.*

> For he *feighliche* went that he his fader were.
> *William and the Werwolf.*

Fear't.   Feared, frightened.

> No foes then could have made him *feared.*—*Bat. of Flod.*

> Yet was this man
> Well *fearder* than,
>   Lest he had slain the frere.—*Sir T. More.*

> The folk fast to toun gan fle
> So war thai *ferde* for that lioun.—*Ywain and Gawain.*

> Warwick was a bug that *fear'd* us all.—*Shak.*

Fearfu'. Frightful.

Feat. Neat, spruce.
>My garments sit on me much *feater* than before.—*Shak.*
>
>Never master had
>A page so kind—
>So *feat,* so *nurse-like.*—*Id.*
>
>This *feat* body of mine doth not crave
>Half of the meat, drink, and cloth, one of your bulk will have.—*Ben Jonson.*

Fecht. To fight; a fight. *E* for *i,* see *dreep. Ch* for *gh,* as in—
>Launfal began to *syche* (sigh).—*Launfal.*
>
>He had a *dochter* fair and bold.—*Amis and Amilom.*
>
>I said, that I sold find a knyght
>That sold me mayntem in my ryght,
>And *feght* with al thre.—*Ywain and Gawain.*
>
>He watz famed for fre that *feght* loved best.
>>*Early E. Alliterative Poems.*

He bare always of usage three feathered darts, and *rycht* well he could handle them.—*Froissart.*

Fechtin. Fighting.
>He wyll set men a *feightynge* and syt hymselfe styll,
>And *smerke,* lyke a smythy kur, at sperkes of steile.
>>—*Skelton.*

Feck, and *fek.* Number, quantity; greatest part.

Feck, many; plenty; quantity. Also the greatest part.—*Halliwell.*

Fecket. Waistcoat.

Fecket. An under waistcoat, properly one worn under the shirt.—*Jamieson.*

I have doubts as to the correctness of Jamieson's explanation. I never heard the word and never met a person who had, and another word, *semmit,* if that be its orthography, has long been in common use for the article of dress spoken of by Jamieson. In the line—

> His *fecket* is white as the new-driven snow,

its colour must have been a matter of indifference—to the public—if the *fecket* was worn under the shirt.

The only E. word the least like *fecket*, and the likeness is not great, is *flocket*, which is said to have been a "loose garment with large sleeves"—

> And yet she wyll jet
> In her furred *flocket*,
> Lyke a jolly fet,
> And gray russet rocket.
> *Skelton's Elynour Rummyng.*

Feckfu'. Large, brawny, stout.

Feckful. Strong; zealous; active.—*Halliwell.*

Feckless. Puny, weak, silly.

Feckless, weak, feeble.—*Halliwell.*

Feckly. Mostly.

Feckly, mostly, most part of.—*Grose.*

Fee. Servants' wages.

> At Michaelmas next my cov'nant comes out,
> When every man gathers his *fee.*—*R. Hood.*
>
> He had spent an hundred pounds,
> And all his mennes *fe.*—*Id.*

Feg. A fig. *E* for *i*. See under *dreep*, and in—

> My helpe, my love, whyll y *leve* (live).—*The Erle of Tolous.*

Fegs ! An exclamation used for faith.

> Art thou my boy? Ay, my good lord.
> I' *fecks ?*—*Shak.*
>
> I'll torture you, i' *fecks.*—*Duke of Buckingham.*

Par ma fy. By my *fecke.*—*Cotgrave.*

> They have been shown and seen,
> *I' fex* have they.—*Fletcher.*
> 'Tis something, *fags!*—*Dr. Wolcot.*
> *Feckins*, I liked it hugely.—*Garrick.*

Feid. Feud, enmity.

> Kyng Phelippe, of great thede (power),
> Maister was of that *feide.*—*Kyng Alisaunder.*

Feirrie or *fierrie.* Bustle.

Fell. Keen, biting, tasty; the flesh immediately under the skin (more properly the cuticle immediately above the flesh—*Jamieson*); a field pretty level on the side of a hill.

Fell, keen, biting.—*Johnson.*

He repayred to the priores(s) of Kyrkesly, who perceyving him to be Robin Hood and waying how *fell* an enemy he was, etc.—*Grafton's Chronicle. Ritson.*

> Were worthy to be brent both *fell* and bones.—*Chaucer.*

Fell is generally, I might say universally, used for skin, and I suspect Burns's sense of the word as "the flesh immediately under the skin," or Jamieson's amendment of it, is not to be found in any other author. And yet there seems to have been at one time a distinction made between fell and skin, unless John of Trevisa has been guilty of tautology. Speaking of Britain, he says:— "Flandres loveth the wolle of this lond, and Normandy the *skynnes* and the *fellys.*" Skelton, too, is tautological, if *fell* means skin, for he writes on "A Deadman's Hed"—

> Nakyd of *hyde*,
> Neither flesh nor *fell*.

Fell, a hill or mountain.—*Grose.*

> He may ger both sle and lif,
> Both by frith and *fell.*—*Sir Penny.*

He and the priests had said, "The Quakers would not come into any great towns, but lived in *Fells* like butterflies.—*Journal of George Fox*.

> Al the se
> Alse a *felle* up sal it stand.—*E. Met. Homilies*.

Felly. Relentless, biting.

Fen. To live comfortably ; a successful struggle.

Fend, to provide for ; he *fends* for his family.—*Bamford*.

To *fend*, to shift for.—*Bailey*. *Grose*.

The contributions (at a pay-wedding) enable the new-married couple to make so good a *fend* as never to look ahint them.—*Loc. His. Table Book*.

> Mete and drink y schal hem *fende*.
> *Horn Child and Maiden Rimnild*.

Sir John Sinclair says *fen* is from find ; Jamieson says he is wrong, but find is sometimes used in nearly the sense of *fend*—

Find, to supply, to furnish. The war in continuance will *find* itself.—*Bacon*. *Johnson*.

In the following passage *finde* comes nearer to *fen*—

> To sweete and swinke I make avowe,
> My wife and children therewith to *finde*.
> *Prologue to the Plowman's Tale, quoted by Skeat*.

Fend. To defend.

The said Master of Kilmaurs will be put to his own *fende* at his liberty in secret manner.—*Dacre to Wolsey*.

> Thar fore he bad I sold me *fend*.—*Ywain and Gawain*.

> All (are) prisoners
> In the lime-grove that weather-*fends* your cell.—*Shak*.

Ferlie or *ferly*. To wonder, a wonder ; also a term of contempt.

> On Malverne hulles me byfel a *ferly* of fairy.—*P. Plowman*.

Sain Jerom telles that fyften
Ferli takenenges sal be sen
Befor the day of dom.—*Early E. Metrical Homilies.*

A boot (boat) he fond by the brym,
And a glysteryng thing theryn
    Therof they had *ferly.*—*Emare.*

Fetch or *fech.* To pull by fits ; to stop suddenly in the draught, and then come on too hastily ; to breathe in termittently.

Fetch, to perform with suddenness or violence.—*Johnson.*

    Note a wild and wanton herd,
Or race of youthful and unhandled colts
Fetching mad bounds.—*Shak.*

She *fetches* a deep sigh.—*Addison.*

She *fetches* her breath as short as a new-ta'en sparrow.
                                                 Shak.

A little is sufficient for a man well nurtured, and he *fetcheth* not his wind short upon his bed.—*Ecclesiasticus xxxi. 9.*

Fey. Strange ; one marked for death ; predestined.

To *fey* it, to do any thing notably (i.e., out of one's usual way).
                                                 Bailey.

    Longe to lyven ichulle forsake
      And *feye* fallen adoun.—*Anc. Song. Ritson.*
But thou arte *fay*, be my faythe.
              MS. quoted by Halliwell.

Fidge. To fidget ; *fidgin' fain*, highly pleased.

Fidge, to be continually moving up and down.—*Bailey.*

    Nay never *fidge* up and down, Numps, and weary itself.
                                       Ben Jonson.

You wriggle, *fidge*, and make a rout,
Puts all your brother puppets out.—*Swift.*

The judge *fidges* as if he had swallow'd cantharides.

                                             Congreve.

Fiel. Some glossarists say *fiel* means *soft, smooth*; others say *clean*. I believe Jamieson is right when he says it means *feil*, i.e., very, and explains the line in which it occurs thus—" Wraps me *very* warm."

Fien, fient. Fiend! a petty oath. *Fien-ma-care,* no matter! *T* for *d*, as in—

> Like commendation *crook't,*
> With "to and from my Love" it *look't.*—*Butler.*

Fier. Sound, healthy; a brother, a companion.

> And seythen hethen kyng
> That ich hol and *fere*
> In land aryved here.—*The Geste of Kyng Horn.*

> The King was blithe and of glad chere,
> For that he saye Gy hole and *fere.*—*Guy of Warwick.*

> Learn what maids havé been
> Her companions and play-*pheers*.
> *The Two Noble Kinsmen.*

> The sisters nyne, the poet's pleasant *feres.*—*Grimoald.*
> Where is my noble *fere?*—*Surrey.*

Fierrie. Bustle, activity.

Ferry-whisk, great bustle; haste. Yorksh.—*Halliwell.*

Fissle. To make a rustling noise, to fidget; a bustle.

Fussle, a slight confusion.—*Suffolk. Fissle,* to fidget.—*Halliwell.*

Come, you put Robin Cupid out with your waters and your *fisling.*—*Ben Jonson.*

Fit. A foot.

> Theyes, legges, *fit,* and al
> Yeoraught of the best.—*Old Love Song. Warton.*
> And now that *fitte* maie not fleye.—*Chester Plays.*

Fittie-lan'. The near horse of the hindmost pair in the plough. Lit. *foot-on-land*, so called because he walks on the unploughed land, while his neighbour, the *fur-ahin*, occupies the furrow.

A note here on the ploughing of Burns's time, from which, I believe, some of the difficulties which he, his father, and, I suppose, other persons, experienced in farming, may perhaps be allowed.

Burns always, in his poems, supposes four horses in a team—

> My pleugh is now thy bairn-time a',
> Four gallant brutes as e'er did draw;

and in the "Inventory" he says distinctly that there were four horses in his plough, and Gilbert says :—" He (Robert) and I were going out with our teams, and our two younger brothers to drive for us." Now, this implies that for each plough there were at least three horses, for no ploughman could need a driver for two horses. This was at Lochlea, a farm of a hundred and thirty acres. These six, and probably eight, horses might have been fairly employed while the ploughing and harrowing were proceeding—though it is to be remembered that Lochlea was a dairy as well as an arable farm—but what could they do during the remainder of the year, seeing that green-cropping was unknown? Simply eat their heads off. In such circumstances a farmer might well say with Triptolemus Yellowlea, "The carls and the cart-avers make it all, and the carls and the cart-avers eat it all."

A *fitty-foal*, from Sax. *fytian*, to follow the mare.—*Thoresby*.

Fizz, to make a hissing noise.

Fiz, a flash, a hissing noise.—*Halliwell*.

If his pulse (I mean his purse) be hot, his fist may cry *fizze*, but want his impression.—*Whimsies. Brand.*

This refers to the burning of the hand of certain malefactors at the time the book was written, 1631.

> And my hand hissing,
> If I scape the halter, with the letter *R*
> Printed upon it.—*A New Way to Pay Old Debts.*

Flae. A flea. *A* for *e*. See under *dail*.

Flaffin. Flapping, fluttering.
> A thousand *flaffyng* flags.—*Sylvester.*

Flandrekins. Natives of Flanders.
> Our nobles are gone
> Among the Burgonyons,
> And Spanyardes onyons,
> And the *Flanderkyns*.—*Skelton.*

> Nel had left her work at home,
> The *Flanderkin* had stayed his loom.—*Martilmasse Day.*

Flang. Past tense of *fling*, which see.

Flannen. Flannel.

Flannen, Var. dial.—Halliwell. Flannel was originally written and pronounced *flannen.*—*Words, Facts, and Phrases.*

Felatin, flannel, or stuff like *flannen.*—*Cotgrave.*

Flee. A fly.
> To inriche their sees,
> The blind men eat up *flees*.—*Image of Ipocrisy.*
> The wing of a pied butter-*flee*.—*Drayton.*
> A nice time this for butter-*flees* to use their little wings.
> —*Bairnsla Foaks' Annual.*
> It helps you not a *flee*.—*R. Hood.*

Flee. To fly.

> Thus with unwearied wings I *flee*
> Through all Love's gardens and his fields.—*Cowley.*

> If you list to *fleen* as high in the aire,
> As doth an egle.—*Chaucer.*

And let your thoughts *flee* higher.—*Beaumont and Fletcher.*

Fleech. To supplicate in a flattering manner.

Fleech, to wheedle.—*Halliwell.*

Fleesh. Fleece. Here we have the reverse of the change of *sh* into *s* as in *buss*; *s* sound into *sh*, as in

Christ commandeth us to *sherch* the Scriptures.—*Tyndale.*

His head was wreathed with a huge *shash* (sash).
—*Thomas Herbert. Trench.*

I believe Burns is alone in this spelling. Dunbar has *flesche*. Chaucer, Gower, Lydgate, and others write *flees*.

Fleg. A kick, a random blow.

To *fleg*, to whip.—*Bailey.*

Flether. To decoy by fair words, to flatter.

Flethers. Flattery.

Fley. To scare, to frighten.

Flay, to fright. *Flaed*, afraid.——*Grose.*

I said to the man, "What made you run away?" His answer was, "You're enough to *flay* owt."—*Sir W. Lawson.*

And ferly *flayed* that folk.—*Early E. Alliterative Poems. Morris.*

> And al the erthe, the achtande day,
> Sal stir and quac and al folc *flay.*
> —*E. Metrical Homilies. Small.*

> Tho was the boy *aflyght*, and dorst not speke.
> —*Octovian Imperator.*

Flichter. To flutter as young nestlings do when their dam approaches.

This seems to be the same as E. *flicker*, which, according to Johnson, is, "To flutter, to play the wings; to have a fluttering motion," and the authorities he quotes quite express Burns's meaning:

> The tuneful lark already stretch'd her wing,
> And *flickering* on her nest made short essays to sing.
> —*Dryden.*

If we compare a passage in the "Cottar's Saturday Night" with the following lines, we shall find a striking similarity, if not identity, in the words:—

> "The expectant wee things, todlin, stacher through,
> To meet their dad, wi' *flichterin*' noise and glee."

> "At all her stretch her little wings she spread,
> And with her feather'd arms embraced the dead;
> Then *flickering* to his pallid lips, she strove
> To print a kiss, the last essay of love."—*Dryden.*

In fact, *flichter* and *flicker* differ no more from each other than *stacher*, in the passage quoted above, does from stagger, or the old form *stakers*.

> Her gost that *flikered* are aloft,
> Into her woful hert ayen it went.—*Chaucer.*

Flicker. To meet, to encounter; to coax, to flatter.

Thise olde dotardes holours, which wol kisse, and *flicker*, and besie hemself.—*Chaucer.*

> Her colde brest began to hete,
> Her herte also to *flacke* and bete.—*Gower.*

Flie. A fly.

Flinders. Shreds, broken pieces.

Flinders, small pieces, fragments; "it's broken into *flinders*."
Bamford.

> The bow and his broad arrow
>   In *flinders* flew about.—*R. Hood.*
>
> The moon was clear, the day drew near,
>   The spears in *flinders* flew.—*The Battle of Otterbourne.*

Sir Walter Scott evidently thought *flinders* an English word, for he prints it at least twice—once in "The Minstrelsy" and once in "The Lay"—without explanation.

> The tough ash spear, so stout and true,
> Into a thousand *flinders* flew.—*Lay of the Last Minstrel.*
> > Canto III.

Fling. To kick, to dance.

> The heedless trunk
>   Still in the saddle seated did remain,
> Until his steed
>   With leaps and *flings* that burden did discharge.—*Fairfax.*
>
> Over the bars the hardy couple leapt,
>   And after them a band of Christians *fling.*—*Id.*
>
> > Then let's flock hither
> > Like birds of a feather,
> > To drink, to *fling*,
> > To laugh and sing.
> > > —*Aristippus or the Jovial Philosopher.*

Flingin-tree. A piece of timber hung by way of partition between two horses in a stable: a flail (properly the *souple* or striking part of a flail).

> > I render thee, fals rebelle,
> > To the *flingande* fende of helle.—*Skelton.*
> >
> > As they ryde talkynge,
> > A rach ther com *flyngynge*
> >   Overwert the way.—*Lybaeus Disconus.*

Flisk. To fret at the yoke. *Fliskit*, past tense of flisk.

> *Flisk*, to skip, or bounce; to fret at the yoke.—*Halliwell.*

Flitter. To vibrate like the wings of a bird. *I* for *u* sound. See *anither.*

Flitter-mouse, i.e., flutter-mouse, a bat.—*Bailey.*

Flunkie. A servant in livery.

Dr. C. Mackay says, "This word was unknown to literature until the time of Burns." This is not quite correct as regards Scotland. Fergusson has it,—

> So *flunky* braw, when drest in maister's claise,
> Struts to Auld Reekie's cross on sunny days.

Carlyle has established its position as an English word,—

Praise-God-bare-bones one discerns to be of considerable private capital, my witty *flunky* friends.

Flyte. To scold.

Flite, to scold or brawl.—*Bailey.*

> With chydyng and with *flytynge,*
> Shewynge him Goddis lawis.—*Skelton.*

> And als, madame, men says sertayne,
> That woso (whoso) *flites,* or turnes ogayne,
> He bygins the mellé.—*Ywain and Gawain.*

Focks. Folk.

Fodgel. Fat; squat and plump.

Fodge, a small bundle.—*Glouc.*

> Her face glystryng like glas:
> All *foggy* fat she was.—*Skelton.*

A *foggy* body.—*Corpus obesum. Ainsworth.*

Foggage. Rank grass which has not been ate in summer, or which grows among grain, and is fed upon after the crop is removed.—*Jamieson.*

Fog, after-grass.—*Ainsworth. Johnson.*

Fogagum (Low Latin). Aftermath, or aftergrass.

Fogage, rank grass not eaten in summer.—*Bailey.*

All these definitions seem to confine *foggage* to food for cattle, but Burns extends it to every thing that could be of service to even so humble a creature as a mouse.

Foor. Went, hastened.

Where *fured* you? Where went you?—*Bailey.*

> Be the dymmyng of the moyre,
> Men myghte se where Richard *fore.*—*R. C. de Lion.*

Swithost he *for* thyder.—*Paul's Life of Alfred. Marsh.*

> And als he *for* hamward, he mette
> A beggar that him cumly grette.
> —*E. Metrical Homilies. Small.*

> This enderday, as I forth *ferde*
> To walk.—*Gower.*

Foord. A ford.

In his hands he bare a shield representing Saint Warburgh crossynge the *foord.*—*Chatterton.*

> Men in summer fearles passe the *foorde,*
> Which is in summer lord of all the plain.—*Spenser.*

In quoting *foord* as answering to S. *foord*, I ought, for the sake of young readers, or those not familiar with old E. authors, to mention that *oo* is often used for the long sound of *o*. Thus in one verse of "The Libel of English Policy," I find *woo* for woe, *agoo* for ago, and *foo* for foe. This is a merely alphabetical arrangement, and does not necessarily imply the Scottish sound of *oo* which as Burns says is that of "the French *u*." But on the other hand, when we find Sir John Cheke writing *moother* for mother; Sackville, *strooke* for struck; and Bishop Pecock using *foormal* for formal, *doone* for done, *anoon* for anon, *oon* for one, etc., it is natural to suspect that it was not a mere peculiarity of orthography, but that it had something to do with the pronunciation.

Foorsday. Thursday. See under *thumart.*

For. In spite of, notwithstanding.

I avyse to speke *for* ony drede.—*Skelton.*

I intend to make merry with my parishioners this Christmas *for* all the sorrow, lest perchance I never return to them again.
—*Latimer.*

For. Near, by, as in "cheek for chow."

For, in this sense, is probably contracted from *forbye,* which is sometimes used for near.

Foreby, before and near to any place.—*Bailey.*

Flyngyth gode skowr him *forby.*—*Kyng Alisaunder.*

For. Against, in opposition to, in competition with, as in "Horn for horn, they stretch and strive."

For. In prevention of, as in "Was timmer propt for thrawin."

Cloth'd with a pitchy cloud *for* being seen.—*Marlowe.*

Walk off, sirrah, and stir my horse *for* taking cold.—*Fletcher.*

The lettres ye send me close them surely *for* opening.—*Letter to Sir Ralph Sadler.*

For roting es na better rede.—*Cursor Mundi.*

Forbears. Forefathers.

Forbye. Besides.

Forby, past, near, besides, in addition to.—*West. and Cumb. Dialect. Halliwell.*

The smelle scholde not greve men that went *forby.*—*Maundeville.*

Fore. Alive.

"To the fore," remaining still in existence.—*Sir W. Scott.*

Except some man (resolved) shall conclude,
With Cesar's death to end our servitude,

> Else (god to *fore*) myself may live to see
> His tired corse lie toiling in his blood.
> —*Thomas Kyd's Cornelia.*

I suspect " to fore " may mean before, and be equal to God being my guide; but it may also mean *if there be a god.*

Fore-hammer. A large hammer requiring both hands to wield it. It is called the fore-hammer because the person using it stands before the anvil, i.e., on the side farthest from the fire, and is the *bout-hammer* of Beaumont and Fletcher,—*bout,* as I understand it, referring to the way it is handled, that is, like Burns's " owre-hip wi' sturdy wheel."

If my wife scold, my *bout-hammer* shall roar.—*The Faithfull Friends.*

Forfairn. Distressed, worn out and jaded; lit. over-travelled.

> As it were a man *forfare.*—*Gower.*
> And all thys worlde in compace to *forfare.*—*Sir T. More.*
> When they seen poore folke *forfare,*
> For hunger die, and for colde quake.—*Chaucer.*
> Madame, sho said, ye er a barn,
> Thus may ye sone your self *forfarn.*—*Ywain and Gawain.*

Forfoughten. Exhausted with fighting.

For-foghten, tired with fighting.—*Halliwell.*

Shakspeare has forwearied in the same sense—

Forwearied in this action of swift speed.—*King John.*

Forspent with toil, as runners with a race.—*Third Part of King Henry VI.*

Thay were so wery *forfaght,* thay myzt not fyzt mare.
—*The Turnament of Tottenham.*

Forgather. To meet, to encounter with.
Forgather.—Halliwell.

Forgie. To forgive. See under *gie.*
> But—old Fortune (God forgie !)
> She's so cross-grain'd.—*Clare.*

Forinawed. Worn out.

Can this be a corruption of *forgnawed*? Of course, it would have a secondary sense, and to be *gnawed*, or eaten away, would come to signify worn out by any means, by the teeth of time as well as of animals.

> He fonde
> The wimpel
> Bebledde aboute and all *forgnawe.—Gower.*

Forjeskit. Jaded with fatigue. Perhaps for *fortaskit*, i.e., overtasked.

Forrit. Forward.
Forrud, forward.—*Bamford.*

Fother. Fodder.
> He ripped the womb up of his mother,
> Dame Tellus, 'cause he wanted *fother*
> And provender wherewith to feed
> Himself and his less cruel steed.—*Butler.*
>
> From the plough soone free your teame,
> Then come home and *fother* them.—*Herrick.*
>
> They *fother* them in the winter with straw.—*Sandys.*

Fou. Full, drunk. This is only a different spelling of *fu.*
> That is a gode yle and plenty*fous.—Maundeville.*

Foughten. Old past participle of to fight.
> On the *foughten* field
> Michael and his angels, prevalent

> Encamping placed in guard their watches round
> Cherubic waving fires.—*Milton*.

> Bidders and beggeres
> *Fayteden* for here fode, *foughten* atte ale.—*P. Plowman*.

Foul thief. The devil.

> The *foul feend* him quelle !—*Chaucer*.

> An ever I may that *foul thief* gette,
> In a fyre I will him burn.—*Marriage of Sir Gawain*.

Founder (a horse). To over-ride, or spoil him with hard working.—*Bailey*.

To founder a horse. To cause such a soreness and tenderness in a horse's foot, that he is unable to set it to the ground.—*Johnson*.

The reason of this word's finding a place here, is that most E. dictionaries, if they have it in this sense, speak of it as Johnson does, whereas Burns speaks of a foundered animal as looking none the worse for his malady, which could only be detected by one skilled in horseflesh. This is the meaning of it in the following passages :—

If you find a gentleman fond of your horse, persuade your master to sell him because he is vicious, and *foundered* into the bargain.

> The stumbling *founder'd* jade can trot as high
> As any other Pegasus can fly.—*Earl of Dorset*.

> He has bought up
> Old horses that your grace had ridden blind, and *founder'd*.
> *Fletcher*.

Four-gill chap. A measure vessel containing an E. pint (jocularly spoken of as " a person ").

Foursome. Union of four. "Foursome reel," dance of four persons.

Fouth. Abundance, plenty. Supposed to be formed from *fou, fou-th,* or *fulth,* like Shakespeare's *spilth,* from spill.

Notwithstanding a general agreement that *fouth* is formed from *full,* I doubt if it is correct. Some of those who advocate this derivation are not quite consistent. One distinguished writer says *fou,* drunk, if formed from full should be written *fu',* and not *fou,* and immediately after says, "Fouth is from full." Is it not possible that *fouth* may be the same as E. *fother,* A.-S., a mass, a load, or connected with it as *food* with *fodder,* and heath with heather. At all events, in Chaucer's line—

> It coste largely of gold a fother,

if we substitute *'fouth* for *fother,* it might have been written by Ramsay, who has—

> And took a fouth
> Of kisses from her yielding mouth.

No doubt *fother* became definite, but this is just what happened to *acre, gill,* etc.

Fow. A bushel, etc.

That is what Burns says of *fow,* meaning apparently any measure-vessel full. He speaks of it indefinitely, as he does also of another measure-dish in the same verse in which *fow* occurs—the *heapit stimpart*—which was a familiar name for the wooden vessel used in distributing grain to horses, whether it contained exactly the "eighth part of a bushel" or not, and the meaning seems to be "so long as I have corn, a large cog-full shall be reserved for thee."

Jamieson, however, says positively that *fow* is a "firlot or bushel." I can only say that I never heard the word applied to any measure.

Frae.   From.

>His pyke-staff they have taken him *frae.—R. Hood.*
>Our fingers are lime-twigges and barbers we be,
>To catch sheetes *fra* hedges, most pleasant to see.
>>*The Three Ladies of London.*
>
>I sal help the *fra* presowne.—*Ywain and Gawain.*
>
>Her ring was noght hir *fra.—The Seven Sages.*

Frammit, or *fremit.*   Estranged from, not related to.

>*Estrangier,* a stranger, alien, a *fremme* bodie.—*Cotgrave.*
>
>So now his friend is changed for a *fremme.—Spenser.*
>
>Never was there yet so *fremed* a caas.—*Chaucer.*
>
>Whether he be *fremd* or of his blod,
>The child is trew and gode.—*Amis and Amiloun.*
>
>As perjured cowards in adversity,
>With sight of fear, from freends to *fremb'd* doth fly.—*Sir Philip Sidney.*

Freath.   Froth, to froth.   *Freath*, in the sense of froth on ale, was, I believe, first used by Burns, and is yet mostly restricted to that and the froth produced in washing.

E for *o* as in—

>First from one coast, till nought thereof be drie,
>And then another, till that likewise *fleat (float).—Spenser.*

Frien'.   Friend.   *Frien* is always pronounced with the *e* long in Scotland, and was probably so enunciated in England also at one time.

>Thereby founde I some holow hertes, and a few faithful *freendes.*
>>—*Sir John Harrington.*
>
>For hate or *frenshippe* they shal ther domys dresse.—*Lydgate.*
>
>So goodly speke and so *freendly.—Chaucer.*

Freit or *freet.*   An omen, to portend; to vex one's self needlessly.

L

Fu'. Full. *Fu' gay*, very gay. See under *a'*.

> Thus was Syr Ywaine sted that sesowne,
> He wrought *fu'* mekyl ogayns resowne.—*Ywain and Gawain.*

Fud. The scut of the hare, coney, etc.

Fuff. To blow intermittently; also an interjection denoting displeasure.

Fuff, to blow or puff.——*Halliwell.*

Fu' han't. Full handed, rich. *Fu'* and *han'*.

Funnie. Full of merriment.

Fun (a low, cant word). Sport, high merriment, frolicksome delight.—*Johnson.*

Both *fun* and *funny* have got into good repute since Johnson's day.

> She swears you are a funny, jolly soul.—*Sterne.*

Funny, comical, pleasing.—*Var. dial. Halliwell.*

Authentic Memoirs of the memorable Joseph Collins of Oxford, commonly known by the name of *Funny Joe.*—*Howe, who quotes from British Magazine for 1747.*

Fur. A furrow.

A *fur*long is the length of a *fur*. *Fur, furh*, a furrow, A. Sax.
Bosworth.

> And setten him upon the molde,
> Where that his fader held the plough
> In thilke *furrgh* which he tho drough.—*Gower.*

Furrgh may have been treated as a dissyllable, as burgh sometimes is, but I think the line would be read or scanned thus by Gower and his contemporaries:—

In thilk—e furrgh—which he—tho drough, making no difference between the digraph gh in furrgh, drough, and plough. The word in another line of Gower's is undoubtedly a monosyllable—

> A *furrgh* of land in which a row.—*Con. Amantis.*

> When Mylys sawe the emperoure,
> He fell downe in a depe *foure*
> Fro hys hors so hye.—*Le Bone Florence of Rome.*

Fur or *foor*, a furrow.—*Thoresby.*

Fur-ahin. The hindmost horse on the right hand when ploughing. Lit. the hinder horse of the pair which walk on the *fur.* See *fur* and *ahin.*

Furder. Further, success.

> It longeth to our order,
> To hurt no man,
> But as we can
> Every wight to *forder.*—*Sir T. More.*

> Forsothe, quod she, theys be
> *Furdrers* of love.—*Skelton.*

> For your own ease, in *furdring* of your need,
> As fast as I may speak, I will you speed.—*Chaucer.*

Hy ne therst (durst) her brynge *forder* est.—*Octovian Imperator.*

Furm. A form, a bench.

Fourm, a seat to sit on at school.—*Bailey.*

You shall find her sitting in her *fourme.*—*Ben Jonson.*

Syr, what *fourme* of preachinge would you appoynte me to preache before a kynge?—*Latimer.*

> And howe a verbe schall be *furmede.*
> *Poem of 15th Century*: *Reliquæ Antiquæ.*

> My lefe chyld, I kownsel ye
> To *furme* the vi. tems.—*Id.*

Fusionless. Without strength or sap.

Fuzzon or *fizon*, the nature, juice, or moisture of the grass, or other herb, the heart or strength of it.—*Grose.*

Which while he lived had *fuysion* of every thing.—*Skelton.*

> Of all manere *fusion*
> Vnough they hadde.—*Lybaeus Disconus.*

Fyftene. Fifteen.

> For hit (the flood) clam vche a clyffe cubites *fyftene.*
> —*Early E. Alliterative Poems.*

Fyke. Trifling cares; to be in a fuss about trifles.

Fyke, to move in an inconstant, indeterminate manner.—*Weber.*

The Sarezynes fledde, away gunne *fyke.*—*R. C. de Lion.*

Fyke. To fidget or shrug, indicating suffering, as in—

> Ye sud be licket
> Until ye *fyke.*

Fyle. To soil, to dirty, to defile.

For Banquo's issue have I *fil d* my mind.—*Shak.*

Sirrah, I scorn my finger should be *fil'd* with thee.—*Beaumont and Fletcher.*

> That byrd is not honest
> That *fylythe* his own nest.—*Skelton.*

He wiped his lips with the hollow of his hand for *fyling* his napkin.—*Rob. Langham's Letter.*

> Take her up in thine armes twaine,
> For *filinge* of her feet.—*Child Waters.*

G.

Ga'. To gall. For omission of *ll* see under *a'*.

Gab. The mouth; to speak boldly or pertly.

Gabb, to prate or tattle.—*Bailey.*

Gab, the mouth. Gift of the gab, faculty of speech (perhaps *fluency* of speech).—*Grose.*

> In'm not leef to *gabbe.*—*Chaucer.*
> That I so *gabbeth* it reweth me.—*Morte d' Arthur.*

Gaberlunzie. An old man.—*Currie.* An old man who takes to beggary. Literally it means a wallet carried at the loins.—*Douglas.* Wallet-man, or tinker.—*Ritson.* On what authority *gaber* is rendered a wallet I have not been able to learn.—*Jamieson.* A mendicant; a poor guest who cannot pay for his entertainment.—*Sir W. Scott.*

The word is out of use. I do not know if it is related to " Gaberliltie, a ballad-singer." A curious thing about this word is that, according to Jamieson, *lunzie* is a wallet, so that if *gaber* is also a wallet, *gaberlunzie* will mean *wallet-wallet*. If *lunzie* be a wallet, then, as to be " a *gude crack*," or talker, was essential to a successful beggar, it may mean the *gabber* or talker with the wallet.

Ga'd. Galled.

Gae. To go.

>He was ful loath to let it *gae*.—*R. Hood.*
>And croked men thar geres he *ga*.—*E. Metrical Homilies.*
>By the eres into the hert it *gase*.—*Ywain and Gawain.*
>At morn the childe cald seriantes twa,
>And bad thai sold his errand *ga*.—*The Ravens.*

Gaed. Went, past tense of *gae.*

>And he *gede* out and myghte not speke to hem.—*Wyclif.*
>The boies *gede* anon doun.—*The Seven Sages.*

Gaet or *gate.* Way, manner, road. In "The Brigs of Ayr" it seems to mean the outlet or mouth of a river.

>*Water-gate*, flood-gate.—*Halliwell.*
>When David was gone his *gate.*—*Gower.*
>A cup in the pate is a mile in the *gate.*—*Swift.*
>Reason went her *gate.*—*Chaucer.*
>Every fairy take his *gait.*—*Shak.*

Gain. Same as *gin* and its original form, meaning against (in relation to time).

Gair. Gore, a triangular piece of cloth inserted in a lady's dress to widen it more at one place than another. *A* for *o*. See under *bane*, and in—

> So schooled the *Gate* (goat) her wanton sonne.—*Spenser.*
> The *goar* of a garment.—*Ainsworth.*

Galligaskins. Loose breeches.

> *Gally-gaskins*, wide loose trousers.—*Halliwell.*
> *Galligaskins*, a sort of wide slops or breeches.—*Bailey.*
> *Galligaskins*, large open hose.—*Johnson.*

Galloway whey. Some old Galloway people say this was *whisky* and water, and in support of their opinion quote from "The Five Carlins" the lines—

> And *whisky* Jean, that took her gill
> In Galloway sae wide.

Other inhabitants of the district say it was *brandy* and water, and in proof of their statement quote from a copy of the same ballad sent by the poet to Mrs. Stewart, in which "Whisky Jean" is called throughout "Brandy Jean," as noticed by Cunningham. This view is supported, if so small a matter were worth supporting at any length, by an extract from a letter of Burns to Mr. Tennant, which also shows how recent is the introduction of whisky to a large part of Scotland :—

They (a John Currie and his wife) keep a country public-house, and sell a great deal of foreign spirits, but all along thought that whisky would have degraded their house. . . . The whisky of this country is a most rascally liquor ; and, by consequence, only drunk by the most rascally part of the inhabitants.

Gallows-tree. English writers use *gallow-tree.*

> He is condemned to the *gallow-tree.*—*Wright's Political Songs.*
>
> A Scot, when from the *gallow-tree* got loose,
> Drops into Styx, and turns a Solan goose.—*Cleveland.*

Gane. Gone.

> Ever, alsone als he was *gane*,
> The ermyte toke the flesh onane.—*Ywain and Gawain.*
>
> Had I spoken with any man,
> To sevyn days war cumen and *gane.*—*The Seven Sages.*
>
> Thoroue lyvar & longes bathe the sharpe arrowe ys *gane.*
> *Chevy Chase.*

Gang. To go, to walk.

> *Gang*, an old word.—*Johnson.*
>> And lard and lady *gang* til kirk.—*Albion's England.*
>> Thereto gan they *gang.*—*R. Hood.*
>> But let them *gang* alone.—*Spenser.*

Gangrel. A wandering person.

> *Gangrel*, one who by the strength of his leg rids much ground.
> *Bailey.*

Longis. A slimme, slow backe, dreaming luske, a drowsie *gangrill.*—*Cotgrave.*

A tall gangrell. Longue eschine.—*Sherwood's E. and Fr. Dictionary.*

Gar. To make, to force to; *gar't*, made.

> Tell me, good Hobbinol, what *gars* thee greet?—*Spenser.*
> *Gar* us have mete and drinke.—*Chaucer.*
> I coude, and I lyst, *garre* you laugh at a game.—*Skelton.*
> Then he *gart* arme of the spyrytualte.
> *Le Bone Florence of Rome.*

Garten. A garter.

Garten, a garter.—*Halliwell.*

Gash. Wise, sagacious, talkative ; to converse.

> He looked wan and *gash*.—*Cobler of Canterburie.*

This is not our meaning, I doubt, at least not primarily, as it refers to the *look*, but it may in a secondary sense apply to the *reality* of seriousness, which is, more or less, implied in *gashness* or wisdom.

Gat. Old p. t. of get.

> They took his head, and *gat* them away.—*2 Samuel, iv.* 7.
> We then did peace desire to keep what we had *gat*.
> *The Disbanded Soldier.*
> I *gat* me men-singers and women-singers.—*Ecclesiastes,* ii. 8.
> His fall *gat* earth with groans.—*Chapman.*

Gaucy or gawsie. Jolly, large.

> *Gaucy,* fat and comely.—*Halliwell.*

Gaud or gad. A rod, a goad.

> *Gad,* a long stick, a goad.—*Grose.*
> In the den are drumming *gads* of steel.—*Stanihurst's Virgil.*
> There would no sword bite upon him more than upon a *gad* of steel.—*Morte d'Arthur.*
> A deputy from Broughton, Lincolnshire, brings a very long whip, called here a *gad*-whip.—*Every Day Book.*

Gaudsman or Gadsman. Ploughboy, the boy that drives the horses in the plough. It is to be remembered that this functionary existed only when there were more than two horses in a plough, or when they were not placed abreast. Now-a-days he is seldom seen, for even when more than two horses are used, by a better arrangement, the ploughman guides them as well as the plough. The gadsman's business is sometimes said to be *to ca'* the plough.

This word affords a curious example of the truth that

language which took its rise in one state of society holds its ground when things are entirely altered. It is long since candles were placed on sticks, or ink was put in horns, yet we still speak of candlesticks and inkhorns. The gadsman of Burns's day was a boy and not a man, and he did not use a *gaud*. Gauds were never, indeed could not be, used for horses. They were employed when oxen drew the plough, and were wielded by men who took their turn in driving and ploughing. These gauds were the ox-goads of Scripture.

The English farmer does not seem to have had any distinctive name for the driver, but he had the gaudsman, as we learn from an enumeration of the desired possessions of a pleasing poet:—

> A serving man not quite a clown,
> A boy to help to tread the mow,
> And *drive* while tother holds the plough.—*Matthew Green.*

Gaun. Going.

Gaunt. To yawn.

Gant, to yawn.—*Halliwell.*

Se how he *ganeth*, lo this dronken wight.—*Wright's Chaucer.*

Why do ye *gane* and gaspe?—*Skelton.*

Gawkie. A half-witted person.

Gawk, a foolish person.—*Johnson.*

Gawky, awkward; generally used to signify a tall awkward person.—*Grose.*

People of England. The grand pensioner, Lord *Gawkee*, etc.—*New Political Dictionary. Life of John Wilkes.*

> Ye fool *gawkies!* ye'll ne'er be believ'd.
> *The Wandsworth Epistle Versified.*

Jamieson quotes *goky* from some edition or MS. of P. Plowman. I have not found it.

They have sent me a tall *gawky* boy to make a servant of.
Garrick.

Gawn. Gavin. *V* is often changed to *w*, as in—

And thei camen ouer the *wawe* of the sea unto the cuntree of Genazareth.—*Wyclif. Morris and Skeat.*

> Swithe mury hit is in halle,
> When the burdes *wawen* (wave, wag) alle!
> *Kyng Alisaunder.*
>
> The kyng tolde hem what sir *Gawayn* had tolde hym.
> *Le Morte d'Arthur.*

Gaylies or *gylie.* Pretty well.

Marry, for this purpose whereof we now write, this would have served *gailie* well.—*Wilson's Arte of Rhetoricke, 1555.*

> Goe thy way, father Grime, *gayly* well you doe say.
> *Damon and Pythias.*

Gear. Riches, goods, of any kind.

> I've an eye and an ear
> To look to our *gear.*—*Ben Jonson.*
>
> Money, plate, and such good *geere*
> They bear away.—*Good Newes from the North, 1640.*
>
> Yet on the *gere*
> That he should wear
>   He reight not what he spent.—*Sir T. More.*

Geck. To toss the head in wantonness or scorn; to sport or rejoice.

To *geck*, to make a fool of.—*Bailey.*

> Made the most notorious *geck* and gull
> That e'er invention play'd on.—*Shak.*

Ged. A pike.

Ged, a pike. Northumb.—*Halliwell.*

Gent. A person. In "Do ye envy the city *gent?*" it seems to mean a merchant or shopkeeper.

Gentle. Aristocratic, in " The Highland Lassie " :—

> Nae *gentle* dames, though e'er sae fair,
> Shall ever be my muse's care:
> Their titles a' are empty show."
> He to-day that sheds his blood with me,
> Shall be my brother ; be he ne'er so vile,
> This day shall *gentle* his condition.—*Shak.*

> I am as *gentle* as yourself, as freeborn.—*Love's Pilgrimage.*

Gentles. Gentry.

> Will you go, *gentles.*—*Shak.*
> I pray you, *gentles*, list to me.—*Love in a Village.*
> Yet served I *gentles.*—*Albion's England.*

The nobles prepared themselves in the best manner ; the ladies spared no cost ; the *gentles* flock'd to please their lord.—*History of Patient Grissell. Percy Society.*

Gentoo. A native of Hindostan.

Genty. Neat, pretty.

Jaunty, dashing, showy, fine, elegant. This word is derived through the forms, *jenty*, *genty*, from Fr. gentil. *Gent*, spruce, fine, handsomely clad, gay.—*Bailey.*

> She that was noble, wise, as fair and *gent.*—*Fairfax.*
> Fayre mote he thee, the prowest and most *gent.*—*Spenser.*
> But, Mr. Bayes, is that too, modest and *gent.*—*The Rehearsal.*
> In men or beast they are so comely, so *jantee*, a-la-mode, and handsome.—*Butler.*
> Your *janty* air and easy motion.—*Spectator.*

Y is often added to adjectives. For example Cowley has *calmy* for calm.

Geordie. Dim. of George, a guinea, and for the same coin *George* is also used.

Strait at Wakefield—
When strength of ale had so much stirr'd me,
That I grew stouter far than *Jordie*, i.e., *George a Green*.
Pinner of Wakefield.

Coins are often named after monarchs, as *Jacobus, Carolus, Napoleon,* &c. Even Milton has not disdained to follow this fashion. In his *Defensio pro Populo Anglicano* he has,—

> Quis expedivit Salmasio suam hundredam
> Picamque docuit nostra verba conari?
> Magister artis venter, et *Jacobæi*
> Centum, exulantis viscera marsupii regis.

I have somewhere seen the following translation:—

> Who to our English tuned Salmasius' throat,
> Who taught the pye to speak our words by rote?
> A hundred golden *Jameses* did the feat;
> He learn'd to prattle—for he wish'd to eat.

There is also this week dead a poulterer that hath left 40,000 *Jacobs* in gold.—*Pepys.*

> He bound up my arm,
> And I gave him two *Georges* which did him no harm.
> *C. Cotton.*

> When the *Georges* are flown
> Then the cause goes down.—*A New Ballade, 1659.*

Germin. A shooting or sprouting seed.—*Johnson. Germina,* pl. of *germin.*

Get, geat. A child, a young one.

He was some gentylmaunes *beyete* (*beget*).—*Octovian Imperator.*
A fendes *bigete.*—*P. Plowman.*
Get, that which is begotten.—*Halliwell.*

Though I know that I have all the glossarists of Chaucer against me, I am of opinion that *get* in the following lines is the word we are now considering—

> And with his stikke, above the crosselet (crucible),
> That was ordained with that false *get*,
> He stirreth the coles.

It must be taken into account that, though Burns so limits it, *get* is not confined to a child, but is applied to grown and even elderly persons. Thus Dunbar calls Kennedie, a rival poet, "Feynds *get*," which perhaps he thought only a Scots, or old English, equivalent for St. Paul's "Child of the Devil," its secondary meaning being rogue. Then who ordained it, whatever it was? *With*, it needs no argument to prove, in Chaucer, as Tyrwhitt's glossary shows, and other old E. authors often, very often means *by*. The only other occasion on which Chaucer uses the word *get*, it signifies fashion, and may be translated *gait* or way. And this, so far as I know, is its meaning wherever it occurs except in "The Chanones Yemanne's Tale," and it has generally new or old joined with it. In the Prologue of the Pardonere he says—

> Him thought he rode al of the newe *get*.

Even in the passage from Occleve, which Tyrwhitt quotes in a note, the word means way, or manner.

> Also ther is another *newe gette*,
> All foul waste of cloth and excessif.

Taking these things into consideration, and noticing also how unlike Chaucer it is to speak of a *false* trick, I submit with deference that the meaning is, "And with this stick, which was prepared, or arranged, by that false *get* (knave), he stirs the coals." I give one example of *with* for *by*—

> But, sertes, alle the rerewarde
> Was i-slayn *with* (by) Kyng Richard.—*R. C. de Lion.*

Ghaist. A ghost.

> As soone as the emperowre yylded the *gast*
> A prowde garson came in haste.—*Le Bone Florence of Rome.*

> That makes thine aungels *gastes* flighand.—*Met. E. Psalter.*

> And ther thai herd a mes (mass) in haste,
> That was said of the haly *gaste.*—*Ywain and Gawain.*

Gie. To give; *gi'ed*, gave; *gi'en*, given.

> New plays and . . . are much akin;
> Much followed both, for both much money *gi'en.*
> *The Two Noble Kinsmen.*

> To their store
> They add the poor man's yeanling, and dare sell
> Both fleece and fell, not *gi'ing* him the fell.—*Ben Jonson.*

> If my daughter there should have done so I wou'd not have *gi'en* her a groat.—*Wycherly.*

> The course y wold that ye had sene;
> In the nownes ye had me the coppe *gene.*
> *The Hunting of the Hare.*

> Daffodils *gi'en* up to thee, There shall be.—*Herrick.*

Gif. If.

> Sir, thai said god *gif* so wer !—*Ywain and Gawain.*

> In al the werld n' is man livind,
> That couth you that sothe finde,
> But *gif* hit were child on,
> That never hadde fader non.—*Herowdes and Merlin.*

Gift. In the line, "I grudge a wee the great folk's *gift,*" Burns seems to use gift as equivalent to fortune or property.

Giftie. Dim. of gift in its usual sense, not as above.

Giga. A musical term signifying, I understand, triple time.

Giglet. A playful girl. *Giglet*, a laughing girl.—*Grose.*

>Thou wilt gad by night in *giglet* wise.—*Fairfax.*

>Aye, Fortune's right hand Mosbie hath forsook,
>To take a wanton *giglot* by the left.—*Arden of Feversham.*

It is for no other end than to make them *giglots.*—*A Touchstone for the time Present.*

Gill. A liquid measure, the fourth of an E. pint.

Gill, a pint.—*Grose. Gill*, the fourth part of a pint, in some places the half of a pint.—*Johnson.*

>Every bottle must be rinced with wine, a *gill* may be enough.
>*Swift.*

>Thee shall each alehouse, thee each *gill*house mourn.—*Pope.*

Gillie. Dim. of gill.

Gilpey. A young girl.

Gimmer. A ewe from one to two years old.

Gimmer-lamb, a ewe lamb.—*Bailey. Gimmer*, an old sheep.—*Bamford.*

Gimmer-lamb, a ewe-lamb; also a two-year's-old sheep.—*Grose.*

>'Twas just like Hob Trumble's *gimmer*
>Which he sold for six-pence a side.—*The Northumberland Garland. Ritson.*

Gin. If, against (in relation to time), i.e., by, as in "I'll aulder be *gin* Beltane," i.e., by Beltane or Whitsunday, which is similar to—

>*Against* his coming were laid many chambers.—*Cavendish.*

>A good foundation *against* the time to come.—*Timothy.*

Against seems to have become *again* and then *gain.*

>It is *again* his kind.—*Chaucer.*

>That unneth I might make resistaunce
>*Agayn* his power, for he was so stronge.—*Stephen Hawes.*

> *Gayne* dangerous stormys theyr anker of supporte.—*Skelton.*
> *Geyne* al sikenes our chief restoratif,
> This sacrament, this blessid brede of lyf.—*Lydgate.*
> *Gin,* if.—*Bailey.*
>
> *Geyne* surfetous suspecte the emerand comendable.—*Skelton.*

Gin is often used in our Northern counties and by the Scotch, as we use *if* or *an;* which they do with equal propriety and as little corruption. It is no other than the participle *given,* gi'en, *gin.*—*Horne Tooke.*

> The Northern man saith, "A (I) sud eat mare cheese *gin* ay had it."—*Verstegan.*
>
> > Oh, dear father, *gin* I be not fair!
> > *The North Country Chorister. Ritson.*

Gin-horse. Engine horse. In Burns's day coals were raised, and cotton-mills were driven by engines called *gins,* drawn by horses.

> He that it wrought, he coude many a *gin.*—*Chaucer.*
> Alisaundre quic hoteth his hynen
> Under heore walles to myne with strong *gynnes.*
> > *Kyng Alisaunder.*

Gipsy. A young girl.

> *Gipsy,* a name of slight reproach to a woman.—*Johnson.*
>
> > A slave I am to Clara's eyes;
> > The *gipsy* knows her power and flies.—*Prior.*
> >
> > Kelly, my things!
> > Be quick, why sure the *gipsy* sleeps.—*Robert Lloyd.*
>
> My shirts! I never had but six, and a cunning *gipsy* of a laundress cut me off the fore-laps of five.—*Sterne.*

Girdle. A thin circular plate of iron for baking cakes and scones,—cakes receiving a supplementary heating *before* the fire: it is a closed gridiron, and the names are from the same root, or one is a corruption of the other.

Griddle, a gridiron.—*Grose*.
Girdle, a round iron plate for baking.—*Halliwell*.

Girn. To grin, to twist the features in rage, agony, &c.; *girnin*, grinning.

Girn, to grin ; *girnin*, grinning.—*Bamford*.
Monstrer la dent. To *girne* or grinne at.—*Cotgrave*.

> He gaped like a gulfe when he did *gerne*.—*Spenser*.
> Some tremblid, some *girnid*.—*Skelton*.
> He ne'er did ope his apish *gerning* mouth
> But to retaile and broke another's wit.—*Marston*.

Girr. A hoop. *Gird* is sometimes used. *D* is frequently omitted after some liquids, but, so far as I know, never after *r* except in this word.

> He, as I said, like dreadful lightning thrown
> From Jupiter's shield, dispersed the armed *gird*
> With which I was environed.—*Massinger*.

Girran. A small horse.

Garran, a small horse ; a hobby.—*Johnson*.
Guaranion, a kind of horse.—*Cotgrave*.

> Yet by my description, you'll find he in short is
> A pack and a *garron*, a top and a tortoise.—*Swift*.

Gizz. A periwig.—*Burns.* A periwig, the face.—*Cunningham.* Withered hair.—*Chambers.* *Gizz*, the face. A cant term.—*Jamieson*.

Glaikit. Inattentive, foolish.

Glaik, inattentive, foolish.—*Halliwell*.

Jamieson thinks *glaikit* is "radically the same as gleek." It may, but so far as I have seen, *gleek* means to do something, and *glaikit* always denotes a state.

Glaive. A sword.

Glave, a broad sword ; a falchion.—*Johnson*.

M

> Sir Guy upon that steed woned,
> With a good *glaive* in his hand.—*Guy of Warwick*.
>
> In litter laid they lead him uncouth ways;
> If so they might deceive Antonius' cruel *glaives*.—*Grimoald*.
>
> Witnesse
> Achilles pressing through the Phrygian *glaives*.—*Spenser*.

Glaizie.   Glittering, smooth like glass.

Glaze, to set a gloss upon, to polish.—*Bailey*.   *Glizzn*, to sparkle.—*Bamford*.

Glaze-worm, a glow-worm.—*Lilly*.   *Glizzen*, glister or sparkle.
Thoresby.

> When the postes wer
> *Englased* glitteringe.—*Skelton*.
>
> All the story of Troy
> Was in the *glaising* ywrought.—*Chaucer*.

Glamour.   Magical delusion.—*Scott*.

Glaum.   To aim, to snatch at with greed.

Glam, to grasp, to snatch.—*Halliwell*.

Gled.   A hawk.

Ye shall not eat the *glede*.—*Deuteronomy*, *xiv. 13*.
The *glead* and swallow.—*Sylvester*.
Milan, a kite, puttocke, *glead*.—*Cotgrave*.

Gleed.   A burning coal.

> He sent hire pinnes, methe, and spiced ale,
> And wafres piping hot out of the *glede*.—*Chaucer*.
>
> As a *glede* glowynge, your ien glyster as glasse.—*Skelton*.
>
> The justyce het men schold her lede
> Out of the cité,
> And brenne anon to smale *glede*
> Hem all thre.—*Octovian Imperator*.

Gleg. Sharp, ready.

Gleg, slippery, smooth. *Cumb.* Also, quick, clever, adroit.
Halliwell.

Gleib. Glebe.—*Currie.* A piece, part, or portion of any thing.—*Jamieson.*

Gleib undoubtedly originally meant *glebe,* land, but the minister's portion of land being distinctively called *the glebe,* the word came to signify a part of any thing, though it is but little used in this sense.

Gley. A squint, to squint ; *agley,* off at a side, wrong.

Gly, to look asquint.—*Bailey.* *Glea* or *a-glea,* crooked. *Gly* or *glea,* to squint.—*Grose.*

Gley, to squint.—*Bamford.* *Glee,* to look asquint.—*Thoresby.*

I garde her gaspe, I garde her *gle.*—*Skelton.*

Gleyde. An old horse.

Glib-gabbet. That speaks smoothly and readily. *Glib* and *gab.*

Glib, slippery, smooth.—*Bailey.* *Gabb,* to prate or tattle.—*Id.*

It comes through you and your rascally *glib-tongu'd* companions.
Green's Tu Quoque.

Glimmer. To look unsteadily in "When my spirits are a little lightened I *glimmer* a little into futurity."— Burns to his father, 1781. For this sense of glimmer Chaucer uses glimse, i.e., glimpse :—

Ye have som *glimsing* (not a transient view, but the power of seeing) and no perfect sight.—*Can. Tales.*

Glimmerous. Having imperfect sight.

Glint. To peep, to glance. Burns always uses *glint ;* other S. writers use glint and glent indifferently. Old E. authors use the latter form.

Glent, glanced.—*Bailey*.

O Earl Brand, I see your heart's blood !
It's nothing but the *glent* and my scarlet hood.—*Earl Brand*

Her browys bent,
Her eyes *glent*.—*Skelton*.

But at the last, as that her eye *glent*
Aside, anon she gan his sworde aspie.—*Chaucer*.

The stroke *glented* downe to his belly.—*Froissart*.
Greahondes thorowe the grevis *glent*.—*Chevy Chase*.

Gloamin. The evening twilight.

Glomung, glommung, twilight.—*Bosworth*.

If the Anglo-Saxons familiarly used this word their successors south of the Tweed forgot it. The author of the following lines which express the thing would have been glad to have it.

> He and y schal stele away,
> *Bitwene the day and the night.*
> *Horn Childe and Maiden Rimnild.*

Gloamin-shot. A twilight interval which workmen within doors take before using lights.—*Jamieson*. Twilight-musing, a shot in the twilight.—*Cunningham*.

Gloom. To look angry, to frown.

To *glome*, to look gloomy, to frown.—*Bailey*.

Which whylome woll of folke smile,
And *glombe* on hem another while.—*Chaucer*.

On me she gave a *glome*
With browes bent.—*Skelton*.

Now *glooming* sadly.—*Spenser*.

What's he who with contracted brow,
Glooms downward with his eyes?—*Congreve*.

Glowr. To stare, to look ; a stare, a look.

Gloar, to look askew.—*Bailey*. *Glowr,* to stare.—*Grose*.

Gloor, to stare fatuously.—*Bamford.*   *Glore*, to look staringly.—*Thoresby.*

> Her dusky mantle Eve had spread;
> The west sky *glower'd* with copper red.—*Clare.*

Glum. Sullen, displeased. Much the same as gloom, but gloom in Burns indicates our feeling towards others, and *glum* to our state of mind without reference to others. This distinction is not always observed by E. writers; thus Hawes, in a passage printed in "Specimens of E. Literature," has—

> Than to the ground he adowne did fall,
> And upon me he gan to loure and *glum.*
> *The Passetyme of Pleasure.*

Glum, sullen, sour in countenance.—*Bailey.*

> They play scylens and *glum*,
> Can say nothing but mum.—*Skelton.*
> If one of all the four has frown'd,
> You ne'er saw people *glummer.*—*Ambrose Phillips.*

Glunch. A frown, to frown. *Glunch* seems to differ from gloom, if one may venture to distinguish between words so nearly identical in meaning, in this respect, that we *gloom* at a person with whom we are angry on any account, but *glunch* at one from whom we expected something and have been disappointed. Burns does not, I acknowledge, bear me out in this, but he does to some extent—

> Does onie great man *glunch* an' gloom?

That is apparently, "does any minister show that he is disappointed at your being less servile than he expected, and then gloom at you in anger."

Goave. To go about staring stupidly.

Gove, to stare vacantly.—*Halliwell.*   *Gofish*, sottish, foolish.——*Bailey.*

> Yet gan she him besech
> For to beware of *gofisshe* people's speech.—*Chaucer*.

Gomeral. A foolish person.

Gomerill, a silly fellow.—*Grose*.

Gor-cock. The red game, red cock, or moor-cock.— *Jamieson* (who doubts if it is a Scotch word). It is now admitted into English dictionaries, though the derivation of *gor* is not certain. It has no connection with *gor* in the name of another fowl.

> Vulture, kite,
> Raven, and *gor-crow*, all my birds of prey.—*Ben Jonson*.

Gos. The gos-hawk or falcon.

Gotten. Old participle of get.

Wealth *gotten* by vanity shall be diminished.—*Proverbs xiii. 17*.

But who can tell how joyful this man was when he had *gotten* his roll again.—*Bunyan*

> Henry the Sixth hath lost
> All that which Henry the Fifth had *gotten*.—*Shak*.

Gowan. The flower of the wild or mountain daisy, dandelion, hawkweed, etc. When gowan is used alone, it always means the mountain daisy.

Ewe-gowan, the common daisy.—*Halliwell*.

Gowany. Abounding in mountain daisies.

Gowd. Gold. For omission of *l* see under *a'*.

Gowd-spink, a goldfinch.—*Craven. Halliwell.*

> Taking from her hand a ring of *gould*.—*Spenser*.
> Aften whan they the *gould* have taken.—*Chaucer*.
> The erle Barnard of Tollous,
> Had fele men chyvalrous
>   Taken to hys presoun;

> Moche *gode* of them he hadd,
> Y can not tell, so god me gladd,
>   So grete was ther raunsome.—*The Erle of Tolous.*

> Than the Steward, Syr Kadore,
> A nobull letter made he there,
>   And wroughte hit all with *gode.*—*Emare.*

Gowdspink. The goldfinch.

Goldspink, the goldfinch.—*Halliwell.*

Gowden. Golden.

Gowff. The game of golf; to strike, *as the bat does the ball at golf.*

Goff, a sort of play at ball.—*Bailey.*

The prince lifted up his *goff*-club to strike the ball.—*Life of Prince Henry.*

> We merrily play
> At *Goff* and at Football.—*Westminster Drollery. London, 1671.*

The game was known in England as early as the time of Edward III., but the name, with which only I have any concern, apparently was not.

Gowk. A cuckoo, a term of contempt.

Gawk, a cuckoo; a foolish fellow.—*Johnson.* *Gowk*, a cuckoo.—*Grose.*

Nay, look how the man stands, as he were *gowked.*—*Ben Jonson.*
Gawkies, tawpies, *gowks*, and fools.—*Epistle to William Creech.*

How does a *gawkie* differ from a *gowk*? Perhaps in this: a *gawkie* is a silly person, but quiet, and a *gowk* obtrudes his folly, speaks out like the cuckoo.

Gowl. To howl.

> For unnethes es a child born fully
> That it ne bygynnes to *goule* and cry.—*Prick of Conscience.*

Sche that whilom was
Dredful to kinges and to emperours,
Now *gaulith* al the pepul on hir, alas !—*Wright's Chaucer.*

Graff. A grave. *F* for *v*, as in

Tydides' life was *saft* (saved).—*Chapman.*

This is said by hem that be not worth two *fetches* (vetches).
Chaucer.

The old emperice, the *fyle* (vile) traytour.—*Octovian Imperator.*

The childe that was so nobull and wysse,
Stode at his fader's *grafe* at eve.—*Wright's St. Patrick's Purgatory.*

So long have I listened to thy speche,
That *graffed* to the ground is my breche.—*Spenser.*

This my deare daughter's deep *engraffed* ill.—*Id.*

I rought of death, ne of life,
Whether that love would me *drife.*—*Chaucer.*

Graip. A pronged instrument for cleaning stables.

Rastelier, the steale of a *grape.*—*Cotgrave.*

Graip, like grapple and grapnel and grape (fruit), comes from *gripe*, and it is sometimes so called.—*Tooke.*

They had *grapers* of yron to cast out of one shyppe into another.
Froissart.

Graith. Accoutrements, furniture, dress.

For over sees it grounded he,
And ouer stremes *graithed* it to be.—*Metrical E. Psalter.*

The new bride was *graithed* with all.—*Lay le Fraine.*

Thise clerkes bete him wel, and let him lie,
And *greithen* hem, and tuke hir hors anon,
And on hir way they gon.—*Chaucer.*

Grane or *grain.* A groan, to groan. *A* for *o* (see under *bane*).

He es ofte seke and ay *granand.*—*Pricke of Conscience.*

Grannie or *graunie*.   Grandmother.

The descendants of *Granny* Campbell would probably be found to exceed 1500 persons.—*Historical Memoirs of Armagh*.

> The wrinkled, blear-eyed, good old *granny*,
> In this same cot, illum'd by many a cranny.—*Dr. Wolcot*.
> I heard my *granny* say.—*Tim Bobbin*.
> Uds Fish, *Granny*, how dost thou?—*Echard*.

Grape.   To grope.   *A* for *o* (see under *bane*).

Grat.   Wept, past tense of *greet*, which see.   *A* for *e* (see under *fallow*).

Scho changyd no chere nor *grette*.—*Sir Amadas*.

Whan he hadde ful long *grete*.—*Robert Mannyng*.

Sche *grette*, and seyde, sche wolde that sche hadde ben ded.
Maundeville.

Great.   Intimate, familiar.

As *great* as the devil and the Earl of Kent.—*Swift*.

When people are intimate, we say they are as *great* as two inkle-weavers.—*Cowper*.

The Chancellor is as *great* as ever with the King.—*Pepys*.

These two were very *great* with Mr. Boyle.—*Wotton to John Evelyn*.

The country talked as if he was *great* with her.—*Trans. of Scarron's Com. Romance*.

Johnson calls great in this sense a low word.   Some very respectable persons, it will be seen, used it.

Gree.   To agree.

Childhood must be maintained by men's authoritye, and slippery youth underpropped with elder counsayle, which neither they can have, but ye geve it, nor ye geve it, yf ye *gree* not.—*Sir T. More*.

We have *gree'd* so well together.—*Shak*.

He *gree'd* with the sexton of the churche to have the key of the churche-dore.—*Skelton's Merry Tales*.

Gree. Highest degree, superiority; *to bear the gree*, to be decidedly victor.

> He is a shepherd great in *gree*.—*Spenser.*
>
> But for the Court gay portaunce he perceiv'd,
> And gallant shew to be in greatest *gree*.—*Id.*

Gre, gree, degree, prize, highest rank.—*Weber.*

> He that bear'th him best in the tournament,
> Shal be graunted the *gree* by the common assent.
> *Tournament of Tottenham.*
>
> The heraudes gaff the child the *gree*.—*Ipomydon.*

Greens. Boiled colewort.

> Thou cook of fat beef and dainty *greens*.—*Burns, to Mr. Hill.*

Greet. To shed tears, to weep.

> Tell me what gars thee *greete*.—*Spenser.*
> And fond that she herselven gan to *grete*.—*Chaucer.*
> He says, "Al er we born *gretand*
> And makand a sorowful sembland."—*Pricke of Conscience.*
> And forthi sal thai *gret* full sar.—*E. Metrical Homilies.*

Grey-nick-quill. In his glossary, Cunningham has Grey-*neck*-quill, and says it is "a quill unfit for a pen," and quotes a proverb which refers to the inferiority of a feather taken from the neck of a goose compared with one taken from the wing.

Grien. To long for, to desire ardently.

By the transposition of *r*, *grien* is formed from Old E. *gern*, or À. S. *geornian*.

> *Gern* he prayd the bischop.—*E. Metrical Homilies.*
> He soht ful *gern* his halie banes.—*Id.*
> *Gern* hi biheld her.—*Orfeo and Heurodis.*

Grieve. Overseer, a superior farm-servant.

> *Wi'-greave*, the overseer of the highways.—*Bailey.*
> *Dike-grave*, an officer who takes care of banks and ditches.—*Id.*

In the "Coke's Tale of Gamelyn," sometimes printed as one of the Canterbury Tales, *greeve* must be some sort of upper servant, though Mr. Wright, from whose version I quote, has not put the word in his glossary. Gamelyn having slain the porter, whose business it was to announce visitors, and forced himself into his brother's house, says to those who accompany him—

> Ye be welcome withouten eny *greeve*,
> For we wiln be maistres here, and aske no man leve,

as if he had said, "Ye are welcome, though not formally introduced by porter, usher, or other official."

Grip. To catch, to seize. *Grips*, embraces.

> The one his pyke-staff *gripped* fast.—*R. Hood.*
>
> And *gripe* the sorer, being *gript* himself.—*Marlowe.*
>
> For *grippel* Edel to himselfe
> The kingdom sought to gaine.—*Argentil and Curan.*
>
> He did fiercely fall
> Upon his sunne-bright shield and *grypt* it fast withall.
> *Spenser.*

My comràde laid him flat by a *grip* of his hair.—*Memoirs of Captain John Creichton. Swift.*

Bi the helpe of that woman and of myne owne *gryppyng* y steied (ascended) uppon that ladder.—*Vision of William Staunton.*

Grip, the past participle of *gripan,* prehendere.—*H. Tooke.*

Then *gript* Æacides his heel.—*Chapman.*

Grissle. Gristle.

This deviation from the usual spelling hardly deserves notice.

> And the emperour of evil trusle
> Carved off his nose by the *grusle.*—*R. C. de Lion.*

Grizzie. Abbreviation of the female name Griselda.—*Jamieson.* More frequently, I believe, a familiar name of Grace.

Grit. Great.

By transposition, *grit* becomes *girt* in some dialects, as in—

> To diddle oud Tommy wad be a *girt* treat.
> *Bell's Ancient Poems and Songs.*

> The lady of Synadowne
> Long lyght in prisoun,
>   And that is *gret* dolour.—*Lybeaus Disconus.*

> Horn dude him in the weye,
> In a *gret* galeye.—*The Geste of Kyng Horn.*

It is not possible to tell whether *gret* is intended for great or grit, but in old writings *e* is more frequently used for *i* than for *ea*.

Groanin'. Groaning, a lying-in; *groanin-maut* (malt), ale brewed for the purpose of being drunk after the lady or goodwife's safe delivery.—*Guy Mannering.*

There's nobody but Mr. Lyrick, and you had as safely tell a secret over a *groaning-cheese* as to him.—*Farquhar.*

Neece, bring the *groaning-cheese* and all the requisites; I must supply the father's place.—*The Vow-breaker.*

Out comes the *groaning-cake.*—*L'Estrange.*

Groat. A coin; *to get the whistle of one's groat*, to play a losing game.

To get the whistle of one's groat means more than to play a losing game, unless a losing game means a total loss; it denotes parting with money for nothing, hearing the sound of it passing away. See *Whissle.*

Grozet. A gooseberry.

Grozet-eyes, goggle-eyes. South.—*Halliwell.*

Gruesome, grousome. Loathsomely grim.

Grew, thrill or curdle.—*Scott.*

Grousome, loathsome, fearful. Cumb.—*Halliwell*.

As connected with this word Jamieson has *groue*, *growe*, and Bailey has, "*Growse*, to be chill before the beginning of an ague fit."

Grumph. A grunt, to grunt.

Grumph, to growl, or grumble.—*Halliwell*.

Grumphie. A sow.

Grun. *U* for *ou*. See under *clud*.

Grunsell, the lower part of a building.—*Johnson, Milton, Fox*.
Grunsel, groundsel.—*Bamford*.

> Fall in a swoun, upon the *grown*.—*Ben Jonson*.
>
> The Frenche men fast to *grunde* gan go.
> *Battallye of Agynkourte*.
>
> The best knyght that on *grund* mai ga.
> *Ywain and Gawain*.
>
> Nor means he after to frequent
> Or court, or stately townes,
> But solitarily to live
> Amongst the country *grownes*.—*Argentite and Curan*.

Grunstane. A grindstone.

Grund, ground.—*Bamford*.

> Shod wele with yren and stele,
> And also *grunden* wonder wele.—*Ywain and Gawain*.
>
> Come to the *grinstane*, Charles, 'tis now too late
> To recollect 'tis Presbyterian fate.
> *Old Sayings, &c. Versified. Lond., 1657.*
>
> He *grunte* his teeth, and fast blew.—*R. C. de Lion*.

Gruntle. The phiz, or visage; a grunting noise.—*Burns*.
A nose.—*Dr. C. Mackay*.

Faire le groin, to pout, lowre, *gruntle*, or grow sullen.—*Cotgrave*.
To grunt or *gruntle*, *grouden*,—*Sherwood*.
Grunt or *gruntle*, *grunnis*.—*Ainsworth*.

We are delighted when wee heare a man *gruntling* like a hogge, yet cannot indure the *gruntling* of the hog itself.—*The Four Degenerate Sons.*

> Pensive in mud they wallow all alone,
> And snore, and *gruntle* to each other's moan.
>
> *The Rehearsal.*

Grunzie. Mouth, snout.

We preach the kingdom of heaven and yet have our *groines* ever wrooting in the ground.—*De Mornay.*

Swine *greun*, a swine's snout.—*Bailey.*

Groyn, a swine's snout.—*Bamford. Grose.*

Grushie. Thick, of thriving growth.

Grutten. Wept, past participle of *greet.*

Gude. The Supreme Being; good.

He, the Supreme *Good*, would send a glittering guardian.—*Comus.*

I Henry of Lancaster—als that I descendit by right line of the blode, coming fro the *gude* King Henry therde—which rewme (realm) was in poynt to be ondone by defaut of governance and ondoying of *gude* law.—*Duke of Lancaster (Hen. IV.). Hume. Hist. of E.*

> For I rek noght, thogh the ryme be rude,
> If the maters thar-of be *gude.*—*Pricke of Conscience.*

Gude-auld-has-been. Was once good. *Gude* and *auld.*

Gude e'en. Good evening.

Good e'en, our neighbours.—*Shak.*

Gudes. Goods, property.

> God grant us grace with hert and will,
> The *gudes* that he has given us till,
> Wele and wisely to spende.—*Sir Penny.*

Gude-willie. Hearty, cordial, cheerful.

> Ah, fair lady, *willy* fond at all.—*Chaucer.*

> O Love, O Charite,
> Thy mother eke, Citheria the swete,
> That after thy selfe, next heried be she.
> Venus I meane, the *well willy* planet.—*Id.*
>
> And all for my *gud wyll*,
> Y am in poynt for to spyll.—*Sir Amadas.*
>
> It semeth love is *wel willende*
> To him.—*Gower.*

Guid faith. In reality, truly. I need hardly say that *gude* and *guid* have the same meaning and pronunciation.

> I heartily could wish you all were gone,
> For if you stay, *good faith*, we are undone.
> Sir W. Davenant.

Guidfather and *guidmother.* Father and mother-in-law.

And it please your Grace, as touching the King your *goodfather*, etc.—*English Ambassador in Spain to Hen. VIII.*

Guidman and *guidwife.* The master and mistress of a house; *young guidman*, one newly married.

> My men should call me lord;
> I am your *goodman.*—*Shak.*
>
> Opon a day, in somers tyde,
> The *gudeman* went by the se-syde.—*The Seven Sages.*
>
> The *godewife* gan before him stand.—*Id.*

Gully, or *gullie.* A large knife. I believe that in Ayrshire *gullie* without any word prefixed always means a *clasp-knife.*

Gully, a common knife.—*Grose.*

Fair *gullies* are little haulch-backed demi-knives.—*Rabelais.*

Gulravage. Joyous mischief.—*Cunningham.* A noisy good-humoured frolic; a tumult; great disorder.—*Jamieson.*

Gumlie. Muddy.

Gumption. Common sense, understanding, talent.

Gumption, talent.—*Halliwell.*

Gawm, to understand, to comprehend. *Gawmless,* without understanding.—*Bamford.*

Gustifie. To give a relish. See under *moistify.*

The palate of this age *gusts* nothing high.—*L'Estrange.*

I shall *gust* it last.—*Shak.*

Gusty, gustfu'. Tasteful.

Gustful, tasteful, well-tasted.—*Johnson.*

Destroy all creatures for thy sport or *gust.*—*Pope.*

Gut-scraper. A fiddler.

Hang your songsters and *scrapers.*—*L'Estrange.*

Out steps Dick the draper,
And he bids, "Strike up *scraper,*
It's best to be dancing a little.—*Arthur O'Bradley.*
For know, thou wretch, that every string
Is a cat's *gut,* which art doth bring
Into a thread.—*The Muse's Recreation.*

I still am a merry *gut-scraper.*—*The Merry Beggars, quoted by Chambers.*

Gutcher. A grandfather, i.e., *guid-syre.*

Gutty. Fat, paunchy.

Burns says to Lapraik, "Till ye forget ye're auld and gutty." Allan Cunningham printed *gatty,* there being probably no such word, and said it means "failing in body." Chambers has *gutty,* which he explains gouty. Now, *gut* does mean gout, and the meaning may be gouty. But gout is a disease with which Lapraik, like farmers in general, and Ayrshire farmers in particular, who wrought and fed as their ploughmen did, was not likely to be troubled. In fact, when Burns, in his "Address to the Toothache," enumerates all the diseases, known to him which produce acute pain, he omits gout, which he certainly would not have done had he ever seen a friend afflicted with it. But Lapraik might well have been corpulent, and his obesity, which has always been a topic for a little good-humoured banter among friends, was more likely to be thus lightly referred to than so serious a malady as gout. And Burns could not but be aware that the *aqua vitae* that was to "make baith sae blythe and witty" was hardly a thing to prescribe for a gouty man.

Is not "auld and gutty" Chaucer's "hem that been *hore and round* of shape," or Falstaff's "There live not three good men unhanged in England; and one of them is *fat* and grows *old*"?

Sir Walter Scott makes Highland Dougal call the Glasgow magistrates—of whom the only one introduced in the novel is spoken of as "stout, short, and somewhat corpulent"—"filthy, *gutty* hallions." If he had meant gouty he would hardly have called them hallions, and if he had meant gluttonous, as the word filthy might suggest, Scott was too great a master of the vernacular not to have put into Dougal's mouth the stronger word *gutsy*.

I have found *gutty* only once in an E. author:—"I am punish'd for carrying the sick, the *gutty*, the lame, to church."— *L'Estrange.* Where this author certainly means gouty he spells it so, and here he may mean obese, for after saying a person was gutty, if he meant gouty, there was little need for adding that he was lame.

H.

Ha'. Hall. In Burns's poems, *ha'* means kitchen. For omission of *ll*, see under *a'*.

In "The Twa Dogs," the *ha'* folk are the servants, and in "Young Jockey who whistled at the gaud, fu' lightly danced he in the *ha'*," ha' is clearly the kitchen.

Ha'-Bible. The great Bible (sometimes called the *family* Bible), which lies in the hall.

Haddin. House, possession; a farm, lit. a holding. See under *haud*.

Holding, tenure, a farm.—*Johnson*. *Holdings* were plentiful.
Carew.

Hae. To have.

> I'll *ha* it proclaimed i' the fair.—*Ben Jonson*.
> Come, you shall *ha'* it.—*Shak*.

Hay any work for Cooper?—*Martin Marprelate Pamphlet*, 1589.
> I could *ha'* undertook to *ha'* kill'd a spider
> With less venom.—*Beaumont and Fletcher*.

Haen. Had; the participle, regularly formed from *hae*, as given from give.

Han, had.—*Bamford*.

Haet. A particle, smallest thing. *Fient haet*, a petty oath of negation, nothing.

In reference to what Burns calls a petty oath, the following extract may be of interest:—"This morning, being the 9th Jan., 1633, the King was pleased to call mee into his withdrawinge chamber, to the windowe, when he went over all that I had croste in Davenant's play-booke, and allowing of faith and slight to bee asseverations only, and no oathes, markt them to stande, and some other few things. The King is pleased to take faith, death, slight, for asseverations and no oathes, to which I doe humbly submit, as my master's judgment; but under favour, conceive them to be oathes."—*Sir Henry Herbert, Master of the Revels.*

Haffet.   The temple, the side of the head.
   Haffet, the forehead or temples.—*Halliwell.*

Hafflins.   Nearly half, partly.
      The leon shall restreyn his ire,
      And turne away *halfing* ashamed.—*Gower.*

Hag.   A scar or gulf in mosses and moors.
   Hag, a sink or mire in mosses : any broken ground.—*Halliwell.*
   This said, he led me over hoults and *hags*,
   Through thorns and bushes scant my legs I drew.—*Fairfax.*
   The mountain was full of bogs and *hags.*—*Swift.*

Haggis.   A kind of pudding boiled in the stomach of a cow or sheep.

The word haggis occurs frequently in E. literature, but as it has been thought to be a different article from that praised by Burns, it may be worth a little examination.

   They sent me word that I was like the first puffe of a *hagasse*, hottest at the first.—*Memoirs of Sir Robert Carey.*

This was no doubt a message of Scotsmen, but Carey evidently understood it, and does not seem to have thought that it required explanation to his countrymen. "The first puffe of a haggasse, hottest at first," is applicable only to the haggis described by Burns, and supposed to be peculiarly Scotch, and not at all to that of Johnson, "A mass of meat, generally pork, chopped, and enclosed in a membrane," in short, a sausage, as

Jamieson says. This passage from Carey, even if it stood alone, might justify us in concluding that *the* Haggis, the "Chieftain of the Puddin race," was once common to England and Scotland. But there is other evidence. Cotgrave, in his Dictionary, published 1632, has "*Gogue*, a sheep's paunch, and thence a *haggas* made of good hearbs, chopt lard, etc." "Thence a *haggas*" is worthy of notice. The ingredients of the pudding, which he describes at length, constitute the French dish, but because it is put in a sheep's paunch it becomes entitled to the English name, *haggas*.

"Our host then invites him to supper, and promises that he shall have a large pudding, a *round haggis*, etc."—*Warton*, who is speaking of a poem of Lydgate's which I have not seen. Now *haggises* are round, but not sausages.

Haggis, a sheep's maw filled with minced meat.—*Bailey.*

"*Hackin* (a word of similar origin with *haggis*), a pudding made in the maw of a sheep or hog. It was formerly a standard dish at Christmas," that is, in England.

Hail. Lead, small shot. *Hail-shot*, small shot scattered like hail.—*Johnson.*

Hain. To spare, to save. *Hain'd rig*, a portion of ground on which the grass has been preserved.

Hain, to save, to preserve. Hence, to exclude cattle from a field so that the grass may grow for hay.—*Halliwell.*

Hair. *Wi' the hair*, smoothly, gently; in accordance with one's humour.

But, Lord! to see how *against the hair* it is with these men, and everybody, to trust us and the King.—*Pepys.*

> He is merry *against the hair.*—*Shak.*

Some young people, when they read Burns's "Wicked strings of hemp or *hair*," or hear of persons so ingenious as to need only " a hair to make a tether," may require to be told that ropes used to be made of hair.

Hairst.   Harvest.   For omission of *v*, see under *ca'* and *gie*.

> *Harrest*, harvest.—*Exmoor. Grose.*

Hairum-scarum.   Hare-brained, unsteady.

> Who's there? I s'pose young *harum-scarum*.
> *Cambridge Facetiæ. Brewster.*
>
> *Hairum-scairum*, a wild fellow.—*Bamford.*
>
> If ever I venture my carcass on such a *harum-scarum* blood again my name is not Hawser Trunnion.—*Smollett.*
>
> Like a Marche *harum.*—*Skelton.*

Haith, a petty oath, faith.

Haivers.   Nonsense.

> *Haver*, to talk nonsense.—*Halliwell.*

Hal or *hald.*   An abiding place, a hold.

> They were bunden fast in *halde.*—*Ywain and Gawain.*
> And also for to fynd the *halde*
> That Sir Colgrevance of talde.—*Id.*
> He was *halden* an hali man.—*E. Metrical Homilies.*

Hale or *haill.*   Whole, tight, healthy.

> *Hale*, i.e., healed or whole.—*H. Tooke.*
>
> God, that for us sufferd wounde,
> Sen us to se him *hale* and sounde.—*Ywain and Gawain.*
> Soon he shall be fresh and *haile.*—*Rich. C. de Lion.*
>
> To Ypocras anon he sent, that he scholde come his sone to *hale.*
> *The Seven Sages.*

Hale and fier. Sound, healthy. See *fier.*

Halesome. Wholesome. *Hale* and *some.*

> No *halesome* breeze here ever blew.—*The Heir of Linne.*

Half-lang. Half grown, short.

Hallachores. See Burns's letter to Mr. Robert Aiken, 1786.

In a letter from a distinguished East Indian scholar, it is said " if *hallachores* is Hindustani, I should take it to be for *halālkhores*, sweepers, persons of the lowest caste, because every sort of food is lawful (*halāl*) for them."

Hallan. A particular partition wall in a cottage.

Hallan, partition between the door of a cottage and the fireplace.—*Scott.*

As neither of these definitions gives a very clear idea of a *hallan*, and as Jamieson's, though quite correct, does not give an account of all connected with it as referred to in "The Cottar's Saturday Night," at the risk of being accounted tedious, I shall endeavour to make it plainer.

The buildings of a farm generally, and those for cottagers always, even when the occupant was so near to the rank of farmer as to possess a cow, were always all in a line, and might be said to be under one roof. At the one end was the byre or cow-house, with a door in front for the entrance and exit of the cattle. Another front door admitted the household into the *trance*, or passage between the cow-house and the kitchen. On each side of the trance was a wall, more or less substantial according to the size of the holding or the liberality of the landlord. In the middle of each of these inside walls was a door, admitting, on the one side, to the kitchen, and, on the other, to the cow-house, so that inmates of the former could enter the latter without exposure to the weather. The wall which separated the kitchen from the *trance* was the *hallan*, and in inferior cottages this was the only inside wall.

As to the origin of the term, I do not think it needs to be sought in Gaelic, Su.-G., or any recondite quarter. That end of the row of building in which was the cow-house, was, and is still in many places, called the *byre-en*, and as the kitchen was the principal apartment in a farmer's or cottager's house, and the principal apartment was called the hall, the wall which separated it from the trance and byre came naturally and in the same way to be styled the *hall-end*, *hall-en*, *hallan*, and it was outside of this wall the Cottar's cow was placed—the Hawkie

> That 'yont the *hallan* snugly chows her cood.

Hallion. A clown, a clumsy fellow, etc.—*Jamieson.* A worthless fellow.—*Scott.*

Halion, a reprobate.—*Halliwell.*

Hallow-day. All Saints' Day.

Hallow-een. All-Hallows-Eve.

> Farewell, thou latter spring, farewell!
> *All-hallown* summer!—*Shak.*

My lord (Wolsey) sitting at dinner upon *All-hallowe'en* day.—*Cavendish's Narrative.*

We rede in olde tyme gode people wolde on *All-hallowe'en* daye bake brade and dele it for all crysten soules.—*Festyval. Ellis.*

Hallowmas. Same as *Hallow-day*. Why it should find a place in S. dictionaries and glossaries I cannot guess, but it is as difficult to understand how Allan Cunningham, a Scotsman, could say in his Life of Burns that Halloween "is the last night of harvest." *Halimas. Bailey.*

To speak puling like a beggar at *Hallowmas.*—*Shak.*

Haly. Holy.

The *hali* water and the cryce.—*Ywain and Gawain.*
Do nothing in *haly* churche
But that thou might by reson wirche.—*Gower.*
And many an ympne for your *haly* dayes.—*Chaucer.*

Hame. Home.

Men calle me Reynolde Grenelefe,
When I am at *hame.*—*R. Hood.*

Think on your love wherever she be,
And on your friends that are at *hame.*
 Sir Eger, Sir Graham, and Sir Gray Steel.

To grind our corn and carry it *hame* again.—*Chaucer.*
This lady was the same
That he had so dremyd of at *hame.*—*The Seven Sages.*

Hamely. Homely, affable.

Down he broght her till his hows,
Hamely as sho war his spows.—*The Seven Sages.*

Hand. Burns seems to use *left-hand* to signify wrong, bad, or incompetent. In "The Battle of Sherramuir" he says, "Their *left-hand* general had nae skill," and in the "Epitaph on Holy Willie," he fears his soul has taken "the left-hand road."

He had his Mittimus and took the *left-hand* road at parting.
 Quevedo. The Last Judgment.

Han' or *haun.* A hand, a person. For omission of *d* see under *afiel.*

And sighing sore her *haundes* she wrong and folde.—*Sackville.*
Now, O thou sacred Muse,
That warlike *handes* (men) ennoblest with immortal name.
 Spenser.

> Sendith (imp. send) ows, to gode *hans*,
> Ane thousand besans.—*Kyng Alisaunder*.

I am aware that *hans* sometimes means multitude, and that Weber says *gode hans* means in great quantity; but surely this was a strange expression to employ when specifying the exact sum to be sent, and I believe it means *by good hands*. *To* is used for *by*.—*Dr. Pauli*.

Hands. In Burns' letters "among my hands" occurs several times for "in or on my hands."

Hang. Used for hung in—

> On every blade the pearls *hang*.—*The Bonnie Lass o' Ballochmyle*.
> But a burde *hang* us beforn.—*Ywain and Gawain*.

Hangie. A name for the devil, found only in Burns, formed perhaps from hang, a very common word for damn. Or it may be meant to denote a hangman, as Burns speaks of him as doing the work of an executioner.

Han's breed. Hand's breadth. See *han* and *abreed*.

> He cleped a barber him before,
> That as a fool, he should be shore,
> All around like a frere,
> An *hand-brede* above the ear.—*Robert of Cyulle*.

Hansel. The first money drawn at market; new.

> *Hansel*, the money drawn upon the first sold of any commodity, or first in the morning.—*Bailey*.
>
> I'll *hansel* his woman's cloaths for him.—*Farquhar*.
>
> Hark! here comes *handsel*.—*Fletcher*.
>
> Geuen glotoun with glad chere good ale to *hansel*.
> *P. Plowman*.

Hantle. A considerable quantity.

> *Hantle*, a handful, much, many, a great quantity.—*Var. dial*. Halliwell.

Hap. An outer garment, mantle, plaid, etc. ; to wrap, to cover.

To *hap*, to cover or wrap warm with bed-clothes.—*Bailey*.

Happe, to cover for warmth.—*Grose*.

Your hede was wonte to be *happed* most drowpy and drowsy.---
Skelton.

Sche schall me bothe hodur and *happe.*—*Le Bone Florence of Rome.*

Hap. A. for *v.* See under *aff.*

They *hypped* on their staves.—*R. Hood.*

Hip, it may be remarked, rather than *hap*, is used in Ayrshire.

He came thedur with an evyll (disease)
Hyppyng on twa stares lyke the devyll.
Le Bone Florence of Rome.

It appears from this that the idea of a lame fiend had occurred to some one before Le Sage got it, for here we have "The Devil on Two Sticks."

Happer. The hopper of a mill.

Hap-shackled. Bound ; the legs on one side of an animal tied together so as to admit of walking with difficulty,—so called probably because an animal so bound has a kind of hopping motion.

To *hamshackle* a horse is to shackle his head to one of his forelegs.—*Dr. Brewster.*

Hap-step-an'-loup. Hop-skip-and-leap. See second *hap* and *loup.*

A *hop and step and jump* way of inditing,
My great and wise relation Pindar boasted.—*Dr. Wolcot.*

A *hop step and loup* on the head lands was often taken by the ploughmen.—*Richardson.*

Harigals. Heart, liver, and lights of an animal; the pluck.—*Jamieson.*

Harkit. Hearkened, listened.
> And pricking up his ears to *hark*
> If he cou'd hear too in the dark.—*Butler.*

Harn. Very coarse linen; cloth made of yarn spun of tow or the coarser part of flax.

Harn and *hearn*, coarse linen.—*Grose.*

In Northumberland a species of coarse linen is called *harn.*
Brand.

Has been. See under *gude.*

Hash. A sot, a term of contempt; a stupid fellow.

Hash, a sloven; one who talks *hash* or nonsense.—*Halliwell.*

I do not know if there is any connection between *hash* and *haskards*, a word used by one or two E. poets. There is at least a curious similarity in its use by Skelton and the Scottish poet. Burns says
> A set o' dull conceited *hashes*
> Think to climb Parnassus;

and Skelton, seeing a great number of people striving to enter the Court of the Queen of Fame, but who cannot get admission, asks the Queen who they are, and
> Forsothe, quod she, theys be *haskardis.*

Haslock woo. Wool of a sheep's throat, the finest wool. *H ause* and *woo.*

Haud. Hold; *hald* with the change of *l* into *u*, for which see under *a'*.

A hipping-hold or *hawd*, a place where people stay to chat when they are sent of an errand.—*Bailey.*

> He left her neane her bed to right,
> Nor neane for to *had* up her head.
> *The Northumberland Garland.* Ritson.

Hauf. Half.

Haugh. Low-lying rich lands, a valley.

Haugh, a green plat in a valley.—*Bailey.*
And came that night to Wooler *Haugh.*—*Battle of Flodden Field.*

Haurl. To drag, to peel. This is Burns's definition, and is evidently intended to cover *haurlin* in "Till skin in blypes came *haurlin,*" but the word has really nothing to do with peeling, but points to the force used.

Haurl, to drag or pull.—*Halliwell.*

Jamieson quotes the following from an E. author:

> To the grounde him caste,
> And *harlede* him vorth villiche.—*R. Glouc.*

Farquhar has *hurl* for strip or peel:

> We'll *hurl* off our cloaths.—*Sir Harry Wildair.*

Hause. To embrace. Literally to put the arms round the neck, from *hals*, the neck, by changing *al* into *au.* See *a'.*

Hause, the throat. *Hauze,* to hug or embrace.—*Grose.*

> I wolde be wreken on this wreeches,
> And don hem hongen bi the *hals.*—*P. Plowman.*

> Well were that lady myght stande in my grace,
> So I wolde *halse* her hartely.—*Skelton.*

> Instead of strokes, each other kissed glad
> And lovely *haulst,* from feare of treason free.—*Spenser.*

Haverel. A half-witted person, half-witted.

Haveril, one who havers.—*Dyce.* A half-fool.—*Halliwell.*

Haver or *hauver-meal.* Oatmeal. *Haversack* is in all E. dictionaries.

Haver, oats.—*Bailey. Johnson.*

Havers, oats. *Haver-*cake, oat-cake.—*Bamford.*

*Haver-*meal, oat-meal.—*Grose.*

A fewe cruddes and creem, and an *haver*-cake.—*P. Plowman.*

She beggers me with *haver* and hey.—*The Northumberland Garland. Ritson.*

Havins. Good manners, decorum, good sense.

Having, behaviour, regularity. This may possibly be the meaning here, i.e., in—

> He is of no *having*.—*Shak. Johnson.*

Surely *havings* in the following passage denotes mental qualities :—

> Lo ! this device was sent me from a nun,
> Or sister sanctified of holiest note ;
> Which late her noble suit in court did shun,
> Whose rarest *havings* made the blossoms dote,
> For she was sought by spirits of richest coat.
> *Shak. A Lover's Complaint.*

Havance, good manners.—*Devon. Grose.*

Havers, manners.——*Thoresby.*

> Sir, the first vertue certaine,
> The greatest, and most soveraigne
> That may be found in any man,
> For *having*, or for wit he can,
> That is his tongue to refraine.—*Chaucer.*

> That man—how dearly ever parted—
> How much in *having*, or without, or in.
> *Troilus and Cressida.*

Hawkie. A cow, properly one with a white face. I believe it is rather a name for a particular cow.

Hawkie, a white-cheeked cow.—*Halliwell.*

Hazle. Hazel.

Healsome. Healthful, wholesome. Another form of *halesome.*

> For seldom a man that has that held
> *Hele* has, and himself may weld.—*Pricke of Conscience.*
> And was comyn to seeke his *hele.*—*Le Bone Flo. of Rome.*
> He was your right good maister while he was in *heale.*
> *Ralph Roister Doister.*

Hearse. Hoarse. *A* for *o* as in *bane.*

Hase, hoarse.—*Ritson.*

> By speech might no man Gawain knaw,
> So was he *hase* and spak ful law.—*Ywain and Gawain.*

Heartie. Dim. of heart.

Heartsome. Cheerful.

Heartsome, merry, lively.—*Halliwell.*

Heather. Heath.

Hadder, heath or ling.—*Bailey.*

The summer will exhibit a more pleasing prospect, for all the *heather* or ling will be in full bloom.—*Rev. C. Dodgson to the Earl of Northumberland.*

He (Mr. Warburton, died 1753) ordered that his body should be inclosed in two coffins, one of lead, the other oak. The first he directed should be filled with green broom, *hather* or ling, which was brought from Epping Forest.—Noble's *History of the College of Arms.*

Hech. Oh! strange! This exclamation is usually printed *hech-ho* or *hech-how.*

> Alas for woe, why should it be soe?
> This makes a sorrowful *heigh-ho.*
> *King of Scots and Andrew Barton.*

> Of no man he had no care,
> But sung, *hey how,* away the mare.
> *The Frere and the Boye.*

They do now with more gaiety and security than ever, sing on a loud note that mad drunken catch, "Heigho! the Devil is dead!"
Dr. Henry More.

Hecht. To foretell or forebode something that is to be got or given, foretold, the thing foretold, promised, offered, threatened; to raise in price. *Ch* for *gh*, see under *fecht*.

> Then out bespoke that lady bright,
> Said, "Ye shall hold that ye have *hight*."—*Sir Amadas.*
> That seke monk *hiht* to come him to.—*E. Metrical Homilies.*
> This knight
> Said, he had hold his day as he had *hight*.—*Chaucer.*
> He schall hold all hys *heghtes*.—*Lybeaus Disconus.*

To *height*, to threaten.—*Thoresby.*

I shall hold my word and *behecht*.—*Sir Ralph Sadler's State Papers.*

Heckle. A board in which are placed a number of sharp pins, used in dressing hemp, flax, etc.

Heckle, an instrument for dressing flax.—*Bailey.*

Heckle and *heckler*.—*Grose.*

> Some laid to pledge
> Their *heckle* and their reel.—*Skelton.*

He balou. A lullaby.—*Jamieson.*

> You musicians, play *Balou!*—*Beaumont and Fletcher.*

Heels-owre-gowdie. Topsy-turvy.

The meaning of this combination of words, like topsy-turvy, which is used to explain it, can be known only by its context. What *gowdie* is, or whence it comes, nobody seems to know.

Heeze. To elevate, to raise. *E* for *oi* sound, as in—

> *Disleal* (disloyal) Knight whose coward courage chose
> To wreake itselfe on beast all innocent.—*Spenser.*

Heft. Haft. *E* for *a*. See under *beld*.

> Her oily side devours both blade and *heft*,
> And there his steel the bold Bermudan left.—*Waller.*

Heich, heigh. High. *A heigh house*, a house of more than one story.

> She is *heigh* beaute withouten pride.—*Chaucer.*
>
> Ther he lay to the larke song
> With notes newe, *hegh* up in the ayr.—*Lydgate.*
>
> Y-take thou schalt be, thurch londes lawe,
> And dempte *heigh* to hong!—*Amis and Amiloun.*

Hein-shinned. Having large projecting shin-bones.—*Jamieson.* Cor. perhaps from *hem-shinn'd*, q., having shins like *haims* or *hems*, i.e., projecting like an ox-collar.—*Longmuir.* In Cunningham's edition it is printed *hem-shinned*. A hem-shinned person is one whose ankles meet as *hems* do at the lower part. It may be as well to mention that *hames, haims,* or *hems*, is not another name for collar, as both Johnson and Jamieson say, but for two pieces of iron or wood placed on the collar which they surround like a hem. That hames and collars are not different words for the same things is shown by the following passage:—

He (the ploughman) shall make ready his collars, hames, treats, etc.—*Gervase Markham.*

Jamieson's mistake is curious. He defines "Brechame, the collar of a working horse" (draught horse), and in connection with *hems*, or *haims*, he quotes Douglas:

> Evir (ivory) *haims* convenient for sic note,
> And raw silk *brechamis* ouir halsis hingis—

making the "Boy-bishop" use two names for the same thing within two lines, if *brechams* and *haims* be both *collars*.

Hellim. Helm. Could Burns know that helm was once a dissyllable, *helma ?* Poets, especially comic poets, claim the liberty of lengthening or shortening words to suit their rhyme or rhythm.

Hent. To seize, to lay hold on.

> The frere to the busche wente,
> Up the byrde for to *hente.*—*The Frere and the Boye.*
>
> And of this crie ne wolde they never stenten,
> Till they the reines of his bridel *henten.*—*Chaucer.*
>
> His harmful Hatchet he *hent* in hand.—*Spenser.*
>
> And merrily *hent* the stile-a.—*Shak.*

Herd. To tend flocks, one who tends flocks.

Herd, a shepherd, or herdsman.—*Bailey.*

Herd is applied both to that which is guarded or kept, and him by whom it is guarded or kept.—*Horne Tooke.*

> There did they find
> The self-same flocks,
> The which, for want of *heards*, themselves they kept.
>
> *Spenser.*
>
> There n'as baillif, ne *herde*, ne other hine.—*Chaucer.*

"Till kye be gaun without the herd" means till, the crop being gathered, the cattle do not need to be watched, but are allowed to pasture on the whole farm. It may perhaps be necessary, for the sake of those who know Scotland only in its present improved condition, to say that in Burns's day there were very few hedges, on many farms none, so that a herd was always required. We do not hear of Burns having acted in this capacity, but his sister, Mrs. Begg, did.

Here awa', there awa'. Here and there, in this district and in that.

> They made more noise than if the king came *there away* with all his clarions.—*Cobbett's State Trials.*

O

Afterwards I went to Mansfield and *thereaway.*—*Journal of George Fox.*

Hern. A heron.

Hairon, a *herne; hern*shaw.—*Cotgrave.*

Hern, contracted from heron.—*Johnson.*

The melancholy *hern* stalks by.—*Song attributed to Prior. Ritson.*

At his siege the *hern,*
Observant stands to take his scaly prize.—*Somerville.*

Herry. To plunder, *most properly to plunder birds' nests.*

And sone assoyl him of his sin,
Hende God that *heried* hell.—*Minot.*

But cumly Crist, that *heried* hell,
Len the grace, that thou may spede
Of thine erand, als thou has nede.—*Ywain and Gawain.*

After them come a poor man making a hevie complainte that he was *hereyet* throw the courtiers taking his fewe in one place and his tackes in another.—*Sir William Ewrie to the Lord Privy Seal of England. 1540.*

Herryment. Plundering, devastation.

Hersel. Herself. *F* omitted as in—

Show *yoursell*
To all the shepherds.—*Ben Jonson.*

Het. Hot.

Her blushing *het* (did heat) her chamber.—*Chapman.*

That one me *hette,* that other did me colde.—*Chaucer.*

Limping Vulcan *het* an iron barr,
And furiously made at the god of warr.—*Old Tom of Bredlam.*

His brayne hath been too *het,*
And with good ale so wet.—*Doctour Double Ale.*

For whan that thai be *hett,*
And Asmodeus grett,
They take, as thei can get,
All fysche that comes to nett.—*Image of Ipocrisy.*

Heugh. A crag, a coal-pit.

Heugh, a rugged steep hill-side ; a ravine.—*Halliwell.*

> Word went east, and word went west,
>   And word is gone over the sea,
> That a Laidley-worm in Spindleston-*Heughs*
>   Would ruin the North Country.—*The Laidley Worm.*

Hide and Hair. The whole of any thing.

Hidin. Hiding ; *under hidin*, in concealment.

Hie (pronounced he). High ; *hie-gate,* high-way.

> This began on a Monday at morn,
>   In Cheviat the hillys so *he.*—*The Hunting of the Cheviat.*
>   *Ritson.*

> To encrese ther glorye and *hie* renoune.—*Lydgate.*

> The golden Phœbus, now ymounted *hic,*
> Hurled his beames.—*Spenser.*

> Tharin stode a towre full *hee,*
> Fairer saw he never with ee.—*The Two Dreams.*

Highlander. Lest Burns should be suspected of cannibalism when he says, "I have just despatched a well-lined rib of John Kirkpatrick's *Highlander,*" it may be as well to mention that a Highland bullock or cow is meant.

Hilch. To hobble, or halt.

Bossu, hulch-backt.—*Cotgrave.*

If Jamieson is correct in supposing that there is some connection—not in the words certainly—between *hilch* and *crouchie*, Cotgrave's *hulch* is in its proper place ; if not Burns is the only authority for the word.

Hiltie-skiltie. Confusedly. Supposed to be *helter-skelter,* which, like *skimble-skamble,* and a host of other words, has no meaning except what it derives from the context. *Hiltie-skiltie*, though a guess at its origin might be made, will probably be explained when we cease hearing that *helter-skelter*, from which it is thought to be corrupted, is formed from " *Heolster sceádo*, the darkness of Hell," or from " *hilariter-celeriter*, cheerfully, quickly."

Himsel. Himself. See *hersel.*

> Now nay, now nay, young Wharton said,
> Sir James Stewart that may not be,
> Unless we were drunkards and quarrelers,
> That had no care of our *sell*,
> Nor caring what we go about,
> Or whether our souls go to heaven or hell.
> *Stewart and Wharton. Ritson.*

Hiney. Honey; also a term of endearment. *I* for *o*. See *anither.*

> He calleth me
> His swetyng and his *hony*.—*Skelton.*
>
> She would me *hony* call.—*Wither.*
>
> To drenchen Alisoun, his *honey* deere.—*Chaucer.*

Hing. To hang.

> Some gnaw the snakes that on their shoulder *hing*.—*Fairfax.*
>
> About her middel twenty score
> Of horse halters and well mo
> There *hingen*.—*Gower.*
>
> Thar sho fyndes the faire lady
> *Hingand* hir hevyd ful drerely.—*Ywain and Gawain.*

Hirple. To walk crazily, to creep, to halt.

> *Herple*, to halt, or limp; "He coom *herplin* after."—*Bamford.*
> *Hirple*, to limp, or walk lame.—*Halliwell.*

Hirsel, hissel. So many cattle (or sheep) as one person can attend.

> *Hirsel*, a flock of sheep or lambs.—*Halliwell.*

Histie. Dry, chapt, barren.

Hitch. A loop, a knot; jerk, sharp movement.
  Hitch, to become entangled.—*Halliwell.*
  To *hitch* is to catch hold of any thing with a hook or rope.
  Bailey.
    Then he began to *hitch* his ear.—*R. Hood.*

Hither-and-yont. Disorderly.

Hizzie. Hussy, a young girl. *I* for *u,* and *z* for *s,* as in *bizz* and *bizzie.*

Hoddin (Hodding). The motion of a sage country man riding on a cart horse.

Bunyan has not the word, but he expresses the idea, showing that while he could picture the Slough of Despond and the Celestial City, he could enjoy and describe what he saw from the window of his prison. It is curious to note that both Burns and Bunyan use the same word, *sage,* in reference to the farmers.

  There's one (farmer) rides very sagely on the road,
  Shewing that he affects the gravest mode.—*Poem in Prison.*

Hoddin-gray. Cloth which has the natural colour of the wool. Perhaps from E. *hoiden,* rustic, clownish.—*Jamieson.* May it not be from Anglo-Saxon *húd,* pronounced *houd,* the hide or skin? As the thing is now unknown, the word is little used, indeed but for Burns it would be forgotten; but I have always heard it pronounced, by very old people, *houden.*
  Her *hoyden-grey* is turned into thirty-piled velvet.—*Don Quixote.*

Hoggie. Dim. of hog, a two-year-old sheep.
  Hog is used in Lincolnshire for a sheep of a certain age.
  Skinner. Johnson.

Hog, a young weather sheep.—*Bailey*.

Hogg-mutton, mutton of a year old sheep.—*Bamford*.

Hog-score. A kind of distance-line, in curling, drawn across the rink.

Hog-shouther. A kind of horse-play by jostling with the shoulder, to jostle. See *shouther*.

As the curling-stone which does not pass the *hog-score* is *pushed* aside, and *hog-shouther* means to *push* with the *shouther* or shoulder, it would seem that *hog* in both words means to push, and that it is a relation of *shog*.

Hole in a' your coats. An error in all your lives.

If I find a *hole in his coat*, I will tell him my mind.—*Shak*.

Hoodie-craw. A hooded crow, carrion-crow, corbie. See *craw*.

Hoodock.

This word is generally explained "miserly." Dr. Mackay objects to this, and says, "It is the French *duc*, an owl. Possibly the first syllable is the E. *hood*. The idea in Burns is that of a greedy bird, or harpy in a minor degree of voracity." Now, not to speak of the hybridism of E. *hood* and F. *duc*, to call people first harpies, vultures, and afterwards mousers, owls, is a bathos of a kind of which Burns could not be guilty. The truth is that very little is known of *hoodock*. Neither Jamieson nor Cunningham takes any notice of it. It is to be found only in Burns, and the only words that resemble it are Skelton's *hoddypeke*, or *huddypeke*, and Dunbar's *hudpikis*. In Skelton, one knave, Crafty Conveyance (i.e., *Skilful Thievery*), speaking of another, says

Can he play well at the *hoddypeke* ?

meaning, apparently, "Is he dexterous at cheating or stealing?" In "The Daunce," Dunbar has

> Catyvs, wretches, and ockerars,
> *Hudpikis*, hurders, and gatherers,
> All with this Warlo went;

that is, caitiffs, niggards, and usurers, hudpikis, erc., were the followers of covetousness. What sort of persons could *hudpikis* be to be fit associates for these characters? Evidently not bold villains, but mean cheats, deceivers, or thieves. If this is the proper interpretation of *hudpikis*, and if there is any connection between *hudpikis*, or *hoddypeke*, and *hoodock*, then Burns's

> The harpy, *hoodock*, purse-proud race

will mean extortioners, cheats, etc.

Hool. Outer skin or case.

Hule, hull or husk, as of corn.—*Bosworth.*

> Then pried he in prively and pertiliche bi-holdes
> Hou hertily the herdes wif *hules* (covers) that child.
> *William and the Werwolf.*

> And bad that counsell should be *hole.*—*Octovian Imperator.*

> The lady lyght on hire bedde,
> Y-*heoled* wel with silken webbe.—*Gest of Alexander. Warton.*

> Above and bynethe is heore *heolyng*
> With botemay, that wol clyng.—*Kyng Alisaunder.*

Hoolie. Slowly, leisurely; hoolie! take leisure! stop!

> When he was on the other side,
> Then fair and *hulie* could he ride.
> *Sir Eger, Sir Graham, and Sir Gray Steel.*

> Oh *hooly, hooly,* ran she up
> To the place where he was lying.—*Barbara Allan. Percy.*

Hooly, tenderly, gently.—*Halliwell.*

Hoord. A hoard, to hoard.

In which he found great store of *hoorded* treasure.—*Spenser.*

He taught men to *hoord* up treasure in heaven.—*De Mornay.*

They *hoorded* up the whole world in the storehouse of their memory.—*Id*.

Horn. A spoon (and comb) made of horn; a drinking vessel.

Horn for spoon is not in Jamieson, nor have I found any evidence of spoons being made of horn in England,* or in any country but Scotland and Alaska.

We found a few spoons made of the horn of the mountain sheep or goat.—*The great River of Alaska. The Century, Oct. 1885.*

Now cut up the haggis and bring me a *horn* spune.—*Local Historian's Table Book.*

Horn, signifying a comb, has also been denied a place in the great Scottish Dictionary. Burns has it in—

> Whare *horn* nor *bane* ne'er dare unsettle
> Your thick plantations.

Horn and *bane* mean a *redding kame* and a *bane kame*. The former is made of horn, whence its name, and the latter, made of bone, is the small tooth comb spoken of by Sidney Smith in his bitter article on the methodists.

His (a barber's) instrument contains his looking glass; a set of *horn*-combs with teeth on one side and wide for the combing and readyng of long, thick and strong heads of hair.—*Randle Holme.*

> Frout and spices sche hem bede,
> Wine to drink, wite and rede
> Bothe of coppe and *horn*.
> *Horne Childe and Maiden Rimnild.*

Hornie. One of the many names of the devil, from the horns he is supposed to wear when he makes himself visible.

> Wert thou the devil, and wor's it on thy *horn*,
> It should be challenged.—*Shak.*

> Had he no *horns* to push?
> As long as your two arms.—*Gam. Gurton's Needle.*

---

* Boswell tells us that Dr. Johnson, when in Scotland, collected "a number of curious things, particularly some *horn spoons.*"

GLOSSARY.   217

Hose. To tie one's hose. To fetter, to imprison.

Host or *hoast.* To cough.
  Houst, to cough. *Haust or hoste,* a dry cough.—*Bailey.*
  Hoast and *host,* cough.—*Thoresby.*
  Host, a cough.—*Palmer.*
  In the winter-time she took a *hoast.*—*The Northumb. Garland.*
  Ritson.

Bosworth evidently thought *host* an E. word; he says, "*Hwóstan,* to *host,* to cough."

Hotch. To shake, to move.
  Hotchin, to keep shifting as if uneasy.—*Bamford.*

Hotch-pot, flesh cut into small pieces, and sodden with herbs or roots. Hence metaphorically (in law) it signifies the putting together of lands, for the equal division of them.—*Bailey.* The metaphorical use of the word cannot be supposed to refer to the cutting or seething, but to the shaking together.

Hotch seems to be only another form of *hitch,* which, says Bailey, is "to wriggle or move by degrees." *Hocher,* Fr. to shake.

Houghmagandie. Fornication.

On this word in his glossary to the first edition of his poems, Burns has the only piece of pure nonsense which I believe he ever printed, but as he left it out in the Edinburgh edition, it is not fair to reproduce it as is sometimes done.

The meaning which Burns has given to *houghmagandie,* whatever the word itself may signify, will for ever cling to it. It is not in Jamieson's dictionary, but is in Longmuir's abridgement of it. It occurs in a volume of poems, and I believe only there, from which Jamieson has made a number of quotations, more, perhaps, than the size or merit of the work justifies. It may therefore be inferred that he did not think it a word having any fixed or definite meaning, and, supposing it to be one of those words that spring up nobody knows whence or how, and that perish in a few weeks unless saved by their adoption by a man of genius, omitted it as unworthy of a place in his great work. But Burns has made it live. Some have thought it was his own creation, but it was used as the name of a tune before his day.

> Play up "Sae merry as ye hae been ";
> Or "Sups of Brandy";
> Or "Gin the kirk wad lat's alane,"
> Or "Houghmagandy."
> *Poems in the Buchan Dialect.*

Houlet or *howlet.*

Eies they have red like *houlets.*—*Philemon Holland.*

There were three fools fell out about an *houlet.*
The Two Noble Kinsmen.

It shall be convey'd in at *howlet* time.—*Middleton.*

I'll sit in a barn with madge-*howlet* and catch mice first.
Ben Jonson.

Houp. Hope. *Ou* or *ow* for *o*, as in—

Taking from her hand a ring of *gould.*—*Spenser.*

She was so diligent withouten *slowth.*—*Chaucer.*

On foure thousand Y hadde ynowe,
To awreke my *wowe* (woe).—*Kyng Alisaunder.*

I should rejoice to hear your desire in seeing me, but I desire to submit to the providens of God, *houping* the Lord will in his good time bring us together again to the praise of his name.—*Mrs. Oliver Cromwell to her husband.*

Housie. Dim. of house.

Hove. To heave, to swell.

Amyd her treasure and wavering richesse,
  Proudly she *hoveth* as lady and empresse.—*Sir T. More.*

Essex was afraid lest the acclamations of the people should have *hoven* him up.—*Memoirs of the Court of Q. Elizabeth.*

  The arc *hoven* watz on hyghe.—*Early E. Alliterative Poems.*
  Hoven-cheese, that is swelled up.—*Bailey.*

Howdie.   A midwife.

In the North of England a midwife is called a *Howdy* or *Howdie-wife.*—*Ellis.*

Howdy, a midwife.—*Grose.*

He (the Bar-guest, a sort of brownie) was a constant attendant on the *howdy* or midwife.—*Richardson.*

Howe.   Hollow, a hollow or dell.

How, deep, or low, hollow.—*Halliwell.*
  They started at neither *how* nor height.—*R. Hood.*

Howe-backit.   Sunk in the back, spoken of a horse, etc.
Howe and *back.*

Howff.   A place of resort.

Hóf (probably sounded *hoof*), a palace, house, dwelling.—*Bosworth.*

And as a house is a place where one remains this may be the root of *hove* and *hover*, stay or tarry.

When Robert the Bruce saw this mischief, and gan to flee, and *hov'd* him (went to some *howff*) that men might not him find.—*MS. in Brit. Mus. quoted by Ritson.*

Howk.   To dig.
Howk, to dig, to scoop.—*Halliwell.*

Hoy.   To urge incessantly.

Hoi, a word used in driving hogs.—*Minshew quoted by Dyce.*
  Such tunges shulde be torne out by the harde rootes,
  Hoyning like hogges that groynis and wrotes.—*Skelton.*

Hoyn here has exactly the meaning of *hoy*, for it does not refer to the kind of noise made by hogs, that is expressed by *groynes*, i.e., grunts, but to its constancy, its iteration.

Hooi, a sound used by shepherds to direct their dogs to drive away the sheep.—*Dr. Adair*.

Hoyse.   A pull upwards.

> I *hoyse* up my sail.—*Damon and Pithias*.
> Some *hoyse* their heels upward.—*New Custom*.
> We *hoyse* up mast and sayle.
>
> *The Mirrour for Magistrates.*
>
> He, mistrusting them,
> *Hois'd* sail, and made his course again for Bretagne.
> *Shak.*

Hoyte.   To amble crazily, a motion between a trot and a gallop.

> There he drinks and *hoits*.—*B. and Fletcher*.

Huchyal.   To hobble. Evidently connected with *hough* with a guttural sound.

To *huckle*, to hamstring (which would cause to huchyal).

Skinner.

Hochel, to walk awkwardly, or lamely.—*Grose*.

Scottish writers sometimes spell hough, *houch;*

> His *houch* senons thai cuttyt in that press.
> *Blind Harry's* "*Wallace*."

Hughoc.   Dim. of Hugh.

Hunders.   Hundreds.

Huird.   To hoard.   *U* for *o*, as in—

> But a *burde* (board) hang us beforn.—*Ywain and Gawain*.
> (Seneca) Chees in a bathe to die in this manere,
>   Rather than han another *turmentise* (torment).
>
> *Chaucer.*

In some editions we read in " The Kirk's Alarm "—

> Singet Sawney, are ye *herding* the penny?

Other editions have *hurding*.

Hunker. To bend the body backward from the knees; *hunkers*, position of the body so bent.

"To hunker" is to adopt the attitude of warriors depicted as in an ambush on archaic Greek vases—at least that is the most dignified description we can give of the position of him who hunkers.—*Saturday Review, May, 1883.*

Those who may not be familiar with Greek vases, may like to see how the Grecian poet describes a warrior *hunkering*.

> (He) croucheth curiously
> On his bent haunches.—*Iliad. Chapman.*
> (He) sits low-crouching on his hams.—*Cowper.*

Hurcheon. A hedge-hog.

> And there ben also *Urchounes* als grete as wylde Swyn here.
> *Maundeville.*

> Like sharpe *urchons* his haire was grow.—*Chaucer.*

Hurchin. Urchin, pigmy, little. The *h* is not easily accounted for.

Urchin is in all E. dictionaries, and is applied to Cupid, as Burns applies *hurchin*.

> Pleas'd Cupid heard, and check'd his mother's pride,
> "And who's blind now, mamma?" the *urchin* cried.
> *Prior.*

Hurdies. The loins, the crupper, the hips.

Hurl. To ride in a carriage.

Hushion. A cushion; a stocking wanting the foot, more correctly—wanting the sole.

A *hushion* by the editors of Burns has been always spoken of as a footless stocking, i.e., a stocking leg. That was, for I hope its day is past as an article of apparel, a *hogger*, or *hugger*, cocker, as it was called in some parts of England, A hushion wanting only the sole and being fastened to the toes protected to some extent the upper part of the foot, and gave the wearer a certain superiority over one who was reduced to the hugger.

How a hushion ever came to be thought a cushion I cannot understand. It would be very difficult to make any person who gives a moment's thought to the subject believe that the line in which the word occurs would be better thus: "She dights (wipes) her grunzie (mouth) wi' a cushion," or that the poet, if he had meant a cushion, would not have said so seeing it makes as good a rhyme as *hushion*. The thing is absurd. It is the poet's intention to represent the woman as "no sae trig," so neat, so cleanly as the cat, and as evidence of her inferiority in this respect, and as a very climax of filthiness she wipes her face with a cushion! If Willie Wastle, her husband, who "was a wabster guid," had taken his *pirn-box* to pare his nails, or his shuttle to shave his beard, we should have said he was not skilful in adapting means to ends, not that he was dirty, and if his wife had wiped her face with a cushion we should have thought her equally unskilful, but should not have called her a slattern, whereas if she kept two or three cows, for Linkumdoddie was doubtless some country village, or pigs, or even hens, and used her *hushion* as a towel, we should have decided at once that if any person "gied a button for her" he had a dear bargain.

Willie Wastle's wife had a prototype in Maude Prate-fast, who loved cleanliness and kept her dishes from all foulness:

> And when she laked clowtes withouten fayle
> She wyped her dishes with her dogges tayle.
> *Stephen Hawes.*

His hosen overhongen his *hokschynes* on euerice a side.
Peres the Ploughman's Crede. Skeat.

Hyte. Angry, mad.

Anglo-Saxon, *héte*, hate, hatred, indignation.—*Bosworth.*

I.

Icker. An ear of corn.

> For they woneth in water, y-wis,
> With *eker* (in one MS. *icker*) and fysch.
> He say (saw) the *ekeris wonynge.*—*Kyng Alisaunder.*

Weber, the editor of this old romance, says, "Eker, watercresses. It may in a more general sense mean weeds." I believe he might have said vegetables. It is in reality *acre*, a field, or *aecer*, the word from which acre with its present meaning has sprung. Ecker seems in English, as distinguished from Anglo-Saxon, to have first signified a vegetable, and then, by a law which, though not so obvious as that under which words degenerate, is as certain, it rose to signify the best part of vegetables, that for which they are cultivated. As an example of this process in a similar word let us take crop, which in Chaucer and Gower means the top of a plant, then the part above ground.

> And ye that ben of beautie *croppe* and root.—*Chaucer.*

Another step was taken when it came to signify the whole produce of a field or farm.

It would seem, I write under correction, that with regard to *icker* this process had begun even in Anglo-Saxon times, for while at one time *aecer* was "a field, land, any thing sown, sown corn, an acre," a little later *æchir*, the same word, had come to mean an ear of corn.

Ier oe. A great-grandchild. Literally, *a grandchild's heir*; from *oe*, a grandchild, and *eer*, an heir.

Oye, a grandchild.—*Halliwell.*

Gif toward Edgar Atheling eni is herte drou,
That was kinde *eir* of this londe hun huld him tho stille.
Rob. of Gloucester.

Ignis fatuus. Will o' the wisp; pl. *ignes fatui*.

If I did not think thou hadst been an *ignis fatuus*, or a ball of wild fire, there's no purchase in money.—*Shak.*

Conjecture, that *ignis fatuus*.—*Churchill.*

Ilk, or *ilka*. Each every.

Of good wine *ilk* man drank a draught.—*R. C. de Lion.*

Stones on *ilka* side.—*Emare.*

Of mouth of childer and soukand
Made thou lof in *ilka* land.—*Metrical E. Psalter.*

Ill-deedie. Mischievous, doing evil deeds.

Deedy, industrious, notable.—*Berks. Halliwell.*

He performed all the manœuvres of a *deedy* battle.—*Cowper.*

Ill-thief. The devil.

The old sacrilegious *theife* when he first tooke possession of thy temple brake in at these windowes.—*W. Streat. Palmer.*

Ill-willie. Ill-natured, malicious, niggardly, unkind.

We on our behalfe shalle be *welle willyng*.—*Lord Grey de Ruthyn.*
Venus, I meane, the *well willy* planete.—*Chaucer.*

Malivole, ill-willie, malicious.—*Cotgrave.*

The loving present of your heartie *well-willer.*—*Rich. Stanihurst.*

Sure you have some *ill-willers.*—*Beaumont and Fletcher.*

Imprimis.   In the first place.

A gentle *imprimis.*—*Massinger.*

Imprimis, I covenant that your acquaintance shall be general.
Congreve.

Incog.   Incognito, disguised,

Incog, unknown, in private.—*Johnson.*

But if you're rough, and use him like a dog, depend upon it, he'll remain *incog.*—*Addison. Johnson.*

Some words are hitherto but fairly split, as *incog*, &c.—*The Tatler.*

In order to remain *incog*,
They always travel in a fog.—*Churchill.*

To bear me hence with many a jog,
From thee my charming dear *incog.*—*Farquhar.*

Indent.   To contract, to bargain.

This is a strange juggler;
Neither *indent* before-hand for his payment,
Nor know the breadth o' th' business.—*Fletcher.*

Shall we buy treason? and *indent* with fears,
When they have lost and forfeited themselves?—*Shak.*

Indite.   To indict, to accuse.   *C* in words formed from *dicto* are often omitted.

They *enderdyted* his land, as the cronicle sayeth, Lady, Lady.
A Newe Ballade.

The Deuyll is *endited.*—*An. Bal. and Broadsides.*

'Twas a rogue
That knew me, and set on by the old Lady;
I'll *indite* him for it.
The Night-walker.   Fletcher and Shirley.

He is for this, I hear, *indited.*
A Hymne to the Gentle Craft.

Jelous the Jayler bound mee fast,
To heare the *verdite* (verdict) of the byll.—*Gascoigne.*

Ingine. Genius, ingenuity. Bailey and Johnson have *ingeny* in this sense. See *engine.*

If thy master be angry with thee I shall suspect his *ingine.*
Ben Jonson.

Ingle. Fire, fire-place; *ingle-cheek,* fireside.

Ingle, fire or flame.—*Grose.*

Engle, or *Ingle*-wood signifies wood for firing.—*Percy.* But it should rather seem to design a wood in which extraordinary fires were made on particular occasions. *Ingleborough* has obtained this name from the fires anciently lighted in the beacon erected on its flat top.

Ritson.

Ingrate. Ungrateful.

Perfidious and *ingrate!*—*Pope.*

Yet 'twere *ingrate* to charge thee with delay.
Clement Barksdale.

Integritive. Honest, with integrity.

Intermingledoms. Entanglements, complications.

Irish blackguard. A kind of snuff so called.

'Tis *blackguard* I like best; them brown snuffs ruin the nose entirely.—*Lever.*

I'se. I shall or will.

I'se try whether your costard or my ballow be the harder.—*Shak.*

Thou'se pay for all.

I'se teche thee a sluttish coy.—*Gammer Gurton's Needle.*

I'se an honest lad as well as another.—*Vanbrugh.*

He's buy me a white cut, forth for to ride,

And I'll go seek him thro' the world that is so wide.
The Two Noble Kinsmen.

Ither.   Other, one another.   See *anither.*

J.

Jad.   Jade; also a familiar term, among country folks, for a giddy young girl; *ă* for *ā.* as in—

>   Mercy on's, a *barn;* a very pretty *barn!—Shak.*

This is evidently intended to be pronounced as *barn,* a granary, and not as *bairn,* for we find, " he shall lack no barns" (with a quibble), as Douce remarks,—pronouncing the two words in the same manner.

Jade, a young woman; in irony and slight contempt.—*Johnson.*

Let the *jade* look to her quarters.—*Vanbrugh.*

A sullen *jade.—Farquhar.*

Spoken by two fathers of two daughters, respectable young women.

Jag.   Prick.

And I saw the *jagges* turn all to addres, to dragons, and todes, and many other orrible bestes, sowking hem, and bitying hem.—
Vision of William Staunton.

Chiquiter, to cut, gash, *jag.—Cotgrave.*

Janwar.   January.

>   Time sure hath wheel'd about this year,
>   December meeting *Janiveer.—Cleveland.*

The month is *Februar.—Gower.*

Jauk.   To dally at work, to trifle.

Jauner.   Idle talk.

Jauntie.   Dim of jaunt, an excursion.

Jaup. A jerk of water, to jerk as agitated water.

Jaup, to splash.—*Halliwell.*

Jaw. Coarse raillery; to pour out, to spurt, to jerk out, as water.

Jaw, the mouth.—*Johnson.* Jaw, in this sense, naturally came to signify what it gives forth or causes.

Hod (hold) your *jaw!* — *Specimen of Durham Language. Richardson.*

Jaw, coarse idle language.—*Var. Dial. Halliwell.*

Jee. To move. This is the word which drivers use when they wish their horses to come more to the left side—that is, nearer. This is the sense in which it is used in "The Vision." See *ajee.*

> But change o' place, and change o' folk,
> May gar thy fancy *jee.*—*Miss Blamire.*

Jenny. Dim. of Janet.

For love of *Jenny,* that faire bonny bell.—*Old Play. Ritson.*
Jenny-wren, a fine song bird.—*Bailey.*

Jillet. A jilt, a giddy girl.

Jill, flirt, a sorry wench, an idle girl.—*Bailey.*

I would have you my-selfe, and a strawe for yond *Gill.*
Gam. Gurton's Needle.

Jimp. To jump, slender in the waist, handsome.

Jimp, neat, tidy.—*Bamford.*

Jimply. Slenderly, tightly, neatly.

Jimps. A kind of easy stays, open before, worn by nurses.—*Jamieson.*

Jump, a kind of loose or limber stays worn by sickly ladies.—
Johnson.

> A weeping Cassock scar'd into a *jump*.—*Cleveland*.
> She scorns the pride of pinching stays or *jumps*.—*Wolcot*.

Jing. A petty oath. Another form of *jingo*.

> One of them, I thought, expressed her sentiments in a very coarse manner when she observed, that, by the living *jingo*, she was all of a muck of sweat.—*Goldsmith*.

> > In haste he to the fire applies it,
> > And turns it round and round, and eyes it,
> > Heigh, *jingo!* worse than 'twas before.—*Fenton*.

Jink. To dodge, to turn a corner; a sudden turning a corner, to move quickly.

Jinker. That turns quickly; a gay sprightly girl, a wag. In prose, *jinker* has only the first meaning.

Jirk. A jerk. *I* for *e*, as in—

> > Thi *tixt* (text) telleth the nought so.—*P. Plowman*.

> > She hath now caught a thorn
> > She shall nat pull it out this next *wike* (week).—*Chaucer*.

Jirkinet. Dim. of jerkin. "A sort of bodice without whalebone, worn by females as a substitute for stays."
Jamieson.

That women wore jerkins is proved by the following—

> > What be they? women? masking in mens weedes?
> > With dutchkin dublets, and with *Ierkins* jaggde?
> > They be so sure, even *Wo* to Men in dede.
> >
> > *George Gascoigne.*

Jirt. A jerk.

Jert, to jerk, to throw a stone by jerking.—*Bamford*.

Jo. Sweetheart, joy, delight.

> > Jocky my jo,
> > To summond our kynge—why dyd ye so?—*Skelton*.

This shows that, if not an English word, it was at least known in England in Henry VIII.'s time.

Jocteleg. A kind of knife.—*Burns.* A clasp-knife.—*Scott.*

Jack-o'-legs, a clasp knife.—*Grose. Jack-a-legs.—Palmer.*

Jorum. A drinking vessel, its contents.

Joram, a large dish or jug of any eatables or liquids.—*Var. dial. Halliwell.*

> Now, Hark to Winchester! we'll sing
> And push about the *Jorum.*
> *The Bishopric Garland. Ritson.*

Jouk. To stoop, to bend the head, to elude.

Jook, to crouch suddenly.—*Halliwell.*

Jow. A verb which includes both the swinging motion and pealing sound of a large bell.—*Burns.*

> And every *jow* the deid-bell gied
> Cried woe to Barbara Allan.—*Percy's Reliques.*

Jowler. The name of a hunting dog or beagle.—*Johnson.*

It has been lately argued that *jowler* means a cudgel. If so, it must be a most remarkable one, for Burns speaks of it in his "Address to Beelzebub" as a fierce growler.

> See him drag his feeble legs about,
> Like hounds ill-coupled; *jowler* lugs him still
> Through hedges, ditches, and through all this ill.
> *Dryden.*

It seems to have been a name not only for a kind of dog, but of an individual.

Joular, there boy. *Joular*, tinker, pedlar, etc.—*Vanbrugh.*

Jundie. To justle, a push aside. Jamieson seems to think this word is connected with *shunt.* "Bailey mentions *shunt* as an E. word signifying to *shove.*"—*Jamieson.*

K.

Kae. A daw.

Kail. Coleworts, a kind of broth.

Kell, a sort of pottage.—*Ainsworth.*

Cole, *keal*, or *kail*, broth.—*Grose.*

Sorbition, a supping; also broth, *cale*, pottage.—*Cotgrave.*

Mother Jenkinson won't furnish me with *cale* and bacon on Christmas day.—*Swift.*

This bogle was a perfect plague to the servant-girls . . during their absence overturning the *kail*-pot, etc.—*Richardson's Table Book.*

> Not worth a shyttel-cocke,
> Nor worth a soure *calstocke*.—*Skelton.*

Kail-blade. A leaf of colewort.

Kail-runt. The stem of the colewort.

Kail-time. Dinner-time.

> 'Tis *pudding-time*, wench, 'tis *pudding-time*.
> *A Match at Midnight.*

Kain and *kane.* Fowls, etc. paid as rent by a farmer.

Kain, rent paid in kind.—*East. Halliwell.*

It would appear from the following lines that it was something different from rent:—

> And when the tenantes come to paie their quarter's rent,
> They bring some fowl at Midsummer, a dish of fish in Lent;
> At Christmasse a capon, at Michaelmasse a goose,
> And something else at New-yere's tide, for feare their lease flee loose.—*George Gascoigne.*

Kame. A comb.

Kame.—*Bamford.*

> And on their heads with long locks comely *kemd*,
> They wore rich mitres.—*Spenser*.

Thou playest the babe, who thinkes his Nurse does him wrong when she *kemes* his hair.—*De Mornay*.

Kebar. A rafter.

Kebbuck. A cheese. *Kebbuck-heel*, end of a cheese, a large piece.

The crustie *heel* of a loaf.—*Cotgrave*.

According to Sir W. Scott a kebbuck is not any kind of cheese, but one made with ewe-milk mixed with cow's-milk.—*Old Mortality*.

Keckle. A laugh; to laugh, to cackle. *E* for *a*. See *beld*.

If *keckle* be *cackle*, as I suppose there is no doubt, the change of *a* into *e* rendered the retention of *c* undesirable, as the word might have been sounded *seckle*.

Keckle, to laugh violently. *Yorksh.*—*Halliwell*.
To prate.—*Bamford*.

Keek. A peep, to peep.

Keikert (of *kiecken*, to see), stared.—*Bailey*.
Keek, to peep, to look slily.—*Halliwell*.

> This Nicholas sat ever gaping upright,
> As he had *kyked* on the newe mone.—*Chaucer*.

> The Robin came to the wren's nest
> And *keeked* in.—*Nursery Rhymes of England*.

Keekin' glass. A mirror.

Keel. Red clay. Ruddle for sheep.—*Halliwell*.

Kelpie. A sort of mischievous spirit, said to haunt fords and ferries at night, especially in storms.

> I lie weltering on the osier'd shore,
> Drown'd by the *kelpie's* wrath, nor e'er shall see thee more.
> *Collins.*

Ken. To know, knowledge, sight.

They talk of witty conceits, and I *ken* not what a deal of prittle-prattle.—*The Muse's Looking-glass.*

> For the luf of symple men,
> That strange Inglis cannot *ken*.—*Rob. of Brunne.*
> Of whence? I *ken* not yet, sir.—*Fletcher.*
> None alive did better *ken* the secretary's craft.—*Fuller.*
> Within a *ken* our army lies.—*Shak.*

Kennin. A small matter, a little.

Kennin, a measure.—*Grose.*

By laws made in the time of Rich. I., "when a vessel arrived at her port of discharge, she was to be hauled up on dry ground, the sails taken down, and everything properly stowed away; and then the master ought to consider an increase of wages '*kenning by kenning*.'"—*Lindsay's History of Merchant Shipping.*

My friends, I see land! Pluck up a good spirit, boys, it is within a *kenning*.—*Rabelais. Motteux.*

> An old *kenning* Edward Hall gave her
> Of comforts the choicest and best.
> *The Northumberland Garland. Ritson.*
> Even within our *kenning*.—*Holland's Pliny.*

Kenspeckle. Well known, easily known, having some peculiarity.

Ken-specked, marked or branded.—*Bailey.*
Kenspeckled, speckled or marked so as to be conspicuous.
—*Halliwell.*

Kep. To catch.

Kep, to catch a ball.—*Grose.* To *kep* a ball, to catch it, or keep it from falling.—*Bailey.*

> These sely clerkes rennen up and doun
> With *kepe, kepe ;* stand, stand ; jossa, warderere,*
> Ga whistle thou, and I shal *kepe* him here.—*Chaucer.*

The editors of Chaucer translate *kepe*, care, attention, to take care. But the passage will not make sense with any of these meanings. To a Scotsman, it is quite clear, and most graphic. The young men are in chase of their horse, and cry to each other, "Kep! kep!" that is, catch or intercept.

The same meaning with the same spelling is found elsewhere:

> But sune King Edward came full still,
> When that he trowed no harm him till
> And *keped* him in the berde.—*Minot.*
> This schip ful gret waves *kepes.*——*E. Metrical Homilies.*
> And hastily that lady hende
> Cumand al her men to wende,
> And dight thaim in thair best array,
> To *kepe* the king that ilk day.—*Ywain and Gawain.*
> Of suche strokes *kepe* I no mo.—*Rich. C. de Lion.*
> The knyght him *keped* ful curtaysly.—*The Two Dreams.*

Ket. A matted, hairy fleece of wool.

Kettle. By *kettle*, which he also calls his "auld mither's pot," Burns means distillation.

Kiaugh. Carking anxiety.

Killie. Kilmarnock.

---

* Though it is going out of my way, I cannot help saying that it might save some trouble to students of Chaucer, if, seeing that "Stand, stand, Jossa," are spoken to the horse, they assumed that "warderere" is also addressed to him, and that it is his name. Who ever tried to catch a horse without calling him by his name, if it was known?

Kiln. A place for preparing grain for grinding. This word has no right to be put here were it not for the fact that in "Hallowe'en" it is spoken of as an appendage to a farm-house instead of a mill, where, I believe, it is only found at present. In the time of Burns, and considerably later, farmers used to *kiln-dry* their grain at home and take it to the mill ready for grinding. Ford, in the "Merry Wives of Windsor," is certainly not a miller, and yet his wife bids Falstaff "Creep into the *kiln-hole.*"

Kiln-pat. Kiln-pot, the empty space under the plates, by millers called the *kiln-head,* on which the grain to be dried is laid. This I take to be Shakspeare's *kiln-hole.*

Kilt. To turn up the clothes.

   Kilt, to tuck up the clothes.—*Halliwell.*

The work *kilt* is Gothic, and used in England and the Lowlands of Scotland to designate the peculiar petticoat worn by the Scotch.—*Edwards.*

   In borrow'd shoes she's *kilted.*—*Ritson.*

Kimmer. A young girl, a gossip.

Kin. Kindred.

>Others in their distress do aid implore
>Of *kin* and friends (i.e., of *kith* and *kin*).—*Fairfax.*

See *kith.*

Kin'. Kind, adj. *D* omitted. See under *afiel',* and in

In the summer they lanced the *rine* (rind) with a stone.—*Sandys's Travels.*

>Of exalacion I finde
>Fire *kinled* of the same kind.—*Gower.*

Kind. Kind, sort. The phrase "Of a' kind coin," meaning, of every kind of coin, has been called a Scotticism, but there is English authority for it.

> Folk was ful fre to fond,
> And brought hem anough to hond
> > Of *al kines thing.—Amis and Amiloun.*
>
> Nought for to borwe of him *no kyn monay.*
> > > > *Wright's Chaucer.*
>
> What *kins thing* is kind? quod I.—*P. Plowman.*

Kind. Nature, in "A woman has't by *kind.*"
> Formed by *kind* for rape and villany.—*Shak.*
> For no man may fordo the law of *kind.—Chaucer.*

King's hood. A certain part of the entrails of an ox, etc. (from its supposed resemblance to some puckered head-dress formerly worn by persons of rank).—*Jamieson.* Literally, a covering for a king's head.

Kintra, kintrie. Country. See *Countra.*

Kintra-side. A district.
> Menstrelles, that walken far and wyde,
> Her and ther in every a *syde,*
> > In mony a dyverse londe.—*Emare.*
>
> The word of hire sprong ful wyde,
> Fer and ner, bi uche a *syde.*—*The King of Tars.*
>
> He let cry in every *syde,*
> > Bothe in felde and towne.—*The Erle of Tolous.*
>
> He dwellyd be Kardyfe *side.—Sir Cleges.*

Kipper. Salmon cured. A.-S. *cypera.*

Kirk. A church.
> The kyng and his knightes to the *kirke* wente.—*P. Plowman.*
> Sone unto the *kirk* thai went.—*Ywain and Gawain.*
> And he herd fra his hali *kirke* mi steuen.—*Metrical E. Psalter.*

Kirk-hammer. Tongue of a church-bell.

Kirn. The harvest supper; a churn, to churn. *Kirn,* meaning churn, is a change of *k* for *ch.* See *birk.*

Kern. This Northern word is plainly a corruption of *corn* baby or image, as is the *kern* supper, of corn supper. In Cornwall people speak of an ill *kerned,* or saved harvest.—*Every Day Book.*

I should have thought that most certainly *kern* supper was no more than corn supper, had not (Eugene) Aram asserted that it was called the churn supper because from immemorial times it was customary to produce in a churn a great quantity of cream, and to circulate it in cups to each of the rustic company, to be eaten with bread.—*Brand.*

The word and the thing, it appears, were once known in England. The word, thanks chiefly to Burns, is alive in Scotland, but the "jovial, rantin' kirn" is dead and gone. *

The Foreman in Nature's shop, the Sune, turned and *kerned* from water into salt.—*Purchas his Pilgrimage.*

Kirsen. To christen.

Kersn or *kersen,* to christen.—*Bamford.*

Are they *cursen'd?* No, they call them infidels. One goodman Ceasar *kersen'd* him.—*Beaumont and Fletcher.*

    I cannot tell
If mine were *kyrsen'd* or no.—*Ben Jonson.*

This is the time when Kent stands out of *Kirsendom,*
For he that's king now was never *kirsen'd.*
     The Mayor of Quinborough.

Kist. A chest, a shop-counter.

The word with the latter meaning is, I believe, found only in Burns.

---

* In some places there is a mockery kept up and called by the name of *kirn,* by the harvest workers subscribing each a small sum to pay for a little festival, to which the farmer contributes the loan of his barn for an evening.

Kyste, a chest, or coffin for the burial of the dead.—*Bailey*.

> In a *kiste*
> The se her threwe upon the londe.—*Gower*.
>
> Fy on the bagges in the *kist*.—*Id*.
>
> "Now, Noe," quod oure lorde, "art thou al redy?
> Hast thou closed thy *kyst* with clay alle aboute?"
> *Early E. Alliterative Poems. Morris*.

Kitchen. Any thing eaten with bread, that serves for soup, gravy, etc.

> *Kitchen*, all sorts of eatables, bread only excepted.—*Halliwell*.

Neither of these definitions is quite correct. The first errs by defect, for more than bread is the better of *kitchen*, potatoes, for example, and Burns expressly mentions *parritch* as requiring some *obsonium*, some addition to make "the wale of food" more palatable. and it seems to limit the terms to liquids, whereas it is applied to cheese, butter, fish, and meat.

Mr. Halliwell's definition, on the other hand, errs by excess, for there are eatables, as already pointed out, besides bread, which are not *kitchen*.

Kith. Circle of acquaintance; neighbours, from *kith*, a country, a region, which is its primary meaning; its secondary is people whom we know and to whom we are known; thus connecting it with *kythe*, to show.

In most of the editions of Burns, *kin* and *kith* are both rendered kindred. If these words mean the same thing, there is a gross tautology in—

> At *kith* or *kin* I need na spier.

This disappears when we translate it—"at relatives or acquaintances or neighbours."

> Thai (the wise men) ferd al sauf in-to thair *kyth* (country).
> *Cursor Mundi.*

Kittle. To tickle ; to excite ; ticklish, likely. In this last sense used by Burns only.

Kittle, uncertain, doubtful.—*Bailey. Bamford.*

Kitelung, a tickling.—*Bosworth.*

Kittle, to tickle ; *kittle* weather, ticklish, changeable, or uncertain weather.—*Grose.*

It stands *kittle,* i.e., ticklishly, ready to fall.—*Thoresby.*

> This done,
> His *kittling* eyes begin to run
> Quite through the table,

i.e., seeking something to eat or drink.

Kittling here may mean kitten. If so, it should be placed under the next word. But I think it means tickling, itching, covetous, like the "itching palm" of Cassius. A young cat's eyes would be out of proportion to the rest of the body of a creature who quenched his thirst on—

> "A chrystal pearl of infant dew
> Brought and besweetened in a blew
> And pregnant violet," and whose buskins were made
> "Of the cow-lady's coral wing."—*Oberon's Feast.*

Kittlin. A kitten.

> Out *kitlings!* what caterwauling's here?—*Fletcher.*
>
> Look for her money, you *kitling.*—*Swift.*
>
> Yet can thy humble roof maintain a quire
> Of singing crickets by the fire ;
> And the brisk mouse may feed herself with crumbs,
> Till the green-eyed *kitling* comes.—*Herrick's Hesperides.*

When the females have brought them their *kitlins,* they etc.—
Littlebury's Herodotus.

Kiuttle. To cuddle, to fondle, to court.

Knaggie. Knaggy, knotty, rugged.

Knap. To break. *Knappin-*hammer, a hammer for breaking stones.

Knap, to snap or break asunder.—*Bailey.*

He thought to give Guy a *knap.*—*Guy of Warwick.*
I would she were as lying a gossip as ever *knapt* ginger.—*Shak.*
He breaketh the bow and *knappeth* the spear in sunder.
Ps. xlvi. of English Prayer-book Version.

Knock. In "But every shot and every *knock,*" it means every stroke of the frame, technically called a *lay,* which drives home the weft.

Knots. Mystic knots play an important part in the history of witchcraft. Most readers will remember—

O wha has loosed the nine witch *knots,*
That were among that ladye's locks?
Minstrelsy of the Scot. Border.

The harmless *knot-grass* from its knots was supposed to have some thing of the witch-knot character about it,—

You minimus of *hind'ring knot-grass* made.—*Shak.*

Middleton, in a passage which can hardly be quoted entire, speaks of the power of knots,—

So sure into what house these are convey'd,
Knit with these charms, and with *retentive knots,* etc.
The Witch.

Knowe. A small round hillock, a knoll. For omission of *l* see under *a'.*

Knowe, a knoll, a hillock. *Knowe-*hill, near Rochdale.—*Bamford.*
It stands on a *knowle.*—*Evelyn.*
In the lower grove as on the rising *knowle.*—*Drayton.*

Knurl. A dwarf.

Knurl, a knot in timber.—*Bailey.*
Knurrs, knots, warts on trees.—*Bamford.*

Knor, or *knurer*, a short, stubbed, dwarfish man; a metaphor from a knot in a tree. In the South we use the diminutive *knurle* in the same sense.—*Grose.*

There shall be no tree, how hard and *knurry* howsoever, but therein we shall write her name.—*Shelton's Don Quixote, 1620.*

Knurlin. Dim. of *Knurl.*

Kye. Cows.

Kye, kine.—*Bailey.*

More meet it were for them to milke *kye* at a fleyke.—*Little John Nobody.*

> Flesh meat I saw never,
> But milk of the *kye*.—*The King and the Hermit.*
>
> Also the good yeman,
> Some tyme in this realme (pronounced ream, as in "Wo is the Ream," *P. Plowman*),
> Had plenty of *kye* and cream.—*Vox Populi, Vox Dei.*

Kyle. A district of Ayrshire.

Kyle Stewart. The district between the rivers Ayr and Irvine.

Kyte. The belly.

Kite, belly.—*Bailey.*

Kythe. To discover, to show one's self.

Kythe, to show, to make known, to discover.—*Bailey.*

> For but Christ upon thee miracle *kythe*,
> Withouten gilt thou schalt be slayn as swithe.—*Chaucer.*
>
> She *kitheth* what she is.—*Id.*
> Than hast thou the fairest chance
> That ever yet had any knight
> That theddur came to *kythe* his might.—*Ywain and Gawain.*
>
> > Pure to the pure, froward thou *kyth'st*
> > Unto the froward wight.—*Psalm xviii.,*

Rous's version, commonly, but erroneously, called the Scotch version, for, it may be a matter of regret or otherwise, neither Scotland's Confession of Faith nor her Psalter is of home growth.

In a letter to Mrs. Dunlop, Burns, speaking of printing poetry, says, "As to the punctuation, the printers do that themselves." He evidently acted on this opinion, and his printers did his punctuation, and after an extraordinary fashion, for very few books have been so wretchedly punctuated as the first and second editions of his poems. Indeed, the most of the editors of his works seem to have thought that even his, or his printer's, commas were stamped with his genius, and refused to touch them, and they still remain to disfigure and render almost unintelligible some of his finest passages. Take, for example, the lines in which the word *kythe*, which has led to this digression, occurs. They look like a conundrum :

> Their faces blithe, fu' sweetly kythe,
> Hearts leal, an' warm, an' kin'.

These words, if read as they are pointed, are impossible to be understood; but take out the unnecessary commas, and as soon as the meaning of the words is known, the sense is obvious—" Their cheerful faces show that their hearts are loyal, warm, and kind." The expression is very much the same as Chaucer's

> His malice in his chere was *kidde*.—*Rom. of the Rose.*

L.

Labour. To work.

In "The Inventory" it means "make to work." According to Cunningham, it signifies thrash, i.e., beat.

I put in this word, which is E. even in Cunningham's sense, as may be seen from Dryden's couplet quoted by Johnson—

> Take, Shepherd, take a plant of stubborn oak
> And *labour* him with many a sturdy stroke,

to protest against the implication that Burns and, of course, other Ayrshire farmers, were in the habit of inflicting corporal punishment on their servants, or they of submitting to it. Honest Allan has libelled both parties. The thing is, and was, utterly unknown. Think of the cottar of the Saturday Night asking his "elder bairns at service out amang the farmers roun'," if their masters had beaten them often since they were last at home, and charging them to take the *labouring* patiently!

Labour, in "The Auld Farmer's Address," has the special meaning of *ploughing*.

Laddie. Dim. of lad.

Lade. A load. *A* for *o*. See under *bane*.
   To *Lade*, to load.—*Bailey.*
   And they *laded* their asses with corn.—*Genesis, xlii. 26.*
   They *laded* them with such things as were necessary.—*Bunyan.*

Lag. Sluggish, slow; to move slowly or delay, as in—
> It only *lags* the fatal hour.
> Some tardy cripple had the countermand
> That came too *lag* to see him buried.—*Shak.*
> Behind her far away a dwarf did *lag*.—*Spenser.*

Laggen. The angle between the side and the bottom of a wooden dish.
   Laggen, as above.—*Halliwell.   Laggins*, staves of a tub.
                                                              Bamford.

Laigh. Low. *A laigh house*, a house of one story.

Lair. To wade and sink in snow, mud, etc.

Lare, a quagmire.—*Grose.*

Lairing, walking through mire, etc.—*Halliwell.*

> The Shad and Tweaf do rather like the *laire*
> Of brackish waves where it doth ebb and flow.
> *Secrets of Angling. Beloe.*

Laird. Owner of land or houses.

But, an' your turns be serv'd, the devil a bit you care for a man after, e'er a *laird* of you.—*Ben Jonson.*

And *lard* and ladie gang till kirk.—*Warner.*

The *laird* of Bukcleugh is not forfeited.—*Sir C. Dacre to Lord Dacre.*

Laith. Loath.

> For to gif dome them is full *lath*.—*Sir Penny.*
> He was a *lathly* creature.—*Ywain and Gawain.*
> Sertes, madam, that es me *lathe*.—*Id.*
> The pouer said, *layth* thinc me
> To selle Goddess charité.—*E. Metrical Homilies.*
> He riped amang the wormes *lathe*.—*Id.*

Laithfu'. Bashful, sheepish. *Laith* and *fu'.*

Lallan. Lowland. *A* for *o*, as in *aff.*

Lallans. Scotch dialect.

Lambie. Dim. of lamb.

Lampit. A kind of shell-fish, a limpet.

Lan'. Land, estate. For omission of *d* see *afiel.*

Lan'-afore. The foremost horse, when there are four, on the left side of the plough; the foremost horse not in the furrow. *Lan'* and *afore.*

Lan'-ahin. The horse behind the *lan'-afore.* *Lan'* and *ahin.*

Lan'-louper. A vagabond. *Lan'* and *loup.* Shakespeare has *land-raker* with the same meaning. *Land-loper.* A vagabond.—*Bailey.*

Villotier, a vagabond, *land-loper.*—*Cotgrave.*

Let mariners learn astronomy; *land-leapers* geography.
Anat. of Melancholy.

The materials of this journal have laid by me several years, expecting that some *land-loper* would have done it more methodically.
Journal of Charles Wolley.

Lane. Lone, alone; my *lane*, thy *lane*, &c., myself alone, thyself alone, &c. The use of *a* for *o* has been shown to be common to E. and S. authors, but I suspect that *my lone* is not to be found among the writings of the former.

Lanely. Lonely.

Lang. Long; to think long, to long, to weary.

His spear he sticked, it was so *lang.*—*Sir Eger, Sir Graham, and Sir Grey Steel.*

Langer there noght he durst bide.—*L. Minot.*

His *lange* heer ykempt behyn' his bak.—*Chaucer.*

Lene he was also *lang.*—*The Seven Sages.*

Do me have him here in my sight,
Me *langes* sar him to se.—*Ywain and Gawain.*

Lang hame. Long home, the grave.

Man goeth to his *long home.*—*Ec. xii. 5.*

This hand hath sent some to their *long home.*—*Butler.*

Lang-kail. Coleworts boiled and eaten with meat. *Lang*, i.e., unshorn and *kail.*

Lap. Did leap: past tense of leap.

Lap, leapt, vaulted.—*Halliwell.*

>The mayde stout and gay
>*Lep* on her palfray.—*Lybeaus Disconus.*
>
>She *lep* on hyr palfray,
>And bad hem all have good day.—*Launfal.*

Lassie. Dim. of lass.

>She cares not for her daddy, nor
>She cares not for her mammy, for
> She is, she is, she is
>My lord of Lowgrove's *lassy.*—*Beaumont and Fletcher.*

Diminutives like *lassy* are not very numerous in English. Here are two others from the same authors:

>Begone, begone, my *juggy*, my *puggy*,
>Begone, my love, my dear.
>
>Ay, little *Larky!* what's the reason,
>Singing thus in winter season?—*Clare.*

Last day. Yesterday.

>A willow garland thou didst send
>Perfumed, *last day*, to me.—*Herrick.*

Last day, yesterday.—*West. Halliwell.*

He saluted me *last day.*—*Marston.*

>My lords, *last day* our state was much impair'd,
> Our friends were slain, kill'd were our soldiers bold.
>
>>*Fairfax.*

Lave. The rest, the remainder.

The *lave*, all the rest.—*Bailey.*

Lave, the remainder or leaving.—*Grose.*

>And last of all among the *lave*
>King James himself to death was wrought.
>
>>*Battle of Flodden.*

Of doughty knights the lusty *lave.*—*Id.*

Laverock. The lark.

>Here see a blackbird feed her young,
>Or a *leverock* build her nest.—*Isaak Walton.*

She made many a wonder soune (sound),
Sometime lich unto the cock,
Sometime unto the *laverock.—Gower.*

The gaynty *lavyrock.—Christmas Carol. Brand.*

Law. To rule, determine, in "Let inclination *law* that."

Law. Low. Also, a hill, as in—

The ship rides by the Berwick-*law.—My Bonnie Mary.*

For to delight each one they draw,
That haunt this work both hie and *law.—Chaucer.*

Ful *law* he lay and likked his fete.—*Ywain and Gawain.*

Now er we hegh, now er we *lawe.—Pricke of Conscience.*

Measure is a meane, nother to hy nor to *lawe.—Skelton.*

Lawlan'. Lowland. *Law* and land.

Lay. Ground unplowed: more frequently and more properly written *lea.—Johnson.*

Fayre fields and pleasant *layes* there been.—*Spencer.*

A tuft of daisies on a flowery *lay*
They saw.—*Dryden.*

And bad hym hold hym at home, and eryen his *leyes.*
P. Plowman.

Lay. To charge, to impute, in—"I'll *lay* my deid," i.e., I'll impute my death.

Lea'e. To leave. For elision of *v*, see under *ca'* and *gie.*

Leal. Loyal, true, faithful.

Tenants by Knights' service were wont to swear to their Lord to be *Feal and Leal*, i.e., faithful and loyal.—*Bailey.*

Disleal knight.—*Spenser.*

His moné, that was gude and *lele,*
Left in Braband ful mekill dele.—*L. Minot.*

> Thou shalt find me true and *leal*.—*Sir Amadas.*
> To love me *leelly*.—*P. Plowman.*

Lear, pronounce *lare.* Learning.

> I did thee *lear*
> A lore repugnant to thy father's faith.—*Fairfax.*
> He was invulnerable made by Magicke *lair.*—*Spenser.*
> Yif thou wilt leve (believe) upon my *lare.*
> *Amis and Amiloun.*
> And thi *lare* in end me righted al.—*Metrical E. Psalter.*

Lea-rig. Grassy ridge: unploughed field. *Lea* and *rig.*

Learn. To teach.

> *Lerne* me my crede.—*P. Ploughman's Crede.*
> Hast thou not *learned* me
> How to make perfumes?—*Shak.*

Lee. A lie.

> Seyde the emperour, "Dame, that ys *leesse.*"
> *Octovian Imperator.*
>
> I woll ou (you) tell thing not *lees.*—*King Robert of Sicily.*
>
> The emerayles dowghter of hethenes
> Made this cloth withouten *lees.*—*Emare.*
>
> They wente, and alle was founde *les.*—*Gower.*
>
> To tamen him withouten *lees.*—*Chaucer.*

Lee-lang. Live-long. *Lee* may seem a long way from *live,* but live was sometimes written *leve* as in Chaucer's—

> Thus may we both *leve.*

Then *v* was omitted as in *lea'e* for leave, *loe* for love.

> O, where have you ridden this *lee-lang* day?
> *Bell's An. Songs and Poems.*

Leesome. Pleasant, happy, gladsome (lovesome).* *Lee* in *leesome*, like *le* in *leman*, is a contraction or corruption of love through the forms *lief, lefe, leve*, and *loe.*

> With *lossum* cheer she on me lough.—*Old Song. Ritson.*
>
> So God me helpe at my nede,
> *Unlossum* is that Kynrede.—*King Alisaunder.*
>
> They are with God both *lefe* and dear.—*Rob. of Brunne.*

Leevin'. Living.

Leeze me. A phrase of congratulatory endearment.— *Burns.* I prefer deriving it from *leif*, dear, agreeable; q. "leif is to me," literally "dear is to me."—*Jamieson.* If Jamieson's derivation is the right one, *leeze* is connected with *leesome.* But does *leeze me* not rather signify, "I praise, commend, or take pleasure in? *Commend* me to the ploughman," and—

> Of a' the thoughtless sons of man,
> *Commend* me to the Bardie clan.

i.e., "I praise the ploughman and poets." The meaning in both passages would be the same if instead of commend we read leeze, "*leeze* me on the ploughman," etc., and "Leeze me on thee John Barleycorn" would have the same meaning, though it would spoil the rhythm, if it were written "Commend me to thee," etc. If this is the meaning of leeze it is an English

---

* The definition here given is proper in most cases, but I suspect that in—

> O, gear will buy me rigs o' lan,
> And gear will buy me sheep and kye;
> But the tender heart o' *leesome* love,
> The gowd and siller canna buy,

it means lawful. *Leful* for lawful is often found in E. authors, and the following will show that in Scotland the word meant lawful:—" It shall be *leisum* to all persons to apprehend any vagabonds who shall be found begging."—*Act Magistrates of Edinburgh, 1685.*

word, derived probably from A.-Sax. *les* or *less*, favour, comfort, happiness.

> Mickle she desireth to show her body,
> Her faire hair, her face rody,
> To have *lees* (commendation, Ellis,) and all praising.
> *The Life of Alexander, quoted by Ellis.*

In Weber's "King Alisaunder" *los* is put instead of *lees*, but this is the same as praising, and Ellis's reading is not so obviously tautological.

> If I herde of thinges straunge,
> Yet for a time it shulde chaunge
> My peine and *lisse* (ease or please) me somedele.—*Gower.*
> Thou might thy time *lisse.*—*Ib.*

Leister. A three-pronged fork for sticking fish.

Leister, a kind of trident used in the North of England for sticking fish.—*Halliwell.*

> Salmons shall leave their cover void of fear,
> Nor dread the thievish net or *triple spear.*—*Gay.*

Gay was a Devonshire man, and as in his native county they had the thing, it is likely that the name also was known, but in his day to use a common name for any thing for which a poetical periphrasis could be found, was considered prosaic, and he had to employ a substitute.

Len'. To lend.

> For hys luf that *lens* us life,
> Gif me my right withouten strife.—*Ywain and Gawain.*
> Fetel (vessel) will I nan *len* thee.—*E. Metrical Homilies.*
> And yf thou have nede of ony more,
>   More shall I *len* thee.—*R. Hood.*

Leugh. Did laugh.

> Tho *lough* this Pandarus.—*Chaucer.*
> "Ough!" quoth Otuel and *lough.*—*Sir Otuel,*

> When Robin had told his tale,
> He *leugh* and made good cheer.—*R. Hood.*

> They *leugh*, and said it was good sport.
> *The Northumberland Garland. Ritson.*

Leuk and *luke*. A look, to look. *Eu* for *oo*. See under *beuk*.

> He *luked* up unto the toure
> And saw the lady, white so flowre.—*The Seven Sages.*

> Full earnestful *luiked* hee.—*Bell's Anc. Poems and Songs.*

> Makes the peur man
> *Leuk* on mony an unkend face.—*The Northumb. Gar.*

Lib. To geld.

Neither grow there any (horns) if they (stags) had none before they were *libbed*.—*Philemon Holland.*

> But now who pares his nails, or *libs* his swine,
> But he must first take counsel of the sign (the stars)?
> *Bishop Hall.*

Lick. To beat, to vanquish, a blow. *Lick*, to beat.—*Grose. Bamford.*

Johnson says it is a low word, but quotes the following:—

He turned upon me as round as a chased boar and gave me a *lick* across the face.—*Dryden.*

> Suppose I've a mind he should drub,
> Whose bones are they, sir, he's to *lick*?—*Fielding.*

Lie. To stay all night, to sleep.

> To my Lord Sandwich's lodgings; who is come hither to *lie*.
> *Pepys.*

Does he *lie* at the Garter?—*Shak.*

Lieve. Willingly, dear.

> I had as *lieve* the town-crier had spoke my lines.—*Shak.*

> Tell hit me,
> As thou wilt to me *lef* be.—*The Seven Sages.*

> A wel fair feste thai made thare,
> O frendes that hem *leve* ware.—*Id.*

Lift. The sky.

> The galey yede as swift
> As any fowle by the *lyfte.*—*R. C. de Lyon.*
>
> Betwix the *lift* an the erth it glade,
> Swa fair a stern was never made.—*Cursor Mundi.*
>
> Nis there hawk no fowl so swift
> Better fleeing by the *lift*
> Than the monkes.—*The Land of Cockayne.*

Lift. A portion, as much as a man may lift, in—

> Gie me o' wit and sense a *lift.*

Lift in Scotland denotes a load or snrcharge of any thing.—*Johnson. Jamieson.*

> Off gold well twenty mennys *lyffte*
> Were layd on mule and rabyte.—*R. C. de Lion.*

In the following passages of Burns and Ramsay, *lift* seems to mean a *drain* or *drawing off*—

> To gie the jars and barrels
>   A *lift* that day.—*The Holy Fair.*
>
> And lent her fresh nine-gallon trees (barrels)
>   A hearty *lift.*—*Lucky Wood s Elegy.*

In Scotland if one is disguised in liquor they say, He *has got a great lift.—Johnson.*

Lightly. Sneeringly, to depreciate. Adverb used as a verb in—

> And whiles ye may *lightly* my beauty a wee.

Like. To please.

In the sense in which Burns uses it in " He rises when he *likes* himsel'," this verb is, as Johnson says, now obsolete. It was once common.

> It *lykes* me
> To suffer for thé.—*Skelton.*

His countenance *likes* me not.—*Shak.*
I can find no company that *likes* me.—*Fletcher.*
It *liketh* hem to be clene in body and gost.—*Chaucer.*
Where *likes* me best I can command.—*Milton.*

Lilt. A ballad, a tune, to sing.

It does not seem ever to have been used in this sense in England. Halliwell says:—"*Lilt,* to jerk or spring; to do anything cleverly or quickly"; and Bamford—"*Lilt,* to walk quickly, lightly," and in addition "*Liltin,* dancing, moving with a jaunty air."

Is *litling,* explained "very little" by Tyrwhitt, not a misprint for *lilting?*

And many a floyte (flute) and *litling* horne.
Book of Fame, Bk. III., v. 133.

Lilting horn would be Gray's "echoing horn" and the "cheerful horn" of other poets. There is or was the word *litling,* but it meant *making little,* rather than *very little.*

Limb. A leg, in—
And there I left for witness an arm and a *limb.*

Limbie. Dim. of limb.

Limmer. A kept mistress, a strumpet.

Foul *limmer,* dretty lown!—*Ben Jonson.*

The *limmer* thieves of Liddesdale.
The Fray of Hautwessell.
I asked one lad, a *lymere,*
"Say, fellow, who shall hunt here?"—*Chaucer.*

Here *limmer* is applied to a man, apparently one who led a *limer,* or dog. Tyrwhitt says a bloodhound.

There overtook I a great rout
Of hunters and eke forresters,
And many relaies and *limers.*
The Booke of the Dutchesse.

Limmer, a mongrel.—*Johnson*.   A mongrel dog.—*Bailey*.

This is the meaning of *limmer*, and, like other opprobrious words taken from the canine race, was applied to male and female indifferently. It is now confined, when used, which I believe it seldom is, to the latter.

Lingo.   Language.

> I have thoughts to learn somewhat of your *lingo* before I cross the sea.—*Congreve*.
>
> I understand no *lingo* but my mother-tongue.—*Don Quixote*.

Link.   To trip along, to walk smartly.

> *Link*, to walk quickly.—*Halliwell*.

Linn.   A waterfall.

> *Lin*, a pool, a cascade, a precipice.—*Halliwell*.

The first sense is the only one I have found in E. authors.

> Tivy cometh down from the capacious *lin*.—*Drayton*.

Lint.   Flax.   *Lint*, the substance commonly called flax.
Johnson.

Lint in the bell.   Flax in flower.

> *Bell* is used for any thing in the form of a bell, as the cups of flowers.—*Johnson*.

> > Where the bee sucks, there suck I.
> > In the cowslips *bell* I lie.—*Shak*.
> >
> > Her apron dy'd in grain, as blue, I trowe,
> > As is the hare-*bell* that adorns the field.—*Shenstone*.
> >
> > With her snowy *bells* the lily of the vale.—*Hurdis*.

Lintwhite.   A linnet; of the colour of flax.

> *Lintwhite*, a lark.—*Suffolk*. *Halliwell*.

As an adjective it is a compound like lily-white.

> *Lylie-whyt* hue (she) is.—*Wright's Specimens of Lyric Poetry*.

Lintie. A linnet.

Lippen. To rely upon.

Lippen, to trust, or rely upon.—*Bailey.* *Lippin*, to expect.
Bamford.

Lippen, to expect, to rely, to trust to, or place confidence in.
Halliwell.

Lippie. Dim. of lip.

Yive-day long. Live-long day. A curious illustration of the straits to which even such a master of rhythm and rhyme as Burns may be reduced.

Loan, loanin'. The place of milking. A place now unknown, as the milking is done in-doors.

Fy-*loan*, a word used to call cows home to be milked.—*Grose.*

Lone, a lane.—*Bamford.*

Lurkede thorw *lones* tologged of Monye.—*P. Plowman.*

When my father was dying, the brag was heard coming up the *lonin* like a coach and six, . . and then went down the *lonin*.
Sharp's Bishopric Garland.

The fiend gae down the *loaning* with her.—*The Northumb. Garland. Ritson.*

Loe. To love. For elision of *v* see under *ca'* and *gie.*

That was a lustie melodie,
Whan every man with other *low.*—*Gower.*

Lo'esome. Lovable, lovely. See *lo'e* and *leesome.*

A *lovesome* lady bright!—*Chaucer.*

Her *lovesum* eighen, her rode so bright.—*Lay le Frein.*

A generous bottle, and a *lovesome* she
Are th' only joys in nature next to thee.—*Otway.*

With *lossum* eis grete and gode.—*The earliest love-song known to Warton.*

Loof. The palm of the hand, plural, *looves* according to Burns, but generally *loofs* or *lufes*.

The *lufe*, the open hand.—*Bailey. Grose.*

Loot. Did let.

Leet, to let.—*Bamford.*

> Death came driving after,
> And all to duste perished;
> He *loot* no man stand.

Dr. Mackay quotes this as from P. Plowman. I have not seen it in any edition that has come under my notice.

Losh. Rustic exclamation.

Lough. A loch or lake.

The Mukel lauande *loghe* to the lyfte rered.—*Alliterative Poems.*
A people
Whom Ireland sent from *loughs* and forests hoar.—*Fairfax.*

Loun. A fellow, a ragamuffin, a woman of easy virtue.

Loon, an idle, lazy, good-for-nothing fellow.—*Bailey.*

> We should have both lord and *lown*.—*Shak.*

> My son's slain, he is falling to swoon,
> And it's all for the sake of an English *loon* (woman).
> *Bell's An. Poems and Songs.*

Loup. To jump, to leap.

To *loup* or *laup*, to leap.—*Thoresby.*

> Thus even on hem I wait and hope,
> Till I may se hem lepe a *lope*.—*Gower.*

> For *loupe* he so lightly laughen he wolde.—*P. Plowman.*

> Then play our casts among the whipsters,
> Throw for the hammer, *lowp* for slippers.
> *A Joco-Serious Discourse, Lond., 1686.*

> He *loop* yn haste on his palfray.—*Octovian Imperator.*

Louper. Leaper. See *lan'-louper.* It may be as well to mention that the word *loup, lope,* means to run as well as to leap.

Lowe. A flame, to flame. *Lowin,* burning, rather blazing.

Low-bell, flame and bell.—*Johnson.*

The rising and falling of the cords at which the *low-bells* were hanged ceased not.—*Shelton's Don Quixotte.*

      Of lightnes sal you se a *lowe.*—*Ywain and Gawain.*

         The dewle hym
      Born (burn) on a *lowe.*—*Sir Cleges.*

      The breath of his mouth that outblow
      As it had been a fire on *low*—*Sir Degoré.*

I hope I have not a shadow of the feeling which animated Ritson when he had occasion to speak of "Mister Ellis," as he always called the celebrated literary antiquary, when I say that I believe he is wrong in explaining *low,* "a small hill or eminence." The body of the dragon, the breath of whose mouth is spoken of, was "like a wine tun," which would be a very small hill, and a lowing or blazing fire is a common expression.

Lowrie. Abbreviation of Lawrence

Do ye hear that, *Lory?*—*Vanbrugh.*

      Lorry has a light heart.—*Sterne.*

The priest *Lowry* was suddenly taken.—*Journal of George Fox.*

Lowrie's burn. The river St. Lawrence.

Lowse. To loose.

And he being with me at supper, the horses of his company brak *lowse.*—*Surrey to Henry VIII.*

      And whan the hors was *laus* he gan to gon
      Toward the fen.—*Chaucer.*

> Then they *lowsyd* hur feyre faxe (hair).—*Le Bone Flo. of Rome.*
> *Louse* me out of bond.—*Tale of Gamelyn.*

Lucerne. A lamp (Ital. *lucerna*), but Burns, in a letter to Nicol, 20th Feb., 1792, uses it for a dim window.

> With Marione clarione, sol, *lucerne.*—*Skelton.*

Luck-penny. Discount, a small sum returned to the payer of the amount agreed on at a sale.

Luck-penny, a small sum of money returned to the purchaser for luck.—*Halliwell.*

> Come, strike me *luck* with earnest, and draw the writings.
> There's a *god's-penny* for thee.—*Beaumont and Fletcher.*

Both the *god's-penny* and the *luck-penny* refer to the belief that it was necessary to the fortunate result of a bargain that money should be returned, but to this Burns's use of the word *luck-penny* does not apply. He must allude to some present that he had received from Mrs. Dunlop on occasion of his marriage, or entering on his farm, when he says to her, "I am indeed seriously angry with you at the quantum of your *luck-penny.*" If this is correct, *luck-penny* is, I believe, used in an uncommon sense.

Lucky. An elderly woman; generally, I believe, a woman in some kind of business, a keeper of a shop, tavern, &c.

Lug. The ear, a handle. *At the lug o'*, near.

> With hair in characters and *luggs* in text.—*Cleveland.*
> I shrewe thy Scottish *lugges.*—*Skelton.*
> *Le mol d' oreille*, the *lug*, or list of the ear.—*Cotgrave.*
> They fanged the remnant of his *lugs*—*Epitaph on Prynne.*

I would take thee such a woundy cut on this spectacle-bearing *lug* of thine.—*Rabelais. Motteux.*

Lugget. (Lit. eared), having a handle.

Luggie. A small wooden dish with a handle.—*Burns.*

The *luggie* is not a very small dish, as it is the milking pail, and must be large enough to hold, if not the milk of "twal-pint Hawkie," at least that of an ordinary cow. It is of cooper's work, and the lug or handle from which it takes its name is one of the staves standing above the rest. If Jamieson had remembered this he would not have said that the handle of a dish was called a *lug* only when it "projected from the side," i.e., stood at right angles to it as the handle of a *caup* does.

Lum. The chimney.

Lum, a cottage chimney.—*Halliwell.*

Lume. A loom, tool, instrument, utensil.

This word is used in all these senses in various parts of Scotland, but I think is seldom heard in Ayrshire, except to denote a weaving-machine.

Loom, any tool or utensil.—*Bailey. Johnson.*

I ha' that wark on hand,
That web upon the *luime* will gar them think.—*Ben Johnson.*

Lunardi. A name given to a fashion of lady's bonnet from Lunardi, the celebrated aëronant, as explained by Burns in a note. He was not the only poet who rhymed of the fashion.

Great is the world's inconstancy.
Fame, like the ocean ebbs as well as flows;
Next year the million pitches on a ruff,
A *balloon-cap,* a shawl, a muff.—*Dr. Wolcot.*

Lunch. A large piece of cheese, flesh, &c.

It is applied to any thing edible, though the poet's definition seems to restrict it to *kitchen.* That he did not intend it to do so his own words show:—" And cheese and bread was dealt about in *lunches*."—*The Holy Fair*. *Lunch*, as much food as one's hand can hold,—*Johnson*, who brackets it with *luncheon*, and quotes a passage from Gay, in which luncheon is used as *lunch* is employed by Burns:—

> When hungry thou stood'st staring like an oaf,
> I sliced the *luncheon* from the barley loaf.

Luncheon, a large lump of food.—*Halliwell*.

A huge *lunshin* of bread, a large piece.—*Thoresby*.

Lunt. A column of smoke, to smoke.

Lunt, the matchcord with which guns are fired.—*Johnson*.

Luppen. Leaped; participle of *loup*.

Luve. Love.

Though a single line would serve my purpose, I cannot resist the temptation to insert the following passage descriptive of the last scene of the Deluge:—

> Bi that the flod to her (their) fete floghed and waxed,
> Then uche a segge (man) segh wel that synk hym byhoved;
> Frendez fellen in-fere and fathmed (embraced) togeder,
> To drygh (dree) her delful deystyné, and dyghen alle samen;
> *Luf* (love) lokez to *luf* and his leve takez,
> For to ende alle at onez and for ever twynne.
> *Morris's Early English Alliterative Poems.*

> Yette hard y never no mon speyke,
> That so mykyll of my *luffe* myght geyt.—*Sir Amadas*.

Luver. Lover.

Lyart. Of a mixed colour, grey.

Liard, mingled roan.—*Johnson*.

> That was wel twight, min own *liard* boy (grey horse).
> *Chaucer.*

> Thou shalt sporeles o' thy *lyard*.
> *Richard of Almayne. Percy's Reliques.*

M.

Mae. More.

> Na *ma* sal wit bot we.—*Ywain and Gawain.*
> The mone and sternes mani *ma.*—*Metrical E. Psalter.*

Magnum-Bonum. Double-sized bottle, containing two English quarts.

> Two bottles in one are excellent fun,
> So waiter, a *magnum* of claret.—*Hor. in London.*

Mahoun. Satan.

> He defy'd *Mahounde* and Apolyne,
> Jubiter, Astarot, and Alcoran also.
> *The Sowdon of Babylone.*
>
> Many Sarezyn hadden her fyn,
> And wenten to *Mahoun* and Apolyne.—*R. C. de Lion.*

The Christians in the crusades were accustomed to hear the Saracens swear by their prophet Mahomet; which thence became for Europeans another name for the devil.—*Warton.*

It is however likely that Burns got the word from Dunbar's "Daunce"—

> But yet luche nevir Mahoun.

Mailen. A farm.

Maling comes from mail, in consequence of rents being originally paid in *mails* or *bags.*—*Sir John Sinclair.*

Jamieson is decided against this theory, but notwithstanding all that has been said in opposition to it, it seems the most plausible that has been suggested. Sir Walter Scott seems to favour it. He says, "*Mail,* payable rent."[*]

---

[*] *Mailen,* however, it must be confessed, did not always mean a farm for which rent was paid:—

A well-stocked *mailen,* himsel for the *laird*—*Last May a Braw Wooer.*

Mainers. Manners. Long for short *a*, as in—
>It were in sothe a *maner* ydylnesse.—*Lydgate.*
>And when this *maister* saw it was time.—*Chaucer.*

Mair. More.
>For, sooth, thou seest me never *mair.*—*Morte Arthur.*
>Both to lesse and eke to *mare.*—*Chaucer.*
>A *mare* payne couthe no man in hert cast.—*P. of Conscience.*
>I wot he might not draw a sword
>>For forty days and *mair.*—*R. Hood.*

Maist. Most.
>Ilkon played the gamen he couth,
>And *maste* had used in his youth.—*Rob. de Brunne.*
>
>Thou Bethleem Juda,
>Thof thou be noght the *maste* cite.—*Cursor Mundi.*

Mak. To make, to make much of, be kind to, to court.
>Fok had wonder that nature
>Myght *mak* so foule a creature.—*Ywain and Gawain.*
>Welcum alle and *mak* good chere.—*Christmas Carol. Ritson.*
>See, Lucius, how much she *makes* of thee.—*Shak.*
>'Tis not enough that I love thee,
>But sometimes thou must *make* of me.—*The Wife's Answer.*
>I am Lyberte, *made* of in every nacyon.—*Skelton.*

Mallie. Molly, Mary.
>*Mall,* contraction of Mary.—*Bailey.*   *Mall,* Mary.—*Bamford.*
>>Three large sowes had she, and no mo;
>>Three kine and eke a sheep that hight *Malle.*—*Chaucer.*
>Sweet *Mall.*—*Sir John Harrington to his Wife.*

I hope my Lord Arran has toulde your Majestie that I did mean to wene *Mall* very shortly.—*Duchess of Buckingham to J. 1.*

Mammie, and *mammy.* Mother.
>By saynt Mary, my lady, your *mammy* and your dady—
>Brought forth a godely babi!—*Skelton.*

Mang. Among. See *amang.*

Manor. An E. word, but used by Burns to signify farm.

Manse. A parsonage house.—*Johnson.*

In "The Holy Fair" *manse* means a living, a benefice, and raises the question, "How could an unbeneficed, and of course unordained, man be there?"

Manteele. A mantle.

> They sawe nothynge but *mantels* of grene.—*R. Hood.*
> *Mantellis*, robes and pavelounes.—*Geste of Alexander.*
> In hys *mantyll* that is so fyne.—*Ipomydon.*
>
> She ne had on but a straite old sacke,
> And many a cloute on it there stacke,
> This was her cote, and her *mantele*,
> No more was there never a dele
> To cloath her with.—*Chaucer.*

Mark, merk. Marks. This, and several other nouns which in English require an s to form the plural, are in Scotch like the words sheep, deer, the same in both numbers.—*Burns.*

This is not peculiar to the Scottish language. Many words are by English writers employed as Burns used mark, this very word being so treated.

> His benefice worthe ten *pounde*,
> Or skante worthe twenty *marke*.—*Skelton.*
> Sixe *mark* yerely and no more but that.—*Occleve.*
> Give me the pencil whose amazing style,
> Makes a bird's beak appear at twenty *mile*.—*Dr. Wolcot.*
> Or, in pure equity the case not clear,
> The chancery takes your rents for twenty *year*.—*Pope.*

Marled. Variegated, speckled, of mingled colours.

> The lanners and the *marlyons* (merlins)
> Shall stand in their morning (mourning) gowns,—*Skelton,*

> There was . . the *merlion* that peineth
> Himself full oft the larke for to seke.—*Chaucer*.

Jamieson has not suggested a derivation for this word which Burns seems to have learned from Mrs. Scott, as he never used it except in reply to her letter. Can it be derived from *merlin, merlen, marlyon*, or *merlion*, or their common source *merula* ? The French have two adjectives, *emerilloné* and *merle*, apparently from this root, and there was once, as we learn from Cotgrave, "A fashion of light gowne or mantle for the summer called Marlotte." Whether this word was any relation of *merula* or of the Scotch *marle* I cannot say.

Mar's year. The rebellion, A.D. 1715. So named from the Earl of Mar.

Mashlum. Meslin, mixed corn.—*Burns*. It is, or was, a mixture of oats and pease; a superior kind, of later introduction, had wheat instead of oats. *Sh* for *s*, see *fleesh*.

Meslin, which Burns uses to explain *mashlum*, now stands, for most people, as much in need of explanation as the word which it is meant to interpret, though it is in Johnson. It is from the same root as *mell*, to mix, or mingle.

Masslin, wheat and rye mixed.—*Cotgrave*.

Mang corn, mixed corn, *masling*.—*Bailey*.

> And wing'd purveyors his sharp hunger fed,
> With frugal scraps of flesh and *maslin* bread.
> *Harte quoted by Johnson.*

The word *meslin* allures me to the insertion of the following passage, and to a short digression :—

> He was of old Pythagoras' opinion,
> That green cheese was most wholesome with an onion;

> Coarse *meslin* bread, and for his daily swig,
> Milk, butter-milk, and water, whey and *whig*;
> Sometimes methiglin, and by fortune happy,
> He sometimes sipped a cup of ale most nappy.
> *John Taylor   On Old Parr.*

It will be seen from this extract that whig is not a Scotch word, and that it is neither milk nor whey. The word, except in its political sense, has apparently died out, but I once heard a moorland farmer's wife say when her buttermilk began to ferment and cast up this substance, "The milk's whigging." Wodrow, Defoe, and others speak of it as having been drunk by the Cameronians in the time of the Persecution. Evidence of this is wanting; but if the poor people did drink this nasty stuff— and surely they first drank the milk—it could hardly have been worth the notice of the historian seeing that it was not uncommon for people in England to quench their thirst with it before the Cameronians came into existence, for Old Parr died in 1635, and the poem from which I have made a quotation must have been written about that time; and Breton, who died in 1624, says in his "Farewell to Town,"—

> With leeks and onions, *whig* and whey,
> I must content me as I may.

Scotland has often been taunted with her poverty, and some of her singing birds, like Breton, have often had difficulty enough to get a living; but there is no record of any of them being reduced to wet their whistle with so thin a potation as *whig*. Indeed, I question very much if ever there were a Scotsman who voluntarily, even in his greatest need, swallowed a tea-spoonful of it.

Mask.   To mash, as malt, etc., to infuse.

Mask, to infuse.—*Grose.*

Maskin-pat. A tea-pot.

Maud. A grey chequered plaid.

Maud, a plaid worn by Cheviot shepherds.—*Halliwell.*

Maukin. A hare. Another form of *Malkin*, a dim. of Mary. See under *a'*.

The severity of the game laws led people to speak of protected animals under ambiguous names. Thus the hare was *maukin, baud, Wat, Mally,* etc.

Malkin was a cat—" I come, Grimalkin," *Shak.*—a cat was puss, puss was applied to the hare, and *maukin* naturally followed.

> He swore that *Maulken* to her cost, etc.—*Vanbrugh.*
>
> Thou took'st me up at every word I spoke,
> As I had been a *Maukin.*—*Fletcher.*

Maukin, cor. of Magdalen.—*Weber.*

Maun. Must.

> Thou *mon* be dede, es noght to laine
> For my lord that thou has slayne.—*Ywain and Gawain.*
>
> To me all prynces to lowte *man* be sene.—*Skelton.*
>
> For dole now I *mun* dye.—*Sir Cauline.*

A gentleman *mun* show himself like a gentleman.—*Ben Jonson.*

> And thou *mun* be ful fayn may fall
> On knees for to serve tham all.—*The Seven Sages.*

Maunna. Must not. *Maun* and *na.*

Maut. Malt. See under *a'*.

The churche-wardes of every parish provide halfe a score or twenty quarters of *mault.*—*Anatomie of Abuses.*

O you ale-knights, you that devoure the marrowe of the *mault*, drinke whole ale-tubs into consumption.—*Jacke of Dover. Ritson.*

Mavis. The thrush.

I put in this word because Burns has it in his glossary, and to show that all Englishmen did not think the mavis was the thrush, as is shown by—

> The *Thrush* replies, the *Mavis* descant sings.—*Spenser.*

Maw. Mow. *Mawn*, mowed. *Aw* for *ow*, as in—

> He hadde more *tawe* (tow) on his distaf
> Than Gerveis knew.—*Chaucer.*
>
> But some than sat ryght sad
> That nothynge had
> There of theyr *awne* (own).—*Skelton.*

Mawn. A basket.

Maund, a Hamper or Basket with handles.—*Bailey.*

> A thousand favours from a *maund* she drew.—*Shak.*
>
> Behold, for us the naked graces stay
> With *maunds* of roses, for to strew the way.—*Herrick.*

Maybe. Perhaps.

May-be. Perhaps. *Var. dial.*—*Halliwell.*

Meere. A mare.

> That on was a *mere* lyke,
> The other a colt, a noble stede.—*R. C. de Lion.*
> In a tabbard he rood upon a *mere.*—*Chaucer.*
> Forthledand hai to *meres* ma.—*Met. E. Psalter.*

Meg. Dimin. of Margaret.

Meg, some wine !—*Fletcher.*

But to our business, *Meg*.—*A New Way to Pay Old Debts.*

Meikle. Much.

> *Mekyll* am I made of nowe-a-days.—*Skelton.*
> To sleep would *mickle* grieve me.—*Fletcher.*
> The one ne'er got me credit, the other *mickle* blame.
>
> *Shak.*

> "I sey for me," quod the mouse, "I se so *mykel* after,
> Shall never the cat ne the kitoun bi mi conseille be greved."
> *P. Plowman.*

Melancholious. Mournful.

This is a regularly formed English word like melodious, harmonious, etc., but like Milton's *thunderous* and *inquisitorious*, Warner's *hospitalious*, and others, it has not been admitted to the rank of a *dictionary* word.

> He was a fumisshe man and *malencolyous.*—*Froissart.*
>
> I am so *malencolious.*—*Gower.*

Henry VII., having some thoughts of marrying the widow of King Ferdinand of Naples, sent me to see what she was like. To report whether her visage was sharp or round, fat or lean, pleasand or amiable and *malencolyous.*—*Bacon.*

The uncleane spirits made the *melancholious* man flye out of the houses, and to live in the graves.—*The Four Degenerate Sons.*

Melder. As much corn as is sent at one time to be milled or ground.

Melder, a kiln-full of oats, as many as are dried at one time for meal.—*Grose.*

We come nearer to Burns's *melder* and *melvie*, if we remember that mill and its compounds were formerly spelled with *e* instead of *i.*

> A *melle* he had of gret maystry.—*R. C. de Lion.*
> Munde the *mellere*, and many moo other.—*P. Plowman.*
> Upon the whiche brook ther stont a *melle.*—*Chaucer.*

Mell. A mallet.

Mell, a wooden mallet or beetle.—*Bailey. Grose.*

> Some made a *mell* of massy lead.
> With leaden *mells* and lances strong.
> *E. Ballad of Flodden Field.*

Knocking-*mell*, a large wooden hammer used for bruising barley.
Halliwell.

Mell.   To meddle, to mix.

> Men are to *mell* with.—*Shak.*
> With his Prowess Policy can *mell.*—*Sylvester.*
> Old Dan Geffrey durst not with it *mell.*—*Spenser.*
> Such is the luck that some men get, while they begin to *mell*
> In setting at one such as were out.—*Gammer Gurton's Needle.*

Mellow.   In liquor.

> Did not some mild-beer Bellman tag the metre?
> If so, I pray, invite the honest fellow,
> Let him partake the praise and make him *mellow.*
> *Samuel Richardson.*

> This honest weaver
> Being a little *mellow* in his ale . . sprung his neck
> *Beaum. and Fletcher.*

> In the morning when sober, in the evening when *mellow.*
> *The Old Man's Song.*

Melvie.   To soil with meal.

I do not know anything of the *v* in this word, nor have I met with any attempt to account for it. If it had not been printed more than once under the poet's superintendence, it might have been supposed a mistake for *z*, which occurs frequently, as in *falzie*, to fail, *plenzie*, to complain, *sonzie*, to excuse, &c.

> Their apprentices are fain to *meal* their faces.—*R. Hood.*

> He thought he had done them wrong in *mealing* their clothes.
> *Montaigne by Peter Coste.*

> Were he *meal'd*
> With that which he corrects, then were he tyrannous.
> *Shak.   Meas. for Measure.*

Burns's *melvie* seems nearer Shakspeare's *meal'd* than Dyce's "mingled, compounded."

Memento mori.   Remember death.

I make as good use of it as many a man doth of a death's head, or a *memento mori.*—*Shak.*

Men'. To mend. For omission of *d* see *afield.*

The *amense* (amends) therof is far to call agayne.—*Skelton.*

Mense. Good manners, decorum.

Menseful, comely, graceful, crediting, or giving reputation to a man.—*Bailey.*

Mense, decency, credit.—*Grose.* *Mensful*, neat and clean.—*Thoresby.*

Or efter werdes *mense* and miht,
That geres foles fal in pliht.—*E. Metrical Homilies. Small.*

Never a soul had the *mense* to come near them.—*The Northumb. Garland.*

Served he wes with *menske* and mirthe.—*Amis and Amiloun.*

Menseless. Ill-bred, rude, impudent, wanting *mense*.
Skelton has *demensy* for want of mense.

Merle. Generally said to be the blackbird. I doubt if this was so at one time. Ramsay says, "*merle*, a merlin, a bird."

Upon his dulcet pipe the *merle* doth only play.—*Drayton.*

Mess. Mass. *Mess John*, a priest.

Here *messe* and here matynes.—*P. Plowman.*
By the *messe*, I shall cleve thy head.—*Skelton.*
The highe *messe* was ydone.—*Chaucer.*

Messin. A small dog, a cur.

He was, notwithstanding his uttermost endeavours to free himself from all untoward noises, surrounded with the barking of curs, bawling of mastiffs, snarling of *messins*, &c.—*Rabelais. Pantagruel.*

Middin. A dunghill.

Midding, a dunghill.—*Bailey. Ainsworth. Middin.*—*Bamford. Midden.*—*Grose.*

It made a noise like a bull stuck fast in a muck-*middin*.—
Bairnslea Foak's Annual.

> A fouler *myddyng* saw thou never nane
> Than a man is, with flesche and bane.—*P. of Conscience.*

Midden-creels. Dung-baskets, panniers in which dung was carried on horseback. Things not in use for a century. I do not believe that Burns ever saw them in operation unless in the Highlands.

Midden-hole. A gutter at the bottom of the dunghill.— *Burns.* Rather, as Jamieson gives it, "a hole or small pool beside a dunghill, in which the filthy water stands." This, too, is now nearly, if not altogether, unknown.

Midge. A gnat.

Midge, a gnat.—*Bailey. Johnson.*

> Where the *midge* dare not venture,
>   Lest herself fast she lay:
> If love come he will enter,
>   And soon find out his way.
>   *Love will find out the way: Ritson.*

Milkin-shiel. A place for milking cows or ewes. See *shiel.*

Mill. Snuff-box. See *sneeshin-mill.*

Mim. Prim, affectedly meek.

Mim, primly silent.—*Halliwell. Mimp*, precise.—*Bamford.*

> Thow mihtest beter meten the Myst on Malverne hilles,
> Than geten a *Mom* of heore Mouth till Moneye weore schewed.
>   *P. Plowman.*

I gat not a *mum* of his mouth for my meed.—*Lydgate.*

Mim-mou'd. Speaking precisely. *Mim* and *mou.*

Min'. Mind, remembrance.

There is nothynge done in any place, but and he set his *myne* thereto he will knowe it.—*Froissart.*

> This writte was gett fra kin to kin,
> That best it couth to haf in *min.*—*Cursor Mundi.*

Minawa and minawae. A minuet.

Mind. To resolve, to intend, to remember, to remind.

I *mind* (resolve or intend) to keep thi league that stands between us.—*Q. Elizabeth.*

O! now it *mindeth* me (I remember) that you was one who saw this man elsewhere.—*Ibid.*

What is man that thou *mines* of him?—*Metrical E. Psalter.*

Which booke I *minde* also to publish.—*Spenser.*

I need not *mind* your ladyship how God hath measured outward happiness to you.—*Fuller.*

Minnnie. Mother, dam.

Minny, mother.—*Halliwell.*

Mirk. Dark.

> A shadow blacker than the *mirkest* night.—*Fairfax.*
> Through *mirksome* aire her ready way she makes.—*Spenser.*
> Dancing in *mirky* night, o'er fen and lake
> He glows.—*Collins.*
> *Mirke* watres that ware of hewe.—*Metrical E. Psalter.*

Misca'. Miscall, to abuse, to call names. See *ca'*.

> My heart will sigh when I *miscall* it so.—*Shak.*

Mischanter. An accident, misadventure. *Mis* and *auntre*, as in

> Of *auntres* that han befelle,
> I can sum telle.—*Sir Orpneo.*
> To the chapell dore he yode
> Mo *anters* for to here.—*Sir Amadas.*

> Gef ye meteth the traitour robbour,
> Geveth (give) him *messantoure.—Kyng Alisaunder*.

Messantoure was doubtless pronounced *misshanter*, for *ss* in old authors is often used for *sh*, e.g.:—

> How longe *ssolle* (shall) her luther heved above her *ssoldres* (shoulders) be?—*Robert of Gloucester*.

A thouzend dyvelen *ssel* (shall) come.—*Dan Michel of Northgate*.

The unright ido to poueremen to such *mesaunture* turnde.
Rob. of Gloucester.

Mislear'd. Mischievous, unmannerly. Literally mistaught. *Mis* and *lear*.

Mislering, misteaching.—*Weber*.

> Traitour, thi schal be quit thi mede !
> For mi sones *mislering*.
> Ye schulle habbe evil ending !—*The Seven Sages*.

Miss. A lewd woman, a kept mistress.

> I had restor'd his fame and bliss
> Long since, but that he keeps a *Miss.—Amherst*.

She was taken to be the Earle of Oxford's *Misse* (as at this time they began to call lewd women).—*Evelyn*.

That which was reported with the boldest confidence was that I had my *misses.—John Bunyan*.

Misteuk. Misteuk. *Eu* for *oo;* see under *beuk*.

> They *tuik* our naigs.—*Richardson*.

> He had the letter by the noke,
> To the erle he it *tuke.—MS. quoted by Halliwell*.

Mither. Mother. *I* for *o;* see *anither*.

> I knaw thee, Jack ! mind an I doont tell thee *mither*.
> *Specimens of Durham Language*.

Mixtie-maxtie. Confusedly mixed.

The effects . . detraction *mixty-maxty*, etc.—*Coleridge*.
Mish-mash, a mingle, a hotch-potch.—*Johnson*.

Moistify.   To moisten.

I have not met with this word, probably the poet's own coinage, and hardly could a word be found better fitted to the place it fills, but similar words are found, e.g., cripplefied occurs in "The Death of Robert Earl of Huntingdon," and Spenser has—

> Whilest she did weepe of no man *mercifide.*
> They flatter the devil here and *smoothify* his name.—*Motteux.*
> The land was *moysted* with blood.—*Maundeville.*
> Art thou one of those wha aim to be *ladyfied?*—*Massinger.*

Mons Meg.   A cannon in Edinburgh Castle.

Mony or *Monie.*   Many.

> There he dwelled *moni* a day.—*Ipoymdon.*
> He sent him to London with *mony* armed groom.
> *Old E. Ballad.*
> Sorwes in Englelond were wel *mony*-volde. —*R. of Glou.*
> Wikked gostes, I wote, fro helle,
> So *mony* that no tonge mygte telle.—*Owayn Miles.*
> Off our folk they schotte *monye.*—*R. C. de Lion.*

Mools.   Earth, mould.

Mullock, dirt, rubbish.—*Bamford.*

> The *mullok* on an hepe ysweped was.—*Chaucer.*
> Let us not *moulen* thus in idlenesse.—*Ib.*
> The other cofre of straw and *mull*
> He fild also.—*Gower.*

> And sithen was Gamelyn graven under *moolde.*
> *Tale of Gamelyn.*

> Show plainly how the pre-existent soul
> Enacts and enters bodies here below,
> And then entire unhurt can leave the *moul,*
> And thence her airy vehicle can draw.—*Dr. Henry More.*

Moony. Moon-struck, lunatic. Johnson has the word but not in this sense.

> The *moony* nights call forth fierce lovers.—*Herrick.*

Moop. To nibble as a sheep.

Moorlan'. Of or belonging to moors.

Morn. The next day, to-morrow.

> Then swere Garcy
> That he wolde brenne all Rome with fyre,
> On the *morne* yf that he myght.—*Le Bone Florence of Rome.*

> I have made vowes fourty and forgete hem on the morne.
> *P. Plowman.*

> Opon the *morn*
> He went to seke that lady bright.—*The Seven Sages.*
> On the *morn*, when it was day,
> The messenger went on his way.—*Emare.*

Mottie. Dusty, full of motes.

Mou. The mouth.

> *Mow*, the mouth.—*Bailey. Hone. Mow*, wry mouth.—*Johnson.*
>> Such beauty as the fair princess
>> Is not for a tyrant's *mow*.—*R. Hood.*
>> Then laugheth she and maketh him the *mow*.
>>> *Chaucer.*

Moudiewort, or *modework.* A mole. *Mould,* i.e., earth and *work.*

> *Mowdywarp,* a mole.—*Bamford. Moudy-rat,* a mole; *moudy-hill,* a mole-hill.—*Halliwell.*

Mousie. Dim. of mouse.

Muckle. Great, big, much. Another spelling of *meikle* and *mickle.*

>> Their practices were such
>> That they wrought *muckle* woe.—*R. Hood.*

> The *mukel* lauande loghe to the lyfte rered.
> *Early E. Alliterative Poems.*

Muckle house. Parliament.

Muir. A moor. *U* for *oo*, as in *beuk*, but muir and moor are pronounced alike.

Munny Begum. Used by Burns for Indian.

Munny Begum was a woman appointed by Warren Hastings, guardian of the young Nawab, or Nabob, of Bengal.

> That Hastings, *Munny Begum*, Scott, must fall,
> And Pitt, and Jenkinson, and Leadenhall.—*The Rolliad.*
> Dames in India, christen'd *Munny Begum.*—*Wolcot.*

Musie. Dim. of Muse.

Muslin-kail. Broth composed simply of water, shelled barley, and greens, i.e., vegetables. See *mashlum*.

Muslin-kail is exactly what is described as the food of the English peasant at one time : "wortes flechles wrought," vegetables cooked without meat.—*Peres the Ploughman's Crede. Skeat.*

Mutchkin. An English pint.

Mysel'. Myself.

> I'll fetch yon pedlars back *mysell—Sir Andrew Barton.*

Mystic tie, *mystic* word and grip. The secrets of Freemasonry.

N.

Na. No, not, nor.

Na, no.—*Bailey.*

> But yet, *na* fors, al sal be for the best.—*Chaucer.*

> To speke of luf *na* time was than.—*Ywain and Gawain*.

Naw, naw, tha was not born then.—Tennyson's *Northern Farmer*.

Nae. No, not any. There is a difference between *na* and *nae*, but I think it is little attended to except in one case, that of the adverb of refusal or denial which to a Scotsman is always *na*, never, *nae*.

> They found hardy men who went *nae* foot back for them.—*Surrey to Cardinal Wolsey*.
>
> Ne his name knew she *na* thing.—*The Seven Sages*.

Naething, or *naithing.* Nothing. *Nae* and *thing*.

Naig. A horse. $\bar{A}$ for $\breve{a}$. See under *shaird*.

> They were a comical sort of people, riding upon *negs*, as they called their small horses.—*North's Life of Lord-Keeper Guilford*.
>
> They tuik our *naigs*,
> And left us eke an empty byre.—*Richardson*.

Naigie. Dim. of naig.

Nane. None.

> Swlk saw I never *nane*.—*Ywain and Gawain*.
>
> Latyn als, I trow, canne *nane*,
> But those that it of scole have tane.—*Pricke of Conscience*.
>
> Ne of thaire wisdom, o *nane* wise,
> Wil I mak no mar marchandise.—*The Seven Sages*.

Nappy. Ale, strong, tasty.

> He'll swear by the *nappy*,
> That man who'd be happy
>   Must be drunk from the womb to the grave.
>   *The Artful Husbana*.
>
> When I my thresher heard
> With *nappy* beer I to the barn repair'd.—*Gay*.
>
> If his head be hard-braced with *nappie* ale.
>   *Old Meg of Herefordshire*.

Natch. A notch.—*Jamieson.* As Burns uses it I should rather think it was something fitted to make a notch,—a large needle perhaps.

Near hand. Nearly. Johnson has *near hand*, but with a different meaning.

> I have been watchman in this wood
> *Near hand* this twenty year.—*R. Hood.*
>
> Bifor hym sone thai come ilk ane,
> *Nerhand* naked and wobigane.—*Launfal.*

Neck-bane. Neck. *Neck* and *bane.*

> And right so als he stouped down,
> Syr Ywain with his brand was boun,
> And strake his *nek-bane* right in sonder.—*Ywain and Gawain.*
>
> Beware, and kepe thy *nekke-bone* from yren.—*Chaucer.*

Neebor. A neighbour.

> Now *neybors* and kynnesmen lete us forth go.
> *Ancient Mysteries.*
>
> But inwardly he chawed his owne maw
> At *neibors* welth that made him ever sad.—*Spenser.*

When you would sneeze, straite turne yourselfe unto your *neibours* face.—*The School of Slovenrie.*

> And, sone, yf thou wylt lyf at ese,
> And warme among thy *neybours* sit.
> *How the Wise Man taught his Son.*

Ne'er-do-weel. One never likely to do well. See *weel.*

Negleckit. Neglected. See *disrespeckit.*

Neist. Next.

Neist, or *niest*, i.e., nighest, superlative of *nie*, a common form of nigh, is really—but for the rule that, whatever is, is right in language—the correct though not the fashionable spelling of next, x having come into use, among other purposes, as a substitute for *s* and *es*, e.g.,—

Till "thow *lixte*" (liest), and "thow *lixte*" lopen out at ones.
—*P. Plowman.*

Daries blod thou art next,
Wyght and gentil, y-bore *hext* (highest).—*Kyng Alisaunder.*
And thanne *neste* (next)
He hath eke foure upon his breste.—*Gower.*
Nest the rote growand,
Es the heved with nek folowand.—*P. of Conscience.*
Melchior him com thair *neist.*—*Cursor Mundi.*

The following shows the word in a transition state, the old spelling being retained, but the new pronunciation adopted:—

Yet some hold opinyon, all is well with the highest;
They are in good saftie when freedome is *niest.*
A Newe Well a Daye.

Neuk. Nook. *Eu* for *oo.* See under *beuk.*

Whore saw you her? I' the chimney *neuk* within.—*B. Jonson.*

New-ca'd. Newly calved. See under *ca'.*

New Light. Newly introduced doctrines at variance with those of the Church of Scotland.

This *New-light* was very different from that of Butler's Ralph. The witty poet of Charles the Second's day ridicules the *New-light* of his time, the Ayrshire bard rather patronized that of his.

Some call it gifts, and some *New-light.*—*Hudibras.*

Nick. A name for the devil. *Nickie-ben*, the same.

Nickie is a familiar name for Nick, but what *ben* is I have never heard any body attempt to explain, nor can I guess, unless we may suppose that as *ben* is sometimes used to express intimacy, the poet had wrought himself

up to a kind of liking for the *patriarch*, as I have more than once heard him called, and had something of the feeling of the old Scottish minister who, after hearing a young man preach, criticised his pronunciation thus:—
" Ye said devil, but I wadna say't that way. I aye say *deevil*, its mair kindly like."

> Nick Machiavel had ne'er a trick
> Though he gave name to our Old *Nick.—Butler*.

Nobody now-a-days needs to be told that Butler is wrong.

Nick. A notch cut into something. *Crummie's nicks*, natural notches on cows' horns.

In his curious letter to Nicol, Burns uses *nick* for notch.

Nick. To cut.

Nick is used by E. writers to signify to *cut into*, but Burns employs it to mean to cut through, as in—

> Sin I began to *nick* the thread.
> *Death and Dr. Hornbook.*

In one passage of Butler it seems to mean cut through—

> For he had drawn your ears before,
> And *nick'd* them on the self-same score.
> *Hudibras.*

Nieve. The fist.

I wu'not, my good two-penny rascal; reach me thy *neif.—Ben Jonson*.

> I kiss thy *neif.—Shak*.

> And yet the thefe, or he wolde leeve,
> He put the hafte in Florence *neeve*,
> For she schulde have the wyte.
> *Le Bone Florence of Rome.*

Neive, neife, a fist.—*Bailey*. *Neyve*, a griped fist.—*Bamford*,

Nievefu'. A handful.

Niffer. An exchange, to exchange, to barter.
To pass from one *neive* to another.—*Jamieson.*

Niger. A negro.

Nines. *To the nines*, to perfection.

Nine appears to have been a favourite number. We still speak of a nine days' wonder. The Romans had their *novendiales feriae*, or nine expiatory days, and Shakespeare makes his witches speak as if they considered their circling nine times perfected their rites—

> The weird sisters, hand in hand,
> Posters of the sea and land,
> Thus do go about, about;
> Thrice to thine, and thrice to mine,
> And thrice again, to make up *nine:*
> Peace! the charm's wound up.—*Macbeth.*

Nine-tailed-cat. A hangman's whip.

Cat o' nine tails, a whip with nine lashes, used for the punishment of crimes.—*Johnson.*

> You dread reformers of an impious age,
> You awful *cat o' nine tails* to the stage,
> This once be just, and in our cause engage.—*Vanbrugh.*
>
> Fine chains for the neck, and a *cat with nine tails.*
> —*Cowper.*

Nipperkin. A small tankard or drinking-cup; a measure.

> We'll drink it out of the *nipperkin*, boys.
> *The Barley Mow Song.*

On one hand was to be seen a long train of flagons, *nipperkins*, etc.—*Rabelais.*

Nit. A nut. *I* for *u.* See under *bizz.*

No. Not, as in—

> O this is no mine ain lassie.

> If there were of my degree
> That wolde sain it was *no* right.—*Gower*.

> Thou art y-falle in hond myne,
> Thé to solace, and *no* pyne.—*Kyng Alisaunder*.

> And round about the valley as ye passe,
> Ye may *no* see, for peeping flowres, the grasse.
> *G. Peele, 1584.*

Nob. The head, knob.

> Nature so slighting the poor Royal *nob*,
> As if she bargained for it by the job.—*Wolcot*.

Nocht. Nothing.

> Gef thou art rich and wel ytold (spoken of),
> Ne be thou *noht* tharefore to bold.
> *Proverbs of Hendyng.*

> To *noght* es lede lither in his sight.
> *Metrical E. Psalter.*

Noosing. In the "Ode sacred to the Memory of Mrs. Oswald," *noosing* probably means tying tightly, though some think it means *nousel*, to nurse. Either signification makes sense of—

> *Noosing* with care a bursting purse.

> O impe of darkness, and seed of the deuyll!
> Born to all wickednesse, and *nusled* in all evyll.
> *New Custom.*

Nor. Though, than.

A man should love his wife better *nor* his father.—*The Four Degenerate Sons.*

Norland. Of or belonging to the north.

Nor-west. North is frequently contracted to *nor*, when joined to other words, as, Norman, Norfolk, Norwich, etc. It is sometimes found even alone so contracted,

> The storm's on wing comes powdering from the *Nore*.
> 'Tis past the Alps already, and whirls forward
> To th' Appenines.—*Brutus of Alba*.

Note. A bank-note for a guinea.

Some of these notes seem to be still in existence. The *Glasgow Weekly Herald*, of Oct. 11, 1884, says, in answer to a correspondent, "Supposing the *guinea bank note* to be genuine, it is worth 21s."

> With not a single *note* the purse supply.—*Crabbe*.

Nowte. Black cattle.

Nowte, neat cattle.—*Grose*.

They brought also ccc *nowt* and lx horse.—*Duke of Northumberland to Henry VIII*.

> All that ever was his and mine,
> Horse and *nowt*, and sheep and swine,
>   Away they drove and bare.—*Sir Amadas*.

O.

Och ! and och-hey. Oh !

Och hon ! och-rie ! Alas !

> But by the way repeated the *och-hones*
> Of his wild Irish and chromatic tones.—*Butler*.
>
> *Oh, hone ! oh, hone !*—*Beaumont aud Fletcher*.
>
> The frier then, that treacherous knave, with *ough ough-hone* lament
> To see his cousin Devill's son to have so foul a shent.
>
>   *Derrick. Sir W. Scott.*

Hone occurs in the old English romance of Ywain and Gawain. Ritson and Halliwell think it means *shame ;* the latter adds *mockery ;* Jamieson says it is *delay*. It may be worth a little examination.

The two knights, as remarkable for their friendship as for their prowess, engaged in battle without knowing each other. The fight, as was to be expected when two such warriors met in conflict, was long and terrible. Night put an end to the battle when

> Thai had bled so mekil blode,
> It was great ferly that thai stode.

They then asked each other's names, and found to their great surprise that they were dear friends. Then said Sir Ywain

> " I grant thou has me overcomen.
> Sir Gawain answered als curtays,
> Thou sal noght do, sir, als thou sais;
> This honour sall noght be myne,
> Bot sertes it aw wele at be thine;
> I gif it the her, withouten *hone*,
> And grantes that i am undone."

There was plainly no room for shame or mockery, and as little for delay, and with deference I think it means without regret or sorrow, that is willingly.

This view is supported by an expresssion of Milton's friend, T. Ellwood :—

" I *honed* after personal conversation with friends," i.e., he *longed* for friends, regretted their absence.

> I had no money, nor ever *honed* after it.—*Ib.*

If this be correct Burns's *och-hon* will be *oh the sorrow!*

Ochtlins, or oughtlins. Somewhat, in any degree.

> Talde thou hir *oght* my name?—*Ywain and Gawain.*
>
> For when he hath *oht* bygeten,
> Al the fredom is forgeten.—*Proverbs of Hendyng. Rel. Antiquae.*

O'ergang. Overgo, to surpass, to excel. *O'er* and *gang.*

O'erlay. A cravat,

O'erword. The chorus, refrain, or burden of a song, any word frequently repeated.

Ony, or onie. Any.

And he had the fairest gardyn that *ony* man might behold.—*Maundevelle.*

> All she thought was lost, by the rode,
> That dyd the lytell boye *ony* good.—*The Frier and the Boye.*

> Thy soveraine temple wol I most honouren
> Of *ony* place.—*Chaucer.*

Ook. A week.

> And yaf hym sowke Fourty *woke.*—*Octovian Imperator.*

> Bot thre *woukes* were set
> And batayle schal there be.—*Childe Horn and Maiden Rimnild.*

> I wolde be gladder
> Than thoughe I had this *woke* ywonne a wey of essex cheese.
> P. Plowman.

> She shall kepe her chambre these three *wookes.*
> *Letter of Lord Dacre and T. Magnus to Hen. VIII. Dyce.*

Or. Ere, before.

> Yet wold he have a ferthing *or* he went.—*Chaucer.*

> The great man was gone out *or* I came.—*Latimer.*

> *Or* I could make a prologue to my brains,
> They had begun the play.—*Shak.*

> He's for a jig, or a tale of bawdry, *or* he sleeps.—*Id.*

Orra. Superfluous, odd.

Otherwhere. Elsewhere, in other places.—*Johnson.*

Ourie. Shivering, drooping.

Oury, dirty, ill-looking, untidy.—*Halliwell.*

Oursel, or *oursels.* Ourselves. See *mysel.*

Out-cast. A quarrel.

Outlers. Outliers, cattle not housed, lying in the fields at night.

Outler, an animal not housed.—*Halliwell.*

These naciouns ben *outelying.*—*Kyng Alisaunder.*

It is but a trifling sport for you to pull down an *out-lyer.*
Cleveland.

Outspak. Spoke out.

Owre. Over, too.

Ourlop, probably of over and leap.—*Bailey.*

> Now er we ryche, now er we pur,
> Now have *or* litel, now pas we measur.—*P. of Conscience.*
>
> He ligges *or* long on bere.—*Sir Amadas.*

V and *u* being used indifferently by old writers, it is not easy to determine when *ouer* should be read *over* or when *ower*, but surely in the following passages *ouer* is a monosyllable. This will appear more evident if it is remembered that the old romances and ballads were sung rather than read or recited.

> But then fare with her esely,
>   And cherysch hur for her gode dede,
> For thyng *ouerdon* unskylfully,
>   Makys wrath to grow where ys no nede.
> *How the Wise Man taught his Son.*
>
> And broke his parks, and slawe his dere,
>   *Ouer* all they chose the best,
> So perelous outlawes as they were,
>   Walked not by easte or west.—*Adam Bell, &c.*
>
> Ute *ouer* that hus than stode the stern,
> Thar Jesus and his moder wern.—*Cursor Mundi.*
>
> *Ower* my 'eäd.—*Tennyson.*

Owre with Burns's spelling occurs in "The Seven Sages"—

> He might han don a better ginne :
> Ibiried hit *owre* priveliche.

> Helle may hold hym be no lawe,
> But that he may pas, at hese lyberte,
> *Ower* swyche.—*Coventry Mysteries.*

Owre hip. A way of fetching a blow with a hammer over the arm.—*Burns.*

Striking with a forehammer by bringing it with a swing over the hip.—*Cunningham.*

Owsen. Oxen.

Ows, an ox.—*Thoresby.* *Owsen*, oxen.—*Bamford.* *Ousen.*—*Bailey.*

Oxter. The arm-pit; to support by putting the hand under the arm-pit.

Oxter, the armpit.—*Bailey.*

P.

Pacing horse. A horse trained to canter.

Before the battle of Dunbar, Major General Lambert having been taken prisoner by the Scottish cavalry, "the valiant Lieutenant Empson, one of Hacker's officers pursued with five or six of our soldiers and hewed him out and brought him to his own regiment, when we procured him a *pacing-horse*."—*Memoirs of Captain John Hodgson.*

> They rode, but authors having not
> Determined, whether *pace* or trot.—*Butler.*

Pack. Intimate, familiar; twelve stones of wool.

Pack, a company. *Pack* of wool, a quantity of about 240 lbs.—*Bailey.*

Pack, to confederate in ill.—*Johnson.*

Pack aff. To go away.

> If she do bid me *pack*, I'll give her thanks,
> As though she bid me stay by her a week.—*Shak.*

Poor Stella must *pack off* to town.—*Swift*.
She should have stay'd, and you *pack'd off*.—*Echard*.

Paidle. To walk in shallow water; a hoe.

Patoüiller, to *padle* or dable in with the feet.—*Cotgrave*.

> As ever thou deserv'st thy daily drink,
> *Padling* in sack.—*Ben Jonson*.

> He may make a *padler* i' the world,
> But never a brave swimmer.
> *Wit at Several Weapons*.

Painch. Paunch.

Painches, tripe.—*Halliwell*.

Pance, the *panch*, maw, belly.—*Cotgrave*.

> Like fowls with Virgins faces, purging still
> Their filthy *panches*.—*Sandys*.

Paitrick. A partridge.

Paitrick, a partridge.—*Halliwell*.

> The painted *partrich* lyes in every field.—*B. Jonson*.

De brave contra where dey killa de *patrich* vid de hawka.—*Duke of Buckingham*.

> There is no flesch so norrysaunt
> Unto an Ynglischeman,
> *Partrick*, plover, heroun, ne swan,
> Cow, ne oxe, scheep, ne swyn,
> As the hed off a Sarezyn.—*Kyng Alisaunder*.

Paly. Pale.

> Fire answers fire; and through their *paly* flames
> Each battle sees the other's umber'd face.—*Shak*.

> Sweet violets, Love's paradise, that spread
>   Your gracious colours, which you couched beare
>   Within your *palie* faces.—*Sir Walter Raleigh*.

Pang. To cram.

Pang, to fill, to stuff.—*Halliwell*.

If in the following lines Skelton does not use *pang* for fill, but for pain, he is the only author I remember who so speaks of heaviness. David says, "I am full of heaviness," Ps. 69 and 20; and to be in heaviness and to have heaviness, are common expressions, but to be pained by heaviness is, I think, unknown.

> No creatuer but that wolde
> Have rewed upon me,
> To behold and se
> What hevynesse dyd me *pange*,
> Wherewith my handes I wrange.
> *Phyllyp Sparowe.*

Parishen. Parish.

> Lewed men they were in clerkes clothyng
> Disguysed fayre, in forme of clerkes wyse,
> Their *parishyns* ful lytle enfourmyng
> In laive devine, or els in God his service.—*Hardynge.*

Quoted by Jamieson, who supposes it means parishes, but it may mean parishioners. The same word is found in Piers Plowman, and seems to stand for people rather than a place,—

> Bote the Parisch-preste, and he departe the selver,
> That have schulde the pore *parisschens.*—*Prologue, v. 79.*

Chaucer has *parishens*, but it also means parishioners.

Park. A field.

Park, a farm, field, or close.—*Devon. Halliwell.*
Parruc, pearroc, a park, an enclosure.—*Bosworth.*

Parle. Speech, courtship.

> Commanders have the power to *parle* with princes.—*Fletcher.*
>   Of all the gentlemen
> That every day with *parle* encounter me,
> In thy opinion which is worthiest love?—*Shak.*
> The creature's jubilee; God's *parle* with dust.—*Henry Vaughan.*

T

> This, if in lengthen'd *parle* the night they pass,
> Shall furnish still his opening to Dundas.—*The Rolliad.*

Parliamentin. Attending parliament. This change of a noun to a verb resembles Butler's—

> And out he rode a *colonelling.*

Parritch. Oatmeal pudding, a well-known Scotch dish. *Porridge.*—*Johnson.* *Porritch.*—*Bamford.*

Ge or *dge* was often changed to *ch*, e.g.,—

> Thu *knowlechest* that thy men breake our parke by nyght.
> *Lord Grey de Ruthyn.*
>
> To whom he bore so fell a *grutch* (grudge).—*Butler.*
> *Charchyng* (charging) hym fast to hie.—*Lydgate.*
> His foul rank blood of bacon and pease *porritch,*
> Must out of you to the last dram.—*Aspasia's Garden.*

Oatmeal porridge must once have been well known in England. We learn this from a scene in one of Beaumont and Fletcher's plays. Wellborn having gone to a house in London, says to his servant, "Have they (the horses) any meat?" to which he replies, "Faith, sir, here are no oats to be got, unless you'll have 'em in *porridge;* the people are so mainly given to spoon meat."

The Scornful Lady.

Speaking of "the halesome parritch," one cannot help recalling that melancholy note which the poet wrote to his wife, seven days before his death:—

> No flesh or fish can I swallow; porridge and milk are the only thing I can taste.

It is curious to notice that E. authors used the plural as they do in Scotland at this moment:—

> They lie on his understanding.—*Fletcher.*
>
> The fool spit in his porridge to try if *they'd* hiss; *they* did not hiss.—*L'Estrange.*

Pat. Did put.
>*Pet*, put.—*Weber.*

Pat to. Did distress, pressed, overtaxed. E. writers use *put to it.*
>This *put* Christian more *to it* than anything he met with before.
>>*Bunyan.*

Pat. A pot. *A* for *o*, see under *aff.*
>>Beth *nat* agast, ne quaketh *nat.*—*Chaucer.*
>>Hee seeth her *nase* (nose) straught and even.—*Gower.*

Pattle or *pettle.* A plough-staff. A small spade with a shaft long enough for the ploughman when at work to reach those parts of the plough which are apt to gather clay. It is the same as *paddle* in "Thou shalt have a *paddle* on thy weapon."—*Deuteronomy.*

Paughty. Proud, haughty, saucy.

Paukie. Cunning, sly.
>*Pauky*, sly, mischievous, pettish, proud, insolent.—*Halliwell.*

Pay. To beat.
>To *pay*, to punish.—*Johnson.*
>>He *paid* good Robin back and side.—*R. Hood.*
>>Mass, you'll *pay* him then!—*Shak.*
>>>Tell their schoolmistress
>>>What truants they are, and bid her *pay* them soundly.
>>>>*The Antipodes.*

Peat-reek. The smoke of peat-fire; Highland whisky, so called from a flavour, real or fancied, given to it by the peats used in its manufacture.

Pech. To fetch the breath short, *as in an asthma.*
>*Pech*, to pant, to breathe heavily. *Cumber.*—*Halliwell.*

Pechan. The crop of fowls, the stomach.

Jamieson calls this an Ayrshire word, which means that he found it in Burns alone. I believe it is unknown in the county.

Pennie or *penny.* Money, riches.

> For never wight he lets to passe that way
> But he him makes his passage-*penny* pay.—*Spenser.*

> My dowry and other thyng y sold,
> And all the *pennys* to them I told.—*Sir Amadas.*

Penny-fee. Wages.

Country servants did not, nor do they yet, receive all their remuneration in money; what money they did get seems to have been called their *penny-fee.* The expression has died out.

They insisted that they must either have the money or the *fee-penny* in merchandise.—*Life of Sir Thomas Gresham.*

Penny-pay wedding. A marriage feast at which the guests pay. Not peculiar to Scotland. See under *fen.*

Penny-wheep. Small beer. See *wheep.*

> What bread how stale !
> What *pennie ale.*—*Tusser.*

Penny ale and podyng ale she poured togederes.—*P. Plowman.*
Penny-whip, very small beer.—*Lanc. Halliwell.*

Perish. To destroy, to cause to perish, as in "And *perish'd* monie a bonnie boat."

I could stand till I had *perished* my lungs with violent laughter.
The Atheist's Tragedy.

Thy flinty heart
Might in thy palace *perish* Margaret.—*Shak.*
And if I wrong the dead, heaven *perish* me.—*Fletcher.*

His wants and miseries have *perished* his good face.—*Beaumont and Fletcher.*

Per se. By themselves.

Pet. A domesticated sheep, &c., a favourite.
> *Pet*, a cade lamb, i.e., one brought up in the house.—*Bailey.*
> *Peat*, a little fondling. It is now commonly called a *pet*.—*Johnson.*
>> This is become a *pet* vice amongst us.—*Swift.*

Pettle. To cherish, to treat as a pet.

Philabeg. A kilt.

Phraise. Fair speeches, flattery; to flatter.
> But Virgil wan the *fraes*,
> And past them all for deep engyen.—*Verses Prefixed to Skelton's Works.*

Pibroch. Music adapted to the bag-pipe.

Pickle. A small quantity, a single grain.
> *Pickle*, a small parcel of land.—*Johnson.*

When the word was once applied to any thing small, though I do not think that in Scotland a *pickle* land was ever heard of, it would not long be confined to that particular thing, but, like other words, would soon be applied to objects very different from that in which it originated. A *pickle land* would naturally lead to its equivalent a *pickle siller*, and so to other small things.

Pickle-herring. A merry-andrew.
> The *pickle-herring* found the way to shake him.—*Spectator.*
> A plague o' these *pickle-herrings!*—*Shak.*

Pier. A quay or harbour.

Pilgarlick. A silly fellow.

> Poor *pilgarlic* is fain to make every body's time his own.
> *Motteux.*
>
> *Pilgarlick* must meet with a dry beating.—*Echard.*

Pin (in "Your *pin* would help to mend a mill"). A wooden pin or skewer used to fasten the end of a pudding or haggis; called also, both in England and Scotland, a pudding-prick. Both terms are now forgotten, modern cookery, I believe, preferring needle and thread to timber.

> They pynche at the payment of a *poddynge prycke*.—*Skelton.*
> I know no use for them so meet
> As to be *puding-pricks*.—*R. Hood.*

Pine. Pain, uneasiness.

> Pierc'd through the heart with sorrow, grief, and *pine*.
> *Fairfax.*
>
> But wel I wote, that in this world gret *pine* is.—*Chaucer.*
>
> The grene coverlet sufferd grete *pine*.—*Skelton.*
>
> By some deadly chance be done to *pine*.—*Spenser.*
>
> Thomne stowue he taught to take two staves
> And fecche felice home for the wyuen *pyne*.—*P. Plowman.*

The Rev. Walter W. Skeat, and nobody has a better right to speak on such a subject, says, "*wyuene pyne* is one more allusion to the *women's punishment*, the *cucking stool*." It seems rather to mean childbed, and to correspond to Barbour's *childill*, and Thomme was "taught" to bring his wife home from gossiping at lyings-in.

Pingle. To be busy about trifles to little purpose.

Pingle had in English some connection with *pickle*, being that which enclosed a *pickle land*, and sometimes meaning the land enclosed.

Pingle, a small enclosure, generally one long and narrow.
Halliwell.

Pingle, a small croft or pycle.—*Grose.*

Pint. Two quarts.

Pit. To put. *I* for *u* sound, see under *fit,* and in—
> And sore hym *hirten* (hurt).—*Kyng Alisaunder.*
> And with that word he for a *quishen* (cushion) ran.
> *Chaucer.*

> What mon art thou this morning mase,
> With *syche* (such) sympell chere?—*Sir Amadas.*
> The small guttes ye shall out *pyt.*—*Book of St. Albans.*

Placad. A public proclamation.

If this word is not a corruption of placard, I cannot guess what it is. Burns apparently meant it for that, and yet a "loud placad," i.e., a writing affixed to a wall, except in the slang sense in which we sometimes hear of a "loud dress," seems nonsense. Chambers thinks it means "cheers," which like "shouts" would give a good enough meaning to—

> The Saxon lads, wi' loud *placads,*
> On Chatham's boy did ca', man;

but then we have the poet's own statement that it is a public proclamation. Placard, however, seems to have been at one time something different from what we now understand it to be, as may be seen in Tusser. The old poetical agriculturalist, having the misfortune to possess a good voice and musical ear, was impressed for the king's choir by some one empowered by *placard* to seize suitable youths. His own words are—

> Thence for my voice, I must, no choice,
> Away of forse, like postboy horse;
> For sundry men had *placardes* then
>   Such child to take.

Plakaot is Dutch for proclamation.

Plack. An old Scotch coin ; used to denote the smallest sum of money.

I found some outlawes of Ingland, some of Scotland at cards, some for ale, some for *plake* and hard-hedds.—*Sadler's State Papers.*

> Though he not worth a *plackis*.
>
> *Northumberland Ballad.*

> Pluck up thyne herte upon a mery pyne
> And lete us laughe a *placke* or tweyn at nale.
>
> *Skelton.*

Plackless. Penniless.

Plaid. A loose upper garment.—*Ramsay.* A long and narrow woollen shawl ; also a kind of cloth.

This word has found a place in all E. dictionaries since Bailey, who spells it *plad*, inserted it in his ; but it was known in England before Bailey's day, as the following curious note shows :—

Waybreg, July 15, 1681.

Sir,—I am encoreged to geve you thes trubell, and beg a favor of you, knoing the regard you ever had for my Lord Duke desest, and his oblegations to you ; which is that you well own, as for yourself, a parsell of Scottch *plad* of ten or leven peses, or geve me leve to order them to be derected to you, that I may with less trubell com by them.—Your Servant,

Norfolk.

Duchess of Norfolk to Mr. Pepys.

The Duchess's morality seems to have been on a level with her orthography, for she tried to entice a Government official to assist her in a smuggling transaction, there being at the time a duty on Scotch woollen cloth brought into England.

> And checker'd *plaid* become their prey.—*Tickell.*

Plaidie. Dim. of plaid.

Plaiding, or *plaiden*. A kind of cloth differing from plaid and flannel.

Allan Cunningham says, "The wives of our husbandmen spun their wool and flax, and sent the yarn and thread to the weaver to be manufactured into cloth. In this way sackcloth for the corn, plaiding for the beds, linen for the body, and broad-cloth and stuffs for daily or even holiday wear were produced." Now, I never heard the word sackcloth used in Scotland except in the Scriptural expression, sackcloth and ashes, or simply sackcloth for mourning; *sacking* is the most used. *Plaiding* was not used for beds. If it had been, what became of the flannel which they manufactured? The *broad-cloth and stuffs* were *plaiding* for coat or jacket, and drugget for vest, in which Allan and many a wealthier man's son, in their schoolboy days, thought themselves well dressed.

That (wetting) is soon effected by the looseness and springiness of the *plaiding.—Letters from Scotland*.

There was a stub-bearded John-a-Styles with a *ploydens* face.
Marston.

This resembles—

Those *linen* cheeks of thine
Are counsellors to fear.—*Shak.*

and—

Peel'd, patch'd, and piebald, *linsywolsy* brothers.—*Pope.*
Russet yeas and honest *Kersey* noes.—*Shak.*

I was wont
To call them *woollen* vassals.—*Ib.*

Plainstanes. The pavement. *Plain* and *stane.*

Plate. A pewter vessel, placed at the door or gate of a church to receive the offerings of the worshippers.

Plate. Dim. of plate, not the previous word but one sometimes used for saucer.

Plea. A disagreement, a quarrel.

Plenish. To furnish a house, to stock a farm.

I have not found *plenish* in an English author, but Chaucer has *plein*, full, and Milton uses *replenish*, not as in "Multiply and replenish the earth," addressed to Noah after the flood, when, of course, it means to furnish or stock again, but in the S. sense, to furnish for the first time. The angel, describing the creation, says—

> The waters thus
> With fish *replenished*, and the air with fowl
> Ev'ning and morn solemniz'd the fifth day.
> *Paradise Lost. B. VII.*

With pileful scriches she *replenishyd* the hole mancion.—*Hall.*

Pleugh, plew. A plough. *Eu* and *ew* for *ou* and *ow*, i.e., the sound of *ū* for that of *ou*, as in *shew* for show, and in—

Til him *bues* (bows) bathe winde and se.—*E. Metrical Homilies.*

Quen (when) Maria sagh thaa bestes *lute* (lout)
First sco (she) was gretli in *dute* (doubt).—*Cursor Mundi.*

And he was in the hynder part of the boot (boat), slepynge on a *pilewe.*—*Wyclif.*

Pliskie. A trick.

Pliver. A plover. *O* into *i*. See *anither*.

Plumrose. A primrose. Jamieson has *plumrock*.

Strange as primrose appears in this disguise, it is not farther from the present spelling than are the following, which, however, are nearer the original *primula* :—

> The honysoucle, the *primerollys*,
> Ther levys splaye at Phebus vp-rysing.—*Lydgate.*

He giveth the firste *primerole.*—*Gower.*

This word is used by Burns in a burlesque letter to Nicol, and may have been made by himself, but the probability is that he had met it somewhere, for *l* and *r* are "so nearly related in sound," to quote Dr. Bosworth, "that they are used promiscuously." Many examples might be given. I give them as they come to remembrance. Shakespeare, Massinger, and Dryden write *Argier* for Algiers, Chaucer has *laurer, purpre,* for laurel and purple, Skelton *flagraunt* for fragrant, Thomas Herbert, *tulipant* for turban, etc.

Grose and Halliwell both give *plum,* very. I do not know that there is any connection, but very, especially if disguised as *plum,* might easily have been changed into having the meaning of *fine* or *good,* and the primrose, from coming early, have been called the *good* or *plum* rose. But how came it to be called a *rose?*

Plum seems to be used in America for very or quite—

You look *plum* fagged out.—*The Century, Feb., 1866.*

Plush. A well-known cloth, but it is so long since ploughmen or gentlemen could say, "Thir breeks o' min that ance were *plush,*" that it may be advisable to show that this material was a common wear.

An old cast pair of black *plush* breeches.—*Sterne.*

I have rent my *plush* and satin,
And now am fit to beg
In Hebrew, Greek, and Latin.—*Dr. Robert Wilde.*

(Modesty) Smiles on the plated buckles in my shoes;
Smiles on my breeches too, of handsome *plush.*—*Dr. Wolcot.*

Poacher-court. Kirk-session.

Pock. A small bag. This is just the E. *poke,* only with the spelling nearer the A.-S. *pocca. Pock* has been preserved in the dim. *pocket*, in *pock*, a pustule produced by small-pox, and in the name of that disease, which the pronunciation shows to be a variation in the spelling of *pocs* or *poks*, and not of *pokes*.

> This pouer man was will of wan
> For *poc* ne sek no havid he nan.
>
> *E. Metrical Homilies.*

Poind. To distrain; to seize a tenant's effects for rent due.

To *pin* or *pen* is the Anglo-Saxon *pyndan*, includere, to close in, and the past participle is *pond, pound, pen, pin, hin.*—*Richardson on the Study of Language.*

Pŭnd, a pound, a fold.—*Bosworth.*

Though differing slightly in use, this is the same as E. *pound*, to confine strayed animals, and is, I believe, in Ayrshire, if not in Scotland, generally pronounced *pin* or *pĭnd*, rather than *poind*.

> George a Green the *pinner* of Wakefield.—*R. Hood.*
> In Wakefield there lives a jolly *pinder.*—*Ib.*
>
> Married once,
> A man is staked or *poun'd.*—*Massinger.*

Poortith. Poverty. Apparently formed from *pouerte*, or *pouert*, by the addition of *ith* or *th*, as in month, tilth, wealth, etc.

> To her wyll I nowe all my *pouerte* lege.—*Skelton.*
> To lyve yn *pouert* and yn servage.—*R. Manning.*

Potence. Potency, power. *Y* omitted, as in—

> And must I own, she said, my secret smart?
> What with more *decence* were in silence kept.
>
> *Dryden.*
>
> O trustlesse state of earthly things, and *slipper* hope
> Of mortal men.—*Spenser.*

Pou and *pu'*. To pull, to gather. For omission of *l*, see under *a'*.

Poo, to pull, *pood*, pulled, *pooin*, pulling.—*Bamford*.

Pouchie. Dim. of pouch, the pocket.

Pouk. To pluck.

> And Pandar wep as he to water wold,
> And *puked* ever his nece new and newe.—*Chaucer*.

Hee also wold to the threshing of the cocke, *pucke* with hens blindfold, and the like.—*Life of Thomas Lord Berkeley*.

> And *pukketh* forth pruyde to prayse thi-selven.
> P. Plowman.

Pouse. To push.

Poss, to thrust, to push violently.—*Bamford*.

> The see by night as any torche brente
> For wood, and *posseth* him up and doun.—*Chaucer*.

> A cat of a courte cam whan hym lyked
> And pleyde with hem perelouslych and *possed* hem aboute.
> P. Plowman.

Poussie. A hare or cat. Dim. of puss, the fondling name for a cat, and here transferred to a hare, owing to a general unwillingness already mentioned to speak of animals protected by the game laws.

Puss, the sportsman's name for a hare.—*Johnson*.

Recent dictionaries have *pussy*.

> Our gunners were rambling the fields,
> So that *pussy* was quickly espy'd.
> *The Bishopric Garland. Ritson.*

Pout. A poult, a chicken.

Powt, a sort of fish, a bird, a young turkey; heath-*powt*, a bird of game.—*Bailey*.

Poot, a young fowl; moor-*poot*, a moor-fowl.—*Bamford*.

Then they housed within his muzzle pheasant-*poots*, turkeys and turkey-*poots*, bustards and bustard-*poots*.—*Motteux*.

Pouther or *powther*. Powder. For change of *d* into *th* see under *blather*, and in—

> I sal tel yow swilk *tithandes*(tidings).—*Ywain and Gawain*.
>
> And the traytour be the *rothe* (rood),
> We shall hym asayle.—*Lybeaus Disconnus*.

But the word *powther* occurs several times in the Records of the Stationers' Company—

> Item, paid *powther* and matche, 7d. Paid for 2 hornes for goune *powther*, 3s.—*Steeven's Illustrations*.

Pouthery. Like powder.

Pow. The head, the skull. Poll, the head, then powl, then *pow*. See *a'*.

> *Pow*, the head, etc.—*Grose*.
>
> And others corne or egges againe, to *poul*-shorne persons sweete.
> B. Googe.
>
> They sett on their nowls
> Good blacke bowls
> To keep their *powls* from battering of battes.
> *Tournament of Tottenham*.
>
> Ac, an the gate weore y-loke,
> Mony *poune* (pl. of *pou*) was to-broke.—*Kyng Alisaunder*.

Was seems to make *poune* singular: had it been so it would not have been *mony poune* but *mony a poune*.

Pownie. A pony. For change of *o* into *ou* sound see under *houp*, and in—

> Ther thei madyn a fowle lowtte
> And begounnon a sore *nowtte* (note).
> *The Huntyng of the Hare*.
>
> I rekyn yow in my *rowllys* (rolls).—*Skelton*.

Poz. Sure.

I believe I can't do it, that's *poz.*—*The Tatler.*

Praise. Figuratively used for God, the object of praise.—*Jamieson.*

Preclair. Super-eminent.

Shakespeare has the word, but in Latin—

Praeclarissimus filius noster Henricus.—*Henry V.*

Preen. A pin.

Prin, a pin; *prin-cod,* a pin-cushion.—*Grose.*

Preen, awl, borer, piercer.—*Repp.*

Her kerchefes were curwuse, with mony a proud *prene.*—*Robson's Romances.*—*Halliwell.*

Pin is said by some etymologists to be a modern form of old English *preon.* Bosworth has *preon,* a clasp, a bodkin.

Prent. Print. *E* for *i.* See under *dreep.*

> The *prente* which he bare in his pilgremage
> Scorn and rebuke cast on his visage.—*Lydgate.*
>
> And with that *prent* he sette a seal.—*Gower.*

And after that might the worke be alowed by the ordinaries, and by their authorities, put unto *prent.*—*Sir T. More.*

Prick-the-louse. A word of contempt for a tailor.— —*Johnson.*

Many men have some scavenger or *prick-louse* taylor to attend upon them.—*Anatomy of Melancholy.*

The poor *prick-lice* were startled at that.—*L'Estrange.*

Prie. To taste.

> There is a horse in my father's stable,
>   He stands beyond the thorn,
> He shakes his head above the trough,
>   But he dares not *prie* the corn.
>   *Blow the Winds, I-ho. Bell.*

Prief.   Proof.

> By evidence to maken open *preef.*—*Lydgate.*
>
> He that seemeth the wisest
> Is most fool, when it cometh to the *prief.*—*Chaucer.*
>
> He gan apply relief
> Of salves and medicines, which had passing *brief.*—*Spenser.*

Prief o' shot.   That cannot be hurt by lead or shot.

It seems he (Æneas) was no warlock, as the Scots commonly call such men, who, they say, are *iron-free* or *lead-free.*—*Dryden. Dedication prefixed to his Translation of the Æneid.*

It is strange that Dryden should refer to the Scots when speaking of this superstition, fresh as he was from—

Quem neque fas igni cuiquam, nec sternere ferro.—*Æ. Lib. VII.*

which he renders—

> Secure of steel, and fated from the fire,

not to speak of the all but invulnerable Achilles, and other examples of persons whose "beginning life from steel was free." I believe that all we find of "arms of proof," "lapt in proof," etc., had its origin in this superstition which is found in many lands.

> He cared not for dint of sword or speere
> No more than for the stroke of straws or bents,
> He was invulnerable made by magicke *leare.*—*Spenser.*

Priest.   For English readers of Burns it may be as well to mention that this word is never applied to clergymen in Scotland, except when some degree of disparagement or dislike is meant to be expressed.

Prig.   To cheapen, to dispute.
Prig, to higgle in price.—*Halliwell.*

Primsie.   Demure, precise.

Propone.   To lay down, to propose.

  Proponent, one that makes a proposal, or lays down a position.
                                                              Johnson.

  Proponent, a propounder.—*Ainsworth.*

  Proponed, proposed.—*Halliwell.*

Proven.   Proved.   *En* for the modern *ed* was once common, as in—

> And that was *gnawen* on every where.—*Spenser.*
>
> Such hunger-*starven* trencher poetrie
> Or let it never live, or timely die.—*Bishop Hall.*

Provoses.   Provosts, chief magistrates of royal burghs.

Jamieson says—"Provost seems to have been used in the same sense in E. in R. Brunne's time," and quotes the following—

> The *provest* of the toun, a wik traitour and cherle,
> He thought to do tresoun vnto his lord the erle.

The word is still well known in England, but the official it denotes is not the same as in Scotland.

Burns's spelling is not to be commended, but as droll plurals are found.

> We are animals no less,
> Altho' of different *specieses.*—*Hudibras.*
>
> Can tell the *oddses* of all games.—*Butler's Mis. Poems.*
>
> As shameful deth as herte can devis
> Come to thise juges and hir *advocas* (advocates).
>   *Chaucer.*

> So is Sibeles of goddesses
> The moder, whom withoute *gesses* (gests)
> The folke prein, honour, and serve.—*Gower.*

Peter English's Moseses, though I do not know there is anything wrong with it, makes a good rhyme with Burns's provoses—

So did Moses. And our *Moseses* ought to do so too.—*The Survey of Policy, 1653.*

> Bailiffes, beadles, *provost*, countours.—*Chaucer.*

From the association of *provost* with these officers, it would seem that in Chaucer's time a provost was a magistrate.

In "Measure for Measure," Shakespeare calls the gaoler Provost.

> Were the stars only made to light
> Robbers and *burglarers* by night.—*Hudibras.*

Puddin. Pudding.

> For guts, some write, ere they are sodden,
> Are fit for music, or for *pudden.*—*Dodsley.*

I don't think these *puddens* are much good unless the seeds are taken out of the raisins.—*Archdeacon Paley. Literary Life of Rev. W. Harness.*

Yf you wyll come you shall be welcome, but I tell you afore hande, you shall have but sclender fare, one dish and that is all. A *puddyne,* and nothynge els.—*Latimer.*

Pudding, more correctly *puddin.*—*Folk-Etymology.*

Puddock-stool. A toad-stool, a mushroom.

> *Champignon,* a mnshroome, toad-stoole, *paddock-stoole.*
>
> *Cotgrave.*

> Euetis, and snakes, and *paddokes* brode,
> That heom thoughte mete gode.—*Kyng Alisaunder.*
>
> The rats brush o'er their faces with their tails,
> And croaking *paddocks* crawl upon their limbs.—*Dryden.*

Pu'pit. Pulpit.

Pulvilised. Scented with powder. Burns underlined this word in a letter to Mr. Hill.

To *pulvil.* To sprinkle with perfumes in powder.—*Johnson.*

Have you *pulvilled* the coachman and postilion, that they may not stink of the stable?—*Congreve.*

How many pound of *pulvil* must the fellow use in sweetening himself from the smell of hops and tobacco?—*Farquhar.*

Pund, or *pun*.   Pound, pounds.   *U* for *ou ;* see under *clud*.

Item, payde for 38 *punde* of butter 4s. 2.—*First Public Dinner in Stationers' Hall, 1557. Stephen's Illustrations.*

> He would *pun* thee into shivers with his fist.—*Shak.*
>
> I can spare you *pownes.*—*The Patient Countess.*

Pursie.   Dim. of purse.

Pyet.   A magpie.

The *piot* ordinarily bring's forth nine Piannets.—*Holland's Pliny.*

This can hardly be our pyet.

In Derbyshire there is or was a public-house with the sign of "The Cock and *Pynot.*"—*Every-Day Book.*

Pynots, magpies.—*Bamford.*

> Swarms there did appear
> Of *piots* hopping at his back.
> *The Northumberland Garland.   Ritson.*

Pyke, pike.   To pick.

> Phylip had leve to go
> To *pyke* my lytell too.—*Skelton.*
>
> Whan hath gadred what him liketh,
> He set him thame down and *piketh*
> And wisshe his herbes in the flood.—*Gower.*

Then cometh the Pye or the ravene and *pyketh* out the one eye. Then cometh the fende and *pyketh* out thir right eye.—*Dives and Lazarus.*

Pyle, a *pyle o' caff.*   A single grain of chaff.

Pile, a blade of grass.—*Halliwell.*

> He has no whiskers, not a *pile.*—*Sterne.*

Chaff not being grain but its covering, a grain of chaff seems a strange expression. Chaff is the *peel* of corn, and, if the pronunciation were not so decidedly against the idea, I should be disposed to say that *pyle* meant *peel*. But the pronunciation is sometimes a disguise for words. Thimble is not very like *thumb*, and *riddle* does not to everybody suggest the verb to read, and so pyle may after all be peel. *Pille* is Danish for to pick and to *peel*, and this is at least as likely to be its derivation as Lat. *pilus*, a hair, which is that of Jamieson. *Pill* is sometimes used for *peel :—*

> His skalpe all *pilde*, and he with elde forlore.—*Sackville.*
> As *pyled* (peeled) as an ape was his skulle.—*Wright's Chaucer.*
> Take 3 hazle sticks, *pill* them fayre and white.—*Percy.*

Pystle. An epistle, a letter.

> The mavys with her whystell
> Shall rede then the *pystell*.—*Skelton.*
> As saith seint Jame, if ye his *pistel* rede.—*Chaucer.*
> Nether Gospell nor *Pystle*.—*Skelton.*

This corruption is found in similar words, e.g.,—

> A faire high-standing cup, and two great *Postle* spoons.
> *Middleton.*

Q.

Quak. To quake, the cry of a duck.

In the second sense it differs from *quack* only in spelling. In the first it differs from quake by the omission of silent *e*, which is often done by old E. writers when the only effect of its insertion is to give a preceding vowel its long sound, as in—

> O suilk a stern the writt it *spak*,
> And of thir offerands to *mak*.—*Cursor Mundi.*
> Al the Kinges o' this werld
> For him sal be *quakand* and ferd.—*Ib.*
> Al the erth, the achtande day,
> Sal stir and *quac* (quake) and al folc fley.
> *E. Metrical Homilies. Small.*

Quarter basin. This occurs in—
> Gat ye me, O gat ye me,
> Gat ye me wi' naething:
> Rock and reel, and spinnin-wheel,
> A mickle *quarter basin.*

What this part of "The Lass of Ecclefechan's" paraphernalia was I cannot say. Perhaps it was like the vessel in " Measure for Measure;" "As it were, a fruit dish, a dish of some threepence." The word *quarter* shows it was a dish of some well-known size. It may have been a "*Bassie, bassy,* a large wooden dish used for carrying meal from the *girnal* (meal-chest) to the *bake-board* (kneading-board), or for containing the meal designed for immediate use."—*Jamieson.*

Quat. To quit. *A* for *i,* as in—
> Thei leyd at her with mallus strong,
> As fast as thei myght *lack* (lick).
>> *The Hunttyng of the Hare.*

> And ho . . skowtes aboute,
> Tyl hyt watz nyghe at *naght* (night).
>> *Early E. Alliterative Poems. Morris.*

Quech (ch gutt.) A drinking cup of cooper's work, with two little knobs for handles.

Questions. The Shorter Catechism of the Westminster Divines. *Getting his questions,* preparing his lessons, or speech.

Quey. A cow from one to two years old.

Quy-calf, a cow-calf.—*Grose. Que,* a cow.—*Linc. Quee,* a female calf.—*Halliwell.*

When it is remembered that *q* is used for *c* or *k* it will be seen that *quey* or *cuey* comes very near E. *cow,* and still nearer A.-Sax. *cu.*

> He was rughher than any *ku.*—*Kyng Alisaunder.*

Quine or *quean*. A woman.

  Queyne, a woman.—*Bamford*.

            Did I not charge thee
  To pinch that *quean* to the heart?—*The Witch of Edmonton*.
  And gan to cry with loud din ;
  "Thou lyest !" he said, " old *quean*."—*Merlin*. *Ellis*.
  Thou like a traiterous *quean*, keep'st twenty devils.—*Fletcher*.
  When lazie *queans* have nought to do.—*Ben Jonson*.

Quirk.   An intricacy.

Quo'.   Quoth.

  Ye are happy (*ko I*) that ye are a woman.—*Ralf Roister Doister*.

R.

Rab.   Dim. of Robert.

Rad.   Afraid.

    This man went ham thoh he were *rad*,
    And did als his bischop him badde.—*Cursor Mundi*.

Rade.   Rode. *A* for *o*, see under *bane*.

    Thair scrippes, quer thai *rade* or yode,
    Tham failed never o drinc ne fode.—*Cursor Mundi*.
    Al that dai as thai *rade*,
    Gret morning both thai made.—*Amis and Amiloun*.

Ragged.   Rugged, rough, as in—

         A *ragged* cowte's been known.
  His men him brought a grisly best, a *ragged* colt.
                             Kyng Alisaunder.
  My voice is *ragged* ; I know I cannot please you.—*Shak*.
  The *ragged'st* hour that time and spite dare bring.—*Id*.

To go into the clefts of the rocks, and into the tops of the *ragged* rocks.—*Isaiah, ii. 21*.

> He left the plain
> To scale the *ragged* cliff.—*Massinger*.

Ragweed. The herb ragwort.

Raible. To rattle nonsense.
  Rabble, to speak confusedly.

> Let thy tunge serve thyn hert in skylle,
> And *rable* not words recheles out of reson.
> *MS. quoted by Halliwell.*

Is this not Douglas's *wrable* for warble ?

> In *wrablis* dulce of hevynly armonyis
> The larkis lowd, releschand in the skyis,
> Lovys thar lege with tonys curyus.—*Eneados.*

Rair. To roar. *A* for *o ;* see under *bane*.

> Both bul and bare,
> That rewfully gan rope and *rare*.—*Ywain and Gawain*.

Raise. Rose. *A* for *o;* see under *bane*.

Raize. To madden, to enflame. Differs only in spelling from E. "*raise*, to excite to war or tumult; to stir up; to excite; to put in action."—*Johnson*.

> He stert up in a brayde,
> And bygan for to *rese* (to be maddened)
> As he wold take hyr by the nese.—*Ipomydon.*
> Saladyn began to *rase* for ire.—*R. C. de Lion.*
> Do thou no thinge in such a *rees*.—*Gower.*

Ramfeezled. Fatigued, overspent.

Ramgunshoch. Rugged, unkind, surly.

Ramp. To rage.
  Ramp, to paw like a mad horse —*Bailey*.

Whan she comth hom she *rampeth* in my face.—*Chaucer.*

And when the king sat in his halle,
Cam in *rampend* among hem alle.—*Gower.*

I've a great *ramping* daughter, that stares like a heifer.
Vanbrugh.

Ram-stam. Forward, thoughtless.

Ram-stam, thoughtless.—*Halliwell.*

Randie. A scolding, sturdy beggar, a shrew.

Randy, boisterous, noisy, obstreperous, disorderly.—*Grose.*

An audatious mouthing-*randing*-impudent, scullery-waistcoat-and-bodied rascal would have hail'd a penny from us for his scullership.—*A Search for Money. Percy Society.*

He was here *randying* for a Knight of his acquaintance.—*Fielding.*

Rant. To be joyous, merry.

We'll *rant* and we'll roar like true British heroes,
We'll *rant* and we'll roar across the salt seas.
The Spanish Ladies.

And doubtless where these brambles claim the ground,
The glass once flow'd to hail the *ranting* song.—*Clare.*

June 10, 1657. A complaint having been made, Sir William Strickland said, "The business needs no examination: the party that informs us is at the door; his name is Robert Ogle, *Anglice* (plainly an error for *alias*), *Ranting Robin.—Burton's Parliamentary Diary.*

Was he, by any chance, like our Ranting Robin? Perhaps he was one of the sect called Ranters or Family of Love.

Rant. To be extravagant in the mode of living.

So many blades that *rant* in silk,
And put on scarlet cloathing.—*The Prodigal's Resolution.*

Now that I'm an elder brother, I'll court, and swear, and *rant* with the best of them.—*Farquhar.*

Rant. Outrage, uproar, tumult.

Rant, to rage.—*Bailey*.

Burns uses *rant* in two or perhaps three senses:—
My wicked rhymes, and drunken *rants* (merry-makings).
While coofs on countless thousands *rant* (live wastefully).
As filled his after life with grief
        And bloody *rants* (outrages).

I do not think the last has any connection with the other two.

Rape, or *raep*. A rope. *A* for *o*. See under *bane*.
    When Ralph of Rokeby saw the *rape*,
    He wist that there had been debate.
                The Felon Sow of Rokeby.

Raploch. A coarse cloth, coarse.

Rare. Fine, excellent.
Her grant holds, sir. O *rare*!—*The Parliament of Love*.
The gentleman is learn'd, and a most *rare* speaker.—*Shak*.

Raree-show. A show carried about in a box, a peep-show.
    No more they pant for public *raree-shows*.—*Churchill*.

Rarely. Excellently, finely, nicely,
How *rarely* does it meet with this time's guise!—*Shak*.
An admirable prince! How *rarely* he talks.—*Massinger*.
I'm acting Sir Courtly, and I do't *rarely*, methinks.—*L'Estrange*.

Rase. Rose. See *raise*.

Rash. A rush. *A* for *u*; see under *backet*.
    Though it avail him not a *reisshe*.—*Gower*.
    All dere ynough a *rishe*.—*Chaucer*.
    And strewed with grene *Rysshes*.—*The Festyval*. *Ellis*,

Rash-buss. A bush of rushes. *Rash* and *buss.*

Ratan. A walking-stick. *Ratan,* an Indian cane.— *Johnson.*

Ratton. A rat.

And praied him that he him wolde sell
Som poison, that he might his *ratouns* quell.—*Chaucer.*

A *raton* of renon most renable of tonge
Seide.—*P. Plowman.*

And alle manere of wylde Beestes they eten, Houndes, Cattes, *Ratouns,* and alle other wylde Beestes.—*Maundeville.*

Raucle. Rash, stout, fearless.

Rakehell, rakil, or *rakle,* seems synonymous with reckless.— *Thomas Campbell.*

To my mind resort
The jolly woes, the hateless short debate,
The *rakehell* life that longs to love's disport.—*Earl of Surrey.*

O *rakel* hand to do so foul a mis.— *Chaucer.*

Thou *rakle* night.—*Id.*

Beth nat to *rakel* of sodayne hastynesse.—*Lydgate.*

Raught. Reached.

And so at length are justly humbled down
Beneath the foot, that *ranght* above the crown.—*Sylvester.*

An aged sire
Clad in a linen robe that *raught* down low.—*Fairfax.*

Come make him stand upon this molehill here,
That *raught* at mountains with outstretched arms.—*Shak.*

Sir Guyon's sword he lightly to him *raught.*—*Spenser.*

Raw. A row.

I wolde not
For all the gold in mery England,
Though it lay now on a *rawe.*—*R. Hood.*

> The princes that war riche on *raw*,
> Gert nakers strike and trumpes blaw.—*Minot*.
>
> Than the lordes, al on *raw*,
> Held them wele payed of this saw.— *Ywain and Gawain*.

Rax. To stretch. *X* stands for *ks* or *es*, so Skelton's *rachchyd* is not far from *raxed*.

> The next halter there sall be
> I bequeth, yt hole to thé;
> Soche pelfry thou hast pachchyd (packed?)
> And so thy selfe houyr wachyd (over-watched)
> That ther thou sculdest be *rachchyd* (raxed or stretched)
> If thow war metely machchyd.—*Poems against Garnesche*.

Ream. Cream, to cream.

Ryem, cream. *Ryemin*, foaming.—*Bamford*.

Ream, rem, cream.—*Bosworth*.

> That on is white so milkes *rem*.—*Arthour and Merlin*.

Reave. To rob.

> Dismounting from his lofty steed
> He to him leapt, in mind to *reave* his life.—*Spenser*.
>
> He wold pull downe my halles and castles,
>   And *reave* me of my life;
> I cannot blame him if he doe,
>   If I *reave* him of his wife.—*King Estmere*.

Rebute. Repulse, denial.

Rebut. To retire back. Obsolete.—*Johnson*.

> Like a bulwark firmely did abyde,
> *Rebutting* him, which in the midst did ryde.
>
> *Spenser.*

Reck. To take heed.

Reck, to care.—*Bailey*.

> Thou *recks* much of thy swinke.—*Spenser*.
> I *reck* not though I lose my life to-day.—*Shak.*

> Goo playe, hym I ne *reke*.—*Skelton*.
> Of night or loneliness it *recks* me not.—*Milton*.

Red. Advised.

Jamieson thinks it is afraid in "I'm *red* ye're glaikit." It may be "I am of opinion." This connects it with the succeeding word *rede*, of which it is the p. p.

> A! mercy, moder, for Mari maide!
> I schal deghghe ; nou *red* me *red*.—*The Seven Sages*.
>
> And so longe criede and bade,
> That him com from heven, *rade*,
> How he scholde heom distroye.—*Kyng Alisaunder*.

Rede. Counsel, to counsel ; part. p. *red* and *rad*.

> Such mercy He by His most holy *reed*
> Unto us taught.—*Spenser*.
>
> If I would follow his *reed*,
> Into your house he would me guide and lead.
> *Gammer Gurton's Needle*.
>
> And luf it noght over wele, I *rede*.—*Sir Penny*.
> If thou *redes* that it sua be.—*Cursor Mundi*.
> The man is blest that hath not bent
>   To wicked *read* his ear.—*First Psalm. Sternhold*.
> She asked what she *rad*.—*Chaucer*.

Red-wud. Stark mad, very angry. See *wud*.

Heat is often applied to some of the passions :—

> A noble emulation *heats* your breast.—*Dryden*.

Neither chasten me in thy *hot* displeasure.—*Psalm xxxviii.*, and as iron heated to redness is very hot, the poet puts *red-wud* or red-mad for a great degree of anger.

Ree. Half-drunk, fuddled.

Ree, as, *All in one Ree*, all in one river, or overflowed with water.
Bailey.

Rie, fun, merriment.—*Halliwell*.

I do not know that either of these words is in any way connected with Burns's *ree*, but in the absence of light on the word, it may be suggested that the first might apply to a tipsy man, seeing that his brain has been overflowed with (strong) water, and the second because if there is any fun in a man it is brought out when he is *ree*, before he becomes maudlin, mad, or imbecile.

Reek. Smoke, to smoke; *reekin*, smoking; *reekit*, smoked, smoky.—*Burns.* Found in all E. dictionaries.

Reekie. Smoky. *Auld Reekie*, Edinburgh.

Reel. A lively dance; to change place in a *foursome* dance. See *cleek*.

> Thornton, aid us in our waltzing;
> Aid us, Bacchus, in our *reels!*—*Hor. in London.*

Reest. To stand restive.

Raisty, or *resty*, a term used of a horse, when he will stand still and will not go backwards or forwards.—*Bailey.* *Reist.*—*Richardson.*

He told me of a *resty* horse.—*The White Devil.*

In the Cleveland dialect a restive horse is said to *reist.*—*Atkinson. Palmer.*

> *Resty* sloth
> Finds the down pillow hard.—*Shak.*

Knight says resty here means *rusty*, spoiled for want of use. Does not *reest* explain it better?

Sometimes by appearing to the horse and making him take the *reist.*—*Richardson.*

Reestet. Stunted, withered, shrivelled, dried or smoked.

Rest, to roast.—*Somerset. Halliwell.*

Reest, or *reast*, rusted, smoke-dried, discoloured; "*Reest* bacon."
Bamford.

Ranci, mustie, fustie, *reasie*, resti.—*Cotgrave*. *Reasie* (or reastie), *ranci*.—*Sherwood*.

Reflec'. Reflect.

Reft. (Past tense of *reave* and rive). Torn, ragged.
> If thou mayest finde any shore,
> Or hole or *reft* whatever it were.—*Gower*.

> Such are the robes that Kings must wear,
> When death has *reft* their crown.—*Margaret's Ghost*.

Relent. To soften. In "Young Peggie," relent is used as a transitive verb.
> And hated earth, and water hated fire,
> Till love *relented* their rebellious ire.—*Spenser*.

Relief. The name given to those who seceded from the Established Church of Scotland that they might be relieved from the yoke of patronage. *Relief minister*, a clergyman of that body.

Remead. Remedy. *Y* omitted; see under *potence*.

Poets often omit more important syllables than *y*.

> In mynd to bene ywroken
> Of all the vile *demeane* (demeanour) and usage bad.—*Spenser*.

> These she to strangers oftentimes would show,
> With grave *demean* and solemn vanity.—*Gilbert West*.

> It's ever alas! but what *remeed?*—*The Northumberland Garland*. *Retson*.

Requite, requit. Requital.
> To *quit* the benefits bestowed.—*Chapman*.

> Exposed unto the sea, which hath *requit* it,
> Him, and his innocent child.—*Shak*.

Resign. This trans. v. is used by Burns as an intransitive, "Teach me to *resign*."

The gallant spirit *resigns*, but *resigns* with an air that speaks a resolution.—*Steele.*

Respecket.   Respected.

Restricked.   Restricted.   See *disrespecket.*

Rew.   To repent, to pity.

> Werke all by conseil, and thou shalt not *rewe.*—*Chaucer.*
> The quene hyt *rew* well sore.—*Launfal.*
> So *rewe* on this robbere.—*P. Plowman.*
> And God so wisly on my soule *rewe,*
> As I shall even juge ben, and trewe.—*Chaucer.*
> And *rewe* on hym of her womanhede.—*Lydgate.*

Rhyme-proof.   Capable of resisting all inducements to write poetry.   See *prief o' shot.*

> No Muse shall tempt me with her siren lay;
> Verse I abjure.—*Churchhill.*

Rickle.   Dim. of rick, which is a small stack put up in the field in which the grain grew. A *rickle* may be made by one man, and is not higher than he can reach from the ground, whereas a *rick* requires a person to stand on it when building, while another forks up the sheaves.

I have been particular with this word, because it does not appear to be generally understood, Cunningham saying, "Rickles are shocks of corn, stooks," and Chambers that they are ricks.

Ridge, an old wife's.   A small piece of land near a cottar's garden.—*Burns to G. Hamilton, 28 August,*

Rief. Thieving, as *rief randies*, thieving or reaving beggars. Another form of *reave*.

Robbers and *rivers* walk at libertie uncorrected.—*Sir T. More.*

Rief, reef. Rife, plenty. *E* for *i*, as in *lee*.

Rig. A ridge.

The place where the Scots and English fought is still called the Battle *Riggs*.—*Percy.*

Her *rigs* thou waterest plenteously. — *Psalm LXV. Rous's Version.*

Oppression the Persoune I leif untill
Pouir Men's corne to hald upon the *Rig*—
   Quhill he get the Teynd all hail at his will.—*Duncan Leider.*

Rig. Back.

This word is not used by Burns except in combination. But it appears in *rigwoodie*, and it is perhaps right to take it by itself.

> She helped him opon his hors *ryg*.—*Ywain and Gawain.*
> Ilk Inglis man on others *rig*,
> Ouer that water er thai went.—*Minot.*
> The graihond on the *rigge* he hit.—*The Seven Sages.*
> He clave him by the *rigge* bone.
>   *Sir Eglamour of Artoys.*

Riggin'. The ridge of a house.

Riggen, the ridge of a house.—*Grose.*

> With bellies top-full to the *rigging*.
>   *The Northumb. Garland. Ritson.*

Rigwiddie, rigwoodie. The rope or chain, originally a withe or withy, that crosses the saddle to support the shafts of a cart. See *rig* and *woodie*.

Of the witches characterised by Burns as—

> *Rigwoodie* hags wad spean a foal,

Chambers says, "worthy of the gallows," i.e., *rigwoodie* means worthy of the gallows. Now, not to dwell on the fact that to deserve to be hanged is not a physical but a moral deformity, and it is the former only that could produce such disgust as would wean a foal, as is proved by Nannie, though as wicked as her old associates, being so attractive that gazing on her Tam—

> Thought his very e'en enrich'd,

the meaning of the word as applied to the "withered beldams" is obvious to any one who has ever seen a *rigwoodie*, *ridge-band*, *ridge-rope*, *ridge-stay*, or *ridge-with*, as it is called in Cheshire, of the poet's day. Instead of being smooth and intended to move easily in the saddle, like the modern chain, it was rough, in order, I believe, that it might remain firm in its place unaffected by the vibration of the cart. To any person who has seen one of these chains, *rigwoodie* will appear appropriate to the bodies of the witches, and has no reference to their moral qualities. To each of them might be applied, and *rigwoodie* means no more, Burns's line—

> Thou's howe-backit now and *knaggie*,

or Spenser's description of a very different character—

> Eche bone myght through her body well be red.

It is only fair to state that Jamieson, as well as Chambers, says that *rigwiddie* means "deserving the *widdie* or the gallows." Probably both of them, from neither of whom in a matter of this kind would one willingly differ, were thinking rather of Lindsay's *widdiefow* than of Burns's *rigwoodie*—

> The *widdiefow* wardens tuik my gear,
> And left me nowthir horse nor meir.

Rin. To run, to melt.

Rivers *rin* not tyll the spryng be full.—*Skelton*.

Nedes must he *rin* that the devyll driveth.—*Id*.

The roo full rekeles ther she *rinnes*.
              Anc. Bal. of the Battle of Otterbourne.

For a best, when it is born, may ga
Als-tite aftir, and *ryn* to and fra.—*P. of Conscience*.

Unto the pleasant river where by Eden it did *rin*.
              The Masonic Hymn.

Ring-bane. Ring-bone, an osseous deposit on the pastern joint, the result of inflammation.—*Williams's Principles and Practice of Vet. Surgery*.

The said horse was thoroughly cured of a *ring-bone* which he had on that foot.—*Rabelais*.

Ring their bells. To blow their own trumpets, to praise themselves.

Rink. The course of the stones, a term in curling. A peculiar pronunciation of *ring*.—*Skeat*.

I borrow the following from Dr. C. Mackay's "Lost Beauties of the English Language":—

"*Rink*, a course or arena for public sports. The word is principally used in connection with skating, and applied either to an open pond, frozen over, where a ring is made, or to a covered enclosure for the same purpose. The word is common in America and Scotland, though but little used in England."

Rip. A handful of unthreshed oats, etc.

Wed-bed Rip, the customary service which inferior tenants yielded their lord in reaping and mowing. *Rip*-towel, a gratuity or reward given to tenants, after they had reaped their lord's corn. *Bed-rip*, same as wed-bed rip.—*Bailey*.

Ripe, a handful of corn, a sheaf.—*Bosworth*.

Ripple. To separate the seed of flax or hemp from the stalk.

Rippel flax, to rub or wipe off the seed-vessels.—*Bailey*.

Ripple.—*Grose*.

Ripples. A weakness in the back and reins.—*Jamieson.*

Burns uses it in the singular, if this be the word, in—

> Auld Orthodoxy lang did grapple,
> But now she's got an unco *ripple* ;

but is it possible that *ripple* is figuratively used to signify a *tearing* or *breaking-up* from the instrument called a ripple or its effect?

Ripple, to scratch slightly.—*Skeat's Etymological Dictionary.*

An *unco ripple* means a severe scratch.

Ripplin-kaim. An instrument for dressing flax. See *ripple* and *kaim.*

Risk. To make a noise like the tearing of roots.

Burns is the only authority Jamieson cites for this word, and he gives the poet's definition.

Road. Track.

To *road.* Applied to small game which, when found by the setting dogs, instead of taking wing, run along the ground before the sportsman.—*Jamieson.*

This, in " He smell'd their ilka hole and *road,*" is probably a corruption of *trod.*

> They never set foot on that same *trode.*—*Spenser.*
>
> As shepherds curre that
> Hath tracted forth some salvage beastes *trade.*—*Ib.*

Rockin. A social meeting of neighbours on a winter evening.

Young ladies now-a-days, when a visit is not intended to be a mere call, take their "work" with them. Formerly this work was almost always spinning, and they took their *rock* or spinning apparatus,—not a spinning-wheel but the less cumbrous rock and distaff,—with them and used during the evening with more or less diligence. Hence a friendly visit of some duration was called a "rockin." A similar meeting had a similar name, *filerie*, a *spinstrie*, in France.—*Cotgrave*.

Reawkin and *rookin*, meeting in neighbours' houses, and spending time in idle gossip.—*Bamford*.

I do not know if rock gave name to a social meeting further south than Lancashire, but it seems to have been constantly in the women's hands, in all parts of England, and to have been frequently employed for other purposes than the making of thread:—

> Some laid to pledge (for ale) their *rock*.—*Skelton*.
>
> The wiffe came yet,
> And with her *rocke*
> Many a knocke
> She gave hym on the crown.—*Sir T. More*.

Roon. A shred, a remnant.—*Burns*. A shred, the selvage of woollen cloth.—*Cunningham*.

Selvage seems to be meant in the lines—

> In thae auld times they thought the Moon
> Woor by degrees, till her last *roon*
> Gaed past their viewin';

but if by selvage is meant *rind*, *rine* and not *roon* is the Ayrshire pronunciation. Jamieson has "roond shoon," from "roond, a list of cloth." I suspect that the principal, if not the only, authority for this spelling is the passage just quoted. At all events selvages or lists are always in Ayrshire called selvages when remaining on the cloth, and *rines* when separated from it. And as for list shoes no Ayrshire woman,—they were not worn by men,—ever knew them by any other name than *rine* or rind shoes, and as for the carpet shoes which Jamieson thinks were also called "roond shoon," in Ayrshire at least, to have so styled them would have seemed to degrade them.

Clogs, pattens wanting the *rines*.—*Bailey*.

Unfortunately he has not told us what *rines* are, but I believe they were strips of cloth, tape, or list, passing over the foot and round the ankle of the wearer of pattens, were in fact rinds with the spelling of Spenser :

> A goodly oake sometime had it bene ;
> And with his nuts larded many swine ;
> But now the graye mosse marred his *rine*.
> *Shepheard's Calendar.*

Probably if Burns had not told us what he meant by *roon*, most Scotsmen would have understood " her last roon " to signify the moon's last visible *round*, or motion for the month.

Roose.   To praise, to commend ; praise.

   Reuse, to extol, or commend highly.—*Bailey*.
   Rooze, to praise, to puff up.—*Bamford*.
   Rooyse, to extol.—*Thoresby*.

> A morn Lybeaus was boun
> For to wynne renoun
>   And *ros* wythoute les.—*Lybeaus Disconnus*.

Roosty.   Rusty.   *Oo* for short sound of *u*, as in—

> Or they twynned them they pekked *mood* (mud).
> *Occleve.*

> The *mooder* (mother) of the Sowdan.—*Chaucer*.
> And in his hand he had a *rousty* sword.—*Id*.
> And *strooke* (struck) the din within our ears.—*Sackville*.
> That conqu'ring look like lightning *strook*.—*Waller*.
> The mizens *strooted* (strutted) with the gale.—*Chapman*.

Rostrum.   Pulpit.

Roun'.   Round, in the circle of neighbourhood.   *D* omitted ; see *afiel*.

Round.   A simultaneous drinking by a company ; a toast.

Their manner of drinking is called Streah, i.e., a *Round*. *Martin*.

Roup.   Sale by auction.   *Roup of parks*, letting of fields for grazing, for the season, by auction.

Rowpand, calling.—*Bailey*.

Out-rope, sale by auction.—*Cotgrave*.

Roupet.   Hoarse, as with a cold.

Roup, hoarseness.—*Bailey*.   *Roop*, hoarseness.—*Grose*.

Rawp and *roup*, hoarseness.—*Thoresby*.

> The emprour fond his emperice
> With lourand chere,   .   .   .
> Hond wringging, and loud *roupe*,
> And here visage al biwope.—*The Seven Sages*.

Roupe here means outcry, that which makes *roupet*. It is probably the same as the previous word.

The goods of this poor man sold at an *outcry*.—*Massinger*.

It has been said that Burns is "guilty of a pleonasm" in

> My *roupet* Muse is *hearse*.

But the words have not the same meaning. A person may be *hearse* without being roupet. An English poet has a similar line:—

Long since my voice is hoarse, my throat is sore.—*Sidney*.

Rousing.   Great.

A *rousing*, a whisking great one.—*Bailey*.

Routhie, rowthie.   Plentiful, from *rowth*, plenty.

Row.   To roll, to wrap.   For omission of *l* see under *a'*.

Roll was sometimes written *rowl*, and the change to *row* was easy.

> I'me no slave to such as you be;
> Neither shall that snowy brest,
> *Rowling* eye, and lip of ruby,
> Ever rob me of my rest.—*George Wither*,

> The burning spit still *rowling* up and down.
>> *Strange Histories. Percy Soc.*

Her mother came out spinning a *rowl* of flax.—*Thomas Shelton.*

The Lolardes set up *srcowis* (scrolls) at Westminster.—*Capgrave's Chronicle. Marsh.*

> For thou'st have forty pounds a week,
>> In gold and silver thou shalt *row* (roll).
>>> *The Lover's Quarrel.*

Rowing (of cloths) is the smoothing of them with a roller.—*Bailey.*

The *rowling* light of heaven.—*Waller.*

Rowte. To low, to bellow.

Rowt, to low like an ox or cow.—*Grose. Rout*, a noise.—*Bailey.*

> Parde, lyke the beating of the see,
>
> . . . .
> And that a man stand out of doute,
> A myle thens, and here it *route*.—*Chaucer.*
>
> It *routes* as it wer a thondyr !—*Kyng Alisaunder.*
>
> The lewid people
> Laughen mereli, and maken *route*.—*Hone's An. Mysteries.*
>
> He bereth him there so stowte,
> That no man dare *rowte*.—*Skelton.*

Rowth, or *routh*. Plenty, abundance.

Routh.—*Halliwell.*

Rozet. Rosin. *Mercurial rozet*, mercury formed into a paste.

A querne of *rosate* of vi. stane.—*Deposition of a Manxman, quoted by Sir W. Scott.*

Ruling-elder. Among Presbyterians, one ordained to the exercise of government in Church courts, without having authority to teach.—*Jamieson.*

As the minister, or pastor, is also an elder, for distinction's sake he is sometimes spoken of as a teaching elder, those conjoined with him, who do not teach, being styled ruling elders. This, which I supposed every person in Scotland knew, seems to have been a matter of which Chambers was ignorant, for he says, in a note to " The Whistle "—" An elder of the Scottish Church is called a ruling-elder when sent to represent a burgh in the General Assembly," the truth being, that a man must be a ruling-elder before he can be such a representative.

Scotsmen sometimes complain that they, their institutions, and ways in general, are misunderstood, and consequently misrepresented by Englishmen; but it would seem to be possible for even a distinguished Scotsman to know very little of some things, and important things, in his own country.

Rumble-gumption. Common sense. Appears not to differ from *gumption*.

Rummel-gumshon, wit, sense.—*Halliwell*.

Rumble-gairie. A rambling or roving person. *Rumble*, to stir, move about.

It seems to be of the same family as *Rumbustuous*, obstreperous.
Grose.

Run-deils. Downright devils.—*Cunningham*.

Rung. A cudgel.

> Be not fear'd, our master,
>   That we two can be dung
> With any bluter base beggar,
>   That has nought but a *rung*.—*R. Hood*.
> And then I'll make a line for every *rung*.
>
> *Swift*.

Runkle. To wrinkle. *U* ior *i*, as in—

> They armed heom and *gurd* (girt) with sweord.
> *Kyng Alisaunder*,

> Theyr *thrust* (thirst) was so great,
> They asked neuer for mete,
> But drynke, styll drynke.—*Skelton.*

Runkle, to crease, to wrinkle.—*Halliwell.*

> Than waxes his gast seke and sare,
> And his face *rouncles* ay mare and mare.
> *Pricke of Conscience.*

Runt. The stem of a colewort or cabbage.

Runt, the stump of underwood. Also, the dead stump of a tree. Also, the stem of a plant.—*Halliwell.*

Runt, a dwarf, a stunted animal or tree.—*Bamford.*

> Before I buy a bargain of such *runts,*
> I'll buy a college of bears.—*Fletcher.*

Ruth. Pity, compassion.

> The better part with Mary and with Ruth
> Chosen thou hast ; and they that overween,
> And at thy growing virtues vent their spleen,
> In thee no anger find, but pity and *ruth.*—*Milton.*

> And in his herte he caught of it gret *routhe.*—*Chaucer.*

> Rue, even for *ruth,* here shortly shall be seen,
> In the remembrance of a weeping queen.—*Shak.*

Ryke. To reach.

This word is not in Jamieson's Dictionary, but it is in Dr. Longmuir's edition of an abridgement, and Burns is given as the only authority. It is apparently derived from A.-Saxon *rœcan,* from which we have reach, *raught,* and *rax,* i.e., racs. The only English form I have found is *reike* and *reyke.*

Reike, to reach or fetch anything.—*Halliwell.*

> A candyll at a lawmpe he lyght,
> And to her chamber *reyked* he ryht.—*Le Bone Flo. of Rome.*

S.

'S for *Has.*

> The busy sun
> Drinks up the sea, and when *he's* done,
> The moon and stars drink up the sun.—*Cowley.*

Sab. Sob. *A* for *o*; see under *aff.*

Sae. So.

> King Estmere he stabled his steede,
> *Sae* fayre at the hall bord.—*King Estmere.*
>
> Elles moght not kinges thre
> Haf raght (reached) to ride *sa* fer awai.—*Cursor Mundi.*
>
> The stately stagge, that seems *sa* stout,
> By yalping houndes at bay is set.—*Anon. 1587.*

Saft. Soft. *A* for *o*; see under *aff.*

> Ye all can spek *safte* words at home.
> —*The Felon Sewe of Rokeby.*

Sagitarre. The constellation Sagitarius.

> Of Scorpio the heved all faire
> Be spreden of the *Sagittaire.*—*Gower.*

Sair. To serve. *A* for *e*; see under *dails*; for omission of *v* see under *ca'* or *gre.*

Sair. Sore.

> So was he woundyd wonder *sare.*—*Ipomydon.*
>
> On knees they fellen alle tho
> With sorrow and sighing *sare.*—*Guy of Warwick.*
>
> His heart was never so *sair.*—*R. Hood.*

Sairie. Poor, silly, feeble. *Jamieson.*

I am by no means certain that Burns ever used this word. In "O aye my wife she dang me" *sa'ar*, is sometimes printed instead of *sairie*. "Some *sairie* comfort still at last" seems feeble for Burns.

> No stivet e'er lived was so much misused
> As *sairy* ald Sawney for claiming the breeks.
> *The Northumberland Garland. Ritson.*

> Ful *sari* life he led.—*The Seven Sages.*

Sairly. Sorely.

Sall or *Sal.* Shall.

> Their idels all *sal* fall dun.—*Cursor Mundi.*
> And knawe na-mare sal he
> His stede, where that it *sal* be.—*E. Metrical Psalter.*
> It *sal* nan other be !—*Wright's Chaucer.*
> Sir, thus *sall* thi maisters wise
> Decayve the with thaire quayntise.—*The Seven Sages.*

Sal-marinum. Sea-salt.

Salt-permit. A note given by an officer of the Excise permitting the moving of salt, on which, in Burns's time, duty was paid.

Sands, to take the. To flee the country or go into concealment.

Sannock. Dim. of Sawnie and Sandy, diminutives of Alexander.

Sang. A song.

> Herdistow ever slik a *sang* er now?—*Wright's Chaucer.*
> The Castel and the Citee rang
> With menstralsi and nobil sang.—*Ywain and Gawain.*
> A *sang* ich schal you singe.—*The Geste of Kyng Horn.*

Sang about. See *about*.

Sapientipotent. Wisely powerful or powerfully wise; the poet's own coinage.

Sappy. Plump.

Sa'r. If there is such a word, it must mean share, portion. This simulacrum of a word is found only in a song referred to under *sairie.* I cannot decide which word is the worse.

Sark. A shirt.

> Gamelyn stood in the place alone without *serk.*
> *Tale of Gamelyn.*

> He had a *sarke* of silk
> About his middle meet.—*The Boy and the Mantle.*

> Stryppyd hem nakyd to the *sarke.*—*R. C. de Leon.*

The minister of Crossthwaite Church had a *whittle-gait* or the valuable privilege of using his knife for a week at a time at any table in the parish, and lastly, a harden *sark* or shirt of coarse linen.—*Brand's Popular Antiquities.*

Sunday's sark. A finer sort of shirt, donned only when its owner put on his best clothes, which for many was only on Sundays.

> Intelligence
> Would for a *Sunday-suit* thy breath condense.—*Cleveland.*

Sarkit. Shirted, provided with shirts.

> But naked now, or *shirted* but with air.—*Dryden.*

Sarkie. Dim. of sark.

Saugh. The willow.

Saugh, a willow, or withen.—*Bamford.*

> They made a bier of the broken bough,
> The *sauch* and the aspin gray.
> *Barthram's Dirge.*

Saul. Soul.

> Methinks it should not be worth your while to risque your *saul.*
> *Vanbrugh.*

Remember, man, thy *sawlys* helthe.—*Skelton.*

Unto his *sawl* was sho feil hulde.—*Ywain and Gawain.*

He makes mani be forsworne
And sum life and *saul* forsworn.—*Sir Penny.*

That yvel the *saul* sal grefe gretely.—*P. of Conscience.*

Saumont. Salmon.

This, except the added *t*, which was frequently applied to words ending in *n*, is the French form of the Latin *salmo*, and that which was used by early English writers.

In the ryver ys gret plenté of *samon.*—*John of Trevisa. Morris and Skeat.*

> They defend them with lamprey,
> With luce, with elis, with *samons.*—*Chaucer.*

> There with his *turbant* (turban) and his robe arrayed,
> I shall convict her.—*Congreve.*

> Give me the *turbant* and the false beard.
> *Beaumont and Fletcher.*

> How can I tell but that his *talants* (talons) may
> Yet scratch my son.—*Spenser.*

> For the *orizont* (horizon) had reft the sonne his light.
> *Chaucer.*

A sorrow so great as brought her to the *margent* of the grave.
Taylor's Holy Living and Dying.

Saunt. A saint.

The insertion of *u* in words like this is common.

Ane brother of the cloystre of *Sauynt* Austin.—*Ayenbite of Inwyte.*

The black Sanctus was a hymn to *Saunte Satan.*—*Dodsley's Old Plays.*

> And I wil nu this ilk tre
> Stand in paradis to be
> To mi *santes* in sted of fode.—*Cursor Mundi.*

> She *straungeth*
> Her love, and longe er that she *chaungeth*.
>
> *Gower.*

Saut. Salt. *To cast saut on one's tail,* to catch or overtake. See under *a'* for omission of *l*.

Sawt, salt.—*Bamford.*

> Such great achievements cannot fail
> To *cast salt on a woman's tail.*—*Butler.*

Sauted. Salted, troubled.

Saw. To sow.

> For on his visage was in little drawn,
> What largeness thinks in paradise was *sawn.*—*Shak.*
>
> Measure and I wyll never be devydyd
> For no dyscorde that any man can *sawe.*—*Skelton.*
>
> He thought on his londes that layen *unsawe.*
>
> —*Tale of Gamelyn.*
>
> And to cause the christen to him to geve confidence
> By the false seede of errour that they *sawe*
> Before his comming, against our fayth and lawe.
> —*Barclay's Ship of Fools.*

Sawny or *Sawnie.* Sandy, Alexander. In "Halloween" it seems to mean Satan.

Sax. Six. *A* for *i* is not common, though it is found, as in—

> Hy ne eteth non othere thing
> Than the erthe youet (gives) withouten *tallyng* (tilling).
> —*Kyng Alisaunder.*

But six is often written *sex,* and thus we have *a* for *e,* for which see under *fallow.*

> It was *sex* months syn.—*Coventry Mysteries.*
>
> Now, als this time *sex* yer,
> I rade allane, als ye sal her.—*Ywain and Gawain.*

A litil village of myne having not past *sex* houses.
—*Earl of Northumberland to Henry VIII.*

Scaith. To damage, to injure, injury.

This trick may chance to *scath* you.—*Shak.*

And of the wyf of Bath
That worketh much *scath.*—*Skelton.*

Tryde often to the *scath* of many deare.—*Spenser.*

But she was somdel defe, and that was *scathe.*—*Chaucer.*

Yet no such quickness for defence he used,
    As did the prince to work him harm and *scaith.*—*Fairfax.*

Scandal-potion. Tea.

At one time satirists joined scandal and tea together. They are not now, I believe, supposed to have any connection.

But chief, all sexes, every rank and age,
Scandal and *tea*, more grateful shall engage.—*The Rolliad.*

Now with mama at tedious whisk I play;
Now without *scandal* drink insipid *tea.*—*Lord Lyttleton.*

Scant. Scarcity. Verb or adjective used as a noun; but surely there must have been a noun *scant* before we could have *scanty*, as there were wind, winter, and sand, before there were windy, wintry and sandy.

Scantling. Burns uses this word for scanty or small in one of his letters to Clarinda.

Scar. To scare. *E* omitted as in

Whar artow!—*whar?*
An hore to Amon the *bar* (bare).
Alisaundre *swor.*—*Kyng Alisaunder.*

For what tyme he to me spak (spake)
Out of hys mouth me thoght *brak* (brake)
A flamme of fyre.—*Robert of Brunne.*

Scar. A cliff. See *scaur.*

Scaud. To skald. *L* omitted; see under *a'*.
  Scaud, skode, or *scode,* to scald.—*Bamford.*

Scauld. To scold. *A* for *o;* see *hald.*
  He was of his tong a *skald.*—*Ywain and Gawain.*

Scaur. To scare, apt to scare. Long sound of *a* changed into *au;* see under *awauken,* and in—

  For penaunce *chaunged* was his hew.—*Rob. of Brunne.*
  Monye he brought of lyf *dawe* (day).—*Kyng Alisaunder.*

Scaur and *scar.* A cliff, a precipice.
  Scar, a steep rock, the cliff of a rock.—*Bailey.*
  Scarr, scaur, a steep, bare, and rocky place on the side of a hill.
  Bamford.

  And eke ful ofte a little *scar* upon the bank,
  Lets in the streme.—*Gower.*

  Whose longitude do swage
  His fury, when his waves on Furnesse seem to war,
  Whose crooked beak is arm'd with many a rugged *scar,*
  Against his boist'rous shocks.—*Poly-olbion.*

Scone. A kind of bread.

A *scone* differs from a *bannock* in being thinner, and both from a cake in not being toasted before the fire as well as above it. A scone, also, is not made of oatmeal, indeed, I am told that unless mixed with some other substance, as potatoes, oatmeal could not be made into scones.

Scone-bonnet. A flat bonnet, like a *scone,* formerly worn by the peasantry of the Lowlands of Scotland, and which continued to be the head-dress of millers till recently.

This word does not occur in Burns's works, but

according to Allan Cunningham, he made use of it in a conversation in Edinburgh.—*Life, p. 361.*

Sconner. A loathing, to loathe.
Scunner, to loathe, to shun.—*Halliwell.*

Scotch mile. Nineteen hundred and eighty-four yards, or two hundred and twenty-four yards longer than an English mile.

Scots. The Scottish language.

Scraich. To scream, as a hen, partridge, etc.
Screik, to shriek.—*Bailey.* *Scrike, skriech, scriech.*—*Weber.*

> The solemn dirge, ye Owls, prepare,
> Ye Bats, more hoarsely *screek.*
> *An Excellent New Ballad.*

Screed. To tear, a rent.
Screade, a shred, leaf. *Screadian*, to shred, cut.—*Bosworth.*

Scriegh. To cry shrilly. Another form of *scraich.*

Scrieve. To glide swiftly along.

Scrievin. Gleesomely, swiftly.

Jamieson has indicated that it is only metaphorically that "gliding swiftly along" can mean gleesomely. He quotes no authority but Burns for the word.

Scrimp. To scant.
Scrimp, to spare, to pinch.—*Var. dial.* *Halliwell.*
Scrimpness, scantiness.—*Bailey.*

Scroggie. Bushy.
Scrog, a stunted bush. *Scroggy*, abounding in underwood.
Halliwell.
Scrog, a fragment, a scrag.—*Bamford.*

Shrogs, a company of bushes, of hazels, thorns, briers.

Thoresby.

Sculduddery. Fornication.

See'd. Did see.

The weak for the strong past tense was often used. In "The Jovial Hunter of Blomsgrove" I find "He *blowed* a blast" and "Then Sir Ryalas *drawed* his broad sword." I could however have been well content if Burns had not used *see'd*.

Some of the old poets seem, as regards this word, to make a sort of compromise:—

> The Devil ne're *see* such two Sir Harrys.
>
> *Wright's Political Songs.*
>
> And there we *see* Thomas.—*R. Hood.*
>
> A damsel come unto me,
> The semeliest that ever i *see*.—*Ywain and Gawain.*
>
> I *seed* an old chap at Bartlemy fair,
> Look more like a king than that chap there.
> *The King and the Countryman.—Bell's An. Poems and Songs.*

Sel. Self; *a body's sel*, one's self alone.

Seln, self,—*Bamford. Sel, seln,* self.—*Thoresby.*

> Which they dig out fro the dells,
> For their bairns' bread, wives, and *sells.*—*Ben Jonson.*
>
> Show your *sell*
> To all the shepherds.—*Id.*
>
> To Perciens Ywol *me seolle* (myself).—*Kyng Alisaunder.*
> Tim Bobbin entered by him *sell.*—*Tim Bobbin.*

Sell't. Did sell. *T* for *d*, see under *akwart*; strong verb conjugated as if it were a weak one, as in

Witness, ye heavens, the truth of all that I have *teld.*—*Spenser.*
The fayrest thorne that ever *groued* (grew).—*Ywain and Gawain.*
He *zeld* her haill hide for a groat.—*The Northumberland Garland. Ritson.*

GLOSSARY.

Semple.   Simple, humble in station, low-born.   *E* for *i*, as in

> He toke hys kyrtyl of, as smert,
> And *ded* (did) hyt on the man above.—*P. of Conscience.*

> I made noght for no disours,
> Ne for no seggours, no harpours,
> Bot for the luf of *symple* men
> That strange Inglıs cannot ken.—*R. of Brunne.*

> Sche made hem in the *pettes* (pits) wete.—*Gower.*

Servan'.   Servant.   *T* is often omitted after *n*.

> For summe of my *servanns* bethe seke other-while.
> *P. Plowman.*

> Sendeth ous
> An C. thousand *besans* (besants).—*Kyng Alisaunder.*

Set.   To face in a dance.   See *cleek.*

Enter young Loveless and his comrades with wenches and two fiddlers—

> Come, my brave man of war, trace out thy darling;
> And you, my learned council, *set* and turn, boys.
> *Beaumont and Fletcher.*

> Thou'st out, says Dick; it's a lie, says Nick,
> For the fiddler play'd it false.
> The fiddler then began to play it over again,
> And every lass did *set* it unto the man.—*Old Ballad.*
> *Nichols's Literary Anecdotes, Vol. VIII.*

Set.   To go, in "His only son for Hornbook *sets.*" *Sets aff,* goes away.

> So let him land
> And solemnly set on to London.—*Shak.*

Set by.   To regard.

> For a greytte lorde was Y tyld,
> And mykell Y was *sette by.*—*Sir Amadas.*

And David behaved himself more wisely than all the servants of Saul, so that his name was much *set by.*—*1 Samuel, xviii. 30.*

> She *settes* not *by* thy love a leeke.
>
> *Lord Vaux.*
>
> Your ladyship can *set*
> As little *by* such tunes as may be possible.
>
> *Shak.*

Settlin. Settling ; *to get a settlin*, to be frightened into quietness.

> He *settled* him at a blow.—*Fuller.*
>
> Till the fury of his highness *settle*
> Come not before him.—*Shak.*
>
> His insolence
> He *settled* with his sceptre.—*Chapman.*

Several. Separate, in "Each took aff his *several* way."

> He was a leper and dwelt in a *several* house.—*2 Kings, xv. 5.*
>
> Thanks to you all, and leave us ; fare you well.
> Good morrow, masters, each his *several* way.—*Shak.*
>
> He does allot for every exercise
> A *several* hour.—*Massinger.*

Sha'. Shall.

Shachlet. Distorted, shapeless.

It is often said that the word is used metaphorically in "Last May a braw wooer" but I think the inquiry about the "shachlet feet" of her rival is to be understood as literally as the question "Gin she had recovered her hearing."

Shaird. A shred, a shard. Long for short sound of *a* as in—

> For either they be ful of jelousie,
> Or *maisterful.*—*Chaucer.*
>
> Hire browe broune, hire eye *blake*
> With middel smal and wel ymake.
>
> *Wright's Specimens of Lyric Poetry.*

Sheard, a fragment.—*Bailey.*

Shangan. A stick cleft at one end for putting the tail of a dog, &c. into, by way of mischief, or to frighten him away.

Shank. To go on foot. From *shank*, a leg.

Shaul. Shallow.

> But this Molaunce, were she not so *shole*,
> Were no less faire and beautiful than she.—*Spenser.*
>
> When *shauldes* and sandie bankes appear,
> What pillot can direct his course?—*Early Naval Ballads. Percy Society.*

Shoal, a shallow.—*Johnson.*

Shaver. A barber, a humorous wag.

> The brace are flinch'd,
> The brace of *shavers* are sneak'd from us, Don.—*Ford.*
>
> Who could imagine now that this young *shaver*,
> Could dream of a woman so soon?—*Farquhar.*
>
> Yet Hampden, Cholmondely, those sinful *shavers*,
> Rebellious, riot in their Sabbath quavers.—*Dr. Wolcot.*

Shavie. A trick, an ill turn. Apparently a trick played by a *shaver*.

Shaw. To show.

> It *schawed* thar ful openlye
> That I led mi lif wrangwislie.—*E. Metrical Homilies.*
>
> For to *shawe* hire gentyll face.—*Life of Alexander.*
>
> Bot Hatherof, thou most me *schawe*,
> Wharbi y schal Wikard knawe.—*Horn Childe and Maiden Rimnild.*
>
> To our Lorde Jeshu Crist in heven,
> Iche to-day *schawe* myne sweven.—*Davies' Visions.*

Shaw. A small wood in a hollow place. "Wild natural wood."—*Sir W. Scott.*

> When *shaws* been sheen.—*R. Hood.*

> Gaillard he was, as goldfinch in the *shawe*.
>
> *Chaucer.*

> In sommer he lyveth by hawys,
> That on hauthorne growth by *schawys*.
>
> *Sir Orpheo.*

> I woll abide under the *shawe.*—*Gower.*

Shear. To reap, to cut grain with a hook or sickle, the only way of reaping known in Burns's day.

He *shears*, he reaps.—*Bamford. Shear*, to reap.—*Bailey.*

> Certain I am full like indeed
> To him that cast in earth his seed,
> But ere he it in his sheves *shere*
> May fall a weather that shall it dere.—*Chaucer.*

> Now o'er our bodies (tumbled up in heaps)
> Like cocks of hay when July *shears* the field.
>
> *Thos. Kyd.*

> Sche fond and gadreth herbes swote;
> Sche pulleth up som be the rote,
> And many with a knyf sche *scherth.*—*Gower.*

> In tyme of harvest men their corne *shere. Skelton.*

Shearer. A reaper.

Shears and *sheers.* Scissors. Johnson makes a distinction between shears and scissors, and the use of the former for the latter is thought a Scotticism.

> I saw a smith
> With open mouth swallowing a tailor's news,
> Who, with his *shears* and measure in his hand,
> Told of a many thousand warlike French.—*Shak.*

> There went but a pair of *sheers* between us.—*Id.*

> Fate urged the *sheers*, and cut the sylph in twain;
> The meeting points the sacred hair dissever
> From the fair head.—*The Rape of the Lock.*

Sheen. Shining, bright. This word, said to be obsolete, is now to be found in all E. dictionaries.

> With spere and schelde and *helmis schene.*—*Minot.*
> Ther as this fresshe Emelia the *shene*
> Was in hire walk.—*Chaucer.*

Sheep-shank. *To think one's self nae sheep-shank,* to be conceited.

Burns, both in prose and verse, speaks of a sheep-shank as if it were a worthless thing. But the peasantry of Ayrshire, who have a high appreciation of a sheep's trotter as an adjunct to a sheep's head, use this metaphor differently, and say of a person supposed to set too high a value on himself, "*He thinks he's nae sma' sheep-shank,*" i.e., he considers himself to be an excellent sheep-shank. I have always heard the emphasis laid on *sma'.*

Sheerly. Entirely. The adjective is common enough, but I do not remember meeting the adverb.

Sheer, clear, entire, through.—*Bamford.*
Sheer, altogether, quite.—*Bailey.*

Sherra-muir. Sheriff-moor, the famous battle fought in the Rebellion, A.D. 1715.

Sherewe, a sheriff.—*Lydgate. Halliwell.*

I have missed this word in Lydgate, but this spelling comes very near *shireues* in the following lines, if we had any means of knowing that *u* did not stand for the modern *v* :—

> Sysours and sompnours, *Shireues* and here clerkes.
> And sette Mede vpon a *Schyreue* shodde al newe.
> —*P. Plowman.*

The Anglo-Saxon, however, gives no countenance to the S. pronunciation.

Sheugh. A ditch, a trench.

Seugh, or *sough,* a wet ditch.—*Grose.*

It is probably allied to *sewer*. It occurs in "Death and Doctor Hornbook," and is said by some editors to mean a *furrow*, though in the same stanza it is said, "Ye need na yoke the pleugh," the only thing that can produce a furrow. In "The Twa Dogs," it means an open drain, or ditch.

Sheuk. Shook. *Eu* for *oo;* see under *beuk.*

Shiel, shieling. A shed, a hut, a temporary dwelling-place.

Shift. To exchange.

> Some to every side and party go,
> *Shift* every friend, and join with every foe.—*Crabbe.*

Shill. Shrill.

> He taketh his harpe anone ryght,
> Into the wode it ringeth *schylle*,
> As he coude harpe at his wille.—*Sir Orpheo.*
>
> And so *schil* schal that noyse bi, and so swete.
> *P. of Conscience.*
>
> Thai ganne arere swich a cri,
> That it *schillede* into the ski.—*The Seven Sages.*

Shog. A shock.

A *shog*, the meeting of two hard bodies which strike against one another with violence.—*Bailey.*

Shog, violent concussion.—*Johnson.*

> Why then capricious mirth make sholders *shog*.
> *Marston.*

After daybreak a *shog* was felt.—*Isaac Littlebury's Herodotus.*

Sagotter, to *shog* or shake.—*Cotgrave.*

> *Shog* on, kind patient.—*Massinger.*

Shool. A shovel.

Shool, a shovel.—*Grose. Bamford. Thoresby.*

GLOSSARY. 345

> Gave him a realm to rule,
> That occupyed a *showell*,
> > A mattoke and a spade.
> From the donge carte,
> The mattocke and the *shule*,
> > To reygne and to rule.--*Skelton.*

> Who dug his grave?
> I, said the owl, with my spade and *showl.*
> > *Death of Cock Robin.*

Shoon. Shoes.

> Do on thy hosen and thy *schoon.*—*Wright's Chaucer.*
> And leav'st such prints of beauty
> As clouted *shoon* do on a floor of loam.—*Bishop Corbet.*
> Some their hose, and some their *shoon.*—*Skelton.*

Shore. To offer, to threaten.

> *Shore*, to threaten.—*Halliwell.*

Shot. A movement of the shuttle across the warp.

> My shuttle's *shot*, my race is run,
> My sun is set, my day is done.—*Thomas Dudley, Gov. of Massachusetts, one of the Pilgrim Fathers.*

> An honest weaver, and as good a workman
> As e'er *shot* shuttle.—*Beaumont and Fletcher.*

Shouther. Shoulder. For change of *d* into *th* see *blather.*

> *Shoother.*—*Bamford.*

> Scho toke hym by the *shouther* bane.
> > *Bell's An. Poems and Songs.*

Schure. Did shear (reap), shore. *U* for *a*; see under *bure.*

> Her kercheves were well *schyre.*—*Launfal.*
> In two yt *share* Guyes stedes body.—*Sir Guy.*
> The god of love, which all to-*share*
> Mine breast.—*Chaucer.*

> The spores of his heles it *schare*.—*Ywain and Gawain*.
> Her throtes he *schar* atwo.—*Amis and Amiloun*.

Sic. Such.

> But *sike* fancies weren foolerie.—*Chaucer*.
>
> And who is yon, thou ladye faire,
> That looketh with *sic* an austerne face.
> *Northumberland betrayed by Douglas*.
>
> And loatheth *sike* delightes, as thou doest prayse.—*Spenser*.

Sicker. Sure, steady.

> And made all *siker* ynow with holinesse.—*Chaucer*.
>
> *Sicker* thy head verie tottie is.—*Spenser*.
>
> Now am I *sicker* I shall never finish my queste.
> *Morte D' Arthur*.
>
> The dancing past, the board is laid,
> And *siker* such a feast is made
>   As heart and lip desire.—*Parnell*.

Side. A district. See *kintra-side*.

> The worde (report) of hire spronge ful wyde
> Ffeor and ner, bi uch a *syde*.—*The Kyng of Tars*.

Sidelins. Sidelong, slanting.

> *Sideling*, sideways, awry.—*Bailey*.
>
> *Sidelin*, shuffling, hesitating.—*Bamford*.
>
> At last, with great *sideling*, my shoulders, and my whole body, got in.—*John Bunyan*.
>
> They had chosen a strong grounde somewhat *sideling* on the side of a hill.—*Hollingshed's Chron.*, *quoted by Jamieson*.
>
> I passed very gently and *sidling* through the two principal streets.
> *Swift*.

Sightless. Used in " The Vision " for unseen or invisible.

> Come to my woman's breasts,
> And take my milk for gall, you murd'ring ministers,

> Wherever in your *sightless* substances
> You wait on nature's mischief.—*Shak.*

Siller. Silver.

> A little thing with a hole in the end, as bright as any *siller*,
> Small, long, sharp at the point and strait as any piller.
> *Gammer Gurton's Needle.*

Siller. Silver ; money.

> Oh dainty duchess, here I bring that knyght,
> Him that your writings, pack'd on every pillar,
> Promised promotion to, and store of *siller.*—*Fletcher.*

Some so-called Scotch words require a double explanation. Their spelling differs from the modern English; and they are used in apparently a different manner. Yet both in form and meaning are they found in English writers. *Siller* is a good example. It is not the conventional orthography, and it is used for money as the French use *argent*. But the spelling, as shown above, was known in England, and the English—as was to be expected in a country in which for two centuries after the Conquest no gold was coined—used silver in the same sense. Indeed, it was long the custom to join silver with gold when money was spoken of, e.g.—

> Ther was gold gyffen in that stonde,
> And plenty of *sylver*, many a ponde.—*Sir Amadas.*

Silver for money—

> On swych chaffare
> Wuld y feyn my *silver* ware.—*Rob. of Brunne.*

One John Pelegrin was corrupted with *silver.*—*Luther's Forerunners, Lond., 1624.*

> So that the king in such manere *sulver* wan ynow.
> *Rob. of Gloucester.*

I expect forty pounds in good *silver*. I am not obliged to take gold ; neither will I.—*Dryden to Jacob Tonson.*

The use of silver was once so common in England, as to give origin to a verb signifying to bribe—

> He has *whytyd* Saladynys hand,
> To be kyng of Surryeland.—*R. C. de Lion.*

Simmer. Summer. *I* for *u* sound; see under *anither, bizz*, and in—

> His lemman *kitte* (cut) hem with hire sheres.—*Chaucer.*

Sin. Son. *I* for *u* sound as above. Son was often spelled *sun.*

> Quen (when) ani deid o that dizein
> His *sun* (son) for him was sett again.—*Cursor Mundi.*

John, *sun* to King Henry, and Fulco fell at variance at chestes.
Leland's Collectanea.

Sin'. Since.

> I could never vaunt of any purse
> I had, *sin'* you were my god-fathers.—*Ben Johnson.*
>
> But when as Calidore was comen in
> And gan aloud for Pastorell to call,
> Knowing his voice, although not heard long *sin'*.
>
> *Spenser.*
>
> For *sin'* he said that we ben jangleresses,
> I shall not sparen.—*Chaucer.*
>
> Was never *syn* Noe floode sich floodes seyn.
> *Wakefield Mysteries.*

Singet. Singed.

Sinn. The sun. *I* for *u*; see under *bizz.*

Sinsyne. Since then. *Sin* and *syne.*

Sirs! and dear sirs! An interjection having no reference to the company. It is not addressed to persons, but expresses the emotion of the speaker, like oh! ah! eh! &c. Shakspeare has *sir* as an interjection twice, and Skelton has

> Kynge Phylyp of Macedony
> Had no such Phylyp as I, No, no, *syr*, hardely.
> *Phyllyp Sparowe.*

> Lo, lo, *sers!*—*Coventry Mysteries.*

Skaith. To injure, to damage; injury, another form of *scaith*.

> To me it es ful mekel *skath*,
> Bot better es lose it than yow bath.—*Ywain and Gawain.*

> It was but in my own defence
> If he has gotten *skaith*.—*R. Hood.*

Skeigh or skiegh. Proud, nice, high-mettled.—*Burns.* Skittish.—*Ramsay.* Timorous, apt to startle; unmanageable, mettlesome, skittish; coy, shy; proud, nice.—*Jamieson.*

Skekie, shy, frightened.—*Halliwell.*

Skellum. A worthless fellow.

Skellum, a rogue.—*Bailey.* *Skellum*, a villain, a scoundrel.—*Johnson.* Chelme, a knave, a *skellam*.—*Cotgrave.*

Skellie. To squint.

Skellut, crooked, awry.—*Bamford.* *Skelly*, to squint.—*Halliwell.*

Jamieson quotes the following from an edition of Piers Plowman which I have not seen:—"Than Scripture scorned me and a *skile loked*." He also gives A.-Sax. *sceol-eáge*, which Bosworth translates squint-eyed, goggle-eyed, and a number of other words as the origin of *skellie*. But whatever the derivation of it, I think it is the same as *skail*, sometimes spelled *skeil*, to disperse, to scatter. This word was known in England.

After his army, to his perpetual shame, *skaled*, he called a council."

But the English word nearest to skellie, both in spelling and meaning, occurs in " Early English Alliterative Poems." I quote from Dr. Morris's excellent edition published in 1869. I make no alteration on the lines except to substitute modern for Anglo-Saxon characters.

The flood is over, and Noah relieves the animals from their confinement in the ark :—

> Therwyth he blesses uch a best & bytaght (gave) hem this erthe,
> Then watz (was) a *skylly* skyualde, quen scaped all the wylde (beasts).

Skylly, skailing, dispersing, divergent, like a *skellie* eye. *Skyvalde*, a scramble, perhaps the origin of our slang word *chivy*.

It will be seen by any one who looks carefully at it that *skile*, in the passage from Piers Plowman quoted by Jamieson, means to scowl rather than to squint, for squinting does not proceed from scorn or any other feeling, but is purely physical.

> The maryners awey gonne *skylle*,
> And yorne awey well hastily.—*Octovian Imperator*.

Skelp. To strike, to slap, to walk with a smart tripping step ; a smart stroke.

> *Skelping*, full, bursting, very large; also a hearty beating.—*Grose*.
> I shall *skelpe* thee on the skalpe.—*Skelton*.

Skelpie-limmer. A technical term in female scolding. See *skelp* and *limmer*.

As Burns does not say what this word means, some people seem to have misunderstood it. Dr. Mackay, for instance, says, " *Skelpie-limmer*, a violent woman, ready both with her hands and tongue."

It is, I think, pretty clear that Burns did not mean a violent woman—that would have been a *skelper*, not a *skelpie*—but one that deserved to be *skelped*, one not too old to be subjected to the chastisement which skelping primarily denotes. Look at the passage in which it occurs :—

> Wee Jennie to her Grannie says,
> Will ye go wi' me, Grannie?

Evidently both from the word *wee* applied to her, and from her desire to secure the presence and protection of her aged relative in what she regarded as a dangerous adventure, she was a mere child, and the grandmother's answer is equivalent to "Ye deserve to be whipped for proposing such a thing." *Skelpie-limmer* is, I believe, the feminine of *stripling*, if the old derivation be allowed, one not too old for corporal punishment, or of Shakespeare's—

I am no *breeching scholar* in the schools.—*Taming of the Shrew.*

This view of the word seems to be countenanced by *whippy*, given by Jamieson as a term of contempt applied to a girl or young woman.

Skink. Drink, anything potable; to serve drink.—*Johnson.*

Bacchus the win hem *skinketh* al aboute.—*Chaucer.*

Skinklin. Shining; a small portion.

Skirl. To shriek, to cry shrilly.
Skirl, to scream, to shriek.—*Halliwell.*
Skyrm, to scream.—*Bamford.*

Sklent. Slant, to run aslant, to deviate from truth, to fib; to glance. See under *asklent.*

Burns's use of *sklented* in "To William Simpson" is like the *squinting* in the following :—

The writers of them seldom or never do attain that end which they propound to themselves, especially if *squinting* at sinister ends.—*Fuller.*

> The observations have a *squint* at the author.—*Cowper*.

Skouth. Room, freedom to act.

> And he get *scouth* to wield his tree,
> I fear you'll both be paid.—*R. Hood*.

Skreigh or **skriegh.** To scream, a scream.

Screek and *scritch*.—*Bailey*. *Skriche*, *scriech*, cry out.—*Weber*.

> Whose fathers struck France so with fear,
> As made poor wives and children *skrike*.
> *Bal. of Flodden Field*.

> Women *scrike*, girles gredyng.—*Kyng Alisaunder*.

Skyrin. Shining, showy.

Scir (A.-Sax.). Sheer, pure, clear, bright, glorious.—*Bosworth*.

Burns uses this word only once—

> But had you seen the philibegs,
> And *skyrin* tartan trews.

The following pretty long extract from an old English romance, is given to show that the word is applied to showy colours by the older as well as the more recent poet :—

> A melle (mill) he hadde of gret maystry ;
> In mydys a schyp for to stand ;
> Swylke on saugh nevyr man in land.
> Four sayles wer thereto,
> Yellw, and grene, red and bloo,
> With canevas layd wel al about,
> Ful *schyr* withinne, and eke without.—*R. C. de Lion*.

> For leuening (lightning) in his sight cloudes *schire*,
> Forthyheden (went forth), haile, coles of fire.
> *Metrical English Psalter*.

Skyte. Very forcible motion.

Skyt, hasty, precipited.—*Dyce*. *Skit*, quickly.—*Weber*.

> Syr skyrgalyard, ye were so *skyt*,
> Your wyll than ran before your wyt.—*Skelton*.

A knyght took him up full *skeet.*—*R. C. de Lion.*

Slade. Did slide. *A* for *o*, as under *bane*, *slode* being the old form.

In hys goynge out of hys schyp a *slod.*—*John of Trevisa.*
Hys hors *slod*, and fel yn the fen.—*Launfal.*

Slae. A sloe. *A* for *o*; see under *bane.*

Slaigh, sloes, berries of the blackthorn.—*Bamford.*

Slap. A gate, a breach in a fence.—*Burns.* A breach in a wall; a gap in a fence.—*Jamieson.*

Slap. Unawares, unexpectedly, as if through a *slap* or gap in a fence, in

Till, *slap*, come in an unco loon.—*The Dumfries Volunteers.*

Slaw. Slow. *Aw* for *ow*; see under *maw.*

Slaw, slow, idle, lazy.—*Bosworth.*

He es swyft to spek on his manere,
And latsome and *slaw* for to here.—*Pricke of Conscience.*

Slee. Sly. *E* for *i* sound; see under *lee.*

Be war for ire that in thy bosom slepeth,
War for the serpent that so *slely* crepeth
Under the gras.—*Wright's Chaucer.*
As wisely and as *slely* as it might.—*Id.*
But Florentyn kidde (showed) that he was *slegh.*
Octovian Imperator.

Sleekit. Sleek. Sleek sometimes takes the participial form.

Yet are the men more loose than they,
More *sleek'd*, more soft, and slacker-limb'd.—*Ben Jonson.*

Sliddery. Slippery.

To a dronke man the way is *slider.*—*Chaucer.*
I trow it be a frost, for the way is *slider.*—*Skelton.*

> He wot not whider
> To go, the waies ben so *slider*.—*Gower*.
>
> The way was so depe and *slider*
> Thai fal doun in the clay.—*Amis and Amiloun*.

Slight. Sleight, art, dexterity, cunning.

Slight, a cunning trick, dexterity.—*Bailey*.

> Thus with *slight*
> Thou shalt disarm them first.—*Ben Johnson*.

I should not have thought of inserting this word, or have supposed its meaning could have been mistaken in the passage,—

> O Willie was a wanton wight,
> And had o' things an unco *slight*,

had I not seen slight called a collection. Not only the lines themselves point out that Willie was an artful manager of affairs, but the other places in which the words occur show clearly that slight is not a collection,—

> And wow! he has an unco *slight*
> O' cauk and keel.
>
> His knife see rustic labour dight,
> And cut it (a haggis) up wi' ready *slight*.

To see a good haggis neatly opened is, to a hungry Scotsman, what the poet calls it, a "glorious sight," but to see it cut up with a collection, say a collection made at the church-door, would be a sight indeed.

Sloken. Quench, slake.

Slocken, soften, as *slocken with overmuch moisture*.—*Bailey*.

Slokened, q. slackened, choked, as a fire is *slokened* by throwing water on it.—*Grose*.

> That bottell swet, which served at the first
> To keep the life, but not to *slocken* thirst.—*Sylvester*.

Slype. To fall over, as a wet furrow from the plough, to slip. Long for short *i*.

There is a slight inaccuracy in Burns's definition of this word, perhaps hardly worth notice. It is not the **furrow** that *slypes* over. A furrow is the trench or hollow made by the removal of the soil by the plough. It is this soil that *slypes* over. But the word itself is interesting for more than one reason. It is a modification of *slip*, and it is interesting to notice what brought about the change. When the soil was short and loose it *slipped* over from the plough at once; but when the ground, from the growth of rushes, *sprits*, or other coarse plants, was tough, it fell slowly, and in masses, often not without a stamp of the ploughman's foot, it was found desirable to have a word which should indicate the longer process, and slip was lengthened into *slype*, which, as Allan Cunningham well explains it, is " To fall over with a slow, reluctant motion." That there should have been such a word shows the low state of agriculture in Burns's day. Owing to better drainage and other improvements in farming, it is now unknown even to ploughmen.

> His mouth upon the gras he wipeth,
> And so with feigned chere him *slipeth.—Gower*.

Sma'. Small ; used as a noun in " Wi' *sma'* to sell, and less to buy." See under *a'*.

Small-pox. Inoculation.

Small-pox was the name generally given to inoculation; vaccination, I need hardly say, was, when Burns used the word (1791), unknown.

Smeddum. Dust, powder ; mettle, sense.

Anglo-Saxon, *Smedema, smedem*, meal, flour.—*Bosworth*.
Smedme, meal. *Dunelm. Smedum*, dust. *West.—Halliwell*.

Smeek. Smoke. *E* for *o*; see under *freath*.

Sméc, sméoc, sméac, vapour, smoke.—*Bosworth*.

Smiddy. Smithy. *D* for *th*; see under *cleed*, and in—

> Now by my *modre* Ceres soul I swere.—*Chaucer.*
> Thou schalt cum *theder* (thither) al so gay
> As any eyrthely mon may.—*Sir Amadas.*
> A myssal newe bound with derys-*ledder* (leather).
> *The Brethren of the Holy Trinity.*

Smit. To infect.

Smiting, contagion.—*Bosworth.*

> Each glance of her eye is so *smittle,*
> That all men are catch'd if they gaze.
> *The Northumb. Garland. Ritson.*

Smoor. To smother.

Smoor, to smother; *smoort,* smothered.—*Bamford.*

To *smoor,* to smother, per contrac.—*Thoresby.*

> Some brains out-bet, some in the guts were gor'd,
> Some dying vomit blood, and some were *smor d.*
> *Sylvester.*

Smoutie. Smutty, ugly, obscene, and perhaps sooty, differing from smutty only in spelling. *Ou* for *u*, as in—

The constable hath of hir so gret pitee,
And eek his wyf, that they wepen for *routhe* (ruth).—*Chaucer.*

> Hit openeth *ous* (us) to the hevene blisse.
> *William of Shoreham.*

Smytrie. A numerous collection of small individuals. No authority but that of Burns can be cited for this word.

Snapper. To stumble, to trip and not fall.

> Count ye your selfe good clerkes,
> And *snapper* in suche werkes?—*Skelton.*

Snash. Abuse, Billingsgate.

Snaw. Snow, to snow.

Your hyghnes subjects was xiii myles within the growndes of Scotland, where great *snawes* doth lye.—*Duke of Northumberland to Hen. VIII.*

> I was drevyn with *snawe* and slete.—*Ywain and Gawain.*
> His heved was whyte as any snawe.—*Lives of the Saints.*
> Now es *snaw*, hail, or rayn,
> And now es fair wedyr again.—*Pricke of Conscience.*

Snaw-broo. Melted snow. *Snaw* and *broo.*

Sned. To lop, or cut off.

Sned besoms. To cut brooms.—*Cunningham.* Rather to dress, to prune, or render *snod.*

It is quite clear that by *snedding besoms* Burns meant making brooms or other sweeping instruments, and it is also true that in "To a Haggis" he uses *sned* for to lop or cut. It is true too that A.-Saxon *sneddun* means cut, and *snidan*, to cut. But it is as true that not all besoms, nor even mostly all, were made of broom. There were, even since I remember, birch-besoms, though often called brooms, for the stable and the cow-house; rush-besoms, and rather expensive things they were, for the cottage, the barn, and the mill. All these, as also the broom proper, required handles, and to supply them was the most important part of the broom-maker's work. Now *sned* is A.-Saxon for a handle or shaft, and both in England and Scotland *sned* is the name for the handle of a scythe to this day. Sned besoms may therefore mean "put handles to them."

Sneeshin. Snuff.

> *Cup o' sneeze*, a pinch of snuff.—*Grose. Bamford.*
> *Snuff*, a *sneeshin* powder. *Snush*, snuff.—*Bailey.*
> He takes *snush*; Mockmode taking *snush* sneezes.—*Farquhar.*

If any young person thinks *snush* or *sneeshin* a strange name for snuff, perhaps he may be enticed to learn Danish when he hears that a snuff-box is called ***snustobaksdaase*** in that language.

Sneeshin-mill. A snuff-box.

> *Sneeze-hurn*, a horn to hold snuff.—*Bamford.*
>
> The *snuff-mill* and gloves came in season.—*The North. Garland. Ritson.*
>
> As tobacco is good here, you had best bring a *Scotch-mill* and make it (snuff) yourself.—*Sterne's Letters.*

Snell. Bitter, biting.

> He was a handy man and *snell*
> In tournament, and eke in fight.—*Morte Arthur.*
>
> In amang all thir wormes *snelle*,
> Als naked als he was borne he felle.—*E. Metrical Poems.*
>
> Than sayd Gyfroun, al so *snell*,
> To all thys y graunte well.—*Lybeaus Disconnus.*
>
> Thyderward Florentyn, well good pas,
> He rood full *snelle*.—*Octovian Imperator.*

Snick, and Sneck. The latchet of a door.

> To *sneck* the door, to latch it.—*Bailey. Grose.*
>
> *Sneck*, a string to pull up the latchet of a door.—*Bamford.*
>
> *Loquet d'une huis*, the latchet or *snecket* of a doore.—*Cotgrave.*

Sir Toby, in "The Twelfth Night," bids Malvolio, whose harangue is disagreeable to him, "Snick up!" This has been guessed to mean "Hang yourself!" May it not mean "Shut up!" a cry which sometimes greets an unpopular speaker?

Snick-drawing. Trick-contriving, synonymous with *latch-drawing*.

> He lived by robbery, . . and principally by and with vaga-

bonds, idle wanderers, night-walkers, and *draw-latches.—Lord Coke.*

The same word occurs in a statute of Ed. III., which mentions " wasters and *draw-laches.*"—*Ritson.*

Snirt, snirtle. To laugh restrainedly, a restrained laugh.
Esbrouër des narines, to *snurt* or snufter.—*Cotgrave.*

Snod. Neat.
A.-S. *sneddun,* cut, pruned (made snod).
Snod, neat, handsome.—*Bailey.*
Snod, smooth, sleek, and snug.—*Bamford.*

Snood. A ribbon for the hair.
Snod, a fillet, cap, hood.—*Bosworth.*
Snoode, a fillet to tie up a woman's hair.—*Bamford.*

Snool. One whose spirit is broken with oppressive slavery, to submit tamely, to sneak.
Sneul, a poor sneaking fellow.—*Halliwell.*

Snoove. To go smoothly and constantly, to sneak.
Snever, slender, smooth.—*Thoresby.*
Sneving, sneaking. *Devon.*—*Halliwell.*

Snowk. To scent or snuff, as a dog, horse, etc.
Snook, to be lurking for a thing.—*Bailey.*
Snuck, to smell.—*Grose.* *Snook,* to smell, to go about smelling.—*Bamford.*
Halener, to *snowk, smell,* search out.—*Cotgrave.*

Sodger. A soldier.
For that sort of *sowdiers* so manfully mand.—*Heywood.*
I dwelled with him as *Soudyour* in his Werres a gret while.
Maundeville.
For y also my selfe am a man undre power and have *Sowdeeres* undre me.—*Tyndale.*

And *sowdears* wyll come to me.—*Le Bone Flo. of Rome.*

Dere be great differentia between the gentlemen officiera and de rogua de *sogiera.*—*Duke of Buckingham.*

Some. Somewhat, rather, as in "We bardies ken *some* better."

This word is not used as an adverb in Ayrshire, but it is commonly used for rather in the eastern counties. See under *clartie.*

Some better will remind those familiar with Chaucer of—

> Alas, why plainen men so in commune
> Of purveyance of God, or of fortune,
> That yeveth hem ful oft in many a gise
> *Wel better* than they can hemselfe devise?
> *The Knightes Tale.*

Something. Somewhat.

He was *something* discouraged by a new pain.—*Temple.*

Sonsie. Having sweet, engaging looks, lucky, jolly.

Soncy, cunning.—*Thoresby.* *Soncy*, lucky, fortunate.—*Grose.*
Soncie, fortunate. It is still in use, and also used in the sense of pleasant, agreeable, plump, fat, and cunning.—*Halliwell.*

Sons of light. Freemasons.

Soom. To swim.

> He *swom* an easy current for his love.
> *The Two Noble Kinsmen.*

> The lady prickt her wanton steed,
> And o'er the river *swom* with speed.
> *The Uugrateful Knight.*

Sooth. Truth, a petty oath.

Johnson says *sooth* is obsolete. It is now in good use, especially in poetry.

> If thy speech be *sooth*,
> I care not if thou dost for me as much.—*Shak.*

GLOSSARY.

Sootie. Sooty.

Sough. A sigh, the sound of wind at a distance.

Sowgh, to sigh; *sooin'*, moaning of the wind.—*Bamford.*

> Ther ran a romble and a *swough* (sound of wind),
> As though a storme shuld bresten every bough.—*Chaucer.*

> With ful many a sory *swough* (sigh),
> He goth and geteth him a kneding trough.—*Id.*

> The well greased wherry now had got between
> And bade her farewell *sough* with her burden.—*Ben Johnson.*

Souk. To suck; a suck.

> As a colte sholde *souk* his dame.—*R. C. de Lion.*

> When that this childe had *souked* but a throwe.—*Chaucer.*

> The waffore *souketh* honeye fro the bee.—*The Libel of E. Policy.*

He hath *sowked* out the most poison that he could find through all Luther's books.—*Sir T. More.*

Souple. Flexible, swift.

Soople, a supple, a stick of hazel or ash.—*Bamford.*

Evidently Bamford's words apply to Burns's "Thresher's weary flingin-tree," which is called a *soople.*

> His botes *souple*, his hors in gret estate,
> Now certainly he was a fayre prelat.—*Chaucer.*

> Hire skyn is tendyr for to towche,
> As of an hownd-fyssh or of an hake,
> Whose tewhyng hath cost many a crowche (cross, coin),
> Hire pylche (shift) *souple* for to make.—*Lydgate.*

Souse. To punish, to hurt in any way. To strike with sudden violence.—*Johnson.*

> The stormy blastes her cave so sore did *sowse.*
> *Sir Thomas Wyat.*

> The falcon
> With sudden *souse* her to the ground shall strike.
> *Sylvester.*

Souter. A shoemaker.

Souter, sowter, a shoemaker or cobbler.—*Bailey.*

A conqueror ? a cobbler ! Hang him, *sowter.*—*Fletcher.*

I saw a *sowter* go to supper or ever he had dined.—*Skelton.*

I have levere here an harlotrie, or a somer game of *souteres.*
P. Plowman.

Souther or sowther. Solder, to solder, to cement. Solder is often written *soder,* and for the change of *d* into *th* see under *blather.*

Sodder, to join or fasten with solder.—*Bailey.*

To *sodder* gold they use the coarser to *sodder* the finer.—*Ray Correspondence.*

It is ready for the *sodering.*—*Isaiah xli. 7.*

The metal's stronger that's well *souder'd.*—*Farquhar.*

Sowens. A sort of pudding made out of oat-flour soured: something resembling that now made of corn-starch.

Sowins, flummery made of oatmeal.—*Johnson.*

Sowings or *sewings,* oatmeal flummery.—*Grose.*

Our lasses fair, say what you dare,
Who *sowens* make with shellings.—*Swift.*

Sowp. A spoonful, a small quantity of any thing liquid. Not confined to liquids unless that term includes porridge, sowens, and puddings in general.

They *sowpen,* and they speken of solace.
Wright's Chaucer.

And whanne they hadde *souped* alle
They token leve.—*Gower.*

Whan they had *sowped,* and the day was gone,
They wente to bedde.—*Launfal.*

Bidde hem go swynke,
And he shal *soupe* swettere.—*P. Plowman.*

And they *sowped* that evenyng wyth grete gladnes.
Caxton. Skeat.

Sowth. To try over a tune with a low whistle.

> *Soud, soud, soud, soud!*—*Taming of the Shrew, Act iv., S. 1.*

This word, when we remember that *d* and *th* are interchangeable, will appear to be Burns's *sowth*, and if Mason had known it he would doubtless have used it to support the first part of his conjecture—" These words seem merely intended to denote the *humming of a tune*, or some kind of ejaculation." The idea of its being an ejaculation is not borne out by the circumstances. Petruchio has just sung a line of one song, and is about to begin another, and is trying—*southing* or *souding*—to get into the tune. The one poet helps to explain the other, if my notion be correct.

Spae. To prophesy.

A purely Danish word; *at spaae i kort*, to tell fortunes on the cards.

Spails. Chips of wood, splinters. E. spill, a splinter.

> *Spails* and *speals*, chips, etc.—*Bailey.* *Spalls*, chips.—*Grose.*
>
>> There men might see spears fly in *speels*.
>>> *Bat. of Flodden.*
>
> *Spalls*, broken pieces.—*Cotgrave.*

Spairge. To dash, to soil as with mire.

> *Spargefaction*, the act of sprinkling.—*Johnson.*
> To *sparkle* away, to disperse.—*Thoresby.*
>
>> But some faire sunne hath *sperst* that lowring clowd.
>>> *Spenser.*
>
> *Sperse* or *sparge* frequently occurs in our old writers.—*Todd.*
>
>> We were *spars't* abroad.—*Sternhold and Hopkins.*
>
> 'Tis now scarce honour
> (For you) To *sparkle* (scatter) such poor people.
>>> *Fletcher.*

Sparseth all the gathered clouds.—*Chapman.*

Spak. Did speak. *E* omitted ; see under *quak.*

And anon he *spak* with hem.—*Wyclif.*

And Frensch she *spak* ful fare and fetysly.

Chaucer.

No worde more she *spacke*.—*The Frere and the Boye.*
More he thoughte than he *spak*.—*Kyng Alisaunder.*

Spate or *speat.* A sweeping torrent after rain or thaw.

Spaetan, to spit.—*Bosworth.* *Spet,* to bring or pour abundantly.—*Johnson.*

Spot is the matter spitten, *spate,* or spilled.—*Tooke.*

When the dragon womb
Of Stygean darkness *spets* her darkest gloom.—*Milton.*

Spaul. A limb.

Spalles, shoulders.—*Bailey.*

Their mightie strokes their haberiens dismayl'd,
And naked made each others' manly *spalles*.—*Spenser.*

(He) smote Ser Thomas
On his *spawdeler* (armour for the shoulder).—*R. C. de Lion.*

Spavie. The spavin.

Spaviet. Having the spavin, spavined.

Spean. To wean.

Spana, teats.—*Bosworth.* *Speene,* or *spene,* a cow-pap.—*Grose.*
Spane, to wean a child.—*Johnson.*

To *span,* or *spene* a child, to wean it.—*Bailey.*

Speel. To climb.

Speel, to climb, to clamber.—*Halliwell.*

Over rocks, over mountains and ditches,
Dike-gutters and hedges it *speals*.—*The Northumb. Garland. Ritson.*

Speet. To spit, to pierce. *E* for *i*; see under *dreep*, and

> She began to preche
> Of the tewsday in the wëke
> When the mare doth *keke* (kick).—*Skelton.*

The truth, dog, or I'll *spit* you like a sparrow.—*Farquhar.*

Spence. The country parlour.

> Al vinolent as botel in the *spence*.—*Chaucer.*
>
> (He) ladde him into *spence* rapely and anon.—*Tale of Gamelyn.*
>
> To compounde
> With Elynour in the *spence*.—*Skelton.*
>
> What do you here within our *spence?*—*An. Songs. Ritson.*

Spier, or *speer.* To ask, to enquire.

> But saw they no man there at whom
> They might the matter *spear*.—*R. Hood.*
>
> My will
> Ben fully set to herken and *spire*
> What any man will speke of hire.—*Gower.*

Howr Kyng bad hes men abeyde,
And he welde *sper* of hem the wey.—*The King and the Barber.*

They passed thorow Pole and Chawmpayne,
Evyr *speryng* ther gatys.—*Le Bone Florence of Rome.*

To *speer the price* of a young woman is to ask her in marriage.—*Jamieson.* To *speer the price* occurs in "O Tibbie, I hae seen the day," and is similar to Benedict's "Rich she shall be, that's certain; wise, or I'll none; virtuous, or I'll ne'er *cheapen her*.—*Much Ado About Nothing.*

Speir in. To go in and ask for.

Splatter. A splutter, to splutter.

Spleuchan. A tobacco seal-skin pouch.

Splore. A frolic, a riot, a noise.

Spontoon. A sort of half-pike carried by officers in the army.

Sprachle. To clamber.

Sprattle. To scramble.

Spreckled. Spotted, speckled.

Spring. A quick air in music, a Scotch reel.

> And strike him such new *springs*, and such free welcomes,
> Shall make him scorn an empire.—*Fletcher.*
>
> There saw I famous old and young,
> Piperis all of the Duche tong
> To lerne love-daunces and *springis*.—*Chaucer.*
>
> I dyde nought elles as I you saye,
> But pyped him a *springe.*—*The Frere and the Boye.*
>
> Come, piper, and play us a *spring.*
>   *Wright's Polit. Bal. Percy Society.*

Sprit, Spret. A tough-rooted plant, something like a rush.

Spreot, a *sprit*, a sprout.—*Bosworth.*

Sprit, to vegetate, to sprout.—*Bamford.*

> His eyn wer carbonkeles bryght,
> As the mone they schon a-nyght,
>   That *spreteth* out ovyr all.—*Launfal.*

Sprittie. Full of sprits, rushy.

Sprush. Spruce, smart, neat. *Sh* for *s* sound. See under *fleesh.*

Spunk. Fire, mettle, wit.

Spunk, match for guns.—*Bailey.*

Spunk, a dried fungus used as tinder.—*Grose.*

Spunk, and *sponk*, touchwood.—*Johnson.*

> In that snug room where any man of *spunk*
> Would find it a hard matter to get drunk.—*Wolcot.*

> She scarcely drinks a dozen drams a day,—
> And, in love matters, is a Queen of *spunk*.—*The Rolliad*.

Spunkie. Mettlesome, fiery, Will o' Wisp, or *ignis fatuus*, ardent spirits.

In the "Epistle to Mr. John Kennedy," the lines—
> But gie me just a true guid fallow
> Wi' right engine,
> And *spunkie* ance to make us mellow,"

are sometimes pointed so as to make spunkie an attribute of the "guid fallow," thus leaving nothing to make them mellow.

Saturday, the 16th of September next, will be sold a strong *spunky* sorrel steed.—*Manchester Hand-bill, 1829.*

Spurtle. A stick used for stirring a pot in cooking.

Spurtle-blade. A jocular name for a sword.

Squad. A crew, a party.
> Monarch of mighty Albion, check thy talk,
> Behold the *squad* approach, led on by Palk.—*The Rolliad*.
> Ev'n Pitt himself once deign'd to court the *squad*.—*Id*.

Squatter. To flutter in water as a wild duck, &c.

Squattle. To sprawl.—*Burns.* Perhaps it rather signifies, to lie squat, from the E. adj.—*Jamieson.* To sprawl in the act of hiding.—*Cunningham.* I believe it is a frequentative of the verb to *squat.*

Squeel. A scream, a screech, to scream, differing only in spelling from E. *squeal.*

Squeel. School in "when there came a yell o' foreign *squeels*."—*Amang the Trees.* This is an Aberdeenshire word. *E* for *oo ;* see under *preef.*

Stable-meal. Liquor consumed in an inn by farmers by way of remuneration for the accommodation of their horses during the day.

Stacher, or stacker. To stagger.

> She riste her up, and *stakereth* here and there.—*Chaucer*.
> All those that he with halbert caught,
> He made to *stacker* in that stound.—*Bat. of Flodden Field*.

Stack. Stuck, the old preterite of stick.

> She ne had on but a straite old sacke,
> And many a cloute on it there *stacke*.—*Chaucer*.
>
> A broche of gold and azure,
> Creseide him yave and *stacke* it on his sherte.—*Id*.
>
> Her hertes depe
> *Stak* in his bounden cofre.—*Occleve*.

Staggie. Diminutive of stag.

After this explicit declaration by Burns himself one would have thought it impossible to mistake the meaning of the word, had not Chambers said it means a *colt*, in

> I've seen the day
> Thou could hae gaen like ony *staggie*
> Out-owre the lay;

that is, when she was a young mare she could run as fast as a young horse. I wonder what old Maggie, could she have understood it, would have thought of such a compliment.

Staig. A stallion. It was doubtless this word that led Chambers astray.

St. Jamie's. The E. Court.

Stalwart. Strong, stout.

> Our king and his men helde the felde,
> *Stalwortly*, with spere and schelde.—*Minot*.
> Thou semyst a *stalward* and a stout.—*R. Hood*.

This Christian and this Saracen togather then soon met,
And as *stalword* men to-gather fast set.—*Rob. of Gloucester*.

A *stalwart* Baron here doth lie.—*The Rolliad*.

Stan'.   To stand.   *D* omitted; see under *blin'*.

The Justice Bramble with Sir Hugh the Canon,
And the bride's parents, which I will not *stan'* on.
Ben Jonson.

Stane.   A stone.   *A* for *o*; see under *bane*.

By the well standes a *stane*.—*Ywain and Gawain*.

Good Robin answer'd ne'er a word,
  But stood still as a *stane*.—*R. Hood*.

When the king had said his will
All the lordes sat *stane*-still.—*The Ravens*.

Stang.   A sting, stung.   Old preterite of sting.

Stang, to sting.—*Bamford*.

The adder so the grey-hound *stang*.—*The Seven Sages*.

The fende which appered in the lyknes of an adder to Eve ande *stange* full evyl.—*Dives and Pauper*.

More stinging than scorpions that *stang* Phaotis.
Skelton.

Stank.   Did stink.   Old preterite of stink.—*Johnson*.

And the river *stank*.—*Exodus, vii. 21*.

Stank.   A pool of standing water.

Stank, a dam or bank to stop water.—*Bailey*.

Ther faure (four) citees were set, . . .
As a stynkande *stanc* that stryed synne.
Early E. Alliterative Poems.

In that Contree ben Bestes, taughte of men to gon in to Watres, into Ryveres, and in to depe *Stankes*, for to take Fysche.
Maundeville.

Stap.   To stop.   *A* for *o*; see under *aff*.

Stark. Stout.

> He had a pike-staff in his hand,
> That was both *stark* and strang.—*R. Hood.*

> I feel my limmes *stark* and suffisant.—*Chaucer.*

Stark beer, boy, stout and strong beer.—*Fletcher.*

Starn. A star.

> And mikel of a *sterne* he tald,
> A *sterne* to cum that suld be sene.—*Cursor Mundi.*

> The twelft day, sal *sternes* fall.—*E. Metrical Homilies.*

> Some lay stareand on the *sternes*,
> And some lay, knocked out thair hernes.—*Minot.*

> And I sal teche him, . . .
> That falles to *sternes* of the sky.—*The Seven Sages.*

Starnie. Dim. of starn.

Startle. To run as cattle stung by the gad-fly, or frightened.

The Queen coming to the place where she was seen of them, though they knew not her estate, yet something there was which made them *startle* aside and gaze upon her.—*Additions to the Countess of Pembroke's "Arcadia."*

Staukin'. Stalking. *L* omitted; see under *a'*.

Stawk, to stride; *stawkin*, striding.—*Bamford.*

Fowling is delightsome, be it with guns, *stawking* horses or otherwise.—*Anatomy of Melancholy.*

Staumrel. Half-witted.

Staw. Stole. *L* changed to *aw*; see under *a'*.

> It befell upon a day,
> That he through out her chambre wall
> Came in all sodeinlich and *stall*
> That thing, which was to him so lefe,
> But wo the while, he was a thefe.—*Gower.*

GLOSSARY. 371

> Tho the dai dawen gan,
> Awai *stal* the young man.—*The Husband shut out.*

Staw. To surfeit.

This word has no connection with the preceding. It is probably *stall*, by the common change of *l* into *aw*, where animals are fed, and it may be *over*-fed, or it may be *stawed*, i.e., stowed, or filled, and of course sated.

Staud, surfeited, tired.—*Halliwell.*

When ye are *staued* (stowed).—*Early E. Alliterative Poems.*

Stech. To cram the belly.

Steek. To shut.

> And when he was out of chaumber gon,
> The dore he *steked* still anon.—*Amis and Amiloun.*

> And at a posterne *unsteke*
> Lybeaus gan out breke.—*Lybeaus Disconnus.*

> This coffre into his chambre brought,
> Which that they finde faste *stoke* (steked).—*Gower.*

Steek. A stitch.

> For the best that sewes her any *styk*
> Takes bot four penys in a wyk.—*Ywain and Gawain.*

> Wight Wallace could hardly have with her kept *steaks*.
> *The Northumberland Garland. Ritson.*

It seems to be used as a verb in—

He *stiked* up his lappes tho, i.e., he stitched up the flaps of his coat.—*Amis and Amiloun.*

Steer. To stir, to molest.

> He woll nought ones *stere* his fote.—*Gower.*

> And in Latin I speke a wordes fewe
> To saffron with my predication,
> And for to *stere* men to devotion.—*Chaucer.*

> Stowtlyche *stere* we us yn were.—*Octovian Imperator.*
> He scarcely then will *steer.*—*Chapman.*

Steeve. Firm, compacted.

This is simply a different spelling of *stiff,* as used by Spenser and others.

> I trust for to slay this fiende
> Though he be *stiff* in stour.—*Sir Cauline.*

Steeve in stour would be accounted good Scotch.

> So *stif* mon he was in armes
> That unnethe eni man mighte is bowe bende.—*R. of Gloucester.*

Sometimes it is spelled with *e* instead of *i* :—

> With coronals *stef* and stelde.—*Lybeaus Disconus.*

Sometimes *f* becomes *v,* as *stive,* strong :—

> The sponges were *stived* into sacks when wet.—*Sandys.*

Stell. A still. *E* for *i;* see under *semple.*

It seems to have been long before E. authors could determine whether to use *e* or *i* in many words,—Spenser, for example, employs them indifferently :—

> He cast him to scold
> And *snebbe* the oak.
> That list at will them to revile and *snib.*

Sten. To rear as a horse.

I suspect that this is an old form of stand. Before he can rear, or at least in the act of rearing, a horse must stand for an instant, but the rearing being more likely to attract observation than the standing, in course of time gave the meaning to the word. The Anglo-Saxon *standan* has *stent,* standest, *stent,* stands.

Sten. A spring or leap.

Stents. Tribute, dues of any kind. E. *stent*, proportion, quantity assigned.

Stent, an allotted portion.—*Var. dial. Halliwell.*

But this I charge that ye the *stents* keepe,
And breke them not for slouth nor ignorance.—*Chaucer.*

Erythius had even nowe attaynde his journeyes *stent.*—*Sackville.*

Stewartrie. Kirkcudbright, which is not a shire or county, but a *stewartry*.

Stey. Steep.

Steegh, steigh, steep.—*Weber.* *Steigh*, a ladder.—*Bamford.*

The Beast
Thought with his winges to *stye* above the ground.—*Spenser.*
This on the wal *steigh* on heigh.—*Kyng Alisaunder.*

King James thought he was writing English, and certainly expected to be understood by his English subjects when he wrote, "If one fall from a high and *stay* rock his breath will be forcibly banished from the body before he can win to the earth."—*Daemonologie.*

Stibble. Stubble. *I* for *u* ; see under *bizz*.

Stibble rig. The reaper, in harvest, who takes the lead.

Stick an' stowe. Totally, altogether.

Sticks, furniture.—*Cumb. Halliwell.*

Stick and stow may be furniture, and all else that one has stowed or stored. There are many adverbial phrases used to express a complete sweep, the separate words of which it is difficult, if not impossible, to explain. In addition to *stick and stow* Jamieson gives *stab and stow*, and *stoop and roop*.

> Godfrey meanwhile to ruin *stick and stone*
> Of this fair town, with battery sore assays.—*Fairfax.*

A' to sticks, completely.

Stilt. A crutch, to halt, to limp.

In one letter Burns speaks of the same things as stilts and crutches.

In modern English *stilt* does not mean a crutch, but in the following passage the word must signify crutches, for they are used by cripples, and it requires an active man to manage what are now called stilts.

> Once at Jerusalem, when the pilgrims kneel'd,
> I strewed powder on the marble stones,
> And therewithal their knees would rankle so
> That I have laughed a good to see the cripples
> Go limping home to Christendom on *stilts*.
> *Marlow. The Jew of Malta.*

Stimpart. The eighth part of a Winchester bushel.

Stirk. A cow or bullock a year old.

Stirk and *sturk*, a young steer or heifer.—*Bailey. Bamford. Grose.*

> They've stolen the *stirks* from half the cows.—*Swift.*

Stock. A plant of colewort, cabbage, etc.

A *stawk*, i.e., a stalk of plants.—*Thoresby. Bamford.*

> Not worth a shyttel-cocke,
> Nor worth a sowre *calstocke*.—*Skelton.*

Stock and horn. A musical instrument.

Stockin. Stocking.

Stocking, corruptly written for *stocken.*—*Horne Tooke.*

> Which our plain fathers erst would have accounted sin,
> Before the costly coach and silken *stock* came in.
> *Poly-olbion.*

Thomas Fuller writes *stocken*. If Dr. Johnson was

puzzled by Shakspeare's reference to *right-and-left shoes*, what would he have thought of right-and-left stockings?

The next morning I found the same usage, the *stockins for one leg* onlie left me.—*Sir James Turner's Memoirs.*

Stoiter. To stagger, to stammer.

Stottar, to stagger. *Stawter*, to stotter, to tumble.—*Bamford.*
Stowter, to struggle, to walk clumsily.—*Halliwell.*

Stook. A rick or shock of corn, consisting of twelve sheaves; to put into shocks.—*Jamieson.*

I give Jamieson's definition that I may have an opportunity of explaining fully what a stook is. A stook is not a rick. In a *rick* the sheaves are placed on the top of each other; in a stook they are set on end, and it may or may not have a sheaf on its top. A stook, also, does not necessarily consist of twelve sheaves, but often of four, more frequently of six, though it appears that twelve was the number in several places.

Stook, a shock of corn of twelve sheaves.—*Bailey.*

Stook, a collection of sheaves of corn, being ten set up together, and covered by two, called also a thrave.—*Grose.*

Treseau, a shocke, *stouke*, rowke, heap of sheaves in a corn-field.—*Cotgrave.*

Stoor. Sounding hollow; strong and hoarse.

Stour, harsh, deep-toned.—*Halliwell.* *Stoure*, strong.—*Weber.*
 The trappure of hym was white sylke,
 The other was rede, bothe styffe and *stoure*.—*Ipomydon.*
 The king and his men ilk ane
 Wend tharwith to have bene slane,
 So blew it *store* with slete and rayne.—*Ywain and Gawain.*
 They are so *stowre*, so frantyke mad.—*Skelton.*

Storm-staid. Hindered from proceeding by a storm.

Stot. An ox.

Stote, a young horse or bullock.—*Bailey*.

Stot, a young bullock or steer.—*Grose*.

A *stot* signified properly a bullock.—*Tyrwhitt*.

Stound. A sudden acute pain.

Stounds, sorrows, dumps, fits.—*Bailey*.

>Begin and end the bitter baleful *stound*.—*Spenser*.

>To put away the *stoundes* strong,
>Which in me lasten all too long.—*Chaucer*.

Stoup. A kind of jug or dish with a handle.

Steop, a drinking cup; the North of England *stoup*.—*Bosworth*.

Stoop or *stoup*, sometimes used to signify a cup, sometimes a much larger vessel.—*Dyce*.

>Set me the *stoups* of wine upon the table.—*Shak*.

>Rutterkin shall bring you all good luk,
>A *stoup* of bere up at a pluk,
>Till his brayne be as wise as a duk.—*Old Song*, quoted by *Dyce*.

Was not thy ale the mightiest of the earth in malt, and thy *stupe* fill'd like a tide?—*Beaumont and Fletcher*.

Stoure, stowre. Dust, more particularly dust in motion; fight, battle.

Stour, formerly in much use, means moved, stirred; and was applied equally to dust, water, and to men.—*Horne Tooke*. *Stour*, dust raised.—*Grose*.

>That es the hard *stour* at the last ende,
>When the saule sal fra the body wende.—*P. of Conscience*.

>Men sene all day, and reden eke in stories,
>That after sharpe *stoures* ben victories.—*Chaucer*.

>Such stormy *stoures* do breed my baleful smart.—*Spenser*.

>Women may maintene no *stowr*.—*Ywain and Gawain*.

Stourie or *stowrie.* Dusty.

Stowlins. By stealth.

> Many of his men and bestes
> *Stelendeliche* drouken of this lake.
> They into the walles *stowe* (stole),
> And defended hem with howe.—*Kyng Alisaunder.*

Stown. Stolen. *L* into *ow*. See under *a'*.

> I have not ridden this lee lang day,
> Nor yet have I *stown* this lady away.—*The Brave Earl Brand.*

> Then he went out of that town,
> Gliding away as dew is *stown.*—*Sir Amadas.*

> The aus *stown* that tit.—*Tim Bobbin.*

Stoyte. To stumble. See *stoiter.*

Strack. Did strike. Final *e* omitted. See under *quak.*

Strake, obsolete preterite of strike.—*Johnson.*

As sone as Sir Renold had given Sir Galahaut that stroke, he *strak* his spurres, and toke the feldes.—*Froissart.*

> On helmes *strake* they so with yre
> At ilka *strake* out-brak the fyre.—*Ywain and Gawain.*

Strae. Straw; *to dee a fair strae death*, to die in bed. *Strae* here is the same as straw in the E. phrase, the *lady in the straw*, still sometimes heard.

Strey, straw.—*Bamford.*

Our peasantry still pronounce *straw* strah.—*Horne Tooke.*

> Me list not of the chaffe ne of the *stree*
> Make so longe a tale as of the corn.—*Chaucer.*

> By his sar set he noght a *stra*,
> Bot for his houn he was wa.—*Ywain and Gawain.*

> I make a vow, quoth Duchman, and swore by the *stra.*
> *Tournament of Tottenham.*

Straik. To stroke. *A* for *o;* see under *bane.*

Strácian, to stroke; *strácung*, soothing.—*Bosworth.*

Strang.   Strong.   *A* for *o ;* see under *aff.*

>He es so worthy and so *strang*,
>That be it never so mekill wrang,
>>He will mak it right.—*Sir Penny.   Warton.*

>He outtoke me thare amang
>Fra mi faas that war sa *strang.*—*Metrical English Psalter.*

>He thoght the towre was so *strang*,
>That thare myght na man do him wrang.—*The Seven Sages.*

Strange.   To become strange.

>And right so as her jargon *straungeth*
>In sundry wise her forme chaungeth.—*Gower.*

>Would not you *strange* now at this?—*Duke of Buckingham.*

Strappan or *strappin.*   Tall and handsome.

Strapping, vast, large, bulky.—*Johnson.*   Huge, lusty, bouncing.—*Bailey.*

There are five-and-thirty *strapping* officers gone this morning to live upon free quarters in the city.—*Farquhar.*

I have two *strapping* daughters.—*Vanbrugh.*

Then that t'other great *strapping* lady—I can't hit of her name.
Congreve.

Strath.   Low alluvial land.

This is certainly one of the few words of Burns that we are perfectly sure is Scotch, though it is found in an English author:

>O'er the wat'ry *strath* or quaggy moss,
>They see the gliding ghosts unbodied troop.—*Collins.*

Strathspey.   A kind of dance; its music.

Straught.   Straight.

>For they anone come out of ship,
>And *straught* unto the king they went.—*Gower.*

>Twenty fadom of brede the armes *straught* (stretched, the same word).—*Chaucer.*

> Thus they schull lye long *straught*
>   Or that they go.—*Octovian Imperator*.

Stravagin. Wandering idly. *Extravagate,* to wander out of limits.—*Johnson.*

Extravagate, to roame, raunge, wander.—*Cotgrave.*
Stravaige, to stroll about.—*Halliwell.*

> The *extravagant* (wandering) and erring spirit.—*Shak.*

Streek. To stretch. *K* for *ch ;* see under *birk.*

To *streik,* to stretch out the limbs.—*Thoresby.*

> You shall have
> A lese (leash) of hounds with you to *streke.*
>   *The Squire of Low Degree.*

> Umlapped (surrounded) als klething with light
> *Strekand* heven als fel with blis.
>   *Metrical E. Psalter. Morris and Skeat.*

In the North of England laying out a body is called *streeking.*—*Brand.*

Striddle. To straddle.

Straddle, q.d., to *striddle* or stride. Umstrid, astride, *astridlands.*—*Bailey.*

Astridlands is an addition to the E. words similar to those in *lins,* as *backlins,* and is important as having the final *s.*

Fy on the, best, thou standest so a *strydlyng* that a man may dryue a cart between thy legges.—*Palsgrave. Halliwell.*

Stroan. To spout, to piss, to pour out like a spout.

This seems as appropriate a place as I am likely to find for the introduction of a paragraph to show that Burns, like other great poets, could "lift unconsidered trifles," and polish them. In "The Dean of Faculty" he says,—

> Which shews that heaven can boil the pot,
> Though the devil p—s in the fire.

Now in an edition of L'Estrange's translation of Quevedo's Visions, published in Glasgow in 1753, and sold as a superior sort of chap-book, these words occur,—"Money will make the pot boil though the devil p—s in the fire."

That Burns's version is an improvement is obvious, for while it is certain that the devil will do his best to frustrate the work of heaven, it is quite possible that a scheme which money promotes may receive his encouragement, Sathanas and Mammon, as Richie Moniplies says, being near akin.

Stroup. The spout.

Strunt. Spirituous liquor of any kind.

Burns is the only authority for strunt in this sense. I believe it is allied to *stroan*.

Strunt, a tail or rump.—*Bailey.* *Strunted*, cut off short.—*Thoresby.*

> No Christian booke
> May thou on looke
> If thou be an English *strunt.*—*Quoted by Ritson.*

Strunt. To walk sturdily.

> This makith men mysdoe more than ought ellis,
> And to *stronte* and to stare and stryve ageyn vertue.
> *Deposition of Richard II.*

Studdie. An anvil. *D* for *th;* see under *cleed.*

Stiddy, an anvil.—*Bamford.* *Stiddy*, a stithy.—*Thoresby.*

He said he did see the *fardest* (farthest) house on fire.—*A Record of the Mercies of God, Lond. 1653.*

Stude. Did stand. *U* for *oo;* see under *beuk* or *gude*, and in

After great *fluddes* (floods).—*A Boke of Counseil, &c., Lond. 1552.*

Naked we come hider and bare,
    An *pure* (poor) swa sal we hethen fare.—*Pricke of Conscience.*

Stuff. Corn or pulse of any kind; goods.

This word is explained by Burns as denoting what farmers are most interested in, viz., their crops. In the same way men of other callings call their materials stuff. Mechanics who receive a quantity of goods to make up speak of "planning their stuff." Shakspeare makes a traveller say, "Therefore away, to get our *stuff* aboard;" and Burns, though in his definition he limits it to grain, applies it to a song,—"The *stuff* won't bear mending." —*Letter to Mr. Thomson.*

Stump. To walk clumsily.

> The old chap to Windsor did *stump.*
> *The King and the Country Man.*

Stumpie. Dim. of stump, a worn quill.

Stumps. Legs.

I'll work thee off thy *stumps* as thou deservest.—*Echard.*

He struts, stands on tip-toes, bustles, and bestirs his *stumps.*— *Rabelais. Motteux.*

We shall have a fellow bestir his *stumps* from chocolate to coffee house.—*Farquhar.*

> I will catch thee up by one
> Of those fat *stumps* thou walkest upon.—*Cotton.*

Sturt. Trouble, to molest, to frighten.

Sturt, to struggle.—*Bailey.   Sturd*, stirred.—*Bamford.*

Sturt is formed in the usual manner from stour (*stur*, A.-S.), *stur-ed, stur'd, sturt.*—*Horne Tooke.*

The following epitaph, in Farlam church-yard, though printed in Camden's Remains, cannot, I am afraid, be deemed an English one. As Farlam is geographically south of the Tweed it may be allowed a place here.

> John Bell of Brekenbrow ligs under this stean,
> Four of mine een sons laid it on my weam.
> I lev'd all my deays but *stirt* (sturt) or strife;
> I was man of my meat, and master of my wife.
> If thou'st done better in thy time than I have done in mine,
> Take the stean off o' my weam and lay it upon thine.

Sturtin. Troubled, frightened.

Styme. A glimmer.

> And with a fling the meal he shook
> Into their face all hail:
> Wherewith he blinded them so close
> A *styme* they could not see.—*R. Hood.*

Stime, a particle, or ray of light.—*Halliwell.*

Sucker. Sugar.

> When venim meddleth with the *sucre*
> And marriage is made for lucre.
> And with the mirre (myrrh) taketh the *sucre.*—*Gower.*

K for *g* sound, as in *tricker* for *trigger*, and in—

> She rist her up, and *stakereth* here and there.—*Chaucer.*

Sud. Should. *S* for *sh*; see under *buss*.

They *sulde* than have good leyser to do yvel.—*Froissart.*

> Gladly thai gaf mete and drink,
> So that they *suld* the better swink.—*Minot.*

The Northern man saith, "Ay *sud* eat mare cheese gin ay had it."—*Verstegan.*

Sugh. The continued rushing noise of wood or water. Another form of *sough*.

Sumph. A blockhead.

Sune. Soon. *U* for *oo*; see *beuk*.

> Lad, wilt thou for Hob Trumble rin?
> That he may *seun* take off her skin.
> *The North. Garland. Ritson.*

Suthron. Southern, English; an old name for the English nation.

All the longage of the Northumbres and specialych at York is so sharp that we *Southeron* men may that longage unnethe understonde.—*John of Trevisa. Morris and Skeat.*

> In *suthrin* Englys was it drawn,
> And I have turned it til ur awn
> Language of the Northern lede,
> That can non other Engles rede.
> *Garnett, Phil. Trans. Latham.*

Swaird. Sward. $\bar{A}$ for $\breve{a}$; see under *shaird.*

Swall. To swell. *A* for *e*; see under *fallow.*

Swale, swelled.—*Bailey.*

> Hire thought it *swal* so sore aboute hire herte,
> That nedely som word hire must asterte.—*Chaucer.*

> Whylom in Kent there dwelt a clerke,
> Who wyth grete cheer and litil werke,
> Up*swalen* was.—*Fenton.*

Swank. Stately, jolly.—*Burns.*

Jamieson says this is not the proper explanation, and that *swank* "often conveys the idea of limber, pliant, agile, and in this sense Fergusson speaks of fallows,

> Mair hardy, souple, steeve, and *swank*,
> Than ever stood on Sammy's shank."

Now *swank* may have the meaning given by Jamieson, but the passage he quotes does not support his view unless we suppose Fergusson, in one line, to have used two words for the same thing, because *souple* means "limber, pliant, agile." Burns may be allowed to have known in what sense he used the word, whatever may be its meaning elsewhere, and, independently of his own statement, we may infer that *swank* did not appear to him equivalent to agile, for of the nineteen stanzas of the poem in which the word occurs four of them are devoted to praise of the mare's agility. In corroboration of Burns's correctness in the explanation of the word, it may be mentioned that Bailey has "*Swanking*, great," and Halliwell "*Swanking*, big, large."

I think the word is connected with *swink*, toil, and refers to her capacity for work:—

> Thar thai offerd, praid, and *swank*,
> Thre dais nother ete ne dranc.—*Cursor Mundi*.

Swankie or *swanker*. A tight strapping young fellow or girl. See *swank*.

Swap. An exchange, to barter.

Swap, to exchange.—*Johnson*.

Swap, to exchange, to barter, to truck.—*Bailey*.

Swarf. To swoon.

Swat. Did sweat.

> Yet did he labour long,
> And *swat*, and chauf'd.—*Spenser*.

> The hakeney
> So *swatte* that it wonder was to see.—*Chaucer*.

> The swapte together tyll the both *swat*.
> *The Hunting of the Cheviot*. Ritson.

> Tells how the drudging goblin *swet*.—*Milton*.

Swatch. A sample.

Swatch, a sample.—*Grose*. *Swatch*, a patch, or fragment.—*Bamford*.

A *swache*, a tally.—*Bailey*. A *swatch*, a shred of cloth.—*Thoresby*.

Swats. Ale. (A.-Sax.) *Swatan*, ale, beer.—*Bosworth*.

Sweer.   Lazy, averse; *dead sweer*, extremely averse.

Swær, heavy, burdensome, slothful, inactive.—*Bosworth.*

One of their company, called *Sweer-to-go*, showed them that this adventure had been foretold.—*Rabelais.*

> Thou art as young a man as I,
> And seem'st to be as *sweer.*—*R. Hood.*

Sweet-milk cheese.   Cheese made of milk as it comes from the cow, opposed to *skim-milk* cheese.

Swinge.   To beat, to whip.

Dober, to beat, to *swinge.*—*Cotgrave.*

> I was in love with my bed;
> You *swinged* me for my love.—*Shak.*

> I' th' end, he *swinged* us
> And *swinged* us soundly too.—*Beau. and Fletcher.*
> I have a plot to *swinge* him.—*Farquhar.*

Swinke.   To labour hard, toil.

> For meat would I *swink* fain.—*Sir Isumbras.*
> And the *swink'd* hedger at his supper sat.—*Milton.*
> All the night he schop him for to *swynke*
> In carying the gold out of that place.—*Chaucer.*

> Thou's but a lazy loord,
> And rekes much of thy *swinke.*—*Spenser.*

Swirl.   A curve, an eddying blast or pool, a knot in wood.

Swire (Dan.), to whirl, to turn round.

Swirl, a whirling wavy motion.—*East.   Halliwell.*

Swirlie.   Knaggy, full of knots.

If this is an adjective connected with *swirl*, its true sense cannot be seen unless we take in Jamieson's explanation of that word: "*Swirl*, the vestiges of a circular motion;" there *swirlie* will be perceived to be, having swirls or knots. However, if Burns had not told us what he meant by *swirlie*, few Scotsmen, I believe, would have thought of knotty as its signification.

Swiss. A native of Switzerland; a mercenary writer.

The Swiss for a long time were notorious for hiring themselves out to fight for any State that would pay for their service, hence any mercenary was called a Swiss.

> Heaven's *Swiss*, who fight for any god or man.—*Pope.*
>
> Like *Swiss*, their force is always laid
> On that side where they *best are paid.*—*Churchill.*

Swith! Get away! Literally, quick or quickly.

> Kyng Estmere threwe the harpe asyde,
>   And *swith* he drew his brand,—*King Estmere.*
>
> This messager, to don his avantage,
> Unto the Kinge's mother rideth *swithe.*—*Chaucer.*
>
> I wot you telle us *swithe* trewly the sothe.—*W. of Palerne.*

Swither. To hesitate in choice, an irresolute wavering in choice.

The use of this word—that is, the sense in which it is understood—is perfectly well known, but its real meaning and origin are matters upon which, so far as I know, no person has been very positive. This being the case, I venture to suggest that it is connected with the previous word *swith*, being in reality its comparative degree, and that it is A.-S. *swither*, rather, and that it has come to signify doubt, hesitation, in the same way that *shilly-shally* has come to mean irresolution. Johnson says: " To stand *shill-I-shall-I*, is to continue hesitating and procrastinating." In like manner, a person who should stand saying, "What shall I *swithur*—i.e., rather do?" would be swithering or in a swither. Where certainty cannot be attained, conjecture may be admitted.

Swoor. Swore, did swear.

> Our Host tho lowh and *swoor.*—*Wright's Chaucer.*
> Kyng Richard
> *Swoor* hys oth, be Seynt Symoun.
> Kyng Richard *swoor* and was agreved.—*Rich. C. de Lion.*

Sybo, or syebow. An onion.

> *Cibol*, a small sort of onion used in salads. This word is common in the Scotch dialect, but the *l* is not pronounced.—*Johnson.*
> *Cibol*, a sort of small degenerate onion.—*Bailey.*

It is said in at least one edition, and that a deservedly popular one, that a *sybo* is a leek. It is not so, and the line quoted by Sir Walter Scott should settle the matter:

> There's nought in the Highlands but *syboes* and *leeks.*

If this word is not rightly understood it might be inferred from what Burns says about a *sybo tail* that the Scotch are in the habit of eating raw leeks which, however palatable to a native of Wales, are to a Scotsman simply disgusting, and not more to his taste than a raw potato; to make him eat one would require a Fluellin.

Syne. Since, ago, then.

> Alle hyt was shewed hym before,
> How he had lyved *syn* he was bore.—*Rob. of Brunne.*
> Was nevyr such a senatour *syn* Crystes incarnacion.—*Skelton.*
> Rowen drank, as her list,
> And gave the kyng; *sine* him kist.—*R. of Brunne.*
> And *syne* go to the tavern house.—*R. Hood.*

T.

Tack. A lease; to *extend a tack*, to draw up its provisions in detail. In the "Earnest Cry and Prayer," "Now stand as tightly by your *tack*" seems to mean "Stand to your bargain, fulfil your promise."

See under *Herry* for the only E. example of *tack* in this sense which I remember, but James V. is reported by Sir Ralph Sadler to have used the word, and as Sir Ralph does not explain it to his master, it must have been known in England.

To hold *tacke*, stand to a bargain.—*Cotgrave.*

Tackets. Nails for shoes, a form of tack, a small nail.

Tae. A toe; *three-tae'd*, having three prongs. *A* for *o*; see under *bane*.

> And ilk a vayne of the mans body
> Had a rote fastened thar-by,
> And in ilk a *taa* and fynger of hand
> Was a rote fra that tre growand.—*Pricke of Conscience.*
>
> Finger and *taes*, fote and hande,
> And alle his touches er tremblande.—*Id.*

Taed. A toad. *A* for *o*; see under *bane*.

> Snakes and nederes thar he fand,
> And gret blac *tades* gangand.—*E. Metrical Homilies.*

Taet. A small quantity.

Taettecan, rags, tatters.—*Bosworth.*

Tairge, or *targe*. A target; to deal strictly with one.

> Ac with *targes*, and hurdices,
> Theo Gregeis heom wryed als the wise.
>
> *Kyng Alisaunder.*
>
> Crystene men made hem a *targe*
> Off dores, and of wyndowes large.—*R. C. de Lion.*

I am utterly unable to explain, and, so far as I know, no one has attempted to explain, how *targe*, a shield, a means of defence, should have come to signify, to deal strictly, to strike, to cross-examine, etc.

It would be interesting to know if Burns, when he wrote—

> And aye on Sundays, duly, nightly,
> I on the Questions targe them *tightly*.

was aware that *tiht* was A.-S. for instruction, discipline.

Tak. To take. Final *e* omitted ; see under *quak*.

> Let delyver him anon, and *tak* him to me.—*Wright's Chaucer*.

> Steward, *tac* thou here
> My fundling for to lere.—*The Geste of Kyng Horn*.

> For he wist noght whederward
> That he sold *tak* the redy way.—*The Seven Sages*.

> No *tak* thou never wreththe non.—*Kyng Alisaunder*.

Tam. Dim. of Thomas.

> You know, *Tam*, your education has been a little at large.
> *Vanbrugh.*

Tane. Taken.

> Keep carefully what thou hast *tane* in charge.—*Sylvester*.
> See, Cupid with a word has *tane* up the brawl.—*Ben Jonson*.
> Therefore my Daphne they have *tane* away.—*Spenser*.

Tangle. Sea-weed.—*Bailey. Halliwell.*

Tangs. Tongs ; *a sheep-head on a tangs*, a sheep's head undergoing singeing.

> Mother Midnight told him she would try whether his scull or the *tangs* were the harder metal.—*John Collier*.

Tap. Top ; *tap o' tow*, the quantity of flax put on the spinning wheel at one time. *A* for *o* ; see under *aff*.

This shows us the meaning of a passage which Mr. Halliwell, with all his extraordinary knowledge of archaic and provincial words and customs could not explain :—

> I take my *tappe in my lappe*, and am gone.—*Morality of Every Man*.

That is, "I take the flax which I brought for my evening's work with me and go away."

Tapetless. Heedless, foolish.

I am not sure that Burns has here hit on the word which most fully expresses, in prose, the meaning of a word used in his verse. It is to be remembered that in explaining Scotch words he had no such assistance as we have. There was no Jamieson's Dictionary of the language, indeed it was hardly allowed to be a language. We need not, therefore, wonder if there should sometimes appear to be a slight discrepancy between the poetical word and its prosaic definition. Perhaps I am wrong in thinking there is one here. Let us examine the passage. It occurs in the Second Letter to Lapraik:

> My awkart Muse sair pleads and begs
> I would na write.
> The *tapetless*, ramfeezl'd hizzie,
> She's saft at best an' something lazy,
> Quo' she, "Ye ken we've been sae busy
> This month an' mair,
> That trouth, my head is grown right dizzie,
> An' something sair."
>
> Her dowf excuses pat me mad;
> "Conscience," says I, "ye thowless jad!"

Here we have *ramfeezl'd, saft, lazy,* and *thowless,* all words indicating inability or unwillingness to perform the task he assigned her, and none of them appropriate to a foolish or heedless personage. Indeed, he represents himself as of opinion that she thought too much, for he says—

> Her dowf excuses pat me mad.

I think it will appear not unreasonable to conclude that *tapetless* must mean something in accordance with ramfeezled and other words in the passage.

Let us now hear what Jamieson—the greatest authority on the Scottish tongue—says : "*Tapetless,* heedless, foolish." This is taken from Burns, and we are no farther advanced. Then he says, "*Tabetless, tapetless, tebbitless*, adj. Not as explained by Shirr. and Sibb. 'without strength,' but destitute of sensation, benumbed." Here he is opposed to Burns and to himself when he adopted heedless, foolish, as the translation of tapetless. Now I believe that destitute of strength, benumbed, is nearer the meaning than his first explanation, but I also believe that Shirref and Sibbald are right, and that *tapetless* means want of strength, energy, or what we should now call pluck. Indeed, I have often wondered that Jamieson, usually so fond of Danish derivations, did not refer this word to *tapper*, brave, valiant, gallant.

Tap-pickle. The grain at the top of the stalk. *Tap* and *pickle.*

Tappit-hen. A tin pot with a knob on the top, containing a quart.—*Scott:* glossary.

In "Waverley" and "Guy Mannering" it is said to be three English quarts.

Tapsalteerie. Topsy-turvy. This seems another form of Barbour's *top-our-tail*, i.e., top-over-tail.

> He lap till ane and can hym ta
> Richt be the neck full felonly
> Till *top our tail* he gert him ly.—*The Bruce.*
>
> He yede down
> Off hys hors, *top on tayle.*—*R. C. de Lion.*
>
> The storm doth *topside-turvey* toss thee.
>
> *T. Kyd.*

Tarrow. To murmur at one's allowance.

In "A Dream," as Chambers correctly says, "To *tarrow* at food is to linger over it from dislike or want of appetite,"

In the "Address of Beelzebub," "If you on your station *tarrow*," it seems to mean "if you are not pleased with the place assigned you, or if you contend about it."

Tarry-breeks.   A sailor.   *Tarry* and *breeks.*

Stainhurst, the translator of Virgil, in 1582, makes Dido call Æneas, hedge-brat, cullion, and *tar-breech* in the course of one speech.—*Malone.*

Tassie.   A cup or goblet.

Tasse.   a cup, a dish.   *Var. dial.*—*Halliwell.*

He distributed among them his whole cupboard of plate, huge pots, large basins, big *tasses*, &c.—*Rabelais.*

Tauld, or *tald.*   *A* for *o*; see under *aff.*

I fand the Bacyn as he *talde.*—*Ywain and Gawain.*

Ther (thir, i.e., these) thre partes er thre spaces *talde*
Of the lyf of ilk man, yhung and alde.—*Pricke of Conscience.*

And he *teld* him how he hadde the steward slain.—*Amis and Amiloun.*

Taupie.   A foolish, thoughtless young person.

Tauted, tawted, or *tautie.*   Matted together; spoken of hair or wool.

I have little doubt that this word is connected with *tease*, which means to take out the *tawts* or entanglements of wool or hair, though I cannot trace the steps by which *ea* became *aw*, but neither can I tell how see has for its past tense *saw*, or teach, *taught.*

Tow, which is really the disordered, i.e., tauted, droppings of flax in dressing, is found written *taw* as well as *tow* in A.-S., and is so spelled by Chaucer—

> He had more *tawe* on his distaf
> Than Gerveis knew.—*The Milleres Tale.*

Tawie. That allows itself to be peaceably handled, spoken of a horse, cow, &c.

This word, which the old farmer applies to his mare, will be best understood by reading what Lord Colchester says of his celebrated horse Cruzier, tamed by Rarey, "He was vicious from a foal, always *troublesome to handle*, and showed temper on every opportunity." *Tawie* means the reverse of all this, in short, the mare was tractable, teachable, which to some may suggest a derivation of the word as probable as any yet *conjectured*.

Teat. Same as *taet*.

'Teen. The evening, abbreviation of *at e'en*.

Teen. Vexation.

> The angry pagan bit his lip for *teen*.—*Fairfax*.
> For hunger I feele so grete *teene*—*Lydgate*.
> Never was there no word them betweene
> Of jalousie, ne of non other *tene*.—*Chaucer*.
> Print in your hart some parcel of my *tene*.—*Surrey*.

Teethin a heckle. Putting new spikes or *teeth* in a heckle.

Temper-pin. The pin of a spinning-wheel, used to slacken or tighten the band which, passing over the wheel, gave motion to the spindle. Also the pin used to *temper* a fiddle string.

> He taketh the harp and *tempreth* it.—*Gower*.

Ten hours' bite. A slight feed to the horses while in the yoke in the forenoon.

In provincial English there are many instances of meals being named from the hour at which they are usually eaten. Thus in Sussex an *elevener* is a luncheon, &c.—*Folk-Etymology*.

Tenebrific. Dark, tenebrous. Johnson has *tenebricose.*

> The radiant brightnes of golden Phebus
> Auster gan cover with clowde *tenebrous.*—*Stephen Hawes.*

Tent. A field pulpit.

I am very far from desiring to give a ludicrous notion of this (once) important part of the ecclesiastical apparatus of Scotland, having some very solemn associations with it, but to those who have not seen it I cannot convey a clearer idea than by saying it closely resembles the structure in which Punch performs his drama. It was a relic of suffering times when very insufficient shelter had to be provided for the preacher.

Tent. Heed, caution, to take heed.

> To *tent*, to tend, or look to.—*Bailey.*
>
> Ya, ya! all olde men to me take *tent*
> & weddyth no wyff, in no kynnes wyse,
> That is a yonge wench.—*Cov. Mysteries.*
>
> Take gode *tent* to thys matere.—*How the Wise Man Taught, etc.*
>
> A madame, takes *tent* to me.—*Ywain and Gawain.*

Tentie. Heedful, cautious.
Tentiff, careful.—*Bailey.*

Tentless. Heedless.

Terraefilial. Belonging to sons of the earth, worldlings.

Terrae filius, a scholar in the University of Oxford, appointed to make jesting and satyrical speeches.—*Bailey.*

Tester. A sixpenny piece.

> There is a *tester* for thee.—*Shak.*
>
> Plums and directors, Shylock and his wife,
> Will club their *testers* now to take thy life.—*Pope.*
>
> Who throws away a *tester* and a mistress loses sixpence.
> *Farquhar.*

GLOSSARY. 395

Teugh. Tough. *Eu* for *ou;* see under *pleugh.*
> And he there caste botemay (bitumen)
> Of Meopante, that *towhe* clay.—*Kyng Alisaunder.*

Teuk. Took. *Eu* for *oo;* see under *beuk.*

Thack. Thatch. *K* for *ch;* see under *birk.*
Thack, thatch, is the past participle of *thecan,* to cover.—*Tooke.*
Thack, thatch. *Thacker,* a thatcher.—*Grose.*
> That they should ever in houses of *thacke,*
> Their lives lead, and wear but blacke.—*Chaucer.*

Thae. Those.
> Fra he was born the dai thretteind
> Thai offerd him *thaa* kinges heind.—*Cursor Mundi.*

> Sir Ywain said, God, maste of myght,
> Sal strenketh us in ilka dede,
> Ogains *tha* devils and al thair drede.—*Ywain and Gawain.*

Thairms. Small guts, fiddle-strings.

Tharms, guts washed for making hogs' puddings.—*Bailey.* And this is a dictionary, and not a very old one either, of the people who profess to be disgusted at a haggis because it is made in the paunch of a cow or sheep!

Tharms, intestines twisted for several uses.—*Johnson.*
Tharms, pudding-skins.—*Thoresby.*
> But *tharmes,*
> The wombe and al down to the kne,
> Of bras they were upo to see.—*Gower.*

Theek. To thatch.
Theak, to thatch.—*Grose.*
> For it is I that other whyle
> Plucke downe lede, and *theke* with tyle.—*Skelton.*

Thegither. Together. *Th* for *t*, as in

> The great lordys of renoun
> *Thold* (told) the kyng.—*Octovian Imperator.*

Th is often used not only for *t*, but for other dentals, as *couthe* for could, *thoth* for doth, etc.

Themsel'. Themselves. See under *mysel.*

Thick. Intimate, familiar.

> We begin now, though contrary to my expectation, to be pretty *thick*, and I thank God who reconciles me to my adversaries.—*Bishop Law.*

Thieveless. Cold, dry, spirited, spoken of a person's demeanour.

This word has been a stumbling-block to many a Scotsman; even to those most familiar with the vernacular it has proved a sort of puzzle. Cunningham omits it from his glossary altogether. Jamieson has "Thewless, i.e., thowless, thieveless," which he regards as synonymous, and his observations on these words are very interesting. *Thowless*, however, it cannot be, for Auld Brig was "bauldly doure," and his speeches were spirited. I believe it means unmannerly, rude, coming from the same A.-S. *theáw* or *theau* as thews in the following passages:—

> For though that ever vertuous was she,
> She was encresed in swiche excellence
> Of *thewes* good, yset in high bountee.—*Chaucer.*
>
> Prowd, peviche, lyddyr, and lewde,
> Malapert, medyllar, nothyng well *thewde.*—*Skelton.*
>
> Blithe was eche a barn ho best might him plese,
> & folowe him for his fredome & for his fair *thewes.*
> *W. of Palerne.*
>
> Upbrought in gentle *thewes* and martial might.—*Spenser.*

A derivative from this, *theáulice* signifies decently, properly, and if the privative affix less be added to *theáu* we have *theauless*, unmannerly, improper. It is to be remembered, as has already been pointed out, that *u* often did duty for both *v* and *u*.

Thigger. A beggar.

Thigan, to receive, accept, take.—*Bosworth.*

Thaym were betere *thygge* thayre mete,
Than any gode on that wyse gete.—*MS. quoted by Halliwell.*

Thir. These.

Many a piece of bacon have I had out of *thir* balkes.
Gam. Gurton's Needle.

The galay men held up thaire handes,
And thanked God for *thir* tithandes.—*Minot.*

Al *thir* men wote, and so wote i,
That she bitrayed hir lady.—*Ywain and Gawain.*

To army *thir* knyghtes wer fayn.—*Libeaus Disconnus.*

Thirl. To thrill. *R* transposed; see under *brugh.*

Thirl, to pierce. It is now pronounced and written thrill.—*Johnson.*

Thirle, to bore or drill, to pierce through.—*Bailey.*

The thik thunder-braste *thirled* hem ofte.
Early E. Alliterative Poems.

With a spere was *thirled* his brest bone.—*Chaucer.*

Thole. To suffer, to endure.

"Lord!" said Guy, "that raised Lazaroun,
And for man *tholed* passioun."—*Guy of Warwick.*

He *tholes* gode men and lele.—*E. Metrical Homilies.*

Mony is jolif in the morning,
And *tholeth* deth or the evenyng.—*Kyng Alisaunder.*

Jesu that was nomen with wrong,
And *tholed* mani paines strong.—*Hist. of Adam and His Descendants.*

Thou's. Thou hast. *Thou'se,* thou art. See *I'se.*

I'se, thou'se, and *thou'st* occur frequently in both E. and S. authors, but, I believe, they generally express the future rather than the present tense.

> *Thou'se* be the next.—*R. Hood.*

> If thou'lt wend thither, my little Musgrave,
> *Thou'st* lig in mine arms all night.
> *Little Musgrave and Lady Barnard.*

The third person of the verb is often used with thou, as in

> Telling the bushes that thou *looks* for wars.—*Shak.*

This may have been the result of inadvertence, but the following must have been done purposely:—

> And, wheresoe'er *thou casts* thy view,
> Upon that white and radiant crew.—*Cowley.*

Thowe. A thaw, to thaw.

Thooant, thawing.—*Bamford.*

> A vale there is
> Where eye-room is from rock to cloudy sky,
> From thence to dales which stormy ruins shroud,
> Then to the crushed water's frothy fry,
> Which tumbleth from the tops where snow is *thow'd.*
> *Robert Southwell's Mœniæ.*

A fresy *thowe,* a meltyng fryse.—*Lydgate.*

Thowless. Slack, lazy. See *thieveless,*

Thrall. Bondage.

> And laid about him, till his nose
> From *thrall* of ring and cord broke loose.—*Butler.*

Thrang. A throng, a crowd. *Thrang.*—*Bamford.*

> Perkyn turned hym about in that ych *thrang,*
> Amang thos wery boyes he wrèst and he wrang.
> *The Tournament of Tottenham.*

About hir was ful mekyl the *thrang.—Ywain and Gawain.*
Alle weore dryven *athrang.—Kyng Alisaunder.*

Thrang. Busy.

Thrang, busy, beset with affairs.—*Bamford.*

> Sir Launcelot *thranged* in the thicke of the presse.
> *Historie of Prince Arthur.*

Throng in the sense of busy is not now an E. word, but it was so once.

Throng, busily employed.—*Grose.* Very *throng,* busily employed. —*Bailey.*

Though I am *thronged* with a multitude of business, &c.—*Mr. Morland to Mr. Pell. Protectorate of Cromwell.*

Thrapple. Throat, windpipe.

Thrapple, the windpipe of a horse.—*Bailey. Thropple,* windpipe.—*Grose.*

Thrapple, the windpipe of any animal.—*Johnson.*

Thrave. Twenty-four sheaves of grain.

A *thrave,* as above.—*Bailey.*

A *threave* of straw, a burden of it.—*Thoresby.*

Diseaux de gerbes, half *thraves* of tenne sheaves a peece.—*Cotgrave.*

> He sends forth *thraves* of ballads.—*Bishop Hall.*
> Gallants
> (Have) been seen to flock here in *threaves.—Ben Jonson.*

The hospital had received, from an ancient grant of King Athelstane, a right of levying a *thrave* of corn upon every plough-land in the county.—*Hume's Hist. of E.*

Thraw. To sprain, to twist, to contradict.

Thraw, to argue, to dispute.—*Bamford.*

Thráwan, to wheel, turn round.—*Bosworth.*

> For I se wel that hit is sothe that alle mannez wyttez,
> To un-thryfte arn alle *thrawen.—Early E. Allit. Poems.*

Thraw. A throe, a pang.

> Time is come the lady schal childe,
> The *thrawes* hire afongon.—*Kyng Alisaunder.*

Threap. To maintain by dint of assertion.

Threap, a country word denoting to argue much or contend.—*Johnson.*

Threpe, to affirm, to blame.—*Bailey.*

It was at Cork that the people of the town first *threaped* upon him that he was the son of the Duke of Clarence.—*Perkin Warbeck's Confession.*

> It's not for a man with a woman to *threape.*—*Percy's Reliques.*
> Sol gold is, and Luna silver we *threpe.*—*Chaucer.*
> But al for Church they cride and *threape.*
>
> *The Wonders of England.*

Threesome. The union of three.

Thresh. To thrash (with a flail); *thresh the barn,* to do a man's work with the flail.

Thresh is the spelling in the Bible, as—

> O my *threshing,* and the corn of my floor.—*Isaiah.*
> The careful ploughman doubting stands,
> Lest on the *threshing*-floor his sheaves prove chaff.—*Milton.*
> The corne is theyrs, let others *thresh.*—*Spenser.*

Threteen. Thirteen.

> For *threttene* is a convent as I guesse.—*Chaucer.*
> Of these sterres which I mene,
> Cor Scorpionis is *threttene.*—*Gower.*
>
> Tyl ten yerdes or twelve hadde tolled out *threttene.*
>
> *P. Plowman.*

Threttie. Thirty.

> *Thretty* thousande stronge and wightes.—*Kyng Alisaunder.*
> And loke even that thyn ark have of heghthe *thretté* (cubits).
> *Early E. Alliterative Poems.*
> He held hir wele al *threty* yer.—*The Seven Sages.*

Thrissle. A thistle.

It were a gode Contree to sowen inne *Thristle* and Breres and Thorns.—*Maundeville.*

Throng. Busy. Very *throng,* busily employed.—*Bailey.*

Through. To go on literally; *to mak to through,* to make good.—*Jamieson.*

I believe the line in "The Brigs of Ayr," in which *to through* occurs should be, "And muckle mair than ye can mak *to-through,*" and it would be at once seen that *to* is joined with through to strengthen the meaning, as in—

A certain woman cast a piece of mill-stone upon Abimelech's head, and all *to-brake* his skull.—*Judges,* ix., 53.

Throuther. Pell-mell, confusedly. Through and other.

Thrum. To pur as a cat.

Blunderbusses planted at every loop-hole go off constantly at the squeaking of a fiddle and the *thrumming* of a guitar.—*Dryden.*

Thud. To make a loud, intermittent noise; the noise so made.

Thoden, a noise, din, whirlwind.—*Bosworth.*

This expressive word is said to have been first used in English in the description given in the *Times* newspaper of the fight between Heenan and Sayers.—*Edwards.*

Thumart. Foumart, pole-cat. *Th* for *f.* In at least one word Shakespeare uses *f* or *th* indifferently.

> An you draw back we'll put you in the *fills.*
> *Troilus and Cressida.*

Thou hast got more hair on thy chin than Dobbin my *thill* horse has on his tail.—*The Merchant of Venice.*

Huet, that hende litel *dwerth* (dwarf).—*William of Palerne.*

Thysel'. Thyself. Se *mysel'.*

Tibbie.   Isabella.

> Then said Perkyn, To *Tybbe* I have hyght.
> *Tournament of Tottenham.*

> And *Tib* my wife, that as her life
>   Loveth good ale to seeke,
> Full oft drinkes she till ye may see
>   The teares run downe her cheeke.
> *Gam. Gurton's Needle.*

Tight.   Strong, active.

Tightest.   Best, in—

And aye the hindmost hour the *tightest.*—*Burns to Nicol.*
Tight, active, alert.—*Halliwell.*

Tightly.   Firmly, severely.

What, beaten with a song? Never more *tightly*, gentlemen.—*Fletcher.*

> Work but *tightly*
> And we will not have a dish-clout in the house
> But of your spinning.—*Massinger.*
> Hold, sirrah, bear you these letters *tightly.*—*Shak.*
> But he stood *tightly* up to them.—*T. Ellwood.*

Till.   To; *till't,* to it.

> *Till* Daniel his dreme he tolde.—*Gower.*
> Whan Philip *till* Acres cam.—*R. C. de Lion.*
> *Till* her that squire bespake.—*Spenser.*
> Sleep and feeding may prorogue his honour
> Even *till* a Lethe'd dullness.—*Shak.*

Till for to is supposed to be a marked peculiarity of Scottish speech, but it was once very common in England, and at one time it seemed not unlikely that till and to would change places:—

> Had I spoken with any man
> *To* sevyn days were comen and gane.—*The Seven Sages.*

Seyvon yere weddeseytt my londes,
To the deyttes that ar woonde
  Be qwytte al bedene,
And owtte of countré wille y wende,
To y have gold and silver to spende.—*Sir Amadas.*

Ther saw I how woful Calistope
Was turned from a woman *til* a bere.—*Chaucer.*

To every tale
Not hastily to yeve thereto credence
Into tyme thou knew that it were trewe.—*Lydgate.*

Timmer. Timber. *timmer-propt*, propped with timber. See under *chamer*.

Timmer, timber.—*Var. dial. Halliwell. Slummer*, slumber. *Bamford.*

Tine. To lose; tint, lost.

His knife was *tint.*—*Sir Eger, Sir Graham and Sir Gray Steel.*

His takyll he shall *tyne.*—*R. Hood.*

Lothe I were him to *tine.*—*Sir Cauline.*

For a flour that semes fayre and bright,
Thurgh stormes fades and *tynes* the myght.—*Pricke of Conscience.*

In that time nothing *tint* he.—*Ywain and Gawain.*

Tinkler. A tinker.

"By the mass!" quoth the *tinkler*, "it's nappy brown ale."
  An. Poems, &c., of the English Peasantry.

A tinker is still called a *tinkler* in the North of England.—*Bell.*

Ale makes the *tinkler* bang his wife.—*Craven Churn Supper Song.*

I once did know a *tinkling* pewterer.—*Marston.*

Tip. A ram. *Tip* and *toop* are only different spellings of tup.

Tip, or *tup*, a ram.—*Grose.*

Tippence. Two-pence. This differs only in spelling from two-pence; scarcely, if at all, in pronunciation.

Tuppence.—Bamford.

He had but a groat, and that was in two *two-pences.—Beaumont and Fletcher.*

Tippenny. A kind of ale, so named from its price.

It was common both in England and Scotland to designate ale by the price at which it was sold.

A kylderkin of *3 half-penny* bere and a kilderkin of single bere, £0 2s. 4d.—*Accounts of Kingston upon Thames.—Antiq. Rep.*

Before the year 1730, the malt liquors in use in London were ale, beer, and *twopenny.—Leigh. Words, Facts, and Phrases.*

Peny-ale and podyng-ale she poured togederes.—*P. Plowman.*

Tipper-taiper. To totter, to walk on tip-toe, or insecurely.

Tirl. To make a slight noise.

Tirl, to put in motion.—*Halliwell.*

> Make rome, syrs, and let us be mery,
> With huff a galand, synge *tyrll* on the bery.
> *The IIII. Elements.*

Tirl. To uncover.

Tither. The other. *I* for *o;* see *anither.*

Tother, contracted from the other.—*Johnson.*

> To tine the gear and Simmy too,
> The ane to the *tither's* nae relief.—*Richardson.*

See where yonder stondeth the *teder* man.—*Skelton.*

Tittie. Sister.

Titty, a sister.—*Cumb. Halliwell.*

Tittle. To whisper, to prate idly.

Titelung (A.-S.), recapitulation.

Tittle-tattle, to prate idly.—*Johnson.*

& te deouel leieth his *tutel* adun to his earen, & *tuteleth* him al that he ever wule.—*The Ancren Riwle.*

GLOSSARY. 405

Tocher, and *tocher gude*.　Marriage portion.

Towgher, a dower, or dowry.—*Grose*.

> A cow and a calf,
> An ox and a half,
> Forty good shillings and three,
> Is not that enough *tocher*
> For a shoemaker's daughter.
> *Nursery Rhymes of England.*

Tod.　A fox.

> Or stew *tods*' hairs.—*Ben Jonson.*
> Driv'st hence the wolf, the *tod*, the brock,
> Or other vermin from the flock.—*Id.*

Toddle.　To totter like the walk of a child.

Ton.　Style or height, as in—

> The *ton* of your fashion.—*The Sons of Old Killie.*

Too fa'.　Twilight, close of the day.　*To* and *fa'*.

> For him in vain at *to-fall* of the day,
> His babes shall linger at the unclosing gate.—*Collins.*

The prefix to- has an intensive or augmentative force.

> His brest *to-brosten* with his sadel bow.—*Chaucer.*
> The lyon . . wolde have him al *to-rent.*—*R. C. de Lion.*

Toom.　Empty. In England and some parts of Scotland this is spelled and pronounced *teem*.

Teem out, pour out.—*Bailey. Bamford.*

> Some busy gin to *teem* the loaded corn.—*Clare.*

Tom, empty, void, exempt.—*Bosworth.*

Toome, or *tume*, empty.—*Grose.*

> Soon the tresowre up they drowe,
> And ther stedys strong ynowe,
> And made ther schyppys *tome.*—*Le Bone Flo. of Rome.*
> A byrdles cage, a key withouten lok,
> A *tombe* shyppe alway ridyng on a rok,
> It may wele ryme, but it accordith nought.—*Lydgate.*

Toop. A tup, a ram. *Oo* for *u*, as in—

> She fond a tred and forthe ys gon,
> To a *noonrie* (nunnery) men call Beverfayre.
> *Le Bone Florence of Rome.*

Toothy. Furnished with teeth, biting.

Toothy, peevish, crabbed.—*Ray.* *Toothy*, having many or large teeth.—*Halliwell.*

Toss. A toast, a celebrated beauty. *T* omitted; see under *disrespecket.*

Tost, the nomination of a person whose health is to be drunk.— —*Bailey.*

Miss Molly, a fam'd *toast*, was fair and young.—*The Tattler.*

Toast, a health proposed, or a belle whose health is often drunk is a corruption of *toss*, which in Scottish has the same meaning.— *Folk Etymology.*

> The plump chalice and the cup,
> That tempts till it be *tossed* up.—*Herrick.*

Tosie. Warm and snug.

Toun and *toon.* A hamlet, a farm-house, a farm; also a town, as "Toun of Ayr."

Toun is the old spelling of town, thus,

> As sone as day he went out of the *toun.*—*Chaucer.*

The modern subaudition, when we use the word *town*, is restricted to any number of houses enclosed together. Formerly, the E. subaudition was more extensive, and embraced also any enclosure, any quantity of land, etc., enclosed.

Sotheli thei dispiriden, and thei wenten awei . . . another into his *toun.* Mat. xxii. 5.—*Wyclif.*

And alle bigunnen togidre to excuse; the first seide, I have bought a *toun*, and I have nede to go out and se it. Luke xiv. 18, —*Tooke.*

The first *town*, though a mere enclosure, gave the name to all other towns.—*Max Muller*.

In "Poor Mailie's Elegy," Burns, though he has not given that meaning in his glossary, uses *toun* for farm:—

> Thro' a' the toun she trotted by him,
> A lang half-mile she could descry him.

As however it is thought a Scotticism to call a farmhouse a town, I must try to show that it was once customary in England to apply the term to a single house. In Anglo-Saxon times *tún*, according to Bosworth, meant, "a dwelling-house, mansion," and in this sense it is found in many English writers. I shall only give one example. In order to see the force of the word, a short explanation of the circumstances in which it was used is necessary.

Sir Ywain, having become insane, wandered in a wood in which he is found naked and insensible by a young woman. She by anointing him with "unement," frees him from his "brayn-wodeness," and lays clothing beside him. Having with difficulty, owing to his extreme weakness, put on the garments provided for him, he addresses the lady, who now rides up to him as if she were passing by and knew nothing of his previous condition, in the following terms :

> Pur charite, i wald ye pray
> For to lene me that palfray
> That in thi hand is redy bowne,
> And wis (direct) me unto som *towne*.

Now I think it is obvious that in his circumstances a town, in the modern sense of the word, would be the last place he would seek, and that he desired to be *wised* to a house of any kind. Fletcher has town for a farmhouse :—

> The woods or some near *town*
> That is a neighbour to the bordering down,
> Hath draw them thither.—*The Faithful Shepherdess.*

Tout. The blast of a horn or trumpet, to blow a horn, &c.

Toot, to blow a horn.—*Bailey.*

Toot was used in a contemptuous sense which I do not understand.—*Johnson.* And he quotes

This writer should wear a *tooting* horn.—*Howell.*

This is surely an insinuation that he was his own trumpeter, blew his own horn, or sang his own praise.

Touzle. To handle roughly, to rumple.

Tussle, or *teawzle,* to struggle in play, to pull, to romp.—*Bamford.* *Touz,* to lug or pull about, to tumble.—*Bailey.*

And farther, not having the fear of your worships before his eyes, but being moved and induced . . did then . . feloniously tear, wound, and *touzle* him . . of which tearings and *touzlings* the said Hare did die.—*The Trial of Farmer Carter's Dog Porter for Murder, 1771.*

> Then they to bete and *tusle* the sayde bedde.
> *The Order of Making the King's (Hen. VIII.) Bed.*
> Father's own son ! he'll *touzle* her.—*Congreve.*

Tow. A rope. This word is given in old dictionaries as a verb only ; in recent ones it is admitted as a noun.

Towmond. A twelvemonth. The substitution of *d* for *th*, by which month became *mond*, has been sufficiently dwelt upon ; but the change of twelve into *tow* is not so easily explained. *Twel* or *twal* was the first step, and the elision of *l* brought it very near its present form.

Towzie. Rough, shaggy. Connected with *touse, touze,* and *touzle.*

> And what sheep, that is full of wulle
> Upon his backe, they *toose* and pulle. —*Gower*.

Toy. A very old fashion of female head-dress.
Tye-top, a garland, a top-knot for the head of maids.—*Bailey*.
Can toy be a corruption of *tye*-top?
> On my head no *toy*
> But was her pattern?—*The Two Noble Kinsmen*.

I do not say this is Burns's *toy*.

Toyte or *tyte*. To totter like old age.
Totty, shaking, unsteady, dizzie. —*Johnson*.
Totty and *tottie*, wavering, tottering, dizzy. —*Bailey*.
> Sicker, thy head very *tottie* is. —*Spenser*.

Tozie. Tipsy. In some editions of Burns's Poems "the martial chuck" of "The Jolly Beggars" is called a tozie, i.e. tipsy, and in others a *towzie*, drab. Which is the right reading must of course be determined by the manuscript, which I have not seen, and have no opportunity of seeing. Unless that document is quite distinct on the point, I should say the poet meant *towzie*, for he had already sufficiently indicated her condition by saying, just two lines before, that she was—
> Wi' *usquebae* and blankets warm.

Tozy, soft like wool.—*Bailey*.

Tram. The shaft of a cart, or carriage of any kind.

Tramp. A journey. This word, now common, was not admitted to English dictionaries in Burns's days.
Tramp, a foot traveller. *Tramps*, travels on foot.—*Bamford*.
Tramp, a walk, a journey.—*Halliwell*.

Transmugrified. Transmigrated, metamorphosed.

Transmogrify, to transform.—*Var. Dial. Halliwell.*

They visibly, without the least hint, *transmogrify* them into such birds as you now see.—*Rabelais. Motteux.*

Those banditti have been long accustomed to chop, change and *transmography* every thing that belongs to my master.—*Don Quixote.*

Trashtrie. Trash. *Trie* in *trashtrie* resembles Spenser's *ree* in—

> Shake off this vile harted *cowardree,*

and may be allowed to pass with the remark of his learned editor: "*Cowardrie*, a word coined by the poet for the sake of the rhyme." *Todd.* See under *wastrie.*

Trews and *trouse.* Trousers.

The leather quilted jack serves under his shirt of mail, and to cover his *trouse* on horseback.—*Spenser.*

Then Dr. Ridley said, "It were best to go in my *trouse*."—*Book of Martyrs.*

Trickie. Tricky, full of tricks.

> Let thought turn exile, while the vacant mind
> To *tricky* words and pretty phrase confin'd
> Pumping for trim description's art,
> To win the ear neglects the heart.—*Cowper.*

Trig. Spruce, neat. *Trick* was used in England instead of *trig.* G and K were often used indifferently. For example, Johnson says:—"*Trigger.* This is often written *tricker*; I know not which is right," and Gayton has "a century of spickets" for spigots.

Oh, dear father gin I be not *trig.*—*Northumb. Garland. Ritson.*

> A neighbour mine not long ago there was,
> But nameless he for blameless he shall be,

GLOSSARY. 411

> That married had a *trick* and bonny lass
>   As in a summer day a man might see.
> —*Sir Philip Sidney.*

> There is a brall come out of France,
>   The *tryxt* ye harde this year a.
> We will trype so *tricke* and gaye.
> —*Ancient Ballads and Broadsides.*

> I saugh a tour on a toft *trighely* i-maked.
> *P. Plowman. Morris and Skeat.*

Trimly. Excellently.

These play and counterfeit the whole passion so *trimly* as though it had been an Enterlude. They do plaie so *trimly* and livelie.
Beehive of the Romish Church.

Trinle, trintle. A wheel of a barrow, to roll. *I* for *u*; see under *bizz*.

Trendel, a sphere, an orb, a circle.—*Bosworth.*

Trindle, the wheel of a barrow.—*Bamford.*

Doest not thou things thyself which men deeme to be without end as strange Mills and *Trindells* and such other kind of selfe-movings.—*De Mornay.*

> In the nekke he hyt him withal
> That the hed *trendelyd* off as a bal.—*R. C. de Lion.*
> His hevid *trindeled* on the sand.
> *Ywain and Gawain.*

He order't th' wheel-barrow with spon-new *trindle* to be fotch't.
John Collier.

Trinkle. To trickle.

To trinkle, to trickle.—*Var. Dial Halliwell.*

Troke. To exchange. E. truck. *O* for *u*, as in Fr. *troq* or *troc*, and in—

> Now up, now down, as *boket* (bucket) in a well.
> *Chaucer.*

Mannes compaignye hy *shoneth* (shunneth).
Kyng Alisaunder.

Whan *note* (nut) brounith in haselrys.—*Id.*

The horse brake loose, and *ron* (run)
The same way other flyers fled.—*Chapman.*

Troggers. Wandering merchants who procured old clothes by purchase or exchange.

This is just another form of *trokers* or *truckers*, from *trucan*, to fail, to truck, to abate, to diminish. *Trog*, *troke*, and *truck*, are different forms of the same word.

Ther ne is non hope of guode, non *wantrokiynge* of kueade.
Dan Michel of Northgate. Morris.

Trugg-corn, an allowance of corn to the vicar of Leimster, for officiating in some Chapels of Ease in that parish.—*Bailey.*

Troggin. What troggers deal in, second-hand clothes.

Trowth. Truth; a petty oath.

Be my *trowth*, I seyd the same.—*Cov. Mysteries.*

We wald that thai were *trowth* plight.
Ywain and Gawain.

In life she is Diana chast,
In *trouth* Penelope.—*Earl of Surrey.*

By my *troth*,
Methought 'twas excellent sport.
Beaumont and Fletcher.

Trump. A Jew's harp.

Crembalum, a Jew's *trump*.—*Ainsworth.*

Here a fiddle, and here a Jew's *trump*.—*Pepys.*

Some take tobacco, some take snuff;
Some play the *trump*.—*Irish Hudibras, 1689.*

There is howlynge and scowlyng, all cast in a dumpe,
With whewling and pewling, as though they had lost a
trump.—*Gam. Gurton's Needle.*

Tongue of the trump, the wire of the Jew's harp;

metaphorically the principal person in a company, or in the management of an affair.

Tryste. To agree to meet, an appointed meeting; a fair.

> Think not, Gray-steel albeit he wold
> Shall hinder you your *tryste* to hold.
> *Sir Eger, Sir Graham, and Sir Gray-steel.*
>
> Under my *trystle* tree.—*R. Hood.*

Notwithstanding all that has been said of *tryst*, it is perhaps only another form of *trust*, which is often spelled *y* or *i*, e.g.:—

And be the more bold and studefast for to *tryste* on the fynal arysyng of ded bodyes.—*John of Trevisa.*

> The erle answered wyth wordys hende,
> Y *tryste* to the as to my frende.—*Le Bone Florence of Rome.*
> I have in you such a *triste.*—*Gower.*

Tug. Raw-hide, *of which, in old times, plough traces were frequently made.*

I can find no evidence that the practice mentioned by Burns ever existed. Burns must have heard it, but it seems impossible now to prove it. Whatever a *tug* may originally have been, it is plain that the poet means that his horse was a "wordy beast as e'er drew" nearest the plough or farthest from it, whether a *fur-ahin* or a *fur-afore.*

Tug is found only as a verb in E. dictionaries, or as signifying a pull, and not that by which a thing is pulled, but Bosworth has "Tige, A.-S., a tie, band, knot, *tug*," and Bailey has "*Tuggae* (old law term), harness, traces, or ropes for drawing." Jamieson also gives *teug*, which is not far from Fletcher's *teugh* :

> Be sure then
> His *teugh* be tith and strong.—*Monsieur Thomas.*

Tulzie. A quarrel, to quarrel, to fight, a fight.

Tumbler. A small cart, lightly formed.—*Jamieson.*

Some old people may have seen carts in which, instead of the wheels revolving on the axle, it revolved with the wheels. It is not easy to determine whether a *tumbler* was a cart of this description, or a *tumbrel* (originally a *tumble*-cart, Scotice, a *coup*-cart), a dung-cart.

Tumbler, a cart.—*Bailey.*

> It cumys thee better for to dryve
> A dogcart or a *tumrelle.*—*Skelton.*

Twa. Two.

> Thai had bene like thai *twa.*—*The Two Dreams.*
> I wat you byne great lordes *twaw.*—*An. Bal. of Chevy Chase.*
> I have herd say, man sal take of *twa* thinges,
> Slike as he findes, or slike as he bringes.—*Chaucer.*
> Was broader than *twa* large span.—*Ywain and Gawain.*

Twa-three. A few; two or three.

'Twad. It would. See *wad.*

Twal. Twelve.

Twel, twelve.—*Weber.*

> On al wise that ye be her
> This day *twelmonth.*—*Ywain and Gawain.*

Twal-hundred. Twelve hundred. This and *seventeen hunner* are technical terms denoting the quality of the cloth.

Twal pennie worth. A small quantity; an English pennyworth.

Twal-pint Hawkie. A cow yielding twelve pints at one milking.

Twalt. Twelfth.

Twang. A twinge. *G* for *ge;* see under *brig.*

Tweedle-dee. An indifferent fiddler.

> *Tweedle,* to handle lightly. Used of awkward fiddling.
>
>> Strange! all this difference should be
>> 'Twixt Tweedle-dum and *Tweedle-dee!—Pope.*

Twin. To part; also, to deprive, as in

> May *twin* auld Scotland o' a life.—*Address of Beelzebub.*
> Which many a lusty love hath *twinned.—Gower.*
> Sith Bialacoil mote fro me *twin,*
> Shette in her prison yond within.—*Chaucer.*
> When the body and the saule salle *twyn.*
>> *Pricke of Conscience.*

Twistle. To twist; a twist, a wrench.

Twistle, that part of a tree where the branches divide from the stock.—*Halliwell.*

Tyke. A dog.

Tike, a dog.—*Grose.* He's a fine *tike.—Bamford.*

Tike. In Shakspeare it is the name of a dog; in which sense it is used in Scotland.—*Johnson.*

If Johnson meant that *tyke* was a word used to signify dog, he has not expressed his meaning with his usual clearness. If he meant, as his words imply, that it was a proper name, like Jowler, Help, etc., he is wrong. It is not used by Shakspeare, or in Scotland, as the name of a dog, but as another word for dog. It was used by Shakspeare and other English writers exactly as it is employed by Burns.

> Bob-tail'd *tike,* or trundle-tail.—*Shak.*
> If you will have a good *tike*
> Of which there are few like.—*Gervase Markham.*

With all the barkand parish *tikes* set at her.—*Ben Jonson.*

Luke Robinson shall go before ye, that snarling northern *tike*.
A Proper New Ballad on the Old Parliament.
Percy Society.

Tysday. Tuesday.

The *Tyseday* tharaftyre.—*Morte d' Arthur.*

On *Tuysday* the xxi day of Apryll.—*Anc. Bal. and Broadsides.*

U

Unback'd. Untamed, not broken, not accustomed to the saddle.

Let me beg of you, like an *unback'd* filly, to kick it.—*Sterne.*
Like *unback'd* colts, they prick'd their ears.—*Shak.*

Uncaring. Disregarding.

Unce. An ounce.

He put this *unce* of copper in the croslet.—*Chaucer.*

Unchancy. Unlucky.

Unco. Strange, uncouth, very, very great, prodigious. *Th* omitted; see under *mou*.

Unto yowre court, sir, have i broght
An *unkouth* (strange) knyght that ye knaw noght.
Ywain and Gawain.

Uncos. News.

The devil cannot stop their mouthes,
But they wyl talke of suche *uncouthes* (*uncos*, news).
Skelton.

I'd ax him what *uncouths* he'd yerd (heard) sturrin.
Tim Bobbin.

Unfauld. Unfold. See *fauld.*

Unkenn'd. Unknown. See *ken.*

Nor seas unused, strange clime, or pool *unken'd.—Fairfax.*

Unsicker. Unsure, unsteady. See *sicker.*

Unskaithed. Undamaged, unhurt. See *skaith.*

Unweeting. Unwotting, unknowing ; *unweeting groan*, involuntary groan.

To weet, to know.—*Bailey. Unweeting*, ignorant, not knowing. —*Johnson.*

Unweeting he fulfill'd
The purpos'd counsel, pre-ordain'd and fix'd.—*Milton.*
Unweting of this Dorigene at al.—*Chaucer.*

Upo'. Upon.

If Burns had not inserted this word in his glossary it would not have been placed here. But, since it is here, it may be pointed out, as a matter of a little interest, that *upon*, which is now mostly displaced by *on*, seemed at one time more likely to drop the second than the first syllable. For from the Anglo-Saxon times down at least to those of Lydgate, we find in English writers *uppe*, *upe*, and *up*, for *on* or *upon*.

He wolde him-sulf *up* is fot (upon his foot).—*Rob. of Gloucester.*
That *upe* the pope's lokinge of Rome he ssolde it do.—*Id.*
His office naturel ay wol it hold,
Up peril of my lif, til that it die.—*Chaucer.*
Ther lith one *up* my wombe and *up* myn hed.—*Id.*
Up peyn of lyf and lesyng of her hede.—*Lydgate.*

Ursa Major. Dr. Johnson.

Usquebae. Whisky.

Usquebaugh, a certain cordial made in Ireland.—*Bailey.*

V.

Valentines' dealing. Drawing of names by lot on St. Valentine's day.

Vap'rin. Vapouring.
Vapour, to huff, brag, or boast.—*Bailey*.

Variorum. Mutability.

Vauntie. Boastful, proud.
Vauntful, boastful, ostentatious.—*Johnson*.
Vauntor, boaster.—*Bailey*.
No *vauntor*, saine men, certain he is none.—*Chaucer*.

Vend. To utter, to give currency to, to vent.
You return fraught with their vices which you *vend* here for fashionable gallantry.—*Farquhar*.
When he (Sir Matthew Hale), took any counterfeit money, he would not *vend* it again.—*Life of Judge Hale*.
Our bishops are all far from making or *vending* heresies.—*Warburton*.

Ventige. A small hole.
Govern these *ventages* with your finger and thumb.—*Shak*.

Vera. Very.
Varra. Very.—*Bamford*.
But it is *vara* fine.—*Shak*.
A man hath *veray* knowleche of himself.—*Chaucer*.
A *verray* few right as am I.—*Gower*.

Virl. A ring round a column, etc.
Verril, a little brass or iron ring at the end of a cane or handle of a tool.—*Bailey*.

Frete, a *verril*, the yron bande, or hoope that keeps a wooden tool from riving.—*Cotgrave.*

> A serving man hath
> His hood and his *verrils* brave.
> —*God speed the Plough.*

Vittle, vittel. Victual, grain of all kinds.

Bothe flessche and fissche, and many other *vitailles.*—*P. Plowman.*

> Pompeys there are of every shape and size;
> Some are the Great y-clep'd and some the Little,
> Some with their deeds that fill the wond'ring skies,
> And some on ladies' laps that eat their *vittle.*
> —*The Rolliad.*

> With other *vittle*, which anon
> We farther shall dilate upon.—*Butler.*

> To all tapsters and tiplers,
> And all ale-house *vitlers.*—*Skelton.*

Vogie. Vain, proud.

W.

Wa'. Wall; *wa's*, walls; *to have one's back at the wa'*, to be unfortunate.

> And there *was* shall be gayly arayed with fayre flowers.
> *The Festyval. Ellis.*

> Then Alex Rydly he lette flee
> A cloth-yard schaft, ahint the *wa'.*—*Richardson.*

Wowes do whiten, and wyndowes glasen.—*P. Plowman.*

She hath been at London to call a *strea* a straw, and a *waw* a wall.—*Cheshire Proverb. Grose.*

Wab. A web. *A* for *e*; see under *fallow*, and in—

> They conne not stinten till no thing be *laft* (left).
> *Chaucer.*

> Gud is bot a *lant* (lent) lone,
> Sumtyme hasse a mon oght, sumtyme non.
>
> *Sir Amadas.*

Wabster. A weaver. *A* for *e*; see *wab*.

Webster, a weaver.—*Johnson.*

> I saugh in that Semble
> Wollene *websteris*, and weveris of Lynen.
>
> *P. Plowman.*

Wad. Would.

Wud, would.—*Bamford.*

I believe this comes nearer the Ayrshire pronunciation than *wad*.

Wald is very common in old E. authors, and as would, by the elision of *l*, came to be sounded *wood*, by the same process *wald* became *wad*.

> A worde to me *wald* he noght say.—*Ywain and Gawain.*
>
> He was ful wroth and grim,
> For no prest *wald* sing for him.—*Chronicle of England.*
>
> Rookhope stands in a pleasant place,
>   If the false thieves *wad* let it be.
>
> *The Bishopric Garland. Ritson.*

Wad. To bet, a bet, a pledge. *A* for *e*; see under *fallow.*

> *Wed* no schalt thou have of me,
> Ac Y wol have *wed* of thee.—*Kyng Alisaunder.*
>
> All the needs full soon are sped,
> Both withouten borgh and *wed*
>   When Penny goes between.—*Sir Penny.*

Wad. Wed, marry.

Wadna. Would not. *Wad* and *na.*

Wadset. A mortgage.

My londes beth *set* to *weddes*, Robyn,
Untyll a certayne day.—*R. Hood.*

Seyvon yere *weddeseytt* my londe,
To (till) the dettes that ar woonde (owing)
Be qwytte all beddene.—*Sir Amadas.*

His maners (manors) he ded to *wedesett.*—*Sir Cleges.*

Wae. Woe, sorrowful.

Wae's me. Woe's me.
Wae's me.—*Bamford.*
Wae's me, woe is the heart, etc.—*Thoresby.*

Waesucks! Alas! O the pity! Plural of *wae's me.*
Usic, usich, us.—*Bosworth.*

Wae worth! Woe worth! unhappy be! woe be to! Anglo-Saxon, *worthan*, to be.

Wo worth the faire gemme vertulesse,
Wo worth that hearbe also that doth no bote,
Wo worth the beauty that is routhlesse,
Wo worth that wight that trede ech under fote.—*Chaucer.*

Woworth the man
That first did teach the cursed steel to bight
On his owne flesh, and make way to the living spright.
—*Spenser.*

Well worth is also found;—
He had his will at Berwick, *wele wurth* the while!—*Minot.*

Wa' flower. Wall-flower. *Wa* and *flower.*

Waft. The woof. E. weft. *A* for *e*; see under *fallow.*

Wage. To carry on a war, to compete, to rival, in—
Warring sighs and groans I'll *wage* thee.
Ae fond kiss.

Troilus. I am as true as truth's simplicity.
Cressida. In that I'll *war* with you.—*Shak.*

Waifs. Strays, wanderers.

Waifs, lost goods or cattle, claimed by nobody.——*Bailey.*

Choses guesves, waifes, strayes, or things left, quitted, abandoned.
—*Cotgrave.*

> Somme serven the kyng . . .
> chalengen his dettes
> Of wardes and wardmotes, *weyves* and streyues.
> P. Plowman.

Wair. To lay out, to expend.

Ware your money, i.e., bestow it well.—*Bailey.*

To *ware* one's money, to bestow it well.—*Grose.*

Both Bailey and Grose, and others, differ from Burns in regard to the meaning of this word. The idea of well or ill is not, I think, included in *wair.*

Wear, to expend, to part with, to lay out money. "Mind heaw theaw *wears* the brass."—*Bamford.*

> On swych chaffare
> Wulde y feyne my sylver *ware.*—*Rob. of Brunne.*
> Hys wyfe
> He walde *ware* no thyng upon.
> *How a Merchant did his Wife Betray.*

Wale. Choice, to choose; *hand-waled,* picked by the hand; the best.

Wailed wine, choice wine; *outwail,* an outcast.—*Bailey.*

> Botte thenne thie soughle woulde throwe thie vysage sheene,
> Yatte shemres oune thie comlie semlykeene,
> Or scarlette with *waylde* lynnen clothe,
> Lyke would thie sprite upon thy vysage.
> *Chatterton. Wrag. of Ella.*

> Most i ridden by rybbes dale, wilde wymmen for to *wale.*
> *Early English Poem. Warton.*

> And he led me in brede to be ;
> Sauf made he me, for he *wald* me.—*Metrical English Psalter.*

Morris and Skeat, in their excellent "Specimens of Early English," translate *wald* would, wanted. *Wald*, as has been shown under *wad*, is undoubtedly often used for would, but here, I believe, it means *waled*, chosen. The Vulgate, from which the version of Psalms in which the lines quoted occur, has—

> Tum est Jehovae pro scipione mihi :
> Et educit me in latum ; liberat me, quia delectatur me.

The authorised version gives "he delighted in me," which is not far from "he chose me." And I suspect "he would me" is an expression very rare if not unknown.

Walie. Ample, large, jolly.

Wally, to cocker, to indulge.—*Bailey*. This may be Burns's *walie*, as to cocker, or feed liberally has a tendency to make the body large and jolly. I have seen it stated that *walie* means choice, but Burns, neither in his definition of the word nor in his use of it, gives any countenance to the idea that it is in any way connected with *wale*. Try the following line with the notion of choice in your mind,—

> Clap in his *walie* nieve a blade,

and you will see that the choice was limited; and as choosing implies the leaving of something, Willie Wastle's wife must have been well stocked with hands if she had "*walie nieves* like midden creels," and had a few over.

By looking carefully at one of the lines in which this word occurs we may perhaps be able to connect it with some word known to be English. Take the line,

> There was ae winsome wench and *walie*.

Why does the poet dwell on her qualities? Because he wishes to prepare us for the parts she has to play. She is described as *winsome* that she might so attract the tipsy gazer that he " thought his very een enrich'd," and uttered the words that broke up the unhallowed assembly. And the other quality *walie* is meant to indicate that she was fitted to take a prominent part in the chase that followed when she

> Far before the rest
> Hard upon noble Maggie press'd.

For this she is made ample, large, jolly, long of limb, and in excellent condition—in a word, *walie*; and Chaucer supplies us with a word which, with changes such as have been frequently indicated, comes very near the one under consideration :—

> For both he had a body, and might
> To doen that thing, as well as hardinesse,
> And eke to seen him in his geare dresse
> So freshe, so yong, so *weldy* seemed he,
> It was an heaven upon him for to se.
>
> *Troilus and Creseide, B. II.*

Weldy, active.—*Tyrwhitt.*

There is no doubt that Douglas by *wallie*, meant large :—

> This warld walteris as dois the *wallie* sey.
> *The Palice of Honour.*

Walie. An interjection of distress.

This is probably a form of A.-S. *Wa'-la' !* Oh ; O if! It occurs in many shapes.

Wally, alas !—*Yorkshire. Halliwell.*

Wala wa the while !—*Chaucer.*

In Wright's Chaucer it is *welaway* and *weylaway ;* Gower has *wailoway ;* Wiat, *weleaway.*

Wallop. To move cumbrously.

Wele a daye, well a day, woe is me.
> *Ancient Ballads and Broadsides.*

Wame. The belly. Womb, originally meant belly Falstaff says "My *womb* undoes me."

Wem, the womb, or belly.—*Grose.*

Wamb, the womb.—*Thoresby.*

> I pray who's this we've met with here,
> That tickles his trunk-*wame.*
>> *Bell's An. Poems and Ballads.*

> Prick't but the *wem* and out there came
> Heroic guts and garbage.—*St. George for England.*

But long they had not digged ere they herde, as it might seme, within the *wam* of the erthe, etc.—*Of wonderful and surprising Eventys.*

> He bled his leggs, and in his *waim*
> Two tapps he there sets running.
>> *Northumb. Garland. Ritson.*

Wamefou'. A belly-full. *Wame* and *fou'.*

Wanchancie. Unlucky. *Wan*, prefix signifying want or luck, equal to *un*, and *chance.*

Wantrust, distrust.—*Bailey.*

> Than shulden I fallen in *wanhope.*—*Chaucer.*

Wangee. A species of Chinese cane.

Wanrest. Inquietude. *Wan* and *rest.*

Wanrestfu'. Restless, unrestful.

Ware. Wore, old past tense of wear, and used by Burns for *worn* in

> The marled plaid ye kindly spare,
> By me should gratefully be *ware.*
> There met him a certain man which *ware* no clothes.
>> *Luke, viii. 27.*

> Above his hanberk strong a coat he *ware*
> Embroidered fair with pearl and rich stone.—*Fairfax*.

> She let make hir self a nonne, and *ware* white clothes and blacke.—*Le Morte d'Arthur*.

Wark. Work.

> God guide thee, Guion, well to end thy *warke*.—*Spenser*.
> And bids me leave my useful *wark*.—*Lord Vaux*.
> Some to make hie wayes, and such like *warks*,
> And some to maintaine preests and clarks.— *The Four P.'s*.
> That wyll syt ydyll all the day,
> And can not set herselfe to *wark*.—*Skelton*.

Wark-lume. A tool to work with. *Wark* and *lume*.

Warl or *warld.* World. For omission of *d* see under *afiel*.

Methinks it should not be worth your while to risque your saul in the next *warld* for, etc.—*Vanbrugh*.

> Where so he in *warld* wende,
> Y schal be to him trewe.—*Amis and Amiloun*.
> All the *warlde* will spy your shame.—*Skelton*.

Warld's worm. A world's worm, a miser.

Warlock. A wizard.

> *Warlock*, a wizzard.—*Bamford*.
> *Warlock*, a male witch; a wizzard.—*Johnson*.
> He was no *warluck*.—*Dryden*.

Warlock-knowe. A knoll on which warlocks held their meetings.

Warly. Worldly, eager on amassing wealth. See *warl*.

Warp. To prepare the warp for the loom. The word warp as a noun is found in all dictionaries, but in none of the older, except Bailey's, is it inserted as a verb.

Warran. A warrant, to warrant. *T* is frequently omitted after *n*, as in

> For lordly love is such a *tyranne* fell,
> That when he rules, all power he doth expell.—*Chaucer.*

> Looke every mannys name thou wryte,
> Upon a scrow of *parchemyn* (parchment).—*Rich. C. de Lion.*

> And ye the sweet savour fele
>   Your *warrans* may right wele.—*Chaucer.*

Warsle or *warstle*. *Wærstlic*, wrestling.—*Bosworth.*

If wrestle and warsle are only different forms of the same word, the change of *e* to *a* is easily accounted for. Indeed *a* is found in several English authors:

> *Wrastling* and casting of the bar.—*Froissart.*
> For ever I *wrastle*, and ever I come behind.—*Gower.*
> At *wrastling* he wold bere away the ram.—*Chaucer.*

But the substitution of *war* for *wr* can only, I suspect, be explained by the supposition, which seems to be that of Jamieson, that *wrestle* and *warsle* come from different roots. If *warsle* had been only an east country word there would have been no difficulty, because, in Forfarshire for instance, *wr* becomes a distinct syllable, wright and wreck being pronounced *wur-right* and *wur-reck;* but in Ayrshire, unless *warstle* be accounted one, not a single case of such a pronunciation can be produced.

As this matter is still, notwithstanding all that has been written about it, *sub judice*, I should be disposed to say that *warstle* comes from warst, that is worst, by the addition of *le* as in sparkle, or Shakspeare's *writhle*. When a competition between two parties is about to take place we often hear the expression, "Now we shall see who is the best;" why may we not say, "We shall see who gets the worst," especially when in the wrestling ring it is the fall, that is, the worst, which is always spoken of? This, I think, gives a force to the word in

> An' owre she *warsl'd* in the ditch.

By the ordinary acceptation of wrestled *warsled* has to have a different meaning given to it. To wrestle, i.e., to contend into, for that is the meaning of it here, is nonsense, but when we say she was *worsted* in her struggle all is plain.*

Warst. Worst.

> Which has shapen us the *werst*.—*Gower*.
>
> The *warst* hors is worthe ten pounde.—*Sir Amadas*.
>
> The *warste* of ther fadurs were barons.
>
> *Le Bone Florence of Rome*.

Washen. Washed. Old part. of wash.

New-*washen*.—*Grose*.

> Hire forehead shone as bright as any day,
> So was it *washen*, whan she lete hire werk.—*Chaucer*.

They *wesshen* hym and wyped hym and wonden hym in cloutes.
P. Plowman.

Wast. West. *A* for *e;* see under *fallow*.

---

* There is a word in *Piers The Ploughman's Creed* which has a curious resemblance to this word. A ploughman is described as having

> His hosen ouerhongen his hokschynes on eueriche a side,
> Al beslombered in fen;

and then it is said,—

> This whit *warselede* in the fen almost to the ankle.

Beslombred undoubtedly means bedaubed. If he was bedaubed to the hokschynes, i.e., gaiters, what need was there for saying he *waselede* to the ancle if *waselede* means bemired himself? I know if a Scotch peasant had seen this *whit* struggling after the plough, drawing his feet with difficulty from the fen his salutation would have been, "Ye're *warslin'* awa!"

Wastrie. Prodigality, wastefulness. A regularly formed E. word like ribaldry, coquetry, &c. It is an E. word, though like Chaucer's *hasardrie*, Bishop Hall's *gawderie*, Gower's *novelrie*, and many others, it is not found in common dictionaries.

Wastrel, a good-for-nothing person.—*Bamford.*

Whan note brouneth in *haselrys.*—*Kyng Alisaunder.*

Wat. Wet. *A* for *e ;* see under *fallow.*

> We were ready to *watte* our feet for that purpose.
> *The Late Expedicion in Scotland. Lond., 1544.*

Wat-shod. Wet-shod.

So he went over at last, not much above *wet-shod.*—*Pilgrim's Progress.*

> And after many wearied steppes
> All *wet-shod* both in dust and myre.
> *The Dutchesse of Suffolke's Calamities.*

My hopes are seam-rent, and go *wet-shod.*—*Massinger.*

Wat. Wot, know.

> I *wat* that he was largely
> By the shoulders mare than I.—*Ywain and Gawain.*

> Noght all the sothe *watte.*—*Sir Amadas.*

> For are we begin our prayer,
> *Wat* he quarof we haf mister.—*E. Metrical Homilies. Small.*

> That he trespasseth well I *wate.*—*Chaucer.*

Wat. A man's upper dress ; a sort of mantle.—*Cunningham.*

In Cunningham's edition of Burns the line which elsewhere appears as

> To make a *coat* to Johnny o't,

is given as "a *wat* to Johnny o't." *Wat*, in this sense, I never met. I insert it, however, lest it turn out the right reading.

Water. A river. *Down the water*, seawards by the river.

In the Confynes of this Countrie (as I take it) I was offered Skirmishe by MacNeill Brian Ertaugh, at my passage over the *Water* at Belfast.—*Henry Sidney, Lord Deputy, to the E. Council.*

Then came he to a *water* brode.—*Sir Guy of Warwick.*

> The wear borne along be the *watter* a Twyde,
> Yth bowndes of Tividale.
> *The Hunting of the Cheviat. Ritson.*
>
> To a *water* they buth y-come,
> The ryver was clere and deop.—*Kyng Alisaunder.*

Water-brose. Brose made of meal and water simply, without the addition of milk, butter, &c. See *brose.*

Eigh, said hoo, an aw stown a loyte *wetur porritch*, an sum thrutchins (whey), an a trecle butter-cake ev yo con eyght um.—*Tim Bobbin.*

Water-fit. Water-foot, mouth of a river.

Wattle. A twig, a wand. *Wattle*, to bind with twigs.—*Johnson.*

Wauble. To swing, to reel. Differs only in spelling from E. *wabble.*

Wabble, to totter as a top sometimes in spinning, to wriggle about as an arrow sometimes does in the air.—*Bailey.*

Waucht. A draught. See *wecht.*

Wauk and wauken. To awake. *Wauken*, waking, watching. See *awauken.*

If you hear a bairn scream it neet-time, its a sign it's *wackan.*—*Pogmoor Olmenack.*

Waukit. Thickened, as fullers do cloth. For omission of *l* see under *a'*.

A *walk*-mill, a fulling-mill; *walkers*, fullers.—*Bailey.*

Wawk-mill, a fulling-mill.—*Bamford.*

> She curst the weaver and the *walker*,
> That cloth that had wrought.
> *The Boy and the Mantle.*

Chambers, notwithstanding Burns's express declaration that *wauket* means thickened, says wauket loof is "dyed palm." The hardness of a workman's palm is so often mentioned by poets that we are forced to the conclusion that it was only by inadvertence that so experienced a writer as Mr. Chambers could have made this mistake. Shakspeare speaks of the "*hard hands* of peasants" and "*Hard-handed* men that work in Athens here," and Browne gives us a word not unworthy to stand beside wauket :—

> The swarty smith spits on his *buckhorn fist.*
> *Britannia's Pastorals.*

Waukrife. Not apt to sleep, wakeful ; from *wauk* and *ryf,* prevalent, full.

Wakker, easily awakened.—*Grose.*

Waur. Worst, to worst.

War and war, worse and worse.——*Bailey. Bamford. Grose.*
> They sayne the world is much *war* than it wont,
> All for her shepherdes been beastly and blont.—*Spenser.*

Wean or *weanie.* A child. As a verb, *wean,* I need not say, is common in E.

Weanel, a child newly weaned.—*Johnson.*

Weanel, a young creature fit to be weaned.—*Bailey.*

Wean, a child, or *wee one.*—*Halliwell.*

It may be as well to remark that whether wean be formed from *wee ane* or not, the pronunciation, which is *wāne* and not *ween,* is rather opposed to the idea, and, as far as I can make out, Jamieson does not approve of this genesis of the word.

Wearie. Weary; *monie a wearie body,* many a different person.

If ever the words *monie a wearie bodie* meant many a different person, it must have been a very long time ago, and in very peculiar circumstances. The expression is found in Burns alone, and I rather think the explanation weakens the line in which it occurs.

> For roads were clad frae side to side
> Wi' monie a wearie body,
> In droves that day.

Here the poet evidently means to show us that the road was crowded with all sorts of people, and to emphasise his description he says there was "monie a wearie body," that is, "there were many people who had travelled great distances," as we know from history was the case at such times. Besides, if "monie a wearie body" means "many a different person," it makes "In droves that day" superfluous. In short, I do not believe Burns intended this part of his explanation to apply to the line in "The Holy Fair."

Wear the plaid. To be a shepherd; figuratively, to be a pastor or clergyman.

Weary. To think long.

Johnson's "Weary, to make impatient of continuance," and his quotation from Shakespeare, "I stay too long, I *weary* thee," are not very different from the Scotch use of the word.

He never forced minister or people to *weary* themselves to wait for his coming.*—*Fuller.*

---

* This quotation is interesting as showing that the delay of public worship till the arrival of the great man of the parish spoken of in "The Heart of Mid-Lothian" was known in England.

> How *wearisome*
> Eternity so spent.—*Milton.*

Weary fa'. A curse, probably from *wery*, A.-S., a curse.

> This Soudanesse, whom I thus blame and *warrie.*—*Chaucer.*

Weason. The weasand, the wind-pipe.

Siflet, the *weason* or wind-pipe.—*Cotgrave.*

Feel, man, whether thy *weason* be not cracked first.—*Ford.*

> The valiant knight his *weason* cut.
>
> *St. George for England.*

> The unerring steel descended while he spoke,
> Pierc'd his wide mouth and thro' his *weason* broke.
>
> *Dryden.*

Weave the stockin. To knit stockings.

> On Fasten-een we had a rockin'
> To ca' the crack, and weave our stockin'.

In Burns's day, and long afterwards, every man and boy about a farm-house, from the master to the herd-laddie, learned to knit, hence the kindly *our* stockin' of the poet, and spent many of the long winter evenings with their knitting-needles, and when they went to pass the evening with a neighbour it was as natural and as common for them to take their stocking as for the women to take their "rock," and had it not been from deference to the ladies these country assemblies might as well have been called "stockins" as "rockins."

To weave for to knit has been called a Scotticism. But it has good English authority:—

Knit, to *weave* without a loom.—*Johnson.*

> The spinsters and the knitters in the sun,
> And the free maids that *weave their thread with bones*,
> Do use to chant it.—*Shak.*

> Yon cottager who *weaves* at her own door,
> Pillow and bobbins all her little store.—*Cowper*

Of *weaving* gray-silk stockings of the webs of spiders, see the Philosophical Transactions.—*Note on the Dunciad by Pope and Warburton.*

Wecht. A species of basket, made of sheep-skin, shaped like a sieve or riddle.

Burns has not admitted the word into his glossary, thinking, perhaps, that he had sufficiently explained it in his note to "Halloween." That note, however, has led to some misapprehension as to the use of the wecht. In the rite described in the note he had occasion to mention only one purpose for which it was employed, and it has been inferred that the winnowing of grain was the sole use to which it was put, whereas that was only one of the services in which it was employed. Its principal use was that of a basket, the winnowing only an incidental one. In short, it was a *vessel*, and this suggests a more probable derivation than that of Jamieson. *Waeg*, *weg*, is a cup, a dish; *wegi*, all kinds of cups.

Waeg, is also, I believe, the origin of *waucht* or *waught*, a cup or glass, in "We'll tak a right guid-willie *waught*." A recent suggestion that *waught* is a corruption of *quaff* cannot, I am afraid, be accepted.

Wee. Little. *A wee*, a short time.

> No forsooth, he hath but a little *wee* face.—*Shak.*
>
> For 'tis, to speak in a familiar style,
> A Yorkshire *wee-bit* longer than a mile.—*Cleveland.*

My pretty *wee* comrade, my half-inch of man's flesh, how run the dice of this cheating world?—*Massinger.*

> Quen sco (she) had sitten thar a *wei*,
> Sco bihild a tre was hei.—*Cursor Mundi.*

Weed. Dress, apparel.

> Ye dide me stripe out of my poure *wede*.—*Chaucer.*

And simple was their *weed.*—*Spenser.*

Gete you monkes *wede.*—*R. Hood.*

Apparayled as a Palmere in pilgrimes *wedes.*—*P. Plowman.*

Weeder-clips. Large wooden pincers, about four feet in length, for extracting weeds, especially thistles, from growing corn. It is now nearly, if not altogether, disused. It was sometimes called a corn-clips, and a line of an old song yet lingers in some memories:

Ye lean'd out owre yere corn-clips.

Clips, a wooden instrument for pulling weeds out of corn.—*Grose.*

Here I *clip*
The anvil of my sword.—*Shak.*

The lusty vine not jealous of the ivy,
Because she *clips* the elm.—*Beau. and Fletcher.*

(The ark was) withouten mast,
Kable, other capstan to *clyppe* to her ankrez.
Early E. Alliterative Poems.

Weel. Well.

The rattling quiver at her shoulders hung,
Therein a flash of arrows feathered *weel.*—*Fairfax.*

Sir, in this hopping I will hop si *weel,*
That my tung shall hop better than my heel.
The Four P's.

He came to the gallows armed *wele,*
Both in iron and in steel.—*The Seven Sages.*

Weelfare. Welfare. See *weel.*

Weel-faur'd or *faurt.* Well favoured.

Faranly, handsome.—*Bailey.*

There is many euil *faueryd,* and thou be foule.—*Skelton.*

Well-faueryd bonne.—*Id.*

Forthy she gan her eye impresse
Upon his face and his stature,

> And thought how never creature
> Was so *welfarend* as was he.—*Gower.*

> Be fore the king in hall scho went
> A coupe with wine scho had in hand,
> And hir hatire was wele *farand.*—*Rob. de Brunne.*

Weepers. Strips of muslin stretched on the cuff of a coat or gown, a token of mourning.

Weet. Rain, wetness, to wet. *Weet our whistle.* To drink.

> We must lodge on the plain dry or *weet.*
> *The Nut Brown Maid.*

> His mouth weel *weet*, his sleeve's right thred bare,
> *Stephen Hawes.*

> With eyhen reed and *wete*
> Throughout the cite, by the maister streete.
> —*Wright's Chaucer.*

> Now have thise lordes but litell nede of bromes
> To sweepe away the filthe out of the streete,
> Setthe side sleves of penyles groomes
> Wole it up likke, be it dry or *wete.*—*Occleve.*

> She sparyd not to *wete* her fete.—*Skelton.*

> As eny jay sche light was and jolyf,
> So was hir joly *whistel wele y-wete.*—*Wright's Chaucer.*

> Let's drink the other cup to *wet our whistles.*—*I. Walton.*

Weird. Fate.

Wird and *wyrd*, fate.—*Bosworth.*

> I beheld the wofull *werd* befall,
> That by the wrathfull wyl of Gods was done.
> *The Mirrour for Magistrates.*

> It were a wondrous *wierde*
> To sen a kynge become an herde.—*Gower.*

> But O Fortune, executrice of *wierdes*,
> O influences of these hevens hie.
> *Chaucer. Troilus and Creseide.*

We'se. We shall. See *I'se.*

We'se have our neele, els dame Chat comes never within heaven-gate. *Thou's* pay for all. *I'se* teach thee.—*Gam. Gurton's Needle.*

Westlin. Westward. Another form of *westland.*

Wha. Who.

Lauerd in thi telde (tabernacle) *wha* sal won?—*Met. E. Psalter.*
But Kay wist not *wha* it was.—*Ywain and Gawain.*
Ask them *wha* sal you defend.—*Id.*
To Perciens Y wol me seolle (myself),
Sywe (follow) me now *wha* so wol!—*Kyng Alisaunder.*

Whaizle. To wheeze. *A* for *e*; see under *dail*. The frequentative *le* is often added at the pleasure of the poet. Both Spenser and Shakespeare from *writhe* have formed *writhle.*

Whalp. Whelp. *A* for *e*; see under *fallow.*

Wham. Whom.

Whidur wol thou go and to *wham*?—*Sir Orpheo.*
The mayden red that thai myght her
A real romance in that place,
Bot i ne wote of *wham* it was.—*Ywain and Gawain.*
Of *wham* God hath don ys wille.—*Percy's Reliques.*

Whang. A leathern string; a piece of cheese, bread, etc.; to give the strappado.

As in the course of time "Monuments themselves memorials need," so the explanations in glossaries and dictionaries which were well understood when first given, require, say after a century, to be explained. *To give the strappado*, which Burns gave as one meaning of whang, is in this predicament. It signifies to punish by blows with a strap or leathern thong, and to *whang* is its literal translation.

Were **I** at the *strappado* **I** would not tell you on compulsion.
Shak.

Whangs, leather thongs.—*Grose*.

A *thwang* for a shoe, the latchet, a thong.—*Thoresby*.

Whang, anything large.—*Yorksh. Halliwell.*

Whang, a blow.—*Ib*.

> His meal-poke hang about his neck,
> Into a leathern *whang*.—*R. Hood.*
>
> And a klub, ful grete and lang,
> Thik fret with mani a *thwang*.—*Ywain and Gawain.*
>
> I'd just streak'd down and with a swish
> *Whang'd* off my hat.—*Clare.*

Threw down with violence.—*Glossary*.

I am not worth to unbynde the *thwong* of hise shoon.—*Luke III.* 16. *Wyclif.*

Whare. Where.

> And knawe namare sal he
> His stede, *whare* that it sal be.—*Metrical E. Psalter.*
>
> Thare strif was Peni makes pese (peace)
> In land *whare* he will lende.—*Sir Penny.*
>
> He went up in a towr on hight,
> *Whare* the Sarzins se him might.—*The Seven Sages.*

Whase. Whose.

> I had wondre what she was, and *whas* wyf she were.
> *P. Plowman.*

> Ne her es nane that the can tell,
> Bot if it be a damysell
> For *whas* sake he heder come,
> And for hir the batayl he nome.—*Ywain and Gawain.*

What-reck. Nevertheless, notwithstanding. The best explanation of this word, which is very much the same as "what does it matter?" or "who cares?" is probably to be found in the poet's own "Louis, *what reck* I by thee?"

Whatt. Past tense of whet, to sharpen, or of *white*, to cut with a knife. It matters not which of these words we suppose Burns to have thought of when he wrote

> Sae my auld stumpie pen I gat it
> An took my jocteleg and *whatt* it

as they both mean what writing-masters were disagreeably familiar with before the introduction of steel pens banished the "Mend my pen" from schools.

White, to cut sticks with a knife and make them white.—*Thoresby.*

Whaup. The curlew.

Whaup, the larger curlew.—*Halliwell.*

Hweop, a cry.—*Bosworth.*

Those who have heard the *eerie* cry of the whaup on a lonely moor will have little doubt of this being the origin of the name.

> The snaw-wreaths are gane frae the gray *Girdlestane*,
> And the *whaups* are at Chattlehope Spout.—*Richardson.*

Wheep. To fly nimbly, to jerk; *penny-wheep*, small-beer. *E* for *i*; see *dreep.*

Whip, to sew after a particular manner.—*Bailey.* This, I am given to understand, refers primarily to the peculiar motion of the arm in sewing, and only secondarily to the kind of seam produced. If this be correct, it interprets, "Oh, rare! to see our elbucks *wheep*," which must sadly puzzle any person who looks to Jamieson for an explanation and finds, "To wheep, 1. To give a sharp whistle at intervals; 2. To squeak;" either of which it would be difficult to do with one's elbow, at least so far as one who has to confess that he never tried, may venture to speak

> Brisk Susan *whips* her linen from the rope.—*Gay.*

Whip-belly, thin weak liquor.—*Linc.* *Penny-whip*, very small beer.—*Lanc. Halliwell.*

They *whipped* us half a dozen hogsheads.—*Spectator.*

Where. Used as a noun in "Wi' you I'll scarce gang ony where."

And if he found *owhere* a good felawe.—*Chaucer.*

Whid. The motion of a hare running but not frighted.

Whid. A lie.

I believe that till Burns used it to denote a lie, *whid* was simply a cant term for word. In Fletcher's "The Beggar's Bush," the new King lays down the rules for his community of rogues :—

Clause. "To give good words."

This is interpreted by the orator of the gang—

Higgen. "Do you mark? To cut bene *whids*.'
Whids, words.—*Bailey.*

Whigmeleeries. Whims, fancies, crotchets.

Whilk. Which.

> Twenty score of bees
> *Whilk* all the summer hum about the hive.—*Ben Jonson.*
> *Whilke* way is he gon? he gan to crie.—*Chaucer.*
>
> And gude it is for many thynges,
> For to here the dedis of kynges,
> *Whilk* were foles and *whilk* were wyse,
> & *whilk* of tham couth mast quantyse;
> And *whilk* did wrong and *whilk* ryght,
> And *whilk* mayntenéd pes and fyght.—*R. of Brunne.*

Whinge. To complain, to whine.

Whinge, to whine, to sob.—*Halliwell.*

Whipper-in. A person who keeps hounds from straying.

This word is found in recent dictionaries, but I believe *whip* is more used in England.

> The *whipper-in* had arrived.—*Life of John Metcalf, the Blind Road-maker.*

Whirligigum.   Useless ornament, trifling appendage ; a whirligig.

Whisht!   Silence ! *to hold one's whisht*, to be silent. *Sh* for *s*; see under *fleesh*.

> *Whist*, an interjection commanding silence.—*Bailey.*
>
> So was the Titaness put down and *whist*.—*Spenser.*
>
> Yonge chyldren can I charme,
> With whysperynges and *whysshinges*.—*John Bale.*

Whisk.   To sweep, to lash.

> *Whisking* is also switching; "there will be *whisking* for't"; also beating, swinging, whipping.—*Thoresby.*
>
> This said, he *whisk'd* his parti-coloured wings.
> *England's Helicon.*
>
> I suppose that he is
> Of Jeremy the *whyskynge* rod,
> The flayle, the scourge of almighty God.—*Skelton.*

Whiskin.   Large ; *whiskin' beard*, a beard like the whiskers of a cat.—*Cunningham.*

This is apparently a guess of Cunningham's, and not a happy one, if it be true, "as some philosophers hold, that the whiskers are a parcel of the beard," for it only says a beard is like a beard.

There is no doubt *whiskin*, I rather think it should not be written *whiskin'*, means large—

> *Whisking*, great, swinging.—*Bailey.*
>
> *Whiskin* or *whisking*, adjectively is great, applied to almost every thing, as floods, fire, winds.—*Thoresby.*

But I believe that whilst Burns meant large, he had a

definite large object in view. He uses the word only once, and in a song written after he had met Captain Grose, and until then the word was unknown in S. literature, though found in E. as far back as 1640—

And wee will han a *whiskin* at every rushbearing ; a wassel cup at yule ; a seed-cake at festens.—*The Two Lancashire Lovers*.

Now, Grose says, " *Whiskin*, a great black drinking pot," and what could be better fitted to give an exaggerated notion, or caricature of a beard ? We know how readily Burns picked up *marled* from Mrs. Scott's lines, and nothing is more probable than that he and Grose enlarged each other's vocabulary.

Whissle. A whistle. To change money.—*Jamieson.* See under groat. *T* omitted ; see *bussle.*

He *whyslede* and hys hondys clapte.—*Octovian Imperator*.

Whitter. A hearty draught of liquor.

Jamieson gives this word and its explanation from Burns, and says, " Perhaps q. *whetter*,* from E. *whet*, applied to a dram, as supposed to sharpen the appetite." The Anglo-Saxon has *hwita, hwotta*, a sharpener. Whether this word has anything to do with *whitter* I cannot say, but it certainly expresses the idea that Burns so often conjoins with drink, viz., that of sharpening, not the appetite, but the intellectual faculties :—

> It kindles wit, it waukens lair,
> It pangs us fou' o' knowledge.

For wet your whistle, Fletcher has—

> Piper, *whet* your whistle.—*The Beggars' Bush*.

---

* Sir W. Scott uses whetter where Burns would probably have written whitter—
This other is a quiet place, where I have ta'en my *whetter* now and then.
The Fortunes of Nigel.

They are commonly known by the name of *Whettiers.*—*The Tatler.*

Whun-stane. Whin-stone, a species of trap. *U* for *i ;* see under *burdie.*

Whyles. Whiles, sometimes.

It is the plural of while, often used as a noun by good English authors, and is equal to *at times*, with this advantage that it does not require the preposition. Burns in his glossary writes as if he thought whiles and sometimes were synonymous ; but whiles is not, so far as I know, found in E. authors with this meaning. Spenser approaches very near it—

> *Somewhile* with merry purpose, fit to please,
> And *otherwhile* with good encouragement.

Whiles, as Burns employs it, would have saved the cumbrous and prosaic some and other.

> Whyles mice and moudieworts they howkit ;
> Whyles scour'd awa in lang excursion.
>
> Whyles owre a linn the burnie plays,
> Whyles round a rocky scaur it strays.

It is, however, sometimes used in the plural by English writers, but seldom without that irritating other—

But these people which *otherwhiles* delight so much.—*De Mornay.*

Don Quixote, sometimes stumbling, *otherwhiles* falling, began to run after the whole Herd.—*Thomas Shelton's Don Quixote.*

> *Otherwhiles*, the famish'd English
> Besiege us.—*Shak.*

Wi'. With.

> God be *wi'* you.—*Shak.*
>
> Yet goe to the court, my lord, she sayes,
> And I myselfe will ride *wi'* thee.
> *The Rising in the North.* *Percy.*

Wick. To strike a stone in an oblique direction, a term in curling.

Is it not rather to touch lightly a corner of a lying stone so that the one in motion may take a new direction? "Take a wick off this one" may sometimes be heard, and it means that the person about to play is to cause his stone to touch the corner of the one indicated, so that it may move at an angle, more or less acute, from its straight course.

It may seem strange to speak of the corner of a round stone, if *wick* really means a corner, which I doubt, but curling-stones were not always circular. In early times they remained as they were found, generally in the channel of a river. If they were of a proper size, and had a tolerably flat and smooth bottom, that was all that was required.

The *wawks*, or corners of the mustachios.—*Thoresby*.

The *wikes* of the mouth, the corners of the mouth.—*Bailey*.

Wikes.—*Grose*.

In "*to wick* a bore," which means to make a stone glide through a narrow passage *wick*, if in the previous paragraph it means a corner, must be a different word, for the most expert curler could hardly be expected to obey his "skip" if he ordered him to "corner a crevice or an opening."

Widde or *woodie.* Properly a rope made of twigs of willow; used to denote a halter.—*Jamieson*. Widdie is simply *withy*, an old form of *withe* or *with*, *th* and *d*, as has been already sufficiently dwelt upon, being interchangeable.

I think there is a greater variety of *Withys* than you mention.—*Ray Correspondence*.

Ash and *withy* poles are best.—*Hist. of Surrey.*

Withy, an ozier.—*Newberry.*

It is generally supposed that Scotland had a monopoly of the *widdie* for punishment; the following passages, the first of which cannot be written or read without a shudder, will show that it was known both in France and England:—

The breasts of many women were cut off, after whose deaths the poor infants died of famine, D'Opede having caused proclamation to be made upon paine of the *with*, that no man should give any reliefe or sustenance to any of them. Others appeared with a *with* about their necks.—*History of the Waldenses, London, 1624.*

A *wyth* take him!—*Beaumont and Fletcher.*

A *withe* had served my turn to hang myself.—*Massinger.*

Widdiefu'. Cross, one deserving the gallows. *Widdie* and *fu.*

In "The Laird was a *widdiefu*, bleerit knurl," he is contrasted with the miller who "was strappin' and ruddy," and I think Burns meant to say, not that he deserved hanging, but that he was cross and ill-tempered. We still say of such a person, "He's as *thrawn as a woodie.*"

Widdle. A struggle.

Widdle, to fret.—*Grose.*

Waedle, poverty, want, indigence.—*Bosworth.*

Widdle waddle, to go sidling first towards one side and then the other.—*Bailey.*

Wiel. A small whirlpool.

Weel, a whirlpool.—*Johnson.*   *Wheel.*—*Grose.*   *Wheel-pit.*—*Thoresby.*

Wifie, wifikie. A diminutive or endearing term for a wife.

Wight. Strong, a person.

> And she could eke
> Wrastlen by veray force and veray might
> With any yong man, were he never so *wight.*—*Chaucer.*

> Gladly thai gaf mete and drink,
> So that thai suld the better swink,
> The *wight* men that thar weire.—*Minot.*

As a substantive wight is found in all E. dictionaries, but with the remark that it is now used ludicrously. It was once a respectable word, and employed in all seriousness by Chaucer, Spenser, Shakespeare, Milton, Dryden, etc. I rather refer to an example from Rous's version of the Psalms, as I have met intelligent Scotsmen who did not know that the word was in their own psalter. See under *kythe.*

Wight was formerly used in England in a more extensive meaning than I have been able to hear of it in Scotland. In Anglo-Saxon it meant creature, any thing, and as late as the seventeenth century it was in use for all living creatures:—

Thou art beholden to the sea for the great number of living *wights* which it fostereth.—*De Mornay.*

It had also other meanings, as the following line indicates:—

I crouche (cross) thee from elves, and from *wightes.*—*Chaucer.*

Wil' cat. Wild cat. *D* omitted; see under *afiel.*
Wilcat, a wild cat, the pole-cat.—*Bamford.*

Wil' fire. Wildfire.

Wilfu'. Wilful, willing. *L* omitted; see under *a'*.

A proud priest may be known when he denieth to follow Christ and his apostles in *wilful* poverty and other virtues.—*Foxe.*

Willyart. Shy, bashful, confused. Perhaps a corruption of *wildered.*

Wimple. To meander, to wave.

Wimple, a muffler or plaited linen cloth which nuns wear about their necks ; also a streamer or flag.—*Bailey.*

> For with a veile that *wimpled* every where,
> Her head and face was hid.—*Spenser.*

Win. The wind; *wins,* the winds. *D* omitted ; see under *afiel.*

Win. To wind, i.e., to dry corn after it is cut.

> Yt felle abowght the Lammasse tyde,
> When husbonds *wynne* ther haye.
> *Anc. Bal. of Chevy Chase.*

It is possible that *wynne* may here mean the in-gathering of " ther haye," rather than the drying of it.

Win, to dry hay.—*Halliwell. Winny,* to dry.—*Skeat.*

Win'. To wind, to winnow.

Winning, winnowing.—*Bosworth.*

Win. Live, dwell.

Win. To wind; *win't,* winded, *as a bottom of yarn.*

Whereby, by all likelihood, weavers, carders, and *winders* of yarn would be destitute. *Stat. Ed. IV.*

Bottom, introduced by way of explanation, to most people now needs explanation.

Bottom, a ball of thread.—*Halliwell.* Originally the spool or knob of wood on which cotton was wound.—*Palmer.*

Win for won, in—

> Like fortune's favours, tint as *win.*—*The Vision.*

Windy door. The door on the side of a barn on which the wind blows.

Before the invention of fanners, barns had always two doors exactly opposite each other. While the winnowing was carried on, the door on the windy side was opened to let the wind perform "its good office," and the other shut to prevent the chaff and lighter grain from being blown away.

Winkers. Eye-lashes.

Winna. Will not. *Will and na.*
  Winno, will not. *Winno do*, will not do.—*Bamford.*
  I *wi' not*, that I *wi' not.*—*Fletcher.*

Winnins. Winnings, earnings.
  He stakes all his *winnings* upon every cast.—*Addison.*
    They shulde bugge (buy) boldely that hem best liked,
    And sithenes selle it agein and save the *wynnynge.*
                                        P. Plowman.

Winnock. A window.

The omission of *d* after *n* is only another example of what has been frequently pointed out. The change of *ow* into *ock* is not so easily explained. But window seems to have had a severe struggle before its present form was firmly established. In addition to *winnock*, *winduck*, *windock*, which, *d* being elided, is Burns's word, *windon*, *windore*, and *wind-door*, which was once thought to be its derivation, are found. Butler has *windore*—

> Love is a burglar, a felon,
> That at the *windore*-eye does steal in;

and Raleigh in his stately History of the World, page 105, has the same form.

Winsome. Gay, hearty, vaunted, attractive.
  Winsum, wynsum, pleasant, delightful, sweet, grateful, prosperous.—*Bosworth.*

Winsome, smart, trimly dressed, lively, joyous.—*Grose.*

> Blisse, mi saule, to Lawerd of alle thinges,
> And nil forgete alle his foryheldinges.
> That *winsom* es to alle thine wickenesses.
> *Winsome* to him be mi speche al.—*Metrical E. Psalter.*

Wintle. A staggering motion; to stagger, to reel.

Found only in Burns, according to Jamieson, but Johnstone says it is heard in Clydesdale and Roxburghshire. It is a common word in Ayrshire, but whether it was so before the publication of Burns's poems or not I cannot say. One thing is certain, many words are now common not only in Scotland, but in England, that owe their currency, perhaps their existence, to his poetry.

Winze. An oath.

This is another word unheard of till Burns used it, and which even his genius could not acclimatise, for it is one of the few words in his poems which are never heard. *Wince, winse,* and *winch* are found, but they all mean to kick:—

> Ware, ware, the mare *Wynsyth* with her wanton hele.—*Skelton.*
> *Tiver,* to yerk, *winse,* to kick.—*Cotgrave.*
>
> Let the gall'd jade *winch.*—*Shak.*

It is to be remembered, however, that Burns does not profess to give the meaning of words, but the sense in which he uses them.

Wiss. To wish. *S* for *sh;* see under *buss,* and in

> The thride dai mersuine and qualle,
> An other *fis* (fish) gret and small
> *Sal* (shall) yel.—*Metrical E. Homilies. Small.*
> Bot for his *fleis* (was pined here,
> His sawel es now til Godd ful dere.—*Id.*

When al was *hust* (hushed) then lay she still.—*Chaucer.*

I have given examples in *s* and not in *ss*, for this digraph was sometimes used for *sh*, as in

> *Bissopes* (bishops) and abbodes were to is wille echon.
> *Rob. of Gloucester.*

Wit. To know, to wot.

> Now please you *wit* the epitaph.—*Shak.*
>
> That sal men se ful sone, I trow,
> And thiself sal noght *wit* how.—*The Seven Sages.*
>
> Assaieth it yourself, than may ye *witen*
> If that I lie or non in this matere.—*Chaucer.*

Wit. Wisdom in "There's *wit* there, ye'll get there."

Who knew the *witte* of the Lord, or who was his counceilour?—*Rom. xi. 34. Wiclif, quoted by Trench.*

> Hath this fellow any *wit* that told you this?—*Shak.*

Thou art both beautiful in thy countenance and *witty* in thy words.—*Book of Judith.*

> When I say *wit*, I wisdom mean.—*Churchill.*

Withouten. Without.

> Still she stood *withouten* let,
> Neither changed hue nor gret,
> That lady mild and dear.—*Sir Amadyce.*
>
> And thou shalt have blys,
> That never shall mys
> *Withouten* nay.—*Skelton.*
>
> And hers be hole *withouten* more.—*Chaucer.*

Wizened. Hide-bound, dried shrunk.

Wisnian, to *wizzen*.—*Bosworth.* *Wizen*.—*Horne Tooke.*

Wizzn, to pine, to waste.—*Bamford.*

Wizen'd, dried, withered.—*Grose.*

> The tre weloid and *wisened* sone,
> And wex olde and dry.—*MS. quoted by Halliwell.*

Won. To dwell.

> Fame blazed hath, that here in Faery Land
> Doe many famous Knightes and Ladies *wonne*.—*Spenser*.
>
> A sturdy pas doun to the court he goth,
> Wher as ther *woned* a man of gret honour.—*Chaucer*.
>
> And is welcome whan he wil and *woneth* wyth hem oft.
> P. *Plowman*.
>
> Ipomydon saw non othyr *won*.—*Ipomydon*.

Wonner. A wonder; a contemptuous appellation. *D* omitted; see under *blin*, and in—

> *An* (and) sone thar wex, withouten fayle,
> Wynd, and *thonor* (thunder), and rayn, and hayle.
> *Ywain and Gawain.*
>
> (The) Lauerd *thonored* fra hevin.—*Metrical E. Psalter*.

Woo'. Wool.

This is the only word in *ool* in which the Scotch elide the *l*, though they use *pu'* for pull, *fu'* for full. The reason may be that wool was originally *wull* or *wulle*.

> *Woo*, wool. Piece-*woo*, wool for a piece of flannel.—*Bamford*.

Woodie. See *widdie*.

Wooer-bab. The garter knotted below the knee with a couple of loops.

Literally, a wooer, lover, or suitor's knot, *bab* or bob meaning an easily moved bunch of any thing.

> An old set-stitched chair, valanced and fringed around with party-coloured worsted *bobs*, stood at the bed's head.—*Sterne*.

The introduction of trousers, which heralded the destruction of so many more important things, put out of fashion this piece of rustic foppery, for it was no more, though Jamieson says they were "formerly worn by a young man who was too bashful to announce in words that the purpose of his visit was to propose marriage."

Not many Scots lads get the credit of being so *mim moued*.

The custom was not confined to Scotland, or to rustics, for Wood says that Dr. Owen, Dean of Christ Church, and vice-Chancellor at Oxford, in 1652, used to go "like a young scholar, with powdered hair, and a large *set of ribbands, pointed, at his knees.*" *Wooer-babs* were, we learn, part of the usual dress of students in the seventeenth century, and may have continued till Burns's day.

> The first that steps up is Lord (any popular lord) you'll see,
> With a *bunch of blue ribbons tied down to his knee.**
>
> *The Masker's Song.*

Woor. Wore.

Wordy. Worthy. *D* for *th;* see under *cleed*, and in—

> A ryche present wyth hym he browght,
> A clothe that was *wordylye* wroght.—*Emare.*
>
> That day full *wordely* he wroght.—*Battalye of Agynkourte.*

Wordie. Dim. of word.

Worset. Worsted. *T* omitted; see under *bussle.* *T* for *d;* see under *akwart*, and in

> And this south-westerne *wynt* on a Seterday at eve.
>
> *P. Plowman.*

> His life upon so yonge a wight
> Besette wolde in *jeopartie.*—*Gower.*

Wow. An exclamation of pleasure or wonder.

---

* *Wooer-babs*, were the dregs of a fashion prevalent in the highest circles:—
At this day men of meane rank weare *garters* and shoe roses of more than five pounds price.—*Stow.*

Farquhar makes a beau say "I'll wear the buckles of my garters behind."
—*Letters.*

Wow is an old spelling of wo or woe, and is equivalent to oh !

Wo worth. Wo be. See *wae worth.*

Howl ye, *woe worth* the day ! *Ezekiel, xxxi.* 2.

Wrack. To tease, to vex.

Wrack, to torture, to torment. This is commonly written rack. —*Johnson.*

> The constabel of the castel down is fare
> To se this *wrak.*—*Chaucer.*

> The beggar then thought all was wrong,
> They were set for his *wrack.*—*R. Hood.*

> Some squire, perhaps you take delight to *rack.*—*Pope.*

Pope's rack and Burns' wrack mean exactly the same thing. Pope speaks of Teresa Blount probably tormenting some clumsy lover ; Burns makes a young matron speak of her purpose to similarly treat her ancient spouse.

Wraith. A spirit, a ghost, an apparition exactly like a living person whose appearance is said to forebode the person's approaching death.

Jamieson has a most interesting article on this word, but comes to no decision as to its derivation. Its root is probably A.-S. *wáer,* a caution, or *warning.*

A *wraith,* or *wauf,* as it is frequently called in Northumberland, is the apparition of a person which appears before his death.— *Richardson.*

Wrang. Wrong, to wrong.

> They dyd our Englyssh men grete *wrang.*
> *Bat. of Otterbourne.*

> Bot he thoght the towre was so strang,
> That there myght no man do him *wrang.*—*The Seven Sages.*

Wrong, however written, whether *wrang*, wrong, or **wrung**, is merely the past tense of the verb to wring.—*Horne Tooke.*

Wreeth. Wreath, a drifted heap of snow.

Wreath, any thing curled or twisted.—*Johnson.*

> His rigge was bristled as with sharp sithen,
> Toeth he had so *wrethen* writhen.—*Kyng Alisaunder.*

> As *wreath* of snow on mountain breast.—*Scott.*

Sir Walter seems to have thought it an E. word, as did also Thomson.*

Write. What is written, writing. Verb for noun.

Writer. An attorney, a solicitor.

Does *writere* in the following mean a lawyer?—

> Now mot ich soutere his sone setten to schole,
> & ich a beggers brol on the booke lerne,
> & worth to a *writere* and with a lorde dwell.
> *Piers the Ploughman's Crede. Skeat.*

Wud. Mad, distracted; angry, *wood*. *U* is often used for *oo*, as in—

There followed a general *flud* (flood).—*De Mornay.*

Wud, mad.—*Bamford.*

> I would be glad to do you good,
> And him also, be he never so *wood*.—*The Four Ps.*

> He lift his sword aloft, for ire nigh *wood*.—*Fairfax.*

> But the two brethren borne of Cadmus blood,
> Blind through ambition, and with vengeance *wood*.
> *Spenser.*

Wumble. Wimble. *U* for *i*; see under *burdie*, and in—

> O fatall *sustren* (sisters).—*Chaucer.*

---

* Thomson has—

> Scarce his head
> Raised o'er the heapy *wreath*, the branching elk,
> Lies slumbering sullen in the white abyss.—*Winter.*

> Withoute batayl, other *dunt* (dint),
> That londe he wan, verrament.—*Kyng Alisaunder.*

Wommel, an auger.—*Grose.*

Wyle. To wile, beguile, persuade; *wyling*, persuasive.

Wyliecoat. A flannel vest.

Jamieson says of this word, "its origin is quite uncertain." I have always understood that it was a *woolly* or, taking the older spelling, *wully coat*, from the material of which it was made, named woolly by way of eminence owing to the flannel composing it being manufactured of the finest wool that could be procured.

When an accession is likely to be made to a family, in the North of England, some nightgowns called *wyllies* are prepared for the expected infant.—*Richardson.*

Wilecoat, a vest for a child.—*Halliwell.*

This is the meaning of the word in Ayrshire—I may rather say was, for it seems now unknown. Gawin Douglas has *welecote*—

> In doubill garmont cled and *welecote*.—*Prologue vii.*

Wyte. Blame, to blame.

> If that I misspeke or say,
> *Wite* it the ale of Southwerk, I you pray.—*Chaucer.*
>
> Alas my wyckydness, that may I *wyte*.—*Skelton.*
>
> That him ne thorst yt not *wyte*,
> For febyl his dint to smyte.—*R. C. de Lion.*
>
> For none would give, but all men would them *wyte*.
> *Spenser.*

Y.

Yard. A garden.

Chaucer applies *garden* and *yard* to the same place.

> I saw a garden right anone;
> Mirthe, that is so faire and fre,
> Is in this *yerd* with his meinie.
> There was many a bird singing,
> Throughout the *yerde* all thringing.
> *The Romaunt of the Rose.*

Garden is *yard* with the addition of the participial termination *en*.

The (initial) Anglo-Saxon letter is pronounced indifferently *G* or *Y.*—*Horne Tooke.*

Yaud. An old mare.—*Jamieson.* I do not think *yaud* has any reference to age or sex. It is only a softened form of jade or *jaud.*

Yaud, a horse.—*Thoresby.*

> Tommy Linn has a mare of the gray;
> It's a running *yade*, says Tommy Linn.
> *The North Country Chorister. Ritson.*
> Your *yauds* may take cold.—*The Jovial Crew.*

Yauld. Strong.

Ye. This pronoun is frequently used for thou.

Yealings. Born in the same year, coevals. Probably a corruption of *yearlings*.

Year. It is used for both singular and plural. See under *merk.*

Yell and *yeld.* Barren, that gives no milk.

Yeld-beasts, animals barren, not giving milk, or too young to give profit.—*Halliwell.*

Yerk. To lash, to jerk; to rouse.

Yark, to strike hard, and suddenly.—*Bamford.*

> Let us alone
> To rule the slaves at home; I can so *yerk* them.—*Massinger.*

> Their wounded steeds
> *Yerk* out their armed heels at their dead masters.—*Shak.*

> A carter a courtier, it is a worthy warke
> That with his whyp his mares was wont to *yark*.—*Skelton.*

Yestreen. Yesternight.

> *Yestreen* to chamber I him led;
> This night Gray-steel has made his bed.
> *Sir Eger, Sir Graham, and Sir Gray-steel.*

> In hope that you would come here *yestere'en*.—*B. Jonson.*

Yett. A gate.

> But with glad chere to the *yate* is went.—*Chaucer.*

> Thee y will follow ham,
> And that y mote with the gan,
> In atté castel-*yete*.—*Horn Childe and Maiden Rimnild.*

> They rode till they came to his mother's *yett*.
> *Brave Earl Brand.*

> If he chance to come when I am abroade,
> Sperre the *yate* for fear of fraude.—*Spenser.*

Yeuk. To itch, to be keenly desirous, to have an uneasy feeling.

Yuck, itch.—*Johnson. Grose. Yeeke.*—*Thoresby.*
Yeuk.—*Bailey.*

> All the best families are laid up with what they call the *yoke*.— *Lady Suffolk's Correspondence, 1702 to 1767.*

> Cassius, you yourself
> Are much condemned to have an itching palm,
> To sell and mart your offices for gold.—*Shak.*

In "If Warren Hastings' neck was *yeukin*," Burns uses it to mean a sign of fear, and in his "Poem on Life" the reverse, "Thy auld elbow *yeuks* wi' joy." Perhaps the former should be *yaukin'*, i.e., aching.

Yill. Ale.

> If I should die, as it may hap,
> My greauve shall be under the good *yeal* tap.
> *Ancient Poems, etc., of the Peasantry of England.* Bell.

I wanted a chappin of *yale* from the public-house.—*Letter (1762) to the Duke of Northumb., from Rev. Charles Dodson, afterwards Bishop of Ossory.*

Yird and *yerd.* Earth; *yerded,* buried. *D* for *th;* see under *cleed.*

> And after Phillis Philliberd
> This tree was cleped in the *yerd.*—*Gower.*
>
> And his ancestors of old time,
> Have *yearded* theere longe.—*Percy.*
>
> She semed non *erdly* thing.—*Emare.*

Yirl. An earl.

> I am a *yerle* callyd within my cuntre.
> *An. Bal. of Chevy Chase.*
>
> The *yerle* of Huntley cawte and kene.
> *Bat. of Otterbourne.*
>
> For many tongs of them will tell,
> How these to *yerles* false did rebell.
> *John Barker, London.*

Yirr. An angry bark of a dog.

Yrre, ire, anger, indignation, fury.—*Bosworth.*
Yarre, like a dog that is angry.—*Cotgrave.*

Yirth. Earth.

> There were many cast to the *yerthe.*—*Froissart.*

Yokin. Yoking, a bout, an engagement. Entering on any employment with vigour or keenness.—*Jamieson.*

Yoking, the ploughing that is done at one putting-to of the horse.—*Scott.*

When the battle of Ancrum was about to begin, a heron soared away betwixt the encountering armies, "O!" exclaimed Angus, "that I had here my white goss-hawk that we might all *yoke* at once."—*Godscroft, quoted by Sir W. Scott.*

It was not part of my design to quote Scotch authors, indeed it was distinctly opposed to it, but this passage was so appropriate to Burns's "hearty yokin," that I could not resist the temptation to give it.

> Ay, tell me that and *unyoke*.—*Shak.*

To haud a yokin at the pleugh, to do a day's ploughing.

Yon.

Burns's use of this word is not in accordance with the explanations given in E. dictionaries. He says, "Yon sang," referring to a song which the gentleman to whom he wrote had in his possession, at a distance, and of course completely out of the poet's sight, while according to Johnson *Yon* is "being at a distance within view." But it is found in good E. authors indicating objects and persons not visible.

> Would *yon* woman
> Had been ten fathoms under ground, when first
> I saw her eyes!—*Fletcher. The Captain.*

And again, the person spoken of being absent—

> Now to be married
> To *yon* strange prince.—*Id. Philaster.*

"I'll go and visit *yon* sick gentlewoman," who was in bed.
Beaumont and Fletcher. The Coxcomb.

> Go get thee gone, and by thyself
> Devise some tricky game,
> For to enthral *yon* rebels all.—*R. Hood.*

Here the speaker is in London, and the rebels are in Sherwood Forest, and, of course, not "within view;" and, not to multiply examples, Shakespeare makes Anne Page say, after Slender has gone out:—

> Good Mother, do not marry me to *yond* fool.
> *The Merry Wives of Windsor.*

And Pandarus in Troy and the girl in the Grecian camp, says:—

> Here's a letter from *yon* poor girl.—*Troilus and Cressida*.

Yont. Beyond.

Geond, adv. yond, yonder, thither, beyond. *G* often becomes *y*, as *gear*, a year.—*Bosworth*.

Be omitted, as in—

> No ceremony that to great ones *longs*.—*Shak*.

Young guidman. New-married man.

Youngling. A youth, but used by Burns as an adjective, young, youthful.

> The *youngling* painter brood.—*Wolcot*.

Younker. A youth.

> A *yonker* then began to laugh.—*Wright's Political Ballads*.
> How like a *younker*, or a prodigal,
> The scarfed bark puts from her native bay.—*Shak*.
> For *yonkers*, such follies fit,
> But we tway been men of wit.—*Spenser*.

Yoursel'. Yourself. See *mysel'*.

Yowden. Yielded, wearied. For change of *l* into *w*, see under *a'*.

> And glader ought his fren ben of his deth,
> Whan with honour is *yolden* up his breth.—*Chaucer*.
>
> Ne had I er now, my swete herte dere,
> Been *yolde* ywis, I were now not here.
> *Id. Rom. of the Rose.*
>
> Barouns and knyghtis of that lond,
> *Yolden* heom to his hond.—*R. C. de Lion*.

Yowe. A ewe. *Ow* for *ew*; see under *browst*.

The orthography differs more than the pronunciation. The *y* sound is heard in both ewe and yowe.

Yowie. Dim. of yowe.

Yule. Christmas.

Yule, the time of Christmas. —*Johnson.*

This was the most respectable festival of our druids called *Yule*-tide.—*Brand.*

> The twenty day of *yowle*, ywys.
> *Le Bone Flo. of Rome.*

At the high feast of *youle.* —*Leland's Itinerary.*

It is good to cry *Ule* at other men's cost.—*Ray.*

> A nother day ye wyll me clothe,
> I trowe, ayenst the *Yole.*—*R. Hood.*

> Was never seen such rule
> In any place but here, at bonfire, or at *Yule.*
> *Drayton.*

WORDS OMITTED.

Craftsmen. Free-masons.

Custoc. See *castock.*

APPENDIX.

Words which occur in verses quoted by Burns.

BLATHRIE. Nonsense.
BOB. A dance.
BRUCKET. Of variegated colours.
BUMBAZ'D. Stupified.
CAULD KAIL. Cold broth; soup left from a previous day.
CHANLERS. Candlesticks, chandeliers.
CLINTIN. Crevice or shelf on the bank of a river.
COGGIN. The teeth of a spinning-wheel.
CUMMIN'. Coming.
CURCHIE. Dim. of *curch*, a female head-dress.
DAUNTON. To subdue, to intimidate.
DOOR-CHEEKS. Door-posts.
DOUK. To duck.
FEE. To hire.
FEETIE. Dim. of feet.
FYE! Haste!
GAES WI' ME. Is easy to me.
GREETIE. Dim. of *greet*, cry.
HEN-BAWKS. Hen-roosts.
HOLLAND. Fine linen.
HOLLIN-BUSS. A holly tree.
JINGLAN, INGLAN. Jingling.
KILL. A kiln.
LINK. A lock of hair.
MENZIE. Serving-men, dependant.
OLIPHANTS. Elephants.
SHAK. Shake.
SHELLIN-HILL. Rising ground whe[re] the shelled oats are winnowed.
SHUTE. Shoot, put over.
STAND WI. To dispute, to diff[er]
SICKEN. Such.
STENT. To stop.
THREE-GIRR'D CAP. This is Sha[kes]peare's *three-hooped pot*.
WANTON. To please.
WARSE. Worse.
WATER-SIDE. Bank of a river.
WONDER. Wondrous.

Foreign Words and Phrases used by Burns.

AB ORIGINE. From the beginning.
A' DIEU, LE BON DIEU, JE VOUS COMMENDE! To God, the good God, I commende you! That is evidently what is meant, but I doubt if the words express it.
A' L' EGARD DE MOI. Concerning me.
A LA FRANCAIS. After the Fren[ch] manner.
ALIAS. Otherwise.
AQUA VITAE. Brandy, whisky.
BELLE ET AIMABLE. Beautiful a[nd] amiable.
BELLE FILLE. Pretty girl.
BELLES LETTRES. Polite literatur[e]

BELLUM. War.
BILLET DOUX. A love-letter.
BON TON. The fashion, good style.
ÇA IRA! This will go, this will do!
CARMAGNOLE. Dress, dance, etc., much in vogue in France at the Revolution; a person who wore the dress; put by Burns for a cruel person.
CHEF D'ŒUVRE. A master-piece.
CHER PETIT MONSIEUR. Dear little Master.
CI DEVANT. Former.
COGNOSCENTI. Connoisseurs.
COMPAGNON DE VOYAGE. Fellow traveller.
COUP DE MAIN. Sudden and successful effort.
CRI DE GUERRE. War-cry.
DE FACTO. Really.
DE HAUT EN BAS. Contemptuously, condescendingly.
DENOUEMENT. The end, catastrophe.
DERNIER RESSORT. The last resource.
DONT J'AI EU L'HONNEUR D'ETRE UN MISERABLE ESCLAVE. Of which I have had the honour of being a wretched slave.
DRAMATIS PERSONAE. The characters in a drama.
DURESSE. Hardness, sternness, Sc. dourness.
ECLAT. Splendour. *Eclatant*, splendid.
ELOIGNEE. Distant.
EMBARAS. Perplexity.
ENBONPOINT. In good condition, plump.
EN PASSANT. By the way.
EN POETE. Like a poet.
ENTRE NOUS. Between you and me.
FAITES MES BAISE-MAINS RESPECTUEUSE. Give my respectful compliments.
FAUX PAS. A false step, an error.
FETE CHAMPETRE. Country festival.
FILLETTE. A young woman.

FINESSE. Artifice, trickery.
FRATER. A brother.
GAIETE DE CŒUR. Lightness of heart, wantonness.
GENS COMME IL FAUT. People as they should be, of the right sort.
GERMINA. Germs.
GRAVISSIMO. Exceedingly grave, musical term.
HARDIESSE. Boldness.
HAUTEUR. Haughtiness.
INTEGER. A whole, not a fraction.
IN TERROREM. To deter.
IO TRIUMPHE! Triumph! rejoice! I suspect that Burns went to Horace for these words. If so, his knowledge of Latin may have been greater than he pretended, or than his biographers have given him credit for possessing.
JEU D'ESPRIT. A witty sally.
LA PLUS AIMABLE DE SON SEXE. The most amiable of her sex.
LAPSUS LINGUÆ. A slip of the tongue.
LENTE LARGO. Slow and grave.
LE PAUVRE INCONNU. The poor unknown.
LE PAUVRE MISERABLE. The poor wretch. Cowper too calls himself *pauvre miserable*.
LE PLUS BEL ESPRIT, ET LE PLUS HONNETE HOMME. The greatest genius and the most honest man.
LES BEAUX ESPRITS. Persons of genius.
LES ENVIRONS. The neighbourhood.
LE VRAI N'EST PAS TOUJOURS LE VRAISEMBLABLE. The true is not always like the truth.
MA CHERE AMIE. My dear friend.
MAITRE D' HOTEL. Steward.
MEMENTO. A remembrance.
MES CHERES MESDAMES. My dear Ladies.
MISERABLE PERDU. Wretched lost one
MOI-MEME. Myself.
MON AMI. My friend.

Mon grand but. My great aim.
Morceaux. Morsels.

Naïveté. Candour, simplicity.
Noblesse. The nobility.
Nota bene. Mark well.
Oublie moi, grand Dieu, si jamais je l'oublie ! Forget me, great God if I ever forget him !

Opinionatre, Opionatreté. Obstinacy.
Ou il plait a' Dieu-et mon Roi. (I go) whither it pleases God—and my King.
Outré. Preposterous, odd.
Pardonnez moi, Madame. Pardon me, Madam.
Pas. Precedence.
Pauvres miserables. Poor wretches.
Peccavi, pater, miserere mei. I have sinned, O father, pity me.
Penchant. Inclination.
Poetæ minores. Minor poets.
Politesse. Politeness.
Primo. Firstly.
Pro and con. For and against.
Probatum est. It has been proved.
Quantum. Amount.
Quem Deus conservet ! Whom may God preserve !
Quondam. Former.
Reveur. Dreamer.
Role. One's place in the world.
Sanctum sanctorum. The holy of holies.
Sans ceremonie. Without ceremony.

Sans culottes. Lit. men without breeches, revolutionists in France.
Scelerat. Villain.
Secundum artem. According to rule.
Solitaire. Recluse, hermit.
Statu quo. As before.
Subscripsi huic. I have subscribed this.
Tant pis. So much the worse.
Tapis. The carpet.
Terra firma. Solid earth, a firm footing.
Tete-a-tete. Private conversation.
Ton. Style. Burns seems to use it to signify *height*.
Tout au contraire. Quite the reverse.
Un but. An aim.
Une bagatelle de l'amitié. A small token of friendship.
Un homme des affaires. A man of business.
Un penchant a'l'adorable moitié du genre humain. A liking for the adorable half of the human race.

Un peu trompé. A little deceived.
Un tout ensemble. A whole.
Vade mecum. Constant companion.
Veni, vidi, vici. I came, I saw, conquered.
Viva voce. By the living voice, by word of mouth.
Vive la bagatelle ! Trifles for ever ! Let us be merry !
Vive l'amour ! Love for ever !

DATE DUE

DEC 13 1983			
MAY 17 1989			
JUN 13 '94			
NOV 7 '95			
GAYLORD			PRINTED IN U.S.A.